W9-AQS-011

A12900 223038

BURT FRANKLIN: RESEARCH & SOURCE WORKS SERIES 599
Essays in Literature & Criticism 92

STUDIES
IN MEDIEVAL
LITERATURE

STUDIES
IN MEDIEVAL
LITERATURE

A MEMORIAL COLLECTION
OF ESSAYS

by Roger Sherman Loomis, 1887-1966,

With a foreword by Albert C. Baugh
and
A Bibliography of Loomis by Ruth Roberts

BURT FRANKLIN
NEW YORK

© 1970 by Burt Franklin.
Published by LENOX HILL Pub. & Dist. Co. (Burt Franklin)
235 East 44th St., New York, N.Y. 10017
Printed in the U.S.A.

S.B.N. 8337-47339
Library of Congress Card Catalog No.: 73-135508
Burt Franklin: Research and Source Works Series 599
Essays in Literature and Criticism 92

FOREWORD

The names of few American scholars have been so intimately associated with the study of the Arthurian legend in the last forty years as that of Roger Sherman Loomis. The only name that comes readily to mind is J. Douglas Bruce, and Bruce died more than forty years ago. Both men had a profound knowledge of Arthurian romance, but Bruce was an inventionist attributing many innovations in medieval treatments to the creative imagination of their authors, whereas Loomis sought the sources in tradition and especially Celtic tradition.

Roger Loomis was born 31 October 1887, in Yokohama, Japan, of missionary parents. He was educated at the Hotchkiss School and at Williams College, where he received his A.B. in 1909. After obtaining his M.A. at Harvard in 1910 he went to New College, Oxford, as a Rhodes Scholar and earned the B. Litt. in 1913. He was married in 1919 to Gertrude Schoepperle, who died two years later; to Laura Hibbard in 1925, who died in 1960; and to Dorothy Bethurum in 1963, all distinguished medievalists in their own right. He was an instructor in English at the University of Illinois from 1913 to 1918. During World War I he edited an Army publication, *Attenshun 21.* From 1920 on he taught at Columbia University, rising in the usual way from instructor to a full professorship. He became Emeritus in 1956. In 1955-56 he was Eastman Professor at Oxford. In 1956-57 he returned to Columbia as a special lecturer. He was one of the founders of the Medieval Club of New York and was twice its president. Among the many honors which he received were degrees from the University of Wales, the University of Rennes, Williams College, and Columbia University. In 1951 he was awarded the Haskins Medal of the Mediaeval Academy of America for his Arthurian Tradition and Chretien de Troyes, and the following year was elected a Fellow of that society.

Roger Loomis came to the study of Arthurian romance by way of his interest in art and art history, and his earliest publications were on medieval Arthurian iconography. But these soon led to the intensive study of the literary texts and the question of the origins of the Arthurian legend His first book in this field, *Celtic Myth and Arthurian Romance,* published in 1927, set the tone of all his subsequent Arthurian publications. It was characterized by a bold originality, almost a daring, that at once marked Loomis as a scholar who would follow the logical implications of his premises to conclusions that might be resisted by others, but which would always be defended with learning and careful reasoning. In some of his later books, *Arthurian Tradition and Chretien de Troyes* (1949) and *The Grail: From Celtic Myth to Christian Symbol* (1963) he felt obliged to retract some of the views he had defended in his first book; but his basic position remained basically unchanged, and his retractions——although they sometimes caused him to discard claims which had been based on much effort of reading and research——did not affect his larger contention that the traditions of the Celtic peoples had played a major part in the growth of the Arthurian legend. Loomis's continuing interest in art is evident in the joint publication with Laura Loomis of *Arthurian Legends in Medieval Art* (1959) and in the volume which he edited under the title *A Mirror of Chaucer's World* (1965).

The standard reference work *Arthurian Literature in the Middle Ages* (1959) was conceived and edited by him and is probably the most widely used of his books. In this encyclopedic survey he organized and infused unity into the contributions of more than thirty scholars here and abroad, and himself contributed several important chapters. But fundamental as this volume is, it must not be allowed to obscure the last Arthurian book which he wrote. In 1963 he published *The Development of Arthurian Romance.* In this small volume of less than 200 pages, intended for the student and general reader, he presented in simple exposition the facts and conclusions accumulated in a lifetime of study of this great body of medieval literature, and it is the best introduction available to the complicated body of medieval texts and modern scholarship concerned.

Few students of Middle English literature can resist the appeal of Chaucer, and Loomis occasionally departed from his main interest to ponder certain Chaucerian problems. His articles, "Was Chaucer a Laodicean? " and "Was Chaucer a Free Thinker? ", both reprinted in the present volume, are sane and well-balanced answers to these questions.

The selection of articles here presented was made by Dorothy Bethurum Loomis. It shows the range of Roger Loomis's learning and makes available essays which originally appeared in widely scattered books and journals often difficult to come by except in the largest libraries. It is published as a tribute to the memory of a great scholar, and these brief introductory remarks are happily contributed by a long-time friend.

Albert C. Baugh

TABLE OF CONTENTS

ACKNOWLEDGEMENTS

For permission to publish the sixteen articles by Roger Sherman Loomis
contained within this work, we are gratefully indebted to the following:

Proceedings of the Society of Antiquaries of Scotland
    "Scotland and the Arthurian Legend" Vol. LXXXIX, Session 1955-1956

Romance Philology
    "Vandeberes, Wandlebury and the Lai de L'Espine" ©1955 by the Regents
    of the University of California. Reprinted from Romance Philology, Vol.
    IX, No. 2, pp. 162-167, by permission of The Regents.

Studies in Medieval Literature in Honor of A.C. Baugh
    "Was Chaucer a Free Thinker? " © 1961 by the University of
    Pennsylvania Press, pp. 21-44.

Essays and Studies in Honor of Carelton Brown
    ' "Was Chaucer a Laodicean? " Reprinted by permission of New York
    University Press © 1940 by New York University.

Franciplegius
    "The Strange History of Carodoc of Vannes" pp. 232-39. Reprinted by
    permission of New York University Press from FRANCIPLEGIUS:
    Medieval and Linguistic Studies in Honor of Francis Peabody Magoun, Jr.
    edited by Jess B. Bessinger, Jr. and Robert P. Creed © 1965 by New York
    University.

Studies in Art and Literature for Belle de Costa Greene
    "The Pas Saladin in Art and Heraldry" Reprinted by permission of
    Princeton University Press © 1954 by Princeton University Press and
    Walter Art Gallery.

Revue Celtique
    "The Head in the Grail" XLVII, 1930, pp. 39-62.

Publications of the Modern Language Association of America
"Malory's Beaumains" Vol. LIV, No. 3, 1939, pp. 656-68.
"The Visit to the Perilous Castle: A Study of the Arthurian Modification of an Irish Theme" Vol. XLVIII, No. 4, 1933, pp. 1000-35.

Comparative Literature
"Breton Folklore and Arthurian Romance" Vol. II, No. 4, 1950, pp. 289-306.

The Journal of English and German Philology
"More Celtic Elements in 'Gawain and the Green Knight' " Vol. XLII, No. 2, 1943, pp. 149-84.

Speculum
"Edward I, Arthurian Enthusiast" Vol. XXVIII, No. 1, 1953, pp. 114-27.

Modern Philology
"By What Route did the Romantic Tradition of Arthur Reach the French? "
© 1936 by University of Chicago Press, Vol. XXXIII, No. 3, pp. 225-38.

Bulletin Bibliographique de la Société International Arthurienne
"Pioneers in Arthurian Scholarship" No. 16, 1964, pp. 95-106.

Romania
"Morgain La Fée in Oral Tradition" LXXX, 1959, pp. 337-67.
"Objections to the Celtic Origin of the 'Matière de Bretagne' " LXXIX, 1959, pp. 47-77.

Morgain la Fée in the Oral Tradition

(Romania LXXX, pp. 337-67)

MORGAIN LA FÉE IN ORAL TRADITION

In much recent Arthurian scholarship there has been a tendency to minimize or to overlook entirely the activities of a
large class of professional entertainers who in the twelfth and
thirteenth centuries wandered far and wide wherever French
was understood and fascinated courtly audiences with narrative songs or prose tales about the adventures of Gawain, the
magic of Merlin, or the loves of Tristan and Isolt. The testimony to their existence, though scattered, is ample. There is
the ex-post-facto prophecy which Geoffrey of Monmouth in
1134-35 attributed to Merlin, namely, that the deeds of the
Boar of Cornwall, Arthur, will be " cibus narrantibus " — which
is correctly interpreted in a manuscript of the late twelfth century : " fabulatores cibos sibi quaerent de eo narrando " [1].
There are the two oft-quoted references in Wace's *Brut*
(1155) [2].

Fist Artus la Roonde Table
Dont Breton dient mainte fable.

En cele grant pais que jo di...
Furent les aventures provees
Et les aventures trovees
Qui d'Artu sont tant racontees,
Que a fable sunt atornees...
Tant ont li conteor conté
Et li fableor tant fablé

---

1. E. Faral, *Légende arthurienne* (Paris, 1929), III, 191. *Collection Lato-
mus*, II (1949), 113. *Arthurian Literature in the Middle Ages*, ed. R.S. Loomis (Oxford, 1959), p. 58, n. 4.
2. Ed. I. Arnold, S.A.T.F., II, vss. 9751 f., 9787-98.

> Pour lor contes ambeleter,
> Que tout ont feit fables sanbler.

The author of a Life of St. Kentigern (1147-64) mentioned
the tales of the *histriones* about Ewen son of Ulien, i. e. Yvain
son of Urien ; and the term *histrio* can mean only a professional [1]. Peter of Blois, later in the century, observed [2] " de Arturo
et Gauganno et Tristanno fabulosa quaedam referunt histriones,
quorum auditu concutiuntur ad compassionem audientium
corda, et usque ad lacrimas compunguntur ". Chrétien de
Troyes, with what is probably a touch of condescension,
asserted about 1170 that the story of Erec was one which

> devant rois et devant contes
> Depecier et corrompre suelent
> Cil qui de conter vivre vuelent [3].

In the *Roman de Renard* the fox, diguised as a minstrel, boasts [4] :

> « Ge fot savoir bon lai breton
> Et de Merlin et de Noton,
> Del roi Artu et de Tristan,
> Del chevrefoil, de saint Brandan. »

In the thirteenth-century burlesque dialogue, *Les Deux Bour-
deurs Ribauds*, one of the minstrels declares [5] :

> « Ge sai des romanz d'aventure,
> De cels de la Reonde Table,
> Qui sont a oir delitable ».

And the other claims : " Si sai de Parceval l'estoire. " Similar
testimony comes from Provençal literature. The Catalan Guiraut de Cabrera, before 1170, gives a long list of the subjects
with which his jongleur should be familiar and includes several

---

1. *Romania*, XXII (1893), 506. R.S. Loomis, « Scotland and the Arthurian Legend », *Proceedings of the Society of Antiquaries of Scotland*, LXXXIX,
11.

2. Migne, *Patrologia Latina*, CCVII, col. 1088.

3. Vss. 20-22.

4. Tome I, vss. 2389-92.

5. E. Faral, *Mimes français du XIIIᵉ siècle* (Paris, 1910), p. 96, 103.

Arthurian personages [1] ; between 1195 and 1200 Guiraut de Calanson urges his jongleur to learn about Lansolet [2]. The author of *Flamenca*, after 1272, describes elaborately the festivities which celebrated the return of the lord of Bourbon with his bride, and shows us a numerous crowd of *conteurs* regaling the guests with a wide repertoire of tales, including several derived from Chrétien's poems [3].

There is also indirect evidence to the same effect. The First Continuation of Chrétien's *Conte del Graal* in the short original version (1190-1200) consists of a number of episodes, strung rather loosely together, and the poet not only addresses his auditors frequently as " Signeur ", but also at one point asks for a draught of wine before he continues his narrative of Gauvain [4]. The poet was obviously a *conteur* or *fabulator* by profession and carried over into his poem — which he may well have intended for recitation — the mannerisms of his trade. What is one to make of the fact that the two illustrations of an Arthurian subject which survive from the twelfth century — the Modena archivolt, which depicts Arthur, Gawain, Ider, and Kay riding to rescue the lady Winlogee from her captors, and the Otranto mosaic, which depicts Arthur mounted on a goat — are based on no surviving literary text of earlier date [5] ? Though it is conceivable, of course, that such texts once existed, the probabilities are that these subjects were brought to the knowledge of the Italian artists, as Wendelin Foerster recog-

---

1. M. de Riquer, *Los cantares de gesta franceses* (Madrid, 1952), p. 358-406.

2. *Romanische Forschungen*, XXII (1906), 151. *Romania*, LXXIX (1958), 59.

3. *Flamenca*, ed. P. Meyer (Paris, 1901), I, vss. 661 ff., 675 ff. On references in Provençal literature to the *Matière de Bretagne* see R. Lejeune in *Arthurian Literature in the Middle Ages*, ed. R. S. Loomis (Oxford, 1959), p. 393-9.

4. J. L. Weston, *Legend of Sir Perceval* (London, 1906), I, 238-43. *Continuations of the Old French Perceval*, ed. W. Roach, III, pt. I (Philadelphia, 1952), 452, 460, 478, 490.

5. R. S. and L. H. Loomis, *Arthurian Legends in Medieval Art* (New York, 1938), p. 32-6. R. S. Loomis, *Wales and the Arthurian Legend* (Cardiff, 1956), p. 72-4.

nized [1], by Breton *conteurs*. The name Winlogee, being derived
from the Breton Winlowen, supports this view [2].

Then there is the tradition, reported by Gervase of Tilbury
about 1211, that a groom, pursuing a runaway palfrey, entered the side of Mount Etna, and within discovered a palace,
where Arthur was lying on a royal bed, and that Arthur, after
restoring the palfrey to the groom, declared that he had lain
thus since the battle with Modred and Childeric, Duke of the
Saxons, his wounds opening afresh every year [3]. Though, of
course, the mention of Modred and Childeric betrays knowledge of Geoffrey of Monmouth's *Historia*, yet Gervase twice
asserted that he had heard the story from the *indigenae*, and
two variant versions provided by Caesarius of Heisterbach and
Etienne de Bourbon show no trace of Geoffrey's influence [4].
But even if we accept Gervase's statement that his informants
were Sicilians, yet they were not the inventors of the legend,
for they knew too well what Etna could vomit forth from its
interior to situate a splendid palace there, and they could have
learned of Arthur only from foreigners. The Normans, who
conquered Sicily in the eleventh century, have often been credited with introducing the tale, but belief in Arthur's survival
was not a Norman but a Breton obsession, to which we have
abundant testimony. There is testimony, moreover, though
scanty, that Breton knights participated in the conquest of
Sicily, [5] and we have just observed that the name Winlogee
on the Modena sculpture indicates the presence of Breton *con-*

---

1. *Zeits. f. rom. Phil.*, XXII (1898), 245.

2. A. de la Borderie, *Histoire de Bretagne*, II, 280. J. Loth, *Chrestomathie bretonne*, p. 147.

3. Arturo Graf, *Miti, leggende e superstizioni del medio evo*, (Torino, 1893), II, p. 304-7, 329 f. Gervase of Tilbury, *Otia Imperialia*, ed. F. Liebrecht, (Hannover, 1856), p. 12 f. Krappe argues convincingly in *Mitteil. d. schles. Gesellsch. f. Volkskunde*, XXXV (1935), 76-102, that this is the source of the Kyffhaüser legend.

4. Graf, *op. cit.*, p. 331 f.

5. *Göttingische gelehrte Anzeigen*, 1890, p. 831. Guillaume de Jumièges, *Gesta Normannorum Ducum*, ed. J. Marx (Paris, 1914), p. 187. Gaufredo Malaterra, *De Rebus Gestis Rogerii Calabriae et Siciliae Comitis*, ed. E. Pontieri, Rerum Italicarum Scriptores, V, pt. 1, p. 66.

teürs in Northern Italy. The ultimate source of the legend of Arthur's survival in a hollow mountain was probably Wales, for in the nineteenth century Rhys collected several folktales which describe Arthur sleeping in a cave surrounded by his warriors [1]. At any rate, since no text antedating Gervase's report describes Arthur as surviving in a cave or hollow mountain, there can be little doubt that this was a tradition spread through oral channels, even though it is not possible to prove that the transmitters were professional *fabulatores*.

All these types of evidence, therefore, converge toward the conclusion that, from the beginning of the twelfth century till well into the thirteenth, there flourished a body of professional entertainers, most of them French-speaking Bretons, who ranged from Scotland to Sicily and earned a precarious livelihood with a repertoire of tales of the Round Table cycle [2]. It is the particular purpose of this article to show that many of the scattered references to Morgain la Fée cannot be derived from any antecedent literary source but give evidence by their ramifications and their wide distribution that their source lay in the repertoire of the wandering Breton *conteurs*.

Let us first consider the direct testimony on this point of Giraldus Cambrensis, in his *Speculum Ecclesiae* (ca. 1216). After summarizing the Glastonbury tradition about the transport of Arthur's body to the isle of Avalon (which is equated with Glastonbury) by his kinswoman Morganis, and his burial there, Giraldus added : [3]

Propter hoc enim fabulosi Britones et eorum cantores fingere solebant, quod dea quaedam phantastica, scilicet et Morganis dicta, corpus Arthuri in insulam detulit Avalloniam ad eius vulnera sanandum. Quae cum sanata fuerint, redibit rex fortis et potens, ad Britones regendum, ut dicunt... Patet et hoc quoque quo pacto dea phantastica Morganis fabulatoribus nuncupata.

---

1. J. Rhys, *Celtic Folklore* (Oxford, 1901), II, 457-64, 477. *Folklore*, LXIX (1958), 13-6.

2. On the *conteurs* see Huet in *Moyen âge*, XXVIII (1915), 234-49 ; Zimmer in *Zeits. f. franz. Sprache u. Lit.*, XIII (1891), 86 f. ; E. Martin, *Zur Gralsage, Quellen u. Forschungen zur Sprach- und Culturgebiete der germanischen Völker*, XLII (1880), 27 f.

3. E. K. Chambers, *Arthur of Britain* (London, 1927), p. 272. Giraldus Cambrensis, *Opera*, Rolls Series, IV, 47.

This testimony is not to be questioned. Giraldus was highly intelligent, sceptical (except when it came to miracles), and widely traveled. We know that by *Britones* he did not mean the *Wallenses*, his own countrymen, the Welsh, but the Bretons [1], and it was notorious that the Bretons passionately believed in Arthur's return. Accordingly, there can be not the slightest doubt that Breton *fabulatores* and *cantores* included in their repertoire the legend that Morgain conveyed Arthur to the isle of Avalon and that they ranked her as a divinity.

About 1190 the German poet, Hartmann von Aue, produced a translation of Chrétien de Troyes's *Erec*, but when he came to Chrétien's reference to the healing plaster which Morgue had given to her brother Arthur, Hartmann substituted for Morgue Fâmurgan, and proceeded to devote 82 lines to her supernatural nature and powers, of which there was not a hint in Chrétien. Let me quote some of these lines :

Sî was ein gotinne.	(5161)	She was a goddess.
Swenne si begunde	(5167)	When she began
Ougen ir zouberlist,		To display her magic art,
Sô hâte si in kurzer vrist		She could in a short time
Die werlt umbevarn dâ		Go round the world
Unde kam wider sâ.		And come back again at once.
Im lufte als ûf der erde	(5177)	In the air as well as on the earth
Mohte sî ze ruowe sweben,		She could quietly fly,
Uf dem wâge und drunder leben.		Live upon or beneath the wave.
Und sô si des gern began,		And as she desired
Sô machete si den man		She made a man
Ze vogele oder ze tiere.		Into a bird or animal.
Und daz mich daz meiste	(5194)	And what to me the greatest
Dunket, die übelen geist,		Seems, the evil spirits,
Die dâ tiuvel sint genant,		Who are there called devils,
Die wâren all under ir hant.		Were all under her control.
Sie mohte wunder machen,		She could work wonders,

---

1. On the meaning of *Britones* see R. S. Loomis, *Wales and the Arthurian Legend*, p. 180 f., 184.

Wan ir muosten die trachen	For the dragons were compelled
Von den lüften bringen	To bring her from the air
Stiure zuo ir dingen,	A contribution for her operations,
Diu vische von dem wâge.	And the fish [to bring a contribution] from the water.
Diu erde deheine wurz entruoc, (5213)	The earth bore no herb
Ir enwaere ir kraft erkant	Whose virtue was not known to her
Alse mir mîn selbes hant.	As well as my hand to me.
Sît daz Sibillâ erstarp ...	Since Sibyl died ...
Sô gewan daz ertrîche	The earth has produced
(Daz wizzet waerlîche)	(Ye may know for truth)
Von zouberlîchem sinne	Of magic skill
Nie bezzer meisterinne	Never a better mistress
Danne Fâmurgàn.	Than Famurgan.

Whence came all this extraordinary information ? From earlier texts ? As has already been observed, nothing, not even the name-form Fâmurgân, came from Chrétien. It is arguable that the faculty of flight through the air and the knowledge of herbs represent a borrowing from Geoffrey of Monmouth's Latin *Vita Merlini* (ca. 1150), in which both attributes are assigned to the mistress of the faery Isle of Apples, Morgen. But the argument is not strong, since no other features of Fâmurgân are derivable from this source, and the *Vita Merlini*, of which only one complete manuscript survives, must have had a very limited circulation.

In 1926 Rudolph Zenker pointed out in a significant article [1] a number of points on which Hartmann's account of Fâmurgân corresponded to other descriptions of the enchantress, descriptions which, for chronological reasons, Hartmann could not have known, and which, conversely, could not have been drawn from a German poem. For these features, common to Hartmann and one or more texts, no literary source is extant, and hence we must postulate the existence of one or more lost traditional sources, whether written or oral. I propose to use Zenker's material and to make considerable additions.

First, Hartmann's statement that Morgain was a goddess (*gotinne*) is found in three later texts. As already noted, Giral-

---

1. *Zeits. f. franz. Sprache u. Lit.*, XLVIII (1926), 22-7.

dus records that the Bretons were wont to speak of her as " dea quaedam phantastica ". In *Gawain and the Green Knight* she is called " Morgne the goddes " [1]. A manuscript of the Prose *Lancelot* reads : [2]

Il fu voirs que Morgains, la suer le roi Artu, sot moult d'enchantement et de charoies sor totes fames ; et por la grant entente qu'ele i mist en lessa-ele et guerpi la covine des genz et conversoit et jor et nuit es granz forez parfondes et soutaines, si que maintes genz, dont il i avoit moult de foles par tot le pais, ne disoient mie que ce fust fame, mes il l'apeloient Morgain-la-déesse.

That Morgain was specifically a divinity of the waters is suggested by Hartmann's statement that she could live on or under the waves. The concept was, at any rate, widespread. Geoffrey of Monmouth in the *Vita Merlini*, vs. 1124, employs the term "nymphae" for Morgain and her sisters, and she herself is called by Etienne de Rouen (1167-69) " nympha perennis " [3]. Chrétien himself in *Erec* (ed. Foerster, vss. 1954-57) says nothing of Morgain's aquatic nature, but makes her the mistress of Guigamor, and the Breton lai of *Guingamor* depicts the faery mistress of the hero bathing naked in a spring [4]. Most remarkable corroboration comes from the Provençal romance, *Jaufré* [5], for the hero, a knight of Arthur's court, was attracted to a spring by the cries of a lady, and when he leaned over it in the attempt to rescue her handmaid from drowning, the lady pushed him in, sprang after him, and, clasped together, they reached the fairest land in the world at the bottom. Though unnamed, the lady revealed her identity later in the poem, declaring : " Jeu sui la fada del Gibel ". Two other romances

---

1. Vs. 2452.

2. W. J. A. Jonckbloet, *Roman van Lancelot* ('s Gravenhage, 1849), II, lxix. *Zeits. f. franz. Sprache u. Lit.*, XXXI (1907), 252.

3. R. S. Loomis, *Wales and the Arthurian Legend*, p. 62.

4. Marie de France, *Lais*, ed. K. Warnke, 3 d. edn. (Halle, 1925), p. 247. See Robert C. Hope, *Legendary Lore of the Holy Wells of England* (London, 1893), p. 112-5.

5. Vss. 8378-9288, 10346-10676. On Morgain's aquatic nature see R. S. Loomis, *Arthurian Tradition and Chrétien de Troyes*, p. 305-7.

concur in calling Morgain " la fée de Montgibel " [1], that is, Mount Etna, where, as we shall see later, her fabulous palace came to be or had already been localized.

These various witnesses combine to assure us that Morgain was widely celebrated as a water-nymph, and this naiad nature was the oldest of her attributes. Ritson and Lady Guest [2], over a century ago, recognized that the Welsh counterpart of Morgain was Modron, both being the mother of Owain or Ivain by Urien ; and Modron derived her name, as all the authorities agree, from the Celtic goddes Matrona, who gave her name to the River Marne [3]. Even in a sixteenth-century Welsh text this aquatic association is preserved, for here the mother of Owain by Urien is described as washing at a ford in Denbighshire [4]. It is plain that of all the supernatural attributes which Hartmann assigned to Fâmurgân none is more archaic and authentic than her power to glide upon or under the waves.

But she had also the gift of flight through the air, and this, though it is ascribed to her in the *Vita Merlini*, could hardly, as we have seen, have been derived by Hartmann from that poem. Indeed, two other authors, who were likewise independent of Geoffrey of Monmouth for their information, show a familiarity with what must have been a wide-spread tradition. Graindor de Brie in the *Bataille Loquifer* (late twelfth or early thirteenth century) tells how Morgain and two other fays conveyed Renouart through the air to Avalon, whither Arthur, Gauvain, and Ivain had already been wafted [5]. A particularly fantastic episode in the *Didot Perceval* [6] (early thir-

1. Lucy A. Paton, *Fairy Mythology of Arthurian Romance* (Boston, 1903), p. 250. This very valuable collection of material on Morgain and Niniane will shortly be reprinted by Burt Franklin, 514 W. 113 St., New York.

2. J. Ritson, *English Metrical Romances* (London, 1802), III, 227. C. Guest, *Mabinogion* (London, 1877), p. 36, n.

3. See R. S. Loomis, *Wales and the Arthurian Legend*, p. 119, n. 68.

4. *Ibid.*, p. 98; T. Gwynn Jones, *Welsh Folklore and Folk-custom* (London, 1930), p. 107.

5. Paton, *op. cit.*, p. 49 f. Le Roux de Lincy, *Livre des légendes* (Paris, 1836), p. 248.

6. *Didot-Perceval*, ed. W. Roach (Philadelphia, 1941), p. 195-202. Cf. Loomis, *Wales and the Arthurian Legend*, p. 91-104.

teenth century) tells how the hero, attacked near a ford by a
flock of black birds, struck one of them down, whereupon it
turned into a beautiful woman and was carried off dead by the
other birds. We are informed that the slain bird was actually
the sister of a fay who dwelt in an invisible castle near the
ford, and that now all was well with her since she had been
transported to Avalon. It becomes quite clear that Hartmann,
Geoffrey, Graindor, and the author of the *Didot Perceval* were
acquainted with various forms of the tradition that the fays of
Avalon, and pre-eminently Morgain, possessed the power of
flight in the shape of birds. There is no literary text in existence
from which the four authors could have derived this information, and we are once more thrown back on the hypothesis of
oral diffusion.

Zenker also pointed out a curious and highly significant correspondence between what Hartman tells us of Fâmurgân and
an episode in the *Prophecies de Merlin* [1], composed by an Italian
in French between 1272 and 1279. While the German poet
mentions that devils and dragons were at the service of the fay,
the unknown Italian author tells of a competition in magic
between her and the Dame d'Avalon (here differentiated from
Morgain), the Queen of Norgales (North Wales), and Sebile.

Lors getta Morgain ses enchantements et fist venir une légion d'ennemis
d'enfer. Et qant il furent venus, Morgain leur dist : « Il vous convient aller
à la dame d'Avalon et la conduisez en cette tour et parmy les airs, et faictes
tant quelle voye appertement aller son corp parmy les airs si comme on
voit aller les oiseaulxs, et s'en voyse la moitié parmi la terre ainsi comme
fait le dragon pour dévorer ». Alors incontinent s'en vont tous au comman-
dement de Morgain, la moitié d'eux en signifiance des oiseaux emmy l'air
les plus hideulx et redoubtés qui oncques mais fussent veus. Et adonc se
lancent pour prendre la dame d'Avalon. Mais de rien ne les doubte pour la
force des pierres, et la noise leva de toutes parts, et fuyrent l'ung ça, l'autre
là, mais pas n'avoyent loysir de fuyr, car ils veoient toute la terre couverte de
dragons enflammés pour dévorer tous ceulx qu'ils trouveroient [2].

When Morgain herself appeared on the scene in the endeavor to prove her superiority as a mistress of spells, she was

---

1. Ed. Lucy A. Paton (New York, 1926), I, 415 f.
2. Quoted from *Zeits. f. franz. Sprache u. Lit.*, XLVIII, 25 f.

ignominiously defeated. For the Dame d'Avalon put on her magic ring and by its virtue forced her rival to remove all her clothes — a trick which she had previously worked on the Queen of Norgales and Sebile. And at the sight of Morgain in the nude, she « ryoit si fort qu'un mot ne sçavoit dire ». A unique text of the *Prophecies,* contained in ms. Bibl. de l'Arsenal 5229 and unknown to Zenker, relates that on another occasion Morgain sent evil spirits in the form of knights to a tournament at Vincestre (Winchester) [1]. Suddenly a dragon, who was really Lucifer himself thus transformed by Morgain, appeared and proceeded to devour the other diabolic knights. Sebile caused fires to burst from the ground at various points. The Round Table knight Segurant attacked the dragon and drove it from the field.

Though much of the *Prophecies* consists of mere invention, only a traditional source can account for the agreement between the German poem of Hartmann and the Italian romance on this matter of Morgain's power over the devils. Neither author could have borrowed from the other, and it is most unlikely that a single French text, even if it once existed, would have inspired treatments so different.

Before leaving Hartmann's account of Fâmurgân, let us note that it agrees with the *Prophecies* also in comparing Morgain with the Sibyl ; Hartmann refers to the classical figure as a forerunner of Morgain in the practice of magic, and the Italian author represents Morgain and Sebile as contemporary practitioners of the art. The significance of this association of the two enchantresses is not diminished by the fact that the author of the *Prophecies* may have taken it over from the French Prose *Lancelot,* where Morgain, Sebille, and the Queen of Sorestan form a trio who put a spell on Lancelot, imprisoned him, and presented themselves to him as rivals for his love [2]. For there is striking evidence to show that Hartmann and the authors of the *Lancelot* and the *Prophecies de Merlin* were not the only ones to associate Morgain with the Sibyl; the extraordinary

---

1. *Prophecies,* ed. Paton, I, 439 f.

2. *Vulgate Version of the Arthurian Romances,* ed. H. O. Sommer (Washington, 1908-16), V, 91-93.

account given early in the fifteenth century by Andrea da Barberino of the visit of Guerino il Meschino to the abode of the fay Alcina, who incidentally revealed herself as the Sibyl who had given Aeneas a vision of Anchises, was actually an elaboration of a visit to the abode of Morgain la Fée. Though Andrea borrowed many details from Dante, the *Fatti d'Enea* of Guido da Pisa, and one of his own works, *Ugone d'Alvernia* [1], and though the geographical setting on a mountain near Norcia in the central Apennines was described with accuracy, the main theme must have been taken from some version of the visit to Morgain's enchanted palace. A comparison of an episode in the long Arthurian romance of *Claris et Laris*, begun in 1268, with Andrea's composite tale will suffice to establish the connection. Incidentally, it is of interest to note that Andrea was not only a prolific author but also a professional reciter : « la sua professione come si rileva dalle portate al catasto riferite dal Vandelli, fu quella di " cantatore ", ossia di narratore o lettore, davanti al publico, di romanzi francesi di cavalleria, da lui rifatti [2] ». In a sense, then, he was a descendant of the Breton *conteurs*. Let me first give a résumé of the passage in *Claris et Laris* [3].

The two titular heroes, riding through the forest of Broceliande, hear exquisite strains of music, but can see nothing to produce them. A fair damsel offers to guide them to an abode whose mistress will give them shelter, and leads them to a valley, adorned with fine dwellings, from which the music issues, so that they seem to be in the heavenly Paradise. But, looking back, they perceive that the road by which they have come has disappeared. They pass through a gate and along streets, behung with the richest fabrics, but empty of people. Entering a palace, they are welcomed by twelve ladies. One

---

1. *Il Guerrin Meschino*, ed. G. Osella, *Pallante* IX-X (Torino, 1932), p. 114, 119. The date of *Guerino* is usually given 1391, but see *ibid.*, p. 16 f.

2. *Ibid.*, p 15. Till late in the nineteenth century *Guerino* itself was read or recited publicly by *cantastorie* in many parts of Italy. *Ibid.*, p. 160 f.

3. Ed. J. Alton, Bibliothek des literarischen Vereins in Stuttgart, CLXIX (Tübingen, 1884), vss. 3548-4142. Paton, *Fairy Mythology*, p. 94 f.

of them reveals herself as Morgain, and assures Laris that she and the other ladies will grant them any request, save leave to depart. Claris protests, in vain, and though the fays serve a delicious repast, the two friends spend the night in lamentation and mutual confidences. At dawn, Laris descends into a garden, and there finds a fay, Madoine, who offers to become his paramour, and he agrees on condition that she reveal to him the way by which he and Claris have come. He lies with her, and she fulfills her part of the bargain by showing him a small stone which, when turned, reveals a broad road leading out of the valley. Two days later Claris and Laris avail themselves of the secret to make their escape.

Andrea's narrative [1], as already noted, is greatly amplified and has been adapted to the localization in a hollow mountain and to the theme of Guerino's quest for information concerning his parents, from whom he had been separated as an infant ; but the resemblance to the French romance is not hard to discern. Arriving at Norcia, Guerino makes inquiries and learns that the wise enchantress Alcina resides in a cavernous mountain near by. Heedless of warnings, he enters the cave, passes a sinner who has been transformed by Alcina into a serpent, and arrives at a large metal door, beside which is an inscription, saying that he who enters and does not leave before the end of a year will live till the Judgement Day, and then both body and soul shall die. Three damsels open the door and lead Guerino to their beautiful mistress. She welcomes him, shows him her treasures, provides a feast, and leads him to a garden which seems like a new Paradise. She tells him the history of the Sibyls and reveals that she is the same whom Aeneas encountered. Instead of answering Guerino's question, she tries to seduce him, even as a last resort lying beside him in the nude. He discovers that every Friday night all the inhabitants of the Paradise take the form of dragons, serpents, and other reptiles. Still, hoping to obtain news of his parents, Guerino remains, but at the end of a year, his efforts proving vain, he determines to leave, and one of the damsels of Alcina

---

1. *Il Guerrin Meschino*, ed. Osella, p. 114-25. Paton, *Fairy Mythology*, p. 53 n. G. Paris, *Légendes du moyen âge* (Paris, 1903), p. 88-91.

conducts him to the door by which he entered. He travels to Rome, confesses to the Pope, and is granted absolution.

In spite of the obvious changes and literary embellishments, the account of Guerino's visit to the Sibyl's sensual Paradise is manifestly derived from some version of Morgain's faery Paradise not unlike that described in *Claris et Laris*. In both tales the beautiful fay who presides over the enchanted realm welcomes the hero or heroes and endeavors to hold them in her power; she is attended by charming damsels; there is an effort, successful or unsuccessful, to seduce the hero; one of the damsels reveals a way of escape. It is, in fact, Morgain's voluptuous nature and her persistent habit of tempting the visitor to her castle which accounts for the behavior of Alcina in a fashion for which neither the Roman nor the Christian concept of the Sibyls offered a precedent. Moreover, the escape from Morgain's prison with the aid of one of her damsels must also have been traditional, for the motif occurs not only in *Claris et Laris* but also in the Prose *Lancelot* and *Alixandre l'Orphelin* [1]. Alcina's nature is best explained, then, as uniting characteristic features of Morgain and the Sibyl : like the former she is a beautiful temptress, whose efforts to keep her victims perpetually in thrall are thwarted by one of her damsels; like the latter she dwells in a cave and possesses preternatural knowledge. If it seems difficult to believe that the legends of Morgain and her enchanted valley were transferred to a mountain in central Italy, let us remember that the tradition of Arthur's survival in the blissful isle of Avalon, over which Morgain presided, was carried even farther and was attached to Mount Etna.

Whether Andrea da Barberino himself was responsible for this fusion of the Sibyl and Morgain into one person and for localizing Morgain's paradise in the Monte della Sibilla, it is impossible to say; but it is highly probable that his activity as a *cantatore* did much to give the legend a vogue. For when Antoine de la Sale, the Provençal tutor of Prince John of Calabria, made a pilgrimage to the moutain in 1420, he seems

---

1. *Vulgate Version*, ed. Sommer, V, 94 f. *Alixandre l'orphelin*, ed. C. E. Pickford (Manchester, 1951), p. 28-30. Paton, *Fairy Mythology*, p. 52, 57.

to have found several stories of visits to the Sibyl's cavern current among « les gens du pais » [1], and one account, which he gives in full in *La Salade* (1438-40) [2], presents such a similarity to Andrea's version that there can be little doubt that Andrea had some influence, either through his book or through his recitals, on the local tradition. But on three important points La Sale's story differs from that in *Guerino* : the adventurous knight was a German ; he did not rebuff the temptress, but yielded ; when he sought absolution from the Pope for his sin, it was refused, and in despair he returned to the Paradise of the Queen Sibille. Now there are numerous testimonies to show that in the fifteenth century this notion of a hollow mountain in Italy, notorious for its sensual delights, was thoroughly familiar to Germans. As early as 1410, Dietrich von Niem wrote of a mount near Pozzuoli, « quem delusi multi Alemani in vulgari appellant ' der Gral ', asserentes prout etiam in illis regionibus plerique autumant, quod in illo multi sunt homines vivi et victuri usque ad diem iudicii, qui tripudibus et deliciis sunt dediti, et ludibriis diabolicis perpetuo irretiti » [3]. This is probably an offshoot from the tradition which La Sale heard ten years later about the Mount of the Sibyl ; at any rate, there can be no doubt of a relationship between La Sale's version and the tales reported by Felix Faber about 1483 [4] :

Et moderno tempore vulgus rudis delirat de quodam Tusciae monte, non longe a Roma, in quo dicunt dominam Venerem deliciis frui cum quibusdam viris et foemenis. Unde de hoc carmen confictum habetur, quod manifeste a vulgo per Alemanniam canitur de quodam nobili Suevo, quem nominant Danhuser, de Danhusen villa prope Dünckelspüchel. Hunc fingunt ad tempus in monte cum Venere fuisse, et cum poenitentia ductus Papae

---

1.Antoine de la Sale, *Le Paradis de la reine Sibyle*, ed. F. Desonay (Paris, 1930), p. 15, 17, 23.

2. *Ibid.*, p. 21-38. Paton, *Fairy Mythology*, p. 52, n. 2. Paris, *op. cit.*, p. 79-84.

3. M. Lexer, *Mittelhochdeutsches Handwörterbuch*, sub *gral*. P. S. Barto, *Tannhäuser and the Mountain of Venus* (New York, 1916), p. 16 f., 119.

4. F. Faber *Evagatorium*, ed. Hassler, III, 221 ; I, 153. Barto, *op. cit.*, p. 21-3, 122 f.

fuisset confessus, denegata fuit sibi absolutio, et ita regressus in montem nusquam comparuit, et in deliciis vivit, ut dicunt, usque ad diem judicii. ..In tantum autem hac fama dementati sunt Alemanni, ut multi simplices ad hos famatos peregrinentur montes... Et hodie plures credunt Venerem in monte Veneris, qui est in insula Cypri, ducere vitam voluptuosam cum suis, cum qua canunt esse quendam dictum Tannhuser.

From these testimonies several highly interesting conclusions can be drawn. First, the Italian legend of the Paradise in the hollow mountain exercised a particular fascination on the Germans, and underwent various ramifications, of which the Tannhäuser legend was one [1]. Secondly, German scholars, who may well have been familiar with German poems depicting a paradisal garden of Venus and who surely realized that the goddess of love was a far more appropriate figure than the chaste prophetess of classical and Christian tradition to preside over a realm of sensual delight, converted the Monte della Sibilla into the Venusberg. Third, some of the more learned, such as Faber, argued from the existence of a mountain sacred to Venus on the isle of Cyprus that the Venusberg had been wrongly localized in Italy and was to be sought rather in the goddess's ancient homeland.

Thus we see how an originally Breton legend of Morgain's Paradise of amorous pleasures was transferred in Italy to the Sibyl, because Morgain, like the Sibyl, could foretell the future; and how, in turn, this Italian legend was transferred by Germans to Venus, because the presiding genius of the Monte della Sibilla retained too much of the lascivious nature of her Breton original to comport well with the established character of the Sibyl. We see, too, from the testimony of contemporary writers that these developments were largely an oral phenomenon, and that it was only after the legends had been the subject of popular rumor and perhaps of professional recitation that literary men set them down and elaborated them on parchment.

---

1. On this legend see Barto, *op. cit.*; Paris, *op. cit.*, p. 113-45; A. F. J. Remy in *Journal of English and Germanic Philology*, XII (1913), 1-45; K. Nyrop, « Tannhäuser i Venusbjaerget », *Fortids Sagn og Sange*, VI (1909), 81-99; H. Dübi in *Zeits. d. Vereins f. Volkskunde*, XVII (1907), 249-64. La Sale, *op. cit.*, p. CX-CXX.

I cannot claim to be the first to detect the affinity between the Sibyl of Norcia, the goddess of the Venusberg, and Morgain la Fée. In a German Shrovetide farce of the fifteenth century on the theme of the Horn Test, Arthur's sister, who can be no other than Morgain, and who, like Morgain in the Prose *Tristan* [1], sent her magic horn to Arthur's court out of malice, is referred to as the Queen of Cyprus (Venus ?) [2]. In the same century Boiardo made Alcina a sister of Morgana, and was followed in the sixteenth by Ariosto. De Reumont and Gaston Paris called attention to the fact that Aretino associated « la Fata Morgana » and the Sibyl of Norcia [3]. Nyrop in 1909 developed the idea that Alcina was a dual personality, a Sibyl-Venus, and traced the latter element in her nature back to Morgain [4]. Whether presiding over a valley or an island or a cavern of libidinous delights, and even though disguised under different names, the three medieval enchantresses displayed such a community of traits that their essential oneness was readily and properly recognized by men of letters as well as scholars.

Andrea da Barberino and Antoine de la Sale may now be added, in view of their transformation of Morgain's Paradise into the Monte della Sibilla, to the three authors previously discussed who associate the fay with the prophetess. There is still a sixth who makes the same connection, though in a different way. The author of an interpolation in the *Wartburg-krieg*, a poem of the latter half of the thirteenth century, introduced in the course of an imaginary riddling contest between Wolfram von Eschenbach and Klingsor, the following curious reference to Arthur's survival in a hollow mountain [5].

---

1. E. Löseth, *Roman en prose de Tristan* (Paris, 1891), p. 39, 136, 137, 178.

2. *Fastnachtspiele aus dem fünfzehnten Jahrhundert, Nachlese*, ed. A. von Keller, Stuttgart Lit. Ver., XLVI (1858), 183-215. *Speculum*, IX (1934) 44.

3. A. de Reumont, *Saggi di storia e letteratura* (Florence, 1880), p. 378-94; Paris, *op. cit.*, p. 94.

4. Nyrop, *loc. cit.*, p. 85-7.

5. *Wartburgkrieg*, ed. T. A. Rompelman (Amsterdam, 1939), p. 185 f. I have adopted the reading Juno from another ms., and have put a comma, instead of a period at the end of the sixth line. For discussions of this pas-

Klingsor : Felîciâ, Sibillen kint,
    Und Jûnô, die mit Artûs in dem berge sint,
    Die habent vleisch sam wir und ouch gebeine.
    Die vrâget ich, wie der künic lebe,
    Artûs, und wer der massenîe spîse gebe,
    Wer ir dâ pflege mit dem tranke reine,
    Harnasch, kleider unde ros — sie lebent noch in vreche.
    Die gotinne bringe her vür dich,
    Daz si dichs unterscheiden, sam si tâten mich,
    Oder dir muoz hôher meisterkunst gebreche.
    Felîciâ ist noch ein maget.
    Bî der selben wirde hât sie mir gesaget,
    Daz sie einen abbet in dem berge saehe...
    Der schreip mit sîner hant vil gar die spaehe,
    Wie Artûs in dem berge lebe und sîne helde maere,
    Der sie mir hundert hât genant,
    Die er mit im vuorte von Britanien lant...
Wolfram : Sybillen kint, Felîciâ,
    Und Jûnô, die sint beide mit Artûs aldâ,
    Daz hât mir Sante Brandan wol betiutet.

(Klingsor : Felicia, the Sibyl's child, and Juno, who are with Arthur in the mountain, have flesh and bones like us. I asked them how the king, Arthur, lives, and who provides the household with food, who there supplies them with pure drink, armor, clothing, and horses. They still live in vigor. Bring the goddesses here before thee that they may tell thee as they did me ; otherwise thou must lack the high mastery. Felicia is still a maid ; by that virtue she told me that she saw an abbot in the mountain... With his hand he wrote the very truth, how Arthur lives in the mountain and his famous heroes ; she named a hundred of them to me, whom he brought with him from Britain... Wolfram : The Sibyl's child, Felicia, and Juno are both with Arthur there ; of that St. Brandan has well informed me.)

We have already met with the concept of Arthur living amidst luxurious surroundings in the cavernous depths of Mount Etna, as a popular tradition reported by Gervase of Tilbury early in the thirteenth century, and though the interpolator of the *Wartburgkrieg* may not have had any particular *berg* in mind, he was doubtles echoing the same basic tradition.

---

sage see Barto, *op. cit.*, p. 11-13 ; Remy, *loc. cit.*, p. 20 f. ; Barto in *Journal of English and Germanic Philology*, XII (1913), 298-302 ; XV (1916), 377-89.

Other texts — the *Bataille Loquifer*, already noted, and some still to be discussed — agree with the lines above in surrounding Arthur in his elysian abode with the knights of the Round Table. A novel feature is the mystifying question as to how Arthur lived and who provided the company with food and drink, armor, and steeds. Modern scholars have answered this question by « The Grail » [1], and there is evidence to be adduced presently, which confirms this answer. What of Arthur's two female companions, Juno and the maid Feliciâ, the Sibyl's child ? The only such companion named in other descriptions of Arthur's survival (except for the eight sisters of Morgen in the *Vita Merlini*) is Morgain herself, and it is easy to guess how the German poet came to duplicate the famous fay. From one source he gathered that she was a goddess and a queen, and therefore called her Juno ; from another source he learned that she was a virgin prophetess and therefore distinguished her from Juno and described her as the Sibyl's maiden child. From no surviving text could he have extracted this composite information about Arthur's sojourn in the Other World. Where, then, could he have got it except from such oral sources as we must postulate to explain other references to Morgain ? The six authors who in such different ways reveal that Morgain and the Sibyl were linked in their minds, or were actually identified, make it clear that this association was a part of the floating Arthurian traditions.

There is possibly a seventh author who dimly and in a still different way shows the influence of this association. About 1195 the Swiss priest Ulrich von Zatzikhoven translated from Anglo-Norman French a romance of Lanzelet [2]. The heroine's name is variously spelled as Yblis or Ibelis, and she dwells in the Vals Iblê [3]. First, let us observe that the name of the damsel forms an anagram of Sibil(e), and we have at least two in-

---

1. Barto, *op. cit.*, p. 12. Remy, *loc. cit.*, p. 20, n. 58. E. Martin, *Zur Gralsage*, p. 34 ff. W. J. Entwistle, *Arthurian Legend in the Literatures of the Spanish Peninsula* (London, 1925), p. 188 f.

2. *Lanzelet*, ed. K. A. Hahn (Frankfurt, 1845). Trans. into English by K. G. T. Webster (New York, 1951). See introd., p. 3-5.

3. Trans. Webster, p. 196-8.

stances in Wolfram von Eschenbach's *Parzival* where he has coined names from anagrams (Sigune from *cusine*, Arnive from Iverne). Secondly, Morgain's Paradise of sensual delights is represented in *Claris et Laris* and in the Prose *Lancelot* as a valley, and Vals Iblê may well represent a misreading of French *Vals Sibile*. Thirdly, Yblis possessed four of the familiar attributes of Morgain [1] : a) she was supremely beautiful ; b) she had foreknowledge of the coming of Lanzelet ; c) she took the initiative in declaring her love to him, and hardly had he won her by combat with her father, when without any marriage ceremony she lay with him ; d) in the wood and the valley where Yblis dwelt the grass was green and the trees bore fruit at all seasons, and no wound was so great but that, if the fruit was bound upon it, it healed at once. Other elements in Yblis' story have no counterpart in the Morgain tradition but show a resemblance to the Welsh *Dream of Maxen* [2]. But if the anagrammatic formation of her name is conceded it is hardly fortuitous that Iblis and the Vals Iblê should present such a similarity to Morgain and her paradisal valley.

With this seventh author who seems to reveal, though not too clearly, the persistent tendency to associate or identify Morgain with the Sibyl we complete the listing of the parallels which demonstrate that Hartmann von Aue's description of the enchantress was neither based on earlier literary sources nor spun out of his own head, but was derived rather from oral traditions, first promulgated by the Breton *conteurs*.

Another branch of the Morgain legend transferred her habitat from Avalon to a Mediterranean island, but it is quite distinct from that, reported by Faber, which identified the island with Cyprus. On the contrary, as in the tradition which situated Arthur's palace in the interior of Mount Etna, Morgain's paradisal abode is more or less explicitly equated with Sicily, and her lecherous aspect is not emphasized. About the middle of the thirteenth century the anonymous author of *Floriant et Florete* told how Morgain and two other fays of the salt sea carried off the infant Floriant to her chief castle of

---

1. Trans. Webster, p. 78-88.
2. *Ibid.*, p. 198.

Mongibel, Mount Etna ; and later, when her foster-son was grown up, she referred to herself as his *amie et drue* [1]. At the end of the romance, she sent a white stag to lure him from Palermo up a mountain, and there in a beautiful castle he found her sitting on a couch. She welcomed him, saying that he would never part from her and that in her castle no one ever died. Arthur, her brother, was destined to come there and when Floriant mourned at being separated from his wife Florete, the fay had her transported that night to join them at Mongibel [2]. Here the traditional elements are : Morgain as one of a trio of fays ; Morgain as mistress, as well as foster-mother, of the hero ; the substitution of Sicily for Avalon as the island abode of Morgain and her brother, and the localization of her palace on or in Mount Etna. Once more let us observe that no surviving literary text could have supplied this information ; it is an elaborated form of the Sicilian traditions recorded by Gervase of Tilbury and Caesarius of Heisterbach.

A much fuller version, with a humorous twist, was given by a Majorcan, Guillem Torrella, in *La Faula* (1360-70) [3]. The poet was floated on the back of a whale from Minorca to an island far to the east, landed, ate of the magic fruit, and was informed by a serpent in French that this was the land where « repaira Morgan la Fee e missire lo reys Artus ». After a sleep, Guillem was waked by the warmth of the sun, and rejoiced in the beauty of the meadows, flowering trees and rivers. A richly caparisoned palfrey appeared and, when humbly requested, carried him to a palace in the midst of a garden where the trees bore fruit and flowers at the same time. A lovely damsel of sixteen years, no other than « Morgan la feya », bade him welcome and led him into the palace, of which the walls were covered with paintings of Arthur's

---

1. *Floriant et Florete*, ed. H. F. Williams (Ann Arbor, 1947), vss. 549-70, 2523 f. See Loomis, *Arthurian Tradition*, p. 88, n. 18.

2. *Floriant et Florete*, vss. 8177-278.

3. Mila y Fontanals, *Poetes catalans* (Paris, 1876), p. 9-22. *Canconer dels Comtes d'Urgell*, ed. D. G. Llabres (Societat Catalana de Bibliofils, 1906), p. 131 ff.

knights, their deeds and loves. Arthur was at first invisible, but when the enchantress placed a ring before Guillem's eyes, he perceived a young man, stretched on a splendid bed and gazing at a sword, and learned that this was indeed the king whose return the Bretons awaited. He had been brought here by Morgain and bathed by her in water of the Tigris, which flowed from the Earthly Paradise. When Guillem expressed suprise that one who had reigned over ninety years could look so youthful, Arthur explained that this was due to annual visits of the Holy Grail. After a gloomy interview, the poet took his leave, the fay pointed out through a window the road by which he had come, and the whale obligingly conveyed him back to Majorca.

Though the poet mentions neither Sicily nor Mongibel and may have imagined an island farther to the east, he was surely drawing upon the same oral tradition reported by Gervase of Tilbury and reflected in *Floriant et Florete*. Here are the palfrey, the palace, the king on his royal couch, brought hither by Morgain. There is also a connection with the *Wartburgkrieg*, for, like the « Sibillen kint », Morgain is quite young, and the Grail preserves Arthur's youth by supplying him with a holy food, whereas in the German poem it supplies the whole company with food and pure drinks. And, taken together, the passage in the *Wartburgkrieg* and that in *La Faula* shed light on the mysterious statement of Dietrich von Niem, quoted above, that the Germans call the mountain near Pozzuoli, where many people live till Doomsday, given over to dancing and wantonness, « der Gral ». In fact, there must have been current, particularly among the Germans, a strong assocition between the Grail as a source of paradisal abundance and a preservative of youth on the one hand and the Paradise of Morgain la Fée on the other. Only thus can we comprehend the many German references to the *Grâl* as a place dedicated to worldly and even lustful pleasures [1]. And were not Wolfram von Eschenbach's account of the *Grâl* as a food-providing talisman and his two references to it as « der wunsch von Pardîs », — translated by Mornet as « ce qu'on peut souhaiter

---

1. Barto, *op. cit.*, p. 8-11.

de plus beau, même au Paradis » — influenced by this sensual aspect of the talisman ?

It is this connection of Morgain with the Grail which explains the curious behavior of the Grail Bearer in the Prose *Lancelot*, behavior so unbecoming in one who was wont to hold in her hands the dish from which Christ and the apostles had eaten the lamb on the eve of the Crucifixion [1]. King Pelles' daughter entered into a plot to bring Lancelot to her bed and lay with him ; she later repeated the performance ; naturally she roused the jealousy of Guenevere ; later still, she dwelt with Lancelot in a castle on the Isle de Joie, where the climate was so summery that she and her damsels could dance every day beneath a pine [2]. Is it not obvious that her conduct strangely resembles that of Morgain in the same romance, and that the Isle de Joie is Morgain's isle of Avalon ? The marked discrepancy between the Grail story of the Prose *Lancelot* and the Perceval versions is due to the fact that the authors took their material from different strands of Celtic tradition. The daughter of King Pelles had a prototype quite distinct from the prototype of Chrétien's Grail Bearer, and that prototype was Morgain [3]. Thus we have three texts which bring the Grail in one way or another into relation with the fay. *La Faula* gives us a girlish Morgain and the Grail which preserves the youth of her brother Arthur ; the *Wartburgkrieg* gives us « Sibillen kint » and the unnamed source of food and drink which modern scholars identify as the Grail; the *Lancelot* models the Grail Bearer on Morgain. It is surely unnecessary to explain why this hypothetical branch of the Grail legend which assigned the high office of Grail bearer to Morgain and converted the Grail realm into the domain of Venus, where feasting, dancing, and amorous play prevailed, has left so few and such obscure traces. When the Grail, originally a platter of plenty [4], had been converted through misunderstanding

---

1. *Vulgate Version*, ed. Sommer, I, 13.
2. *Ibid.*, V, 107-10, 379 f., 402 f.
3. Loomis, *Arthurian Tradition*, p. 143, n. 43 ; p. 375-9.
4. *Ibid.*, p. 387 f.

into a sacramental vessel or holy relic [1], — and this had begun before Chrétien's time, — then everything and everybody connected with it had to be in some degree sanctified.
Morgain herself, because of her scandalous reputation, was the
most difficult person to purge, so that even where she survives
most clearly as King Pelles' daughter, her name is suppressed
and her motive in acquiescing in the plot to bring Lancelot to
bed with her is exalted into joyful submission to the divine
will.

After this excursus on the Grail, let us turn our attention to
the longest and most amusing of the accounts of Morgain and
Arthur in the Isle of Avalon, namely, that found in *Ly Myreur des Histors* of the waggish chronicler, Jean d'Outremeuse
of Liège, who died in 1400 [2]. It deserves to be reprinted en-
tire, but a brief summary will serve our purpose. In the year
896, Ogier the Dane, the paladin of Charlemagne, left Cyprus
in a dromond and was wrecked on a rock near the isle of Avalon, to which he was conveyed by angels. He fought with
many monsters and was attacked as an intruder by Arthur and
Gawain. Summoned by Alberon, her son, Morgain interrupted the combat and, after assuring the Dane that she was no
evil spirit, led him to her castle, made of precious stones and
surrounded with gardens and odorous trees. The great hall was
adorned with paintings of Arthur and his knights. But, the author tells us, the whole show was merely « vens et fantomme »,
and had been created through the magic arts which Morgain
had learned from Merlin. She now placed a ring on Ogier's
finger, and at once it seemed that he was but thirty years
old. Jean interrupts the narrative to tell us that the damsels

---

1. *Romans du Graal dans la littérature des XIIᵉ et XIIIᵉ siècles, Colloques
internationaux du Centre National de la Recherche Scientifique*, III (1956), 233-
45.

2. Ed. S. Bormans (Bruxelles, 1877), IV, 47-58. Another 14th century
narrative which places Arthur and Morgain in the East is *Le Bastard de
Bouillon*, ed. A. Scheler (Bruxelles, 1877), p. 119-32. Baudoin learned from
the princes of Mecca that beyond the Red Sea lay the land of faerie. With
twelve barons he crossed over in a boat; they were welcomed by Arthur
and his sister, and losing all desire to return to their homes spent five years
in a garden where a thousand fays disported themselves.

and ladies of Morgain's household lived chaste lives, but he notes that some say that they love the sin of lechery and that Ogier had children by Morgain, one of them a giant, but Jean admits that he does not know. Morgain entertained her guest by making paintings disappear and appear on the walls. When the tables were set, she gave him a cloth on which no melancholy man, murderer, or coward could partake of food without its turning black and burning ; but when Ogier ate, it gleamed more brightly than before. The episode concludes with the statement that Ogier remained a long time on the island in joy and sanctity, forgetful of the world, and that though the marvels recounted may seem beyond belief, the author is inclined to accept them because all were wrought by invoking the Trinity !

It is certain that for much of this fantastic story d'Outremeuse was dependent on three literary sources which have come down to us. The fourteenth-century expansion of Ogier's history provided the wreck near Avalon, the magic ring which restores the hero to young manhood, the birth of a son named Meurvain, and the long sojourn with Morgain [1]. The *Bataille Loquifer* provided the combat with monsters and the presence of Gawain in Avalon. *Huon of Bordeaux* is probably the romance from which Morgain's son Alberon or Auberon was borrowed [2].

But two elements in the story were not inspired by any written texts that we know. To be sure, *La Faula*, as we have just seen, also gives a description of the mural paintings in Morgain's palace ; but that the chronicler of Liège had read the Catalan poem is out of the question ; and though the French Prose *Lancelot* informs us that the hero, when imprisoned by Morgain, covered the walls with frescoes depicting his triumphs in arms and his love for Guenevere [3], yet the details of this account differ so completely from the treatment of the theme by Jean d'Outremeuse that no direct relationship can be inferred. In short, there was no common literary source,

---

1. Paton, *Fairy Mythology*, *p.* 74-7.
2. *Ibid.*, p. 115.
3. *Vulgate Version*, ed. Sommer, V, 217 f.

but we must assume a vague tradition to explain the agreement of *Ly Myreur*, *La Faula*, and the Prose *Lancelot* as to the
elaborate mural decorations of Morgain's palace.

Moreover, there is the miraculous table-cloth, which distin-
guishes between base and noble knights. I have yet to find in
any medieval text a precise analogue, and the talisman may
be a product of the chronicler's imagination. But I would call
attention to the fact that the Grail in the Prose *Lancelot*, where
King Pelles' daughter, the Grail Bearer, gives clear signs of
being modeled on Morgain, the Grail seems to function as a
discriminating talisman [1]. All the knights assembled in the
hall of Corbenic are richly served with whatever viands they
wish, as the damsel passes before them with the holy vessel.
Gawain, smitten by her beauty, gazes after her till she leaves
the hall. « Si regarde la table devant lui et il ne voit rien...
Et quant il vit chou, si en fu si esbahis qu'il ne sot que faire
ne que dire. Car bien quide avoir mespris en aucunes choses. »
It seems possible, therefore, even probable, that Jean d'Outremeuse did not supply the table-cloth from his imagination but
preserved a tradition about Morgain's discriminating talisman
found in no other extant text, though akin to the tradition of
Morgain's vessel, dimly reflected in the Prose *Lancelot*.

Having noted already the fascination which Morgain exercised upon the imagination of the Germans from 1190 to
1500, let us turn our attention back to Wolfram von Eschenbach, who in his masterpiece *Parzival* (1200-1210) made two
allusions to a « berc ze Fâmorgân » and two to a land called
« Feimurgan » — allusions which have puzzled the critics. Gawan
met a King Vergulaht, a splendid knight; « sîn geslähte sante
Mazadân vür den berc ze Fâmorgân; sîn art was von der
feien [2]. » (Mazadan sent forth his [Vergulaht's] family from the
mountain of Famorgan; his origin was from the fays.) Later
Parzival's uncle, Trevrizent, recounts his youthful travels as
a knight errant : « 'Ich hân ouch manege tjoste getân vor dem
berc ze Fâmorgân. Ich tet vil rîcher tjoste schîn vor dem berc

---

1. *Vulgate Version*, ed. Sommer, IV, 344.
2. *Parzival*, 400, 5-9.

ze Agremontîn.' '» (I have also engaged in many jousts before the mountain of Famorgan. I rode in more splendid
jousts before the mountain of Agremontin.) Martin in his
note on the second passage identified Agremontîn as Agri-
monte in the Basilicata, east of Salerno, but he thought the
« berc ze Fàmorgân » must lie in the Celtic West ². However,
nearly all the place-names on Trevrizent's itinerary were genuine and were located in the Mediterranean region. If Agremontîn was a mountain near Salerno, it would be very natural
to couple with it an even more famous mountain in Sicily,
Etna, which we know from Wolfram's contemporary, Gervase
of Tilbury, was popularly regarded as the abode of Arthur,
and where forty years or so later the author of *Floriant et Florete* placed Morgain's palace. Can there be much doubt that
« der berc ze Fâmorgân » was Etna ?

The two occurrences of Feimurgan form something of a
crux. The first, referring to Mazadân as Gahmuret's ancestor,
reads ³ : « Den fuort ein feie in Feimurgân diu hiez Terdelaschoye. » (A fay named Terdelaschoye led him to Feimurgan.) The second reads ⁴ : « Den ze Famurgâne Terdelaschoye
fuorte. » (Terdelaschoye led him to Fâmurgân.) It is obvious
that the names of the fay and of her Land of Joy have
been interchanged in both passages. But why ? Some have
argued that this « gaffe » supports Wolfram's assertion that he
was ignorant of letters, but today there are not many scholars who take that assertion seriously. Wolfram is notorious
for his penchant for mystification and playful humor. Professor Sparnaay ⁵ is right, I believe, in rejecting the notion that
the poet did not understand such common French words as
« terre de la joie » and that he blundered crudely in applying
them to the fay; Sparnaay is right, too, in interpreting the
confusion of names as deliberate, a spark of the author's hu-

---

1. *Ibid.*, 496, 7-10.
2. *Parzival*, ed. E. Martin (Halle, 1903), II, 375 f.
3. *Parzival*, 56, 18 f.
4. *Ibid.*, 585, 14 f.
5. *Neophilologus*, XVI (1930-31), 256.

mor, perhaps, indeed, an exaggerated example of the sort of mistranslation which he attributed to Hartmann von Aue.

But, however one interprets this strange allusion to Feimurgân, its significance for the main thesis of this article remains unimpaired. Neither Chrétien, nor any other author whose work has survived and who wrote before Wolfram, referred to Morgain's realm as « terre de la joie ». The phrase must have come either from a lost text or from oral tradition. And it is not irrelevant in this connexion to recall that the most persistent of all the traditions of Morgain is one for which no literary text of the Middle Ages can be quoted as a source — the belief that she called up by her spells the mirage known as the Fata Morgana. Let me quote from Graf's classic essay, « Artu nell' Etna » [1].

Ora é noto che col nome di fata Morgana si designa un fenomeno ottico (ciò che i francesi chiamano *mirage*) solito a lasciarsi vedere con maggiore frequenza e perspicuità appunto nello stretto di Messina. Quel nome designa presentemente il fenomeno stesso, e non accenna più ad alcuna individuata e soprannaturale potenza che ne sia cagione ; ma in origine non dovette essere così. Si credette allora alla reale presenza della fata in quei luoghi, e il fenomeno si considerò come un' opera dell' arte sua, forse com'uno dei giuochi o degli allettamenti ond'ella abbelliva l'ore e il soggiorno a' suoi compagni di *faerie*.

Surely in this instance, where no literary form of the belief has survived from the Middle Ages or later, there can be no doubt of the existence and the creative activity of a local oral tradition.

As we began our investigation of the fascinating enchantress with the Breton fables about her conveying Arthur to Avalon at the end of his mundane career, so let us in concluding glance back at the fables which introduced Morgain at his cradle at the beginning of his life. Layamon is the first (ca. 1200) to report a tradition that three « elves » appeared at Arthur's birth and bestowed on him prowess, long life, and liberality [2]. Not long after, the French author of the Second Continuation of Chrétien's *Perceval*, who could not, of

1. A. Graf, *op. cit.*, II, 324.
2. Layamon, *Brut*, ed. F. Madden (London, 1847), II, 384 f.

course, have read Layamon, introduced the same episode [1]. Though neither poet assigned any names to the fays, yet, when in the romances of *Floriant, Ogier,* and *Garin de Monglane* [2] the same motif was employed in describing the births of the respective heroes, Morgain was included among the supernatural visitants; and in view of the history of this tradition it may be inferred that she was prominent in it from the very first. Though the notion of the prophetic function of the Parcae or Fatae at the birth of a child was widespread in pagan times and survived as such into the eleventh century [3], and though it became a favorite theme of medieval fiction and modern fairy tales in many lands [4], yet in the case of Morgain a specific provenance can be detected. Not only did Giraldus Cambrensis, as we have observed, ascribe to the Bretons the legend of the transporting of Arthur to Avalon by Morganis, but Maury can be quoted as follows [5] : « Longtemps, à l'époque des couches de leurs femmes, les Bretons servaient un repas dans une chambre contiguë à celle de l'accouchée, repas qui était destiné aux fées dont ils redoutaient le ressentiment. » And as late as 1888 a man of Gouray near Loudéac told the folklorist Sébillot [6] that the fairies called Margots were wont to gives names to infants, especially those of noble houses, bestowed gifts on them, and predicted what they would become — precisely the functions ascribed to Morgain la Fée in the Middle Ages. These Margots of Haute Bre-

---

1. C. Potvin, *Perceval le Gallois* (Mons, 1866-71), V, 123.

2. *Floriant et Florete,* vss. 549-62. Le Roux de Lincy, *Livre des légendes,* p. 178 f. *Enfances Garin de Monglane,* ed. O. Bisinger (Greifswald, 1915), p. 57 f.

3. Paton, *Fairy Mythology,* p. 193, n. 1. A. Maury, *Croyances et légendes du moyen âge* (Paris, 1896), p. 26, 29, 66 ff. Migne, *Patrologia Latina,* CXL, 971. *Germanic Review,* XIX (1944), 128 f. Robert of Brunne, *Handlyng Synne,* ed. Furnivall (London, 1901), I, 21.

4. Gustave Cohen, *Roman courtois au xiie siècle* (Paris, 1938), p. 64. Bolte et Polivka, *Anmerkungen zu den Kinder- und Hausmärchen der Brüder Grimm* (Leipzig, 1913-18), I, 434. *Annales de Bretagne,* LVI (1949), 215, n. 44.

5. Maury, *op. cit.,* p. 22.

6. P. Sébillot, *Traditions et superstitions de la Haute Bretagne* (Paris, 1882), p. 110.

tagne, it is well known, were called Morgan in Basse Bretagne and on the islands of Molène and Ouessant, and their identity with the medieval Morgain has been demonstrated [1]. In fact, stories told of Morgain in *Jaufré* and *La Pulzella Gaia* were still told of Marie-Morgan or Margot la Fée in Brittany, presumably their homeland, hardly more than a century ago [2].

It is the fashion in some quarters today to maintain that the development of Arthurian romance can best be understood by ignoring Celtic parallels, even the most obvious, and by denying not only the importance but even the existence of oral tradition; and the whole vast proliferation of story, we are told, was almost exclusively engendered in the imaginations of clerics and literary men, who borrowed material only from their literary predecessors. To this hypothesis I submit that the legend of Morgain la Fée constitutes a sufficient refutation. With her Celtic antecedents I have dealt elsewhere [3], and, if I am correct, they go back to the Gaulish goddess Matrona on the one side, and to the Irish goddess known as Morrigan or Macha on the other. If the facts presented in this article can stand critical examination, there must have been a prodigious circulation of tales about the fairy queen by word of mouth, partly in elaborate forms devised by professional entertainers, and partly in the simpler forms of local gossip and travelers' yarns. By no manner of means could these multifarious traditions have developed from the earliest references to her in literature — Geoffrey of Monmouth's *Vita Merlini,* Benoît de Ste. Maure's *Roman de Troie* [4], and Chrétien's brief allusions to Morgain's healing plasters and to Morgain as the mistress of Guigamor. Far be it from me to dispute the ingenuity and art with which many literary men handled the matter supplied by oral tradition, or to question their frequent borrow-

---

1. *Annales de Bretagne,* LVI, 210-5.

2. *Ibid.,* LVI, 211-4.

3. *Speculum,* XX (1945), 183-203. Reprinted in Loomis, *Wales and the Arthurian Legend,* p. 105-30.

4. *Speculum,* XX, 183-5. Reprinted in Loomis, *Wales,* p. 106-8. I am greatly indebted to my friend, Prof. Carl Bayerschmidt, for help with translations.

ing from earlier literary sources, or to deny that there are some Arthurian romances (e. g. *Cligès, Gliglois, Estoire del Saint Graal*) which owe almost nothing to the *conteurs*; that would be to fly in the face of the evidence. But it is also to fly in the face of the evidence to deny the power and persistence of oral tradition in fashioning the *Matière de Bretagne*.

———

The Head in the Grail

(Revue Celtique XLVII, pp. 39-62)

THE HEAD IN THE GRAIL

One of the most puzzling enigmas in the Grail legend is furnished by the account in the Welsh romance of *Peredur* of the mysterious procession in the castle of Peredur's uncle. Whereas in all French versions of the procession there is a vessel called a *graal* and often one or more *tailleors*, in *Peredur* alone do we hear of a vessel containing a man's head. *Graal* is a rather rare French word, meaning, according to the well-known passage in Helinandus' *Chronicle* (ante 1216 A. D.) : " scutella lata et aliquantulum profunda, in qua preciosae dapes divitibus solent apponi. " [1] *Tailleor* means a carving platter. Both words, therefore, signify large dishes, and it is only because the *graal* came to be regarded as the cup of the eucharist that it was equated with a chalice.

The date of *Peredur* is uncertain, but Prof. Mary Williams, M. Loth, and Dr. Gwenogvryn Evans regard it as early.[2] It is generally admitted to be in large measure a redaction from a French romance,[3] but the precise degree of its indebtedness to the *Conte del Graal* is in dispute. My personal opinion is that, though *Peredur* is, for the most part, of immediate French origin, it owes nothing to Crestien, and I trust that this brief discussion of one feature will justify that opinion.

We read that the young Peredur, on leaving Arthur's court, comes first to the castle of an uncle of his, who is lame and

---

1. On the word see especially Nitze in *Modern Philology*, XIII, pp. 681 ff, and W. Foerster, *Christian v. Troyes, Wörterbuch*, pp. 174* ff.

2. J. Loth, *Mabinogion*, ed. 1, I, pp. 17 f. Mary R. Williams, *Essai sur la composition de Peredur*, p. 26. *White Book Mabinogion*, ed. J. G. Evans, p. xv. Cf. *Zts. f. Celt. Phil.*, XV, (1925), 66 ff.

3. M. R. Williams, *op. cit.*, p. 121. J. Loth, *Mabinogion*, ed. 2 (1913), I, p. 53.

whose attendants fish from the bank of a lake. The next day he comes to the castle of a second uncle, and after a repast he is tested thrice in the cutting of a bar and the rejoining of the parts. As Peredur then sits conversing, two youths (*gwas*) bear in an immense spear, from the point of which run three drops of blood. " ar hynny llyma dwy vorwyn yn dyuot ymywn, a dyscyl vawr y rygthunt, a phen gwr ar y dyscyl, a gwaet yn amhyl ygkylch y pen. (Then behold two maidens coming in, and a large platter between them, and the head of a man on the platter, and blood in plenty around the head.) "[1] At the appearance of both the lance and the platter great lamentation breaks out. Finally all is silent, and Peredur retires to his chamber. Many years after, when he is at Arthur's court at Caerleon, a loathly damsel rides in on a yellow mule, upbraids him for having failed at the castle of the lame king to ask concerning the story and the cause of the bleeding lance and the other marvels. If Peredur had done so, the king would have obtained health and peace ; because the youth failed, there has been war and slaughter. Peredur then vows to learn the story of the lance. After many adventures he comes to a castle, finds there a gray-haired lame man, and sits down beside him. A yellow-haired youth then informs Peredur without his asking, that he (the aforesaid youth) had been the bearer of the head in the platter and of the bleeding spear. The head was that of Peredur's cousin, slain by the sorceresses of Gloucester, and Peredur is destined to avenge the murder. The romance concludes with the slaying of the sorceresses.

It is, of course, generally admitted that, in spite of the palpable omissions and inconsistencies of detail, the story of the bloody head is fairly clear [2]. Its motif, as Nutt pointed out, is the duty of avenging the death of a kinsman. But no

---

1. *White Book Mabinogion*, ed. J. G. Evans, col. 130. Cf. J. Loth, *Mabinogion* (1913), p. 65. Slight verbal differences appear in MS. Peniarth 7 ; cf. *White Book Mabinogion*, col. 613.

2. A. Nutt, *Studies on the Legend of the Holy Grail*, p. 143. M. R. Williams, *op. cit.*, p. 44. J. D. Bruce, *Evolution of Arthurian Romance, Hesperia, Ergänzungsreihe*, VIII, I, p. 346.

where else in the many versions of the visit of Perceval or Gawain
to the Grail castle is there any bloody head in the vessel or
even a hint that the vessel was connected with a feud. Inas-
much as these other versions in French and German show
many primitive traits not found in *Peredur* and since *Peredur*
itself is manifestly corrupt, the chances are overwhelming
that the introduction of the head in the platter and the vengeance motif are afterthoughts. The question is : what could
have led to the introduction of this barbaric element into the
graal ?

Many explanations have been offered for the enigma,[1] but
I shall concern myself here only with two. One was put forward by Miss Weston in *Romania*,[2] and may be summarized
as follows. The redactor of *Peredur* knew the Grail tradition
in its fully developed form as known to Crestien de Troyes
and his continuators. He therefore knew of the identification
of the Graal with the vessel of the eucharist, whether chalice
or paten. In saying that Peredur was the son of Evrawc he
seems to have given the name of the town Evrawc, York, to
Peredur's father, who was presumably its lord. In this connection with York *Peredur* of all the Grail romances is unique.
Another connection of the name Peredur with Yorkshire is
found in the statement of the seventeenth century antiquary
Stowe to the effect that Peredurus, a British prince, founded
the town of Pickering between B. C. 270-61. Now in the York
breviary and nowhere else occurs the statement, " Caput Johannis : signat Corpus Christi : quo pascimur in sancto altari. "
" Thus," Miss Weston concludes, " there is at least a possibility that the curious form given to the Grail in *Peredur* may
be due to the fact that the redactor, familiar with the equation,
Caput Johannis = Corpus Christi, was desirous of doing honor
to his local cult. "

Miss Weston seems to have been quite unaware of the difficulties which this hypothesis raises, for she offers no answer

1. Bruce, *op. cit.*, I, p. 346. W. Golther, *Parzival und der Graal*, 116 f.
E. Windisch, *Das Keltische Brittannien* Abhandlungen, phil.-hist. Kl., König-
liche Sächsische *Ges.* der Wissenschaften, XXIX, N° 6, p. 193.

2. *Romania*, XLIX (1923), pp. 273 ff.

to the following pertinent questtons : 1. Are we by any means
so sure that the whole *Conte del Graal,* which was probably
not complete before 1225, antedates *Peredur* that we can assume
that the former is the basis of the latter? 2. If the author
regarded the Grail as a vessel of the eucharist, and equated it
with the charger containing the head of John the Baptist, how
is it that he failed to bring the sword, which is found in so
many of the Grail adventures, into harmony with his conception, by making it the sword with which John the Baptist
was beheaded? How is it that he invented a dénouement so
grossly incongruous with his symbolism as to make the bloody
head that of Peredur's cousin, slain by the sorceresses of Gloucester? 3. Is not the assumption that the author of *Peredur*
in the twelfth century was attached to Yorkshire, and was
drawing upon local traditions concerning his hero, most improbable, since the only real evidence for the existence of such
a tradition is a passage in a seventeenth century historian
obviously inspired by Geoffrey of Monmouth and concerned
with Peredur entirely different from Arthur's warrior, [1] and
since Celtic tradition in Yorkshire must then have been
extinct for centuries? On the whole, Miss Weston's explanation raises more questions than it answers.

The other explanation of the head in the platter is that of
Miss Williams, published in 1909. [2] " L'idée de rappeler la
mort du cousin de Peredur en exposant sa tête n'est qu'un
développement différent de la légende de la tête de Bran, telle
qu'elle figure dans le Mabinogi de *Branwen merch Llyr.* On la
retrouve dans le conte suivant extrait du *Reductorium Morale*
de Pierre Bercheur, qui écrivait au XIVᵉ siècle. ' Quid dicam
de mirabilibus que in historiis Galuagni et Arcturi ponuntur;
quorum vnum de omnibus recito, scilicet de palatio quod
Galuagnus sub aquam casu raptus reperit, vbi mensam refer-
tam epulis et sedem positam inuenit : ostium uero per quod
exire valeret non vidit; qui cum famesceret et comedere vellet,

1. John Stowe, *Annales or General Chronicle of England* (London, 1615),
p. 12.

2. M. R. Williams, *op. cit.*, p. 47. Cf., however, *Rev. Celt.*, XLVI, 23.

statim caput hominis mortui positum in lance [platter] affuit;
et gigas in feretro iuxta ignem iacuit; giganteque surgente et
palatium capite concutiente, capite uero clamante et cibos
interdicente, nunquam de cibis comedere ausus fuit : qui
post multa miracula exiit : sed nesciuit qualiter exiuit. ' " [1]

Miss Williams thus briefly suggests an interesting theory
of a connection between the bloody head in the platter in
the castle of Peredur's uncle, a head in a platter in the tale of
Gauvain told by Bercheur, and the severed head of Bran,
which was present at the banqueting of his followers. But the
relationship as she presents it is not obvious, and it is my
present purpose to offer some evidence for it [2].

Though the story of Bercheur is generally supposed to have
no extant source or close analogue in Arthurian romance, I
believe such an analogue exists in Pseudo-Wauchier's continuation of the *Conte del Graal* (1180-1210). We shall call the
story, for convenience, Pseudo-Wauchier I. Arthur and his
knights come to a very fair land, and Gauvain rides ahead
to seek hostel. He follows a troop of horsemen up a hill, but
when he reaches the top they have disappeared. He descries a
fair castle beside a broad river. As he approaches, he finds a
fountain and two maidens beside it, who have been drawing
water in pitchers of gold. After exchanging greetings with
them, he rides into the castle, and is astonished at the treasure displayed, — coins, precious vessels, and rich stuffs [3].
But no one can he see. He rides into the hall of the castle,
and finds cloths spread and wine set out, but no living
thing

---

1. I have introduced slight variations on the basis of Kittredge's reprint in
his *Study of Gawain and the Green Knight* (Cambridge, 1916), pp. 180 f.
The same work contains a vast quantity of material and a bibliography on
severed heads.

2. C. Potvin, *Perceval le Gallois*, Mons, 1866, III, pp. 251 ff. Miss Weston has translated this whole episode from another MS. in her *Gawain
and the Lady of Lys*, London, 1907.

3. Cf. the wealth of Annwn as described in *Pwyll*. J. Loth, *Mabinogion*,
ed. 2, I, p. 87. *White Book Mabinogion*, ed. J. G. Evans, col. 5.

4. Cf. the empty island palace, with abundant food and drink in
Imram Curaig Mailduin.

Et en un estre la devant
Vit sor graaus d'argent ester
Plus de cent tiestes de sangler,
Tous pres et tous escueles,
Et li poivres estoit dales.
Mesire Gauwains esgarda,
Leva sa main, si se sainna. [1]

Still seeing no one, Gauvain returns through the castle,
hoping to see at the bridge the maidens, " qui samblent fees, "
but they too have disappeared. Riding back, he brings Arthur
and his company to the seemingly empty castle. They prepare
to eat the abundant food, but suddenly Gauvain stops, having
espied the shield of a certain Bran de Lis, whose sister he had
ravished some years before. Bran, a large knight on " un gran-
disme destrier, " had engaged in combat with Gauvain, and
they had agreed to fight it out when next they met. Accordingly, Gauvain arms himself precipitately and refuses to eat
more. Kay follows a fairy brachet though the castle till he
comes to a garden, where a multitude of folk are making
merry. Their lord, Bran de Lis [2], learning that Gauvain has
come to his castle, goes at once, half-armed, to the hall, and
parting the folk, scowls at his foe. " Quant il ot un poi pense,

1. Potvin, *op. cit.*, III, p. 254, vv. 16760-66. *Sor graaus* is the reading
of MS. B. N. fr. 1429, fol. 151 v., and is surely correct.
2. The origin of the word Lis in this connection lies not, I believe, in
the Welsh word *llys*, " castle, " as M. Lot in *Romania*, XXIV, p. 322, has
proposed but in the name of Bran de Lis' sister, which was probably Flor
de Lis. The *Livre d'Artus*, *Diu Krone*, and *Wigalois* agree that Gawain's
amie was called Florie or Floree, — a name which rests on ancient Irish
tradition. Cf. my *Celtic Myth and Arthurian Romance*, 10-15, 21f, 303, 327.
Now it is odd that in the very passage in which Gauvain describes his
amour with Bran de Lis' sister he says :

" Et por faire tout mon delit
Les eus li baisai et le vis,
Qui fu blans come flors de lis. " (vv. 17088-90)

I believe therefore that in Pseudo-Wauchier's source the damsel was called Flor de Lis and her kinsfolk were logically called Bran de Lis, Morre
de Lis, and Melian de Lis. Pseudo-Wauchier, not realizing that the words
Flor de Lis, undistinguished of course by capitals, were the damsel's name,
merely used them as a hackneyed simile.

si a amont son cief leve." Both Bran and Gauvain mount, and by torch-light hold desperate combat in the hall. Finally, in one of the most picturesque and moving scenes in Arthurian romance, Gauvain's *amie* brings her little son in, and holds him up between the flashing blades of his father and his uncle. Arthur intervenes, and Bran becomes his liegeman and Gauvain's friend.

Despite the obvious modification and elaboration which the story of Gauvain at the castle of Bran de Lis has undergone, it still presents the following points of resemblance to Bercheur's anecdote of Galuagnus. 1. In Bercheur the palace is under water; in Pseudo-Wauchier it lies by a river, and fountain fays stand near the entrance. 2. In both a meal is ready laid, but no person is at first to be seen. 3. In Bercheur the head of a man suddenly appears in a platter. In Pseudo-Wauchier Gauvain spies more than a hundred "tiestes de sangler sor graaus [1]," and crosses himself. This act is hardly justified by the sight of a number of boars' heads, but if he had seen more than a hundred "tiestes sanglenter sor graaus" it would be amply explained. Since such misreadings are recognizable elsewhere in Arthurian romance, [2] it is by no means inconceivable that Pseudo-Wauchier found in his source bleeding heads on grails. [3] 4. In Bercheur there is a giant lying

1. The syntax is possible in Old French. The meaning is supported by Godefroy, *Dictionnaire*, VII, 305, quoting *Chanson d'Antioche* : la terre senglenta.

2. For example, Miss Weston notes in *Legend of Sir Perceval*, I, p. 279 n. 4, that " li contes del ciel " mentioned in the *Elucidation* must be a mistake for " li contes del cigne. "

3. I believe the multiplication of the heads is due to a confusion in Pseudo-Wauchier's source between the one head in the platter and the " more than a hundred heads " impaled on stakes which Gauvain in *Vengeance Raguidel* sees on approaching just such a magic castle as that of Bran de Lis. A shepherd tells Gauvain that at the castle of Le Noir Chevalier

> " La vi je testes plus de cent
> Que li chevaliers ot trencies,
> Si estoient totes ficies
> De cief en cief el hireçon.
> Jamais n'irai en sa maison ;
> Qui i vait n'en puet revenir. "

Gauvain, however, enters the castle, sees no one, and sits down to a feast on a bier by the fire; in Pseudo-Wauchier there enters Bran de Lis, a big knight, who, as we shall see, is to be identified with the Fisher King, described by Crestien as lying in his castle hall on a couch beside a fire. 5. In Bercheur the giant strikes the roof with his head; in Pseudo-Wauchier Bran lifts his head before approaching Gauvain. 6. In both Gauvain is interrupted as he is about to eat. If our interpretation is correct, then, both Bercheur and Pseudo-Wauchier have given us variants of the adventures of Gauvain in the palace of Bran de Lis or the Fisher King.

Two other stories in the *Conte del Graal* seem to confirm this interpretation. The first is in Pseudo-Wauchier also, and will be referred to as Pseudo-Wauchier II. [1] Its hero is Gaheries, who, as I have shown elsewhere, was in origin identical with Gauvain. [2] He comes to a very fair castle on the bank of a river, and in the streets finds great riches and beauty, but no living person. He enters the hall and several chambers, empty also. At last he descends into a garden, and sees a dwarf enter a tent with a silver hanap. Within the tent he finds a damsel, feeding from the hanap a huge wounded knight in purple, lying on a bed. At Gaheries' greeting, the tall knight is enraged, his wounds bleed, and he orders the intruder removed. Presently, a small but beautifully formed " Petit Chevalier " rides into the tent, and forces Gaheries with insults to mount and joust with him. To his utter humiliation Gaheries is thrown by the dwarf knight; who then places his foot on his neck and tells him that a year hence he must return and choose between three alternatives : to become a weaver, [3] to fight once more, or to let his head be struck off. Gaheries agrees and departs amidst the jeers and insults of many folk, who now fill the once empty rooms and streets of the castle.

---

spread. He is interrupted by Maduc le Noir, with whom he is forced to combat. Cf. *Vengeance Raguidel*, ed. M. Friedwagner (Halle, 1909), vv. 622 ff. On heads impaled on stakes see *Romanic Review*, IX, pp. 21 ff.

1. Potvin, *Perceval le Gallois*, IV, vv. 21135-21714.

2. R. S. Loomis, *Celtic Myth and Arthurian Romance*, p. 84. *Publications of the Modern Language Association*, XLIII (1928), pp. 386-8.

3. Cf. Crestien de Troyes, *Yvain*, vv. 5188-5324.

Ultimately the adventure is concluded by Gaheries' return and the slaying of both the " Petit Chevalier " and the lord of the castle, presumably the huge knight whom he had seen before lying on a couch.

Two clues lead us to suspect that this huge knight, lord of the castle, was Bran. First, in Crestien's *Erec* we read of two brothers, Belin or Bilis, the dwarf king of the Antipodes, and Brien, his gigantic brother, half a foot taller than any knight of Arthur's court. [1] This association of dwarf and giant seems to fit the antagonists of Gaheries in the enchanted castle. Secondly, the huge, wounded knight in purple, lying on a bed, and fed from a goblet by a maiden, suggests various descriptions of the Fisher King. In Crestien the wounded Fisher King lies in purple robes on a great couch by a fire ; [2] his father, also wounded, is sustained in life by a wafer (the Host) brought in the Graal; [3] in Heinrich von dem Türlin's account of Gauvain's first visit to the Grail castle the aged king drinks blood from a crystal cup, brought by a beautiful maiden; [4] in Heinrich's account of the second visit the old man drinks three drops of blood from a salver, and eats a piece of bread from a reliquary, salver and reliquary both brought by maidens in procession. [5] Now in the *Didot Perceval* the Grail King, whose rôle in the story is very close to Crestien's Fisher King, is called Bron.

On the relation of these two stories of Pseudo-Wauchier to each other and to other tales certain curious points should be noted. First, is it credible that Pseudo-Wauchier, having once described the castle of the tall knight, Bran de Lis, should then have made researches into Crestien's *Erec* and discovering there a certain tall knight Brien with a dwarf brother Belin, have identified Brien and Bran de Lis, and concocted a story in which a tall knight, unnamed, and a dwarf knight should dwell together in a palace like that of Bran de Lis? Second-

1. Crestien de Troyes. *Erec*, vv 1993 ff.
2. Crestien de Troyes, *Contes del Graal*, ed. G. Baist, vv. 3046-56.
3. *Ibid.*, vv. 6373-93.
4. Heinrich von dem Türlin, *Krone*, ed. Scholl, vv. 14754 ff.
5. *Ibid.*, vv. 29380 ff.

ly, is it credible that Pseudo-Wauchier should have hit
upon the notion of attaching the characteristics of Crestien's Maimed King to his composite figure of Bran-Brien, and
that the author of the *Didot-Perceval* should independently have
attached certain other characteristics of Crestien's maimed
king to Robert de Borons's Bron? It seems to me that those
scholars who deny the existence of tradition in Arthurian
romance must assume precisely these extraordinary procedures
or else ascribe all this convergence of evidence toward the
names Bran, Brien, and Bron to an almost miraculous coincidence. Thirdly, is it coincidence that Pseudo-Wauchier's
two tales of the enchanted castle by the river with its empty
streets and chambers, combine neatly to furnish almost all the
features of Bercheur's story? The castle of Bran de Lis provides the aqueous suggestions, the spread table, the head in
the grail, the interrupted Gauvain ; while the castle of the giant
knight (presumably Brien) provides the giant lying on a bed
and showing great anger at the intrusion. Fourthly, is it accident that our investigation of the head in the platter has
brought us back to a scene so reminiscent of the Grail castle
as the wounded knight on the bed, fed from a hanap by a maid-
en? A study of these stories will, I believe, lead to the inevitable conclusion that all draw upon a reservoir of common
tradition, and not upon each other or upon a single narrative
source. The head which Peredur sees in the platter, surrounded by blood, the " tiestes de sangler. . sor graaus, " seen by
Gauvain, and the " caput hominis mortui in lance, " which
suddenly appears to Galuagnus, — these are all derived from
the same general mass of Grail tradition.

Before we proceed to ascertain whether Miss Williams was
right in pointing to the Welsh traditions of Bran as the source
of the severed head, let us note that the damsels with their
golden pitchers beside the spring described in Pseudo-Wauchier I are also traditional features. In the so-called *Elucidation* prefixed to the *Conte del Graal* they play a far more significant part. It has been recognized, — and probably with justice, — that the *Elucidation* corresponds in many of its details
concerning the Grail to the account given by Pseudo-Wau-

chier of Gauvain's visit to the Grail castle [1], and that its author
may have known both Crestien and Pseudo-Wauchier. But
there are dangers in assuming that because both the author
of the *Elucidation* and Pseudo-Wauchier dilate on the sympathetic relation which exists between the success of the Grail
quest and the flowing of the waters, one author is borrowing
from the other. Grimm records instances of a belief that when
a river dried up, the lord of the land would languish, and
that conversely the health of the lord would affect the flow
of the river. [2] Even if the *Elucidation* derives this feature from
Pseudo-Wauchier, it cannot have derived the following account
of the fountain-maidens from that source. We read [3] that
the land of Logres (Welsh Lloegyr = England) was waste
and desolate because the wells had failed and the damsels
within them had disappeared. [4] Formerly a traveler could
find at any of these wells whatever food and drink he desired.
There issued from the well a fair damsel bearing meat, pasties,
and bread in a golden cup, followed by another damsel bringing a napkin and a dish of gold and silver, containing whatsoever one desired. But King Amangon [5] had ravished one
of the maidens and stolen her cup, and his followers had imit-

---

1. R. Heinzel, *Französische Gralromane*, p. 11. Bruce, *Evolution of Arthurian Romance*, II, p. 87.

2. Jacob Grimm, *Deutsche Mythologie*, ed. 4 (1815), p. 491.

3. Potvin, *Perceval le Gallois*, II, vv. 28-111. Cf. Prof. A. C. L. Brown's inadequate discussion in *Modern Philology*, XXII (1924), pp. 124-130.

4. Miss Weston, Prof. Brown, and others have concluded that " puis " here means "hills." The fact that a German so translated the word proves nothing, since admittedly the word could have that meaning nor does the analogy from Gervase' folktale, presently to be considered, prove much. The fact is that ancient Welsh literature knows a maiden as a " well cup-bearer, " and that Arthurian literature knows several fays associated with springs or lakes, but none, so far as I am aware, who dwell in hills. Cf. Potvin, *Perceval le Gallois*, III, p. 252; V, p. 38. For an extensive biblio-graphy on Celtic and Arthurian water-fays cf. *Modern Philology*, XII (1915), 599 ff ; also E. M. Grimes, *Lays of Desiré, Graelent, and Melion*, (N. Y. 1928), pp. 20 f. For ancient Celtic water-divinities cf. A. Bertrand, *Religion des Gaulois* (Paris, 1897), pp. 191-212. For modern survivals of fountain worship cf. J. Rhys, *Celtic Folklore*, (1901), I, 354 ff ; E. Hull, *Folklore of the British Isles* (London, 1928), pp. 106-117.

5. On Amangon cf. Heinzel, *Französische Gralromane*, p. 78 note ;

ated his example with the other spring-maidens. Thus the realm became waste ; trees, meadows, and flowers withered ; waters ceased to run. No longer could one find the court of the Rich Fisher, which made the land resplendent with gold, silver, furs, hawks, and falcons. But when the court and the Grail were found, the waters and the fountains ran through the meadows, and the fields and woods were leafy and green again.

Is the author merely elaborating out of his imagination the hint supplied by Pseudo-Wauchier in the two damsels with their golden pitchers by the spring ? Let us see. A Welsh poem from the *Black Book of Carmarthen* (twelfth century MS.) on the flooding of the plain of Gwaelod attributed the calamity to a maiden, " who at a time of feasting suffered the wave of a magical well which was under her charge to escape and over-flow the country round. " [1] Here are the pertinent lines : [2]

Boed emendiceid y morvin	Accursed be the maiden,
achellygaut guydi cvin	Who let loose after supping,
finaun wenestir mor terruin	Well cup-bearer of the mighty [main.

Boed amendiceid y vachteith	Accursed be the damsel,
ae golligaut guydi gueith	Who let it loose after battle,
finaun wenestir mor diffeith	Well cup-bearer of the high sea.

Clearly, then, the Welsh of the twelfth century believed in maidens who controlled the flow of springs and who were cup-bearers, and surely not even the staunchest anti-Celtist will assert that the Welsh derived this belief from Pseudo-Wauchier or the *Elucidation*. The reverse is the true relation-ship. And the Welsh, in turn, derived their belief in the well-maidens doubtless from old British cults of well-divinities, attested by inscriptions to the *Nymphae.* [3]

A story from the borders of Wales related by Gervase of

Bruce, *op. cit.*, I, p. 87 note. He is probably identical with King Mangon in the *Lai du Cor* and with the Welsh Manawydan, brother of Bran.

1. J. E. Lloyd, *History of Wales*, (1911), I, p. 26.
2. Rhys, *Celtic Folklore*, I (1901), p. 383.
3. Holder, *Altceltischer Sprachschatz*, II, p. 811.

Tilbury early in the thirteenth century sheds a further light on the well-maidens of the *Elucidation*. [1] " Erat in comitatu Claudii Cestriae (Gloucestershire) sylva venatoria... In hujus nemoroso saltu erat monticulus ad staturam hominis in apicem exsurgens, in quem milites et alii venatores ascendere consueverunt, cum aestu ac siti fatigati aliquod instantiae suae quaerebant remedium. Verum ex loci ac rei conditione relictis a longe sociis, solus quivis ascendit, cumque solus quasi ad alterum loquens diceret : ' Sitio, ' statim ex improviso e latere propinator adstabat celebri cultu, vultu hilari, manu exposita cornu grande gestans, auro gemmisque ornatum... Vice calicis nectar ignoti sed suavissimi saporis offerebatur, quo hausto totus calescentis corporis aestus et lassitudo fugiebat... Sed et ,umto nectare minister mantile ad ora siccanda porrigebat, et expleto suo ministerio disparens, nec mercedem pro obsequio nec colloquium pro inquisitione expectabat... Uno aliquo die miles in civitate illa venator illuc accessit, et postulato potu ac sumto cornu, non illud.. pincernae restituit, sed ad proprium usum retinuit. " The horn eventually found its way into the possession of King Henry I. This story presents so close a parallel to an Irish tale of Finn's horn, Midlethan, a tale which also contains a hunt, a fairy mound, a man upon it, a horn adorned with gold, a draught which fills the huntsmen with pleasure, [2] that we may feel certain that Gervase' story is Celtic in origin. Now in the light of the *Elucidation*, telling of well-maidens robbed of their cups, the Welsh belief in well-maidens who bore cups, and Gervase' tale .of the stealing of the horn, consider this episode found in certain MSS. of the *Conte del Graal*. [3] Gauvain meets a damsel riding a mule and carrying an ivory horn in her right hand. Suggesting that Gau-

---

1. Gervasius von Tilbury, *Otia Imperialia*, ed. F. Liebrecht, p. 28. For similar stories of the theft of a fairy vessel cf. E. S. Hartland, *Science of Fairy Tales* (1890), pp. 140-60.

2. Kuno Meyer, *Fianaigecht*, *Todd Lecture Series*, XVI (Dublin, 1910), pp. 57-63.

3. For example, Bibl. Nat. Ms. fr. 12577. Rotographs of this MS. are in the Library of Congress and the New York Public Library. Cf. J. L. Weston, *Legend of Sir Perceval*, I, p. 217.

vain may need refreshment, she sounds her horn, and at once knights, valets, and maidens appear and prepare a feast under a spreading tree. As Gauvain and the maiden sit down, a knight rides up and carries off the horn, but Gauvain pursues and brings it back. The damsel's name is La Pucele au Cor d'Yvoire. Is it not highly probable that we have here a rationalized account of the theft of the food-providing vessel? Originally the horn itself provided by magic all the refreshment that Gauvain needed. At any rate, we may legitimately regard the *Elucidation* as containing genuine Welsh traditions of maiden cupbearers of the springs, and conclude that Pseudo-Wauchiers's comparatively pointless introduction of two maidens with gold pitchers beside a spring, though likewise derived from Welsh tradition, could not have been the source of the *Elucidation* on this point. The only rational explanation of the correspondence between Pseudo-Wauchier, the *Elucidation*, the episode of the Pucelle au Cor d'Yvoire, and Gervase' local legend is that they all go back to Celtic tradition.

In order to make the relationship of the various stories we have considered more clear, I submit a chart showing features common to two or more of them as well as the corresponding features in the Mabinogi of *Branwen*, which we shall presently consider. I have attempted to place the versions in roughly chronological order.

The chart may prove convincing as showing the correctness of Miss Williams' identification of the head in the platter in *Peredur* with the head in the dish in Bercheur, but it may not prove so convincing as regards the relationship of all these stories to the Welsh traditions of Bran. But let us now proceed to note how many of the details in the stories of Bran de Lis, Brien, and Bron, the Fisher King, which we have considered, are accounted for by what we can learn concerning Bran. 1. Bran is gigantic. [1] This feature, in a greater or less degree, is ascribed to Bran de Lis, to the knight in Pseudo-Wauchier II, whom we have identified with Brien, to the

---

1. J. Loth, *Mabinogion* (1913), I, p. 124. *White Book Mabinogion*, ed. J. G. Evans, col. 40.

Mabinogi of *Branwen*	Crestien	Pseudo-Wauchier I	Pseudo-Wauchier II	*Peredur*	*Eluci-dation*	Bercheur
		two damsels with gold vessels by spring		two damsels with gold vessels at well		
hall on island	castle near river	castle by river	castle by river	castle		palace under water
tent			tent			
		riches in street	riches in street		riches at court	
		no one visible	no one visible		folk vanish	no one visible
feast spread		feast spread				feast spread
giant	old man	tall man	tall man	hoary man		giant
King	King Rich Fisher			King	King Rich Fisher	
Bran	(Bron)	Bran de Lis	(Brien)			
	in purple		in purple			
wounded in foot	wounded in thighs		wounded	lame		
	on bed		on bed			on bier
	by fire					by fire
severed head	*graal*	heads *de sangler* on grails	hanap	head on *graal* platter, blood		head on platter
	borne by maiden		served by maiden	borne by maiden		

figure on the bier in Bercheur, who when he rises strike
the roof with his head. 2. Bran was too large for any house
and was obliged to feast in tents. [1] In Pseudo–Wauchier II the wounded knight, presumably Brien, lies in a
tent. 3. Bran was wounded in battle in the foot. [2] Crestien's
Fisher King was wounded in battle ; [3] the tall knight (Brien)
in Pseudo-Wauchier II is wounded ; and Peredur's uncle,
whose rôle is so close to that of Crestien's Fisher King, is
described by the Loathly Damsel as lame. [4] It is significant
that Boron's *Joseph* and the *Didot Perceval* call the Rich Fisher
Bron. 4. Bran must have possessed vessels of plenty. This
point must be gone into thoroughly, for some of the evidence
is indirect. First there is the probability that Bran son of Llyr
shares something of the nature and properties of the Irish
Manannán mac Lir and of the Welsh Manawydan son of Llyr.

The Irish Manannán evidently had a reputation as " a good
provider. " He settled the Tuatha Dé Danann in their abodes,
" and the Feast of Goibne [the divine smith] and the swine
of Manannán were made for the warriors, that is.. the Feast
of Goibne to ward off age and death from the high-kings, and
the swine of Manannán to be killed and to exist for the warriors. " [5] In one version of the *Echtra Cormaic* we learn that
Manannán himself dwells in Tír Tairngire, the Land of Promise, and he and his wife are recognized not only by the provision of swine which though eaten are never consumed, but
also by the possession of inexhaustible supplies of wheat and
of cows which would furnish milk for the men of the whole
world [6]. By reason of a strange hiatus in our evidence Manannán is not specifically provided with any cup, caldron, or
horn that supplies unlimited food or drink. But in two island

---

1. *Ibid.*
2. Loth, *op. cit.*, I, p. 144. *White Book Mabinogion*, col. 56.
3. Crestien de Troyes, *Conte del Graal*, ed. G. Baist (Freiburg), vv.
3471 f.
4. Loth, *op. cit.*, II, p. 104. *White Book Mabinogion*, col. 166.
5. This passage from the *Book of Fermoy* was kindly supplied me by
Miss Eleanor Hull.
6. *Irische Texte*, ed. Stokes and Windisch, III, pp. 213-5.

palaces of the gods described in terms almost identical with those applied to Manannán's palace in the *Echtra Cormaic* we discover magic vessels of plenty. In the *Echtra Airt* [1] Conn sees food-laden boards rise up suddenly before him, a drink-horn appears without a bearer. There is a vat, in the oversea palace of Labraid, Manannán's brother-in-law, described in the *Serglige Conculaind* [2]. " Dabach and do mid medrach oc a dáil for in teglāch ; maraid beós — is búan in bes — conid bithlan eo bithgrés. (A vat is there with joyous mead, distributing to the household; it continues ever, — enduring is the custom, — so that it is always constantly full.) " Among the Welsh, Manawyd, Manannán's counterpart, is perpetual guardian of the Caldron of Britain. [3] This is doubtless identical with the caldron mentioned among the Thirteen Treasures of the Isle of Britain, though assigned in this list to Dyrnog Gawr. [4] " Pair Dyrnog Gawr. Os rhoid ynddo gig iw ferwi i wr llwfr, ni ferwai byth ; ond bwyd i was dewr, fo ferwai ddigon yn y man. (The Caldron of Dyrnog the Giant ; if flesh should be put into it to boil for a cowardly man, it would never be done ; but food for a valiant youth, it would soon boil enough)." This caldron of Dyrnog is probably to be identified with the caldron of Diwrnach the Irishman in *Kilhwch* [5] and the caldron of the Head of Annwn in the *Preiddeu Annwfn* ; " ny beirw bwyt llwfyr ; " (it does not boil a coward's food). [6] " It is highly significant that both in the list in *Kilhwch*, which dates back at least as far as the year 1100, and in the later list of the

---

1. *Eriu*, III (1907), p. 157. Cf. E. Windisch, *Irische Texte*, III, p. 213.

2. Windisch, *op. cit.*, I (1880), p. 218.

3. *Irish Nennius*, ed. J. H. Todd, p. lviii.

4. Edward Jones, *Bardic Museum*, p. 48. That this list is substantially ancient is indicated by the fact that according to Jones, p. 49, it can be traced back to a parchment MS. and therefore must be as old as the fifteenth century. Furthermore, a number of the objects occur in *Kilhwch and Olwen* and must therefore belong to traditions as old as the year 1100. Furthermore, I can detect no trace of outside influence.

5. Loth, *op. cit.*, I, pp. 307, 334 f.

6. Skene, *Four Ancient Books of Wales*, II, p. 181. R. S. Loomis, *Celtic Myth and Arthurian Romance*, pp. 91 f.

Thirteen Treasures of Britain the Caldron of the Head of
Annwn has been euhemerised and is assigned to a giant Dyrnog or to Diwrnach the Irishman, purveyor of the Irish King.
In other words, the Thirteen Treasures were, at least in some
cases, divine possessions belonging to the Head of Annwn
which have been transferred by euhemerization to mere mortals. There is every probability that Bran son of Llyr, like
his brother Manawyd, possessèd a caldron of plenty besides
his healing caldron. More than that, there are among the
Thirteen Treasures a number of objects, including vessels
of plenty, which either are said expressly to belong to Bran
or are to be detected in the French romances among the possessions of the Fisher King, presumably Bron. There is the
Horn of Bran : [1] " Corn Bran Galed, or Gogledd ; y ddiod
y ddymunai ynddo, fo ai ceid can gynted ag i dymunid.
(The Horn of Bran the Hard from Cumbria ; the drink that
might be desired in it would appear as soon as it was wished for). " The sword of Rhydderch and the Chessboard
of Gwenddollau mentioned in this list I have shown in my
Celtic Myth and Arthurian Romance are to be recognized in
Perlesvaus (ca. 1200) as the sword of Gurgalain and the magic
chessboard, both wonders placed in the castle of the Fisher
King. [2] There appears in the same list of the Thirteen Treasures a " dysgl Rhydderch, [3]" " a platter of Rhydderch ; "
whatever food was desired thereon was instantly obtained ;
" y bwyd a chwenychai fe fyddai arno, fo ai caid yn y man, "
This is highly significant, since here is the very word, *dyscyl*,
which is applied to the vessel in the castle of Peredur's uncle ;
here the object possesses precisely the feeding properties attributed to the Grail ; here it is among a list of objects of which
two have a place in the castle of the Fisher King, and one is
specifically assigned to Bran himself. It does seem strange that
when so many Celtic vessels of plenty have been discussed in
connection with the Grail, the only one which can be accur-

1. Jones, *Bardic Museum*, p. 48.
2. Loomis, *op. cit.*, pp. 246-8.
3. Jones, *op. cit.*, p. 48.

ately called a "*graal*" should have been overlooked. Surely it is no mere chance which has combined in the Grail these attributes of other divine vessels of the Celts : inexhaustibility ; the power to discriminate the worthy from the unworthy ; and the power of automatic motion. It would seem that the caldron and the horn of Welsh mythology have not survived as such in French Grail romance, [1] but have bequeathed their properties to the one famous vessel of plenty, the Welsh *dyscyl*, the French *Saint Graal*.

5. Naturally the Celtic sea-gods who possessed these vessels of plenty were famous for their feasts. Manannán held the Feast of Age, where there was neither more nor less than sufficient for every comer. [2] The Irish Bran on arriving in the Land of Women, Manannán's island home, feasted with his men ; there was no taste wanting to them. [3] They became immortal. [4] Of the Welsh Manawydan, too, we learn that after Bran's death he held repeated feasts with Pryderi. [5] The feast of the Welsh Bran must have been famous, because the Mabinogi refers to " The Entertaining of Bran " and " The Entertaining of the Noble Head " (*yspadawt vran, yspydawt urdaul benn*) as proverbial. [6] Needless to say, the feasts in the castle of the Fisher King as related in the Grail romances are equally splendid and rich. The account in *Perlesvaus*, moreover, emphasizes the immortality of the company : [7] " Atant en fu menez misires Gauvains en la sale et treuve XII chevaliers anciens, tous chanuz, et ne sanbloient pas estre de si grant aage con il estoient ; car chascuns avoit C anz ou plus, et si ne sanbloit pas que chacuns an eust XL. " Clearly we have been on the right track in following back the clues which connected the Grail tradition with Bran.

---

1. The horn, however, survives in many disguises. Cf. Loomis, *op. cit.*, pp. 234-6.
2. E. Hull, *op. cit.*, p. 35. Todd, *R. I. A., Irish MS. Series*, I, i, p. 46.
3. K. Meyer, A Nutt, *Voyage of Bran*, I, p. 30.
4. *Ibid.*, pp. 32-34.
5. J. Loth, *Mabinogion* (1913), I, pp. 153 f.
6. *White Book Mabinogion*, ed. J. G. Evans, cols. 59, 61.
7. Potvin, *Perceval le Gallois*, I, p. 87. Cf. p. 328.

Now taking into consideration this wide-spread Celtic tradition of the feasts in the sea-god's palace, often situated in an
island, and of the vessels of plenty which there fed the company of immortals, let us examine the story of the " Entertainment of the Noble Head " in the Mabinogi of *Branwen*. [1]
Bran, after his wounding, commanded his followers, including
Pryderi and Manawydan, to cut off his head. " A chymerwch
chwi y penn, heb ef... yn hardlech y bydwch seith mlyned
ar ginyaw Ar penn a uyd kystal gennwch y gedymdeithas. ac
y bu oreu gennwch ban uu arnaf i eiryoet. Ac y guales ym
penuro y bydwch pedwarugeint mlyned... ar penn yn dilwgyr
genhwch... Ac yna y kyrchyssant wynteu hardlech ac y dech-
reussant eisted ac y dechreuwyt ymdiwallu o uwyt allyn. Ac
y dechreuyssant wynteu uwyta ac yuet... Ac ar hynny o ginyaw y buant seith mlyned. Ac ym penn y seithuet ulwydyn
y kychwynyssant parth a gualas ympenuro. Ac yno yd oed
udunt lle teg brenhineid uch benn y weilgi... Ar nos honno y
buant yno yn diwall ac yn digrif ganthunt... Ac yno y treu-
lyssant y pedwarugeint mlyned hyt na wybuant wy eiryoet
dwyn yspeit digriuach na hyurydach no honno. Nyt oed anesmwythach nac adnabot o un ar y gilyd y uot yn hynny o
amser no fan doethan yno. Nit oed anesmwythach ganthunt
wynte gyduot y penn yna no phan uuassei uendigeituran yn
uyw gyd ac wynt. (" And take ye the head, " said he... " In
Harlech shall ye be seven years at a banquet... And the company of the head you will love as much as when you loved it
most when it was upon me. And in [the isle of] Grassholm
in Pembroke ye shall be four score years... and ye shall have
the head with you uncorrupted. "... Then they went to Harlech, and they began to sit, and they began to provide themselves with food and drink, and they began to eat and drink...
And at that banquet they were seven years. And at the end
of the seventh year they set out towards Grassholm in Pembroke. And there was for them there a fair and kingly place
above the ocean... And that night they were there well-sup-
plied and joyous... And there they spent four score years so

1. *White Book Mabinogion*, cols. 57-9.

that they never knew a happier period nor pleasanter than
that, nor did one ot them know of the other that he was
older by that time than when they came there. No more un-
easy were they to be in the company of the head than when
Blessed Bran had been alive with them. " When we recollect
that Taliessin, Manawyd, and Pryderi were among Bran's tol-
lowers who feasted in this island palace, [1] we recall the passage descriptive of Caer Siddi (the Fortress of the Fays) or
Annwn in a poem attributed to Taliessin : [2]

Ys kyweir vyg kadeir ygkaersidi	Perfect is my seat in Kaer Siddi.
Nys plawd neb heint a hencint a ue yndi	Nor plague nor age harms him who dwells therein.
Ys gwyr manawyt aphryderi..	Manawyd and Pryderi know it..
ac am y banneu ffry dyeu gweilgi	Around its corners ocean's current flows.

It is obvious that the feasting of Bran's followers in the Isle
of Grassholm is a slighty euhemerized account of the ambro-
sial banquets of the sea god and his immortal companions in
an island of the western seas. [3] The " Entertaining of the
Noble Head" has left its impress clearly in Arthurian romance,
for in the *Didot Perceval* we read : [4] " Li Rois Peschieres [Bron]
si converse en ces illes d'Irlande en un des plus biaus lius del
monde. Et saces qu'il est a le gregnor mesaise que onques fust
hom, et est cheus en grant maladie. " Except that this passage knows nothing of the severed head, could there be a more
succinct description of the wounded Bran abiding in " a fair
and kingly place above the ocean, " in an island of the Irish
sea ?

I venture to suppose that Miss Williams' suggestion needs
no further vindication. The head surrounded by blood seen
by Peredur in the Lame King's castle, the " tiestes de sangler"
in the castle of Bran de Lis, the " caput hominis mortui "

1. *Ibid.*, col. 56.
2. Skene, *op. cit.*, I, p. 276 ; II, p. 155. Cf. *Cymmrodor*, XXVIII (1918), p. 236.
3. Concerning modern belief in a subaqueous land near Grassholm cf. Rhys, *Celtic Folklore*, I, 171.
4. J. L. Weston, *Legend of Sir Perceval*, II, pp. 12 f.

in the underwater palace, — not to mention a multitude of other details, — have their explanation in the severed head of the sea-god Bran. The " dyscyl, " the " graaus, " the " lanx " in which the heads are placed are in all probability derived from the " dysgl " which supplied whatever food one desired, the original of the " Graal " itself. Now it is a curious fact that the wounded Bran and his head seem to exist side by side in *Peredur*, in Pseudo-Wauchier I, and in Bercheur, and that the traditions preserved in *Branwen* and the *Didot Perceval* show the sojourning in an island elysium of the " Noble Head, " in one case in a physiological sense and in the other in a figurative sense. I believe all this is explained, as well as the appearance of the head in the platter, if we suppose that Bran's title, " the Noble Head ", was taken physiologically. Thus we account for the joyous feasts in the presence of Bran or the Fisher King himself, for similar feasts in the presence of his severed head, for other feasts in which both traditions have been conflated. The same explanation suffices to account for the presence of the head in the grail, for doubtless just as the caldron of Pwyll was called " the caldron of the Head of Annwn (peir Pen Annwfyn), " so the food-providing platter was called " dyscyl Pen Annwn " or simply " dyscyl Pen. " Thus the " platter of the Head " came to contain the head of Bran.

Let us glance back once more at certain features in the *Peredur* story, for I believe they shed light on a most tantalizing scene in the *Perlesvaus*. We remember that before the court of Peredur's uncle there passes a damsel bearing a head in a platter. Later she appears in hideous guise at Arthur's court riding a mule and rebukes Peredur for failing to ask concerning the wonders he had seen on the previous occasion. Now in *Perlesvaus* [1] we read of a bald damsel who rides into Arthur's hall on a mule, " et portoit a son col son destre bras pendu a une estole [2] dor... Et tenoit an cele main le chief dun roi seele en argent et couronne dor. " Her attendant holds the head of a queen, and one hundred and fifty heads of knights

---

1. Potvin, *op. cit.*, I, pp. 24 f.
2. This is the reading of the Berne MS. Brussels has *astele*.

remain in a chariot outside, drawn by three white stags. Later
she meets Gauvain, [1] and her attendant rebukes him because
he had failed to ask why her mistress' arm was slung in the
stole of gold. Still later [2] Gauvain is informed that the hand
in which the bald damsel held the head is the hand with
which she had served Perceval with the *graal*. One is moved
strongly to suspect that this Grail-bearer who bears the head
of a king in her hand and rebukes Gauvain for failing to ask
concerning her arm, really carried the head in a platter like
her counterpart in *Peredur*. This suspicion is strengthened by
the observation that the word *estole* is close to *escuele*, almost a
synonym of *graal*. It seems probable that the author of *Perlesvaus* had before him a text saying in effect that the damsel
on the mule " portoit a son destre bras une escuele dor, "
and that in it was the head of a king. It is also noteworthy
that in Irish legend a certain Liban daughter of Eochaid Finn, [3]
clearly a pagan sea-goddess, was drawn in a chariot with two
stags, and that in the *Serglige Conculaind* a Liban, [4] presumably the same, daughter of Aed Abrat (= the Dagda) [5] comes
to Cúchulinn, laughs at him in scorn, and later invites him
to her island home to fight against its enemies. It seems as if
certain characteristics of Liban survived in the bald damsel of
Perlesvaus. Oddly enough, too, the number of warriors in the
household of Liban's husband are one hundred and fifty. [6]
Though this correspondence with the number of heads of
knights who presumably had in origin belonged to the bald
damsel's household may be accidental, yet the number of
strong suggestions that we are dealing in this scene with

1. Potvin, *op. cit.*, I, p, 35.
2. *Ibid.*, p. 54.
3. S. H. O'Grady, *Silva Gadelica*, II, 269. Liban's story is much like
that of the " well cup-bearer " in the old Welsh poem and the modern
tradition of the Welsh fairy Grassi or Grace. Cf. Rhys, *Celtic Folklore*, I,
pp. 367, 383.
4. Windisch, *Irische Texte*, I, 207 ff. Cf. on Liban, *Beihefte zur Zts. für
Rom. Phil.*, LXX (1921), 11-16.
5. *Medieval Studies in Memory of Gertrude Schoepperle Loomis* (Paris and
N. Y., 1927), 402-4.
6. Windisch, *op. cit.*, I, 218.

fundamentally Celtic material, added to the identity of the bald damsel with the Grail bearer and of her lord, the Fisher King, with Peredur's uncle, render it highly probable that the head she bears is " The Noble Head " and that the " estole " which supports her arm is really an " escuele " which her arm supports. In brief, once more we have what seems to be the head in the Grail.

This discussion may legitimately give rise to two reflections. In the first place, far more in the Grail legend finds its explanation in the hypothesis of Celtic origin than most scholars have been willing to concede. In my book and other articles I have called attention to the Celtic origin of many of the most important names and of other features and episodes. What is left of Miss Weston's ingenious hypothesis of Grail origins ? [1] I am still convinced that her emphasis on the association with fertility and her diagnosis of the nature of the Grail King's wound, are correct. Perhaps, also, the question test is a survival of ritual. But I retract my support [2] of her hypothesis that the ritual had sexual meaning, and that lance and grail were sexual symbols. The answer to the question, " Whom does one serve with the Grail ? " was simply " Bron " or whichever Maimed King it happened to be.

A second reflection justified, I hope, by this discussion has already been expressed in my book. If Celtic literature sheds light on Arthurian romance, the converse is also true. A knowledge of Arthurian romance is essential to a full understanding of Celtic literature and mythology. The two are complementary studies [3].

---

1. Developed in her books, *The Legend of Sir Perceval* (London, 1906, 9), *The Quest of the Holy Grail* (London, 1913), and *From Ritual to Romance* (Cambridge, 1920).

2. R. S. Loomis, *op. cit.*, 260 ff.

3. I wish to acknowledge with gratitude the helpful criticism of Prof. Hilka and Prof. Krappe.

Malory's Beaumains

(Publications of the Modern Language Association of America Vol. LIV, No. 3, pp. 656-68)

MALORY'S BEAUMAINS

IN his book entitled *Malory* Professor Vinaver propounds a plausible hypothesis that certain features of the romance of Gareth in the seventh book of the *Morte d'Arthur* were inventions of the author.[1]

The hero—Beaumains—is Malory's own hero, and his name, impossible in any French romance, strangely resembles that of Malory's patron [Richard Beauchamp, Earl of Warwick]. His successive battles with the Black, Green, and Red Knights, and particularly his behaviour at the tournament at the castle of Lady Lioness, at once call to mind the romantic adventure of Richard Beauchamp. At that tournament the King of Ireland wondered who Beaumains might be, "that one tyme semed grene, and another tyme at his ageyne comyng he semed blewe. And thus at every cours that he rode to and fro he chaunged his colour so that ther myght neyther kynge nor knyghte have redy congnyssaunce of hym." The parallel is so close as to lead me to believe that some parts of the book of Beaumains were written in remembrance of Beauchamp's gallant deeds.

Such a picture of the aged Sir Thomas recalling the feats of arms which he may have witnessed in his youth and piously transferring them from the knightly noble under whom he had served in France to a noble knight of Arthur's court appeals to our imagination and our sentiment. But sentiment is not always a safe criterion.

A more critical examination reveals certain difficulties. For one thing, we do not know that Beauchamp was a "patron" of Malory's; all we can be sure of is that the Warwickshire knight served in the military retinue of the Earl of Warwick.[2] It is probable that as comrades in arms they were well known to each other, and that the younger admired the older as the pattern of chivalry that he was;[3] but more we cannot say. Moreover, the association of the two goes back to 1414; the Earl died in 1439, and the *Morte d'Arthur* was not completed till 1469[4] and may well have been the work of the decade preceding. There is a gap, then, of fifty years, more or less, between the gallant deeds which Malory is supposed to have commemorated in his seventh book and any probable date of composition of that book. Furthermore, it is quite unlike his procedure in any other part of his work to introduce a considerable narrative

[1] E. Vinaver, *Malory* (Oxford, 1929), p. 3.   [2] *Ibid.*, p. 12.

[3] On Beauchamp as "the Father of Courtesy" cf. Viscount Dillon and W. H. St. J. Hope, *Pageant of the Birth, Life, and Death of Richard Beauchamp* (London, 1914), p. 69.

[4] If Malory witnessed Beauchamp's exploits near Calais, it must have been between Beauchamp's appointment as Captain of Calais in 1414 and his embassy to the Emperor later in the same year. *Dictionary of National Biography*, II, 29.

element from his own experience or observation; the only additions of any length are in the nature of moralizing reflection. None of these negative considerations is decisive; they merely suggest caution.

The chief weakness of the hypothesis lies in the fact that the parallel between Beaumains' and Beauchamp's exploits is far from close, and that it is better explained by the fact that both the literary and the historic hero were following a commonplace of Arthurian romance. As for the parallel, Beauchamp on three successive days jousted in trappings bearing three inherited heraldic coats; his French opponents were in turn the "Chevaler Rouge," "the Chivaler Blanke," and Sir Colard Fynes.[5] Beaumains, on the other hand, early in his career overthrew on one day a Black Knight and a Green Knight, the next day a Red Knight, the next a knight in blue, and two days later the Red Knight of the Red Launds—altogether five knights on four days.[6] Later in his career Beaumains himself in a single day appeared magically in successive green, blue, and yellow arms.[7] Neither in his earlier nor in his later feats of prowess does Beaumains seem to be patterned on Beauchamp. Such resemblance as exists is more naturally and simply accounted for by the fact that a tournament in which the hero adopts a different disguise on each of three days is one of the earliest and most familiar motifs of Arthurian romance.[8] Richard Beauchamp, like his near-contemporaries, the Maréchal de Boucicaut and Jacques de Lalaing,[9] was playing at being an ·Arthurian knight; no wonder that his performances exhibit a remote likeness to those of Malory's hero. If in the adventures of Beaumains there were a single clear hint of contemporary interest, any allusion to the Warwick family, however indirect, one would readily grant the association of names in the author's mind, and the possibility—though by no means the certainty—that Malory developed the conventional theme of the three days' tournament in novel ways, remembering the spectacular exploit of his commander at Calais some fifty years before. But such a clinching fact is not to be discovered.

What were the circumstances in which the name Beaumains first appeared? We know, of course, that Beaumains was an epithet applied to Gareth by crusty Sir Kay.[10]

I dare undertake he is a vylayne borne . . . And sythen he hath no name, I shall

---

[5] Dillon and Hope, *op. cit.*, pp. 56–61.   [6] Bk. vii, ch. 7–17.

[7] Ed. Sommer, Bk. vii, ch. 30, 31. Other editions, ch. 29, 30.

[8] J. L. Weston, *Three Days' Tournament* (London, 1902); C. H. Carter, "Ipomedon, an Illustration of Romance Origin," in *Haverford Essays* (Haverford, 1909).

[9] *Mediæval Studies in Memory of A. Kingsley Porter* (Cambridge, Mass., 1939), p. 87. Cf. also G. F. Beltz, *Memorials of the Most Noble Order of the Garter* (London, 1841), pp. liii, 401–407.   [10] Bk. vii, ch. 1.

yeue hym a name that shal be Beaumayns, that is, fayre handes, and in to the kechen I shalle brynge hym. . . . He shall be as fatte by the twelue monethes ende as a porke hog.

There are about this explanation of the epithet two suspicious features: so flattering a sobriquet is quite out of harmony with the rest of Kay's insulting speech; and the gross disregard of gender in combining masculine adjective with feminine noun suggests not so much that Kay's grammar was a match for his manners, ~~but~~ that we are here faced with a late bungling attempt to explain a traditional name.

This brings us to another hypothesis which, though not as appealing at first or second glance, has, I think, more evidence in its favor. Twelve years ago in *Celtic Myth and Arthurian Romance* I endeavored to show that Gawain's name and Gareth's, when traced back to the Welsh stage, stood to each other in the relation of epithet to name.[11] In brief, the argument was this. In the *Mabinogion* are discoverable three names, each with its epithet attached, which rouse curiosity because of their similarity: Gwri Gwallt Euryn, Gware Gwallt Euryn, and Gwrvan Gwallt Avwyn, meaning respectively Gwri of the Golden Hair, Gware of the Golden Hair, and Gwrvan of the Hair Like Reins. The first of these, Gwri, is that of the hero of the *Four Branches of the Mabinogi*,[12] the four tales oldest in substance.[13] Since we find figures from the *Four Branches* listed among Arthur's warriors in *Kilhwch and Olwen*, it is hard not to recognize Gwri Gwallt Euryn in Gware Gwallt Euryn.[14] Two eminent Welsh scholars have conceded the *possible* identity also of Gwrvan Gwallt Avwyn.[15] In this possibility, we have a ready explanation for the names of three sons of King Lot as they are found on the Continent: Guirres or Gurehes and Guahries or Gaeres are simply derivatives from two forms of one name, Gwri and Gware. (It will be remembered that *h* in Old French was not sounded, and that *s* is the normal termination of the masculine nominative singular.) Gauvains, then, derives, through what is probably its earliest recorded form, Galvagin,[16] from the epithet Gwallt Avwyn. Gareth, who is likewise a son of King Lot, manifestly

[11] R. S. Loomis, *Celtic Myth and Arthurian Romance* (New York, 1927), pp. 84–89.

[12] W. J. Gruffydd, *Math Vab Mathonwy* (Cardiff, 1928), pp. 326–329. Pryderi, it will be remembered, was first named Gwri.

[13] Professor Ifor Williams places the composition about 1060. Cf. I. Williams, *Pedeir Keinc y Mabinogi* (Cardiff, 1930), p. xli.

[14] J. Loth, *Mabinogion* (Paris, 1913), I, 278, n. 4.

[15] *Ibid.*, p. 277. *PMLA*, XLIII (1928), 384, n. 2.

[16] R. S. Loomis, L. H. Loomis, *Arthurian Legends in Medieval Art* (New York, 1938), p. 32 f. The name Gwelchmai is, as Bruce recognized, a Welsh substitution for French Galvain. Cf. J. D. Bruce, *Evolution of Arthurian Romance* (1923), I, 192; also *MP*, XXXIII (1936), 234.

owes the origin of his name to a mistaken inference that the nominative Gaheres implied a stem Gaheret. Thus his name originally stood to that of Gauvains as name to epithet. That is precisely the relation which Malory ascribes to Gareth and Beaumains.

The question arises: is it possible that Beaumains is a corruption of Gauvains which still retained its original nature as a sobriquet? Or are we faced merely by some odd coincidences? So far as the possibility of corruption is concerned, the substitution of the initial *B* for *G* in manuscript transmission is fairly common, for there is a form of capital *g* in some French manuscripts which resembles a *b*. The historian Ferdinand Lot has noted:[17] "Le *g* initial du *Lanzelet* a été lu *b* par le *Lancelot*, faute qui n'est pas rare." Bruce perceived the same confusion between the Brulans of the *Estoire del Saint Graal* and the Garlans of the *Huth Merlin*.[18] One manuscript of Manessier's continuation of the *Conte del Graal* gives the name Goot Delsert, another Boon Desert.[19] Sommer's *Index of Names and Places* offers the following variants illustrating the same confusion: Galiane, Balienne; Glaalant, Braolans; Grandoines, Brandoines. It is entirely possible therefore that at some stage Gauuains was read Bauuains. An epithet beginning *Bau-* would inevitably suggest the French adjective *biaus* (*beaus*), later *beau*, since two Arthurian heroes were called by their mothers "biaus filz,"[20] and one of these received from Arthur on his arrival at court the sobriquet of "Li Biaus Descouneus."[21] The name being read Bauuains and inevitably suggesting that the first element of the epithet was *Biau-*, the next question before the medieval redactor was the meaning of *-uains*. What could it be but a scribal error for *mains?*

Professor Vinaver has rightly asserted that so gross a grammatical crime as Beaumains for Belles-mains was impossible for a Frenchman.[22] But an Anglo-Norman would have been capable of it;[23] the very spelling of the name Gareth goes to show that Malory's source was Anglo-Norman. The Continental form of the oblique case was Ga(h)eret, and it

[17] F. Lot, *Etude sur le Lancelot en prose* (Paris, 1918), p. 148 n.

[18] *M. P.*, xvi (1918), 348.

[19] C. Potvin, *Perceval le Gallois* (Mons, 1870), v, 158.—Note that the Norse *Parcevals saga*, E. Kölbing, *Riddarasögur*, (Strassburg, 1872), p. 30, says that the French word for the object borne by the maiden in the Grail King's hall was *braull*.

[20] Chrétien de Troyes, *Conte del Graal*, ed. A. Hilka (Halle, 1932), vv. 347, 373 ff., etc. Renaut de Beaujeu, *Le Bel Inconnu*, ed. G. P. Williams (Paris, 1929), v. 117.

[21] Renaut de Beaujeu, *op. cit.*, 131. I discard my original suggestion that the epithet Beaumains was related to the Irish epithet Finn.   [22] Vinaver, *Malory*, p. 3.

[23] L. E. Menger, *Anglo-Norman Dialect* (New York, 1904), p. 112. F. J. Tanquerey, *Recueil de lettres anglo-françaises* (Paris, 1916), p. lv, notes "le nombre considérable de cas pour lesquels l'accord ne se fait pas entre l'adjectif et le nom. . . . Une irrégularité du même genre accouple un singulier et un pluriel."

was in England that Anglo-Norman scribes habitually confused *t* and *th*, because they pronounced both indifferently as a dental voiceless stop.[24] We have in the thirteenth-century manuscript of *Havelok*, for instance, the adjective *gret* written as *greth*.[25] The man who first wrote Gareth for Garet, was probably not incapable of the solecism Beaumains. If we grant the possibility of such a development, we cannot wonder that Kay's nickname for the youth, "Fair-Hands," harmonizes so ill with Kay's scornful speech. Tradition insisted upon Kay's playing his churlish rôle; on the other hand, tradition, curiously distorted, insisted that Gareth was called Beaumains. We seem to have here a good example of that incomplete harmonizing of clashing traditions which is a familiar phenomenon in the literature of the Round Table.

To be sure, such a development of Beaumains, however possible the various steps and however harmonious with other facts, may seem purely imaginary. Let me offer in evidence a case somewhat different but not without marked analogies to the course we have been tracing, in order to show that such things do happen. Mr. A. G. Bradley writes:[26]

The Golden Valley [in Herefordshire] was not so named from any fatness of its soil, . . . nor yet from any treasure buried in its hills, but merely from the inability of the French monks to pronounce Welsh. The little river Dore which waters the valley and the abbey precincts was originally of course "dwr," a familiar Welsh word for water that stands for the modern name of a score of Welsh streams. This was clipped into "Dore" or "Dor" by the unaccustomed tongue of the strangers, and then in later generations was curiously enough treated by the Anglo-Herefordians as Norman-French and translated into English with an undeniably pleasant effect.

As with Beaumains, then, we have a name of Welsh origin undergoing corruption in oral transmission, mistaken for French, and finally translated into English. Thus Dwr became Golden; thus, by hypothesis, Gwallt Avwyn became Fair Hands.

Despite the analogy, however, the evidence for this hypothesis is not yet conclusive. We have seen that everything could have happened as suggested, and much that is baffling about the names of Gareth and Beaumains would be thus explained; but we look for definite confirmation. Now Professor Vinaver has demonstrated the equation of Gareth with Gaheret in the *Vulgate Lancelot* by citing three adventures which are told of both heroes.[27] It should be manifest that if we can show seven parallels between the careers of Beaumains and Gauvains, and if it is apparent that these parallels are not explicable as arbitrary borrowings

[24] *Havelok*, ed. W. W. Skeat (Oxford, 1902), pp. ix, xv, xvi.   [25] *Ibid.*, v. 1025.
[26] A. G. Bradley, *In the March and Borderland of Wales* (London, 1905), p. 55.
[27] *Medium Aevum*, i (1932), 157 ff.

by Gareth from the story of his more famous brother, then we have definite corroboration of our whole hypothesis that both Beaumains and Gauvains had their origin in the epithet Gwallt Avwyn, which must have been once attached to Gware as we find it attached to Gwrvan. Let us examine the parallels.

1. Gauvains, in the *Mule sans Frein*,[28] is summoned by a damsel who arrives at Arthur's court, to go to the castle of her sister, reaches it after sundry hazards, there finds that his predecessors in the adventure have been ignominiously done to death, but, undeterred, finds his way into the castle and twice encounters a personage with a great ax and replaceable head. Exactly the same statements may be predicated of Beaumains, yet no one who has read the two stories attentively will propose that Malory's seventh book is an adaptation of the *Mule sans Frein*. If no other considerations were valid, the independence of Malory is proved by the fact that he preserves the original Irish feature of the light emanating from the knight with the ax,[29] which is absent in the *Mule sans Frein*. A common origin is therefore the best explanation of the similarity between these adventures of Gauvains and Beaumains.

2. Gauvains, in Chrétien's *Conte del Graal*,[30] comes to the castle of the King of Escavalon, and with his encouragement conducts a love affair with his sister to such a point that it is interrupted by men bearing axes; he defends himself successfully; and his host on his arrival regrets the attack and is reconciled to Gauvains. Likewise Beaumains comes to the castle of the lord of Avylyon, with his encouragement conducts a love affair with his sister to such a point that he is interrupted by a knight with an ax; he defends himself successfully; and his host on his arrival regrets the attack and staunches his wounds.[31] Once more the parallelism is remarkable, but once more it is incredible that Malory's version should have been derived, even indirectly, from Chrétien. For one thing, Malory's account is far closer to the pattern of the beheading test, which is of Irish origin,[32] and, for another, Malory's Avylyon is not likely to be derived from the corrupt Escavalon.[33]

3. Gauvains, in the *Chevalier à l'Espée*,[34] comes, after due warning by some shepherds, to a castle, is welcomed by the lord, and at table falls violently in love with his daughter and she with Gauvains. The host encourages the affair, but when that night the lovers lie together, they

---

[28] *La Damoisels à la Mule*, ed. B. Orlowski (Paris, 1911), vv. 304–633.

[29] *PMLA*, xlviii (1933), 1004, 1022 ff.

[30] Chrétien de Troyes, *Conte del Graal*, ed. Hilka, vv. 5703–6215.

[31] Bk. vii, ch. 21, 22.   [32] *PMLA*, xlviii, 1004–07, 1021–23.

[33] On derivation of Avalon, of which this is a corruption, cf. *Romanic Review*, xxix (1938), 176 f.

[34] *Chevalier à l'Epée*, ed. E. C. Armstrong (Baltimore, 1897). Cf. *PLMA* xlviii, 1011 ff.

are interrupted by a flying sword. The next morning the host bestows his daughter on Gauvains. Beaumains comes, after due warning by a poor man, to a castle, is welcomed by its lord, and at table falls violently in love with his sister, and she with Beaumains. The host encourages the affair, but when that night the lovers lie together, they are interrupted by a mysterious intruder. The host some time later bestows his sister on Beaumains. Once more, it is impossible to believe that the Gareth version is derived from the poem; the one satisfactory explanation is a common source.

4. Gawain, in *Gawain and the Green Knight*, deals a parlous blow at a Green Knight, is entertained hospitably in his castle, and is escorted on his way by his host's servant. Beaumains deals a parlous blow at a Green Knight, is entertained hospitably in his castle, and is escorted on his way by his host.[35] Any one acquainted with the masterpiece of English romance will realize that it is not the source of the Green Knight episode in Malory.

5. Gauvains, in Chrétien's *Conte del Graal*,[36] meets a damsel, who refuses to let him touch her with his dirty hands, but rides with him, and to all her mockeries Gauvains replies with courtesy. He first overthrows one knight beside a river; then after a brief separation from the damsel he vanquishes a second keeper of a river passage, crosses a perilous ford, meets there a knight with whom he engages to fight a week later. The damsel now asks pardon for her mockeries. All this will doubtless remind the reader of certain of the most familiar adventures of Beaumains with the scornful damsel Lynet; and whereas in Malory the narrative is abundantly clear and well-motivated, Chrétien's story is extraordinarily confused. At least two other traditional stories of ultimate Irish derivation[37] have been interwoven with the traditional theme of the scornful damsel, which may possibly have the same origin.[38] Malory's uncontaminated version of this theme cannot be based on Chrétien; there must be a common source.

[35] Bk. VII, ch. 8, 9.

[36] Chrétien de Troyes, *Conte del Graal*, ed. Hilka, vv. 6828–7370, 8371–8973.

[37] *Romania*, LIX (1933), 558 f. R. S. Loomis, *Celtic Myth and Arthurian Romance* (New York, 1927), pp. 165–170. *PMLA*, XLVIII (1933), 1004 f., 1013 ff.

[38] In the *Serglige Conculaind* Líban, daughter of Aed Abrat (*i.e.*, the god Dagda; cf. *Medieval Studies in Memory of G. Schoepperle Loomis*, pp. 402, 404), comes to Cúchulainn in a vision, laughs at him, and strikes him. Later she comes to him in reality, summons him to combat with three champions in order to win possession of her sister Fann. Though refusing at first he goes at last, accompanied by Líban, to the beautiful land where her sister dwells. He slays the hostile champions and enjoys the love of Fann for a month. She then repulses him, and he wanders for a time on the mountains, half crazed. Cf. A. C. L. Brown, *Iwain* (Boston, 1903), 35–38, 142–144. On Líban cf. also *Revue Celtique*, XLVII (1930), 60 ff.

6. Gauvains, in the *Atre Périlleux*,[39] rides with a damsel and encounters a knight who has carried off another damsel in order to provoke a combat with Gauvains. This knight bears red arms and has the strength of three knights till the hour of *none*, when his strength gradually wanes with the sinking of the sun. In the combat Gauvains loses his own sword, later wrests the red knight's sword from him, and finally kills him. Likewise, Beaumains[40] rides with a damsel and encounters a knight who is besieging a lady with intent to provoke a combat with Gawain or some other champion of the Round Table. This knight bears red arms and his strength increases till the hour of *none*, when he has seven men's strength. In the combat Beaumains exchanges swords with the Red Knight and finally vanquishes him. There are two other versions of this story, and a detailed study of all four would yield interesting results. In Chrétien's *Erec* we read of the hero's encounter with a huge knight in red arms who after the hour of *none* wearies and loses his breath and is finally conquered.[41] In the fifteenth century *Eger and Grime* (Percy version) Grime overcomes in combat a knight with red shield and spear, whose strength increases from midnight to noon and decreases from noon to midnight.[42] It is interesting to note that in the opinion of scholars the name of Chrétien's hero derives from Breton Guerec,[43] and that in the Scotch romance a minor character bears the name Gares. Mere coincidence, perhaps, but suggesting that all four versions drew upon French variants of a story whose original hero was the Welsh Gware or Gwri. At any rate, it is certain that the Beaumains version is not based on the Gauvains version of the *Atre Périlleux*, because it retains certain features of the plot found in Chrétien's *Erec* and not found in the *Atre*, namely, the grisly exhibition of the heads or bodies of knights slain by the red champion and the blowing of a horn. Neither can this adventure of Beaumains' be borrowed from Chrétien for the obvious reason that Malory's narrative is free from any trace of the contaminating elements which have been generally recognized in this part of *Erec*.[44] Once more, then, we are forced to the conclusion that the Beaumains-Gauvains parallel is due to a common source.

7. Gauvains, according to Chrétien's *Ivain*, became the lover of Lunete.[45] Likewise Beaumains, it is fair to believe, was the destined

[39] *L'Atre Périlleux*, ed. B. Woledge (Paris, 1936), vv. 1513–1627, 2070–2462.
[40] Bk. VII, ch. 13–17.
[41] Chrétien de Troyes, *Erec*, ed. W. Foerster (Halle, 1890), vv. 5878–6009.
[42] *Eger and Grime*, ed. J. R. Caldwell (Cambridge, Mass., 1933), pp. 188 f., 266, 272. A superficial discussion of these features is found on pp. 111–117.
[43] *Romania*, xxv (1896), 588. R. Edens, *Erec-Geraint* (Rostock, 1910), p. 141. *Romanische Forschungen*, XL, 479.   [44] *Romania*, xxv, 258 ff. *PMLA*, LI (1936), 13 ff.
[45] Chrétien de Troyes, *Ivain* (*Der Löwenritter*), ed. W. Foerster (Halle, 1887), vv. 2415–41.

lover of Lynet according to some early version of the story. Though it may not be of much significance that Tennyson preferred such an outcome to Malory's dénouement,[46] yet Malory himself tells us that Lynet married Gaherys,[47] whose name is simply the nominative form on which Gareth is based. Here is a seventh reason for supposing that in the past Beaumains and Gauvains had shared a common legend.

Now one of the most noteworthy observations to be made regarding this series of parallels is that in the two cases where the Beaumains story corresponds to Chrétien's *Conte del Graal* and in the one case where it corresponds to *Erec*, it retains a version which is manifestly less confused by the intrusion of other plots. I do not impute to Chrétien this complication of motifs; he doubtless found them in his sources. But the comparison between his versions and those preserved by Malory in the book of Beaumains leaves little doubt that the common traditions behind them must go back well into the twelfth century. And we need not hesitate to accept such a view when even so conservative a scholar as Professor Kittredge asserts that Chrétien's romances "come late in the development of the story which each tells,"[48] and the sculpture on the archivolt of Modena cathedral proves the circulation of Arthurian tales early in the twelfth century.[49]

One final consideration not only confirms a certain degree of antiquity for the adventures of Gareth, but also strengthens the probability that his sobriquet Beaumains is a survival from the Welsh. We read that Arthur was able to recognize him throughout his magical changes of color at the tournament of the Castle Perilous by his hair.[50] Now it may be stated with some confidence that no knight could be recognized by his hair in any tournament of the fifteenth or fourteenth century, for usually his whole head was covered by the great helm.[51] This would also be true, I believe, of the latter half of the thirteenth century.[52] Even in the twelfth, Chrétien's Lancelot is able to maintain an incognito in a tourney,[53] and it seems clear that Gareth's recognition by means of his hair is an archaic feature, a carry-over from a time before even the

[46] Alfred Tennyson, *Gareth and Lynette*, vv. 1392–94.

[47] Ed. Sommer, Bk. VII, ch. 36. Other editions, ch. 35.

[48] G. L. Kittredge, *Study of Gawain and the Green Knight* (Cambridge, Mass., 1916), p. 241.

[49] R. S. Loomis, L. H. Loomis, *Arthurian Legends in Medieval Art* (New York, 1938), pp. 32 ff.   [50] Ed. Sommer, Bk. VII, ch. 30. Other editions, ch. 29.

[51] R. S. Loomis, L. H. Loomis, *op. cit.*, Figs. 76, 77, 92a, 94a, 101–105, 143, 174, 177, 188, 261, 262, 273, 277, 282, 284, 292, 306, 311, 342, 346, 369. In a few exceptions, such as Figs. 354, 381, the hair is certainly not visible.

[52] *Ibid.*, Figs. 43, 44, 162, 165, 215, 219, 356, 359, 361.

[53] Chrétien de Troyes, *Chevalier de la Charrette (Karrenritter)*, ed. W. Foerster (Halle, 1899), v. 5546 ff.

tournament existed. That being so, is it not pertinent to ask whether there is a connection between this fact and the fact that Gware enjoyed the epithet Gwallt Euryn, "Golden Hair," and presumably enjoyed also the epithet Gwallt Avwyn, "Hair Like Reins." All the evidence we have been able to discover points to a connection.

Let us summarize that evidence.

1. There is no satisfactory reason to believe Beaumains was named after Richard Beauchamp, and there are some objections.

2. The origin of the name as a studied insult on the part of Kay is preposterous.

3. Beaumains might well be a corruption of Gauvains since (a) initial *g* and *b* are sometimes confused; (b) *biau* as part of a nickname was familiar in Arthurian story; (c) the originator of the form Gareth was an Anglo-Norman and was probably capable of creating a Beaumains out of what he read as *Bauuains*.

4. This supposition is confirmed by the fact that there are seven parallels between the adventures of Beaumains and those of Gauvains.

5. Three of these parallels indicate a source antedating Chrétien.

6. The sobriquet Beaumains supports the theory that Gauvains itself is derived through the form Galvagin from the Welsh epithet Gwallt Avwyn, and for these reasons: (a) it retains the memory of the fact that it originated as an epithet; (b) Gareth probably derives through Garet, Guahre(s), from Welsh Gware, to whom the epithet Gwallt Euryn is attached; (c) both Welsh epithets emphasize the hair as a distinctive feature; and Gareth was recognized at the tournament by his hair, an obviously archaic survival.

To offset this fabric of evidence three objections may legitimately be raised. First, is it probable that not only Beaumains, but also so prominent, so ubiquitous a character in Arthurian romance as Gawain should derive their names from an epithet recorded only once in Welsh literature and then attached to the obscure figure of Gwrvan? The answer might well be "No," unless one realized that the remains of the original Welsh Arthuriad are so scanty[54] that one cannot test the popularity of any personage by the degree of prominence he achieves in those remains. For example, Trystan, whose renown from 1150 on equalled that of any knight of the cycle, is merely listed in the *Dream of Rhonabwy* and is

---

[54] The original Welsh Arthuriad does not, of course, include *Peredur*, *Owain* (*The Lady of the Fountain*), or *Geraint*, which are generally conceded to be based on French originals, though not necessarily on the corresponding romances of Chrétien. The only uncontaminated Welsh materials dealing with Arthur are *Kilhwch and Olwen*, *The Dream of Rhonabwy*, *The Harryings of Annwn*, a poem in the *Black Book of Carmarthen*, and a few triads.

briefly mentioned in a few late triads.[55] The single occurrence of the epithet Gwallt 'Avwyn is not a criterion of its familiarity. Furthermore, its bearer Gwrvan was not a nonentity. M. Lot recognized him as the Gorvain Cadrut who plays a considerable rôle in *Meraugis de Portlesguez* and *Hunbaut* and whose name in various scribal corruptions occurs in the Vulgate cycle and the *Livre d'Artus*.[56] And after all, the importance of Gwrvan and his onomastic descendants matters little to our case, for, by hypothesis, the epithet Gwallt Avwyn, like the epithet Gwallt Euryn, was borne by Gwri or Gware, and Gwri, later dubbed Pryderi, was the hero of the *Four Branches*. Gware, the prototype of Gareth, was no mere supernumerary, and it is entirely probable that any sobriquet applied to him should have survived, especially when we remember Loth's dictum that "l'épithète est souvent plus significative et plus tenace que le nom."[57]

A second plausible objection to the thesis of this article may be raised on the ground that there is no complete and exact parallel between the attributes and careers of Gwri or Gware and those of Gareth or Gawain. This argument, however reasonable, loses most of its cogency in the face of four considerations. (1) The *Four Branches of the Mabinogi*, which supply all that we know concerning Gwri, though containing much ancient material, present it in an extraordinarily muddled form. Professor Gruffydd has demonstrated that the branch of *Math* is "a vast conglomeration of themes, most of them, if not all, appearing in a truncated and sometimes hardly distinguishable form,"[58] and he has pointed out that in the first branch the very story of the birth of Gwri, which directly concerns us, has been seriously distorted.[59] Though the prominence of Gwri in this branch proves his importance, the lack of a complete and close correspondence between his story and those of Gawain and Gareth does not disprove the original identity of these characters. (2) Similarly, on the other hand, the lack of a complete correspondence can be accounted for by the lack of any tale of the birth of Gaheret or Gareth and the acknowledged contamination of the story of Gawain's birth by ecclesiastical legend.[60] (3) Despite the demonstrated corruption of the

---

[55] J. Loth, *Mabinogion* (Paris, 1913), I, 373, n. 2.

[56] *Romania*, XXIV, 326. H. O. Sommer, *Vulgate Version, Index of Names and Places* (Washington, 1916), gives Gornains Cadrus, Gosnayns Cadrus, Gosenain, and Osenain, which represent progressive corruptions of Gorvain.

[57] Loth, *op. cit.*, I, 79 f.

[58] W. J. Gruffydd, *Math Vab Mathonwy* (Cardiff, 1928), p. 47.   [59] *Ibid.*, p. 51 n.

[60] *Historia Meriadoci and De Ortu Walwanii*, ed. J. D. Bruce (Baltimore, 1913), p. xli ff.—The theory of the common derivation of the Gregory and the Gawain legends from a legend of Gwri Gwallt-Avwyn influenced by the pious Coptic tale of King Armenios still seems to me a better explanation of the facts than Bruce's theory. Cf. R. S. Loomis, *Celtic Myth*, p. 331 ff.

enfances of Gwri on the one hand and those of Gawain on the other, a
marked parallelism does exist.[61] Both are born under circumstances
which bring shame to their mothers; both are discovered as foundlings
swaddled in a rich cloth and their gentle birth is recognized; both are
baptized, one as Gwri Wallt-Euryn, the other as Walwanius or Gauvain;
both after a precocious boyhood in charge of foster-parents are given in
charge to a king or emperor; both after his decease succeed to the throne.
Moreover, it will be recalled, both Gwri-Gware and Gareth are distinguished by their hair. (4) The fact that the later career of Gwri under
his new name of Pryderi offers no parallel to that of Gareth or Gawain is
satisfactorily explained by the supposition that the story of Pryderi is
a graft from another hero-tale upon the stock of Gwri's birth-tale. This
postulate is confirmed by striking correspondences between Pryderi's
relation to King Bran and certain of his adventures on the one side and
Perceval's relation to the Fisher King, Bron, and certain of his adventures on the other—correspondences too elaborate to detail here but
easily accessible in other articles of mine.[62] In other words, an extraordinary amount of evidence leads to the conclusion that the Welsh hero
Gwri-Gware, later called Pryderi, is a composite figure, whose early
career under the first name parallels that of Gawain, and whose later
career under the second name parallels that of Perceval. Originally, there
can be little doubt, Gwri and Pryderi were distinct personages whose
stories were telescoped in the *Four Branches* for reasons which we can
only surmise. When all these facts are taken into consideration, we find
as much similarity between what we know of Gwri-Gware and what we
know of Gareth or Gawain as we have any right to expect.

A third natural objection is this: if Beaumains is Gawain, is it not absurd to discover them in Malory's book giving each other great strokes
till the blood trailed to the ground? Well, however preposterous such
conduct may be in the world of reality, the duplication of characters
through misunderstanding and the appearance of these doublets side by
side is one of the curiosities of Arthurian literature.[63] In Malory's seventh
book Gareth and Gaherys, unquestionably variants of the same name,
are separate persons, brothers. In Chrétien's *Ivain* Keus quarrels with
his *alter ego* Calogrenant, that is, Kay the Grumbler.[64] Morgan le Fay
and the Dame d'Avalon, patently the same person, figure as rival enchantresses in the *Prophecies de Merlin*.[65] In the evolution of romance
many strange things are possible, and one of them is the representation

[61] Loth, *op. cit.*, I, 106–116. *Historia Meriadoci*, pp. xxxvii–l, 55–59. *Perlesvaus*, ed.
Nitze and Jenkins (Chicago, 1932, 1937), I, 307 f., II, 327 f. *Romania*, XXXIX (1910), 1 ff.
[62] *Speculum*, VIII (1933), 427–429. *M. L. R.* XXIV (1929), 427–430. *Romanische
Forschungen*, XLV (1931), 83.   [63] *M. P.*, XVI (1918), 347.
[64] *M. L. N.*, XLIII (1928), 215 ff.   [65] Ed. Lucy A. Paton (New York, 1926), I, 415 f

of two developments from one original character as separate or even an-
tagonistic persons.

Since, then, the three objections to the derivation of the name Beaumains from Gauvains and ultimately from Gwallt Avwyn are invalid and
since there are several more or less cogent arguments in its favor, there
should be no bar to its acceptance. The derivation of a proper name in a
late fifteenth-century romance may seem a matter of small moment.
Quite the contrary. It involves conclusions regarding the most vital
issues in the history of the Matter of Britain. It disposes, for one thing,
of the suggestion that Malory's source for his seventh book was simply a
remaniement of the plot of La Côte Mal Taillée related in the French
Prose Tristan.[66] It was the author of the *Prose Tristan* who arbitrarily
transferred the adventures properly belonging to Gaheret Gauvain to
Brunor le Noir, alias La Côte Mal Taillée. An elaborate *conte* of Gaheret
must have existed some time before the flourishing of Chrétien de
Troyes, since Chrétien's stories of Gauvain and Erec represent highly
contaminated versions of certain episodes which are related in simpler
forms of Beaumains. Certainly the late Joseph Bédier was right in concluding that between 1066 and 1168 there developed "toute une floraison
de poèmes [I should prefer to say 'contes en prose'][67] arthuriens."[68] These,
though circulating in French and adapted to the tastes and the standards of the French nobility, retained much of their original Celtic matter.
Not on the basis of late localizations and an artificial atmosphere did certain legends of Arthur and the Round Table come to be called "la Matière de Bretagne," but on the basis of historic origin.

[66] *Medium Aevum*, I (1932), 162–167.   [67] *Mod. Phil.*, XXXIII (1936), 235 ff.
[68] Thomas, *Tristan*, ed. Bédier, II (Paris, 1905), 154.

Breton Folklore and Arthurian Romance

(Comparative Literature. Vol. II, No. 4, pp. 289-306)

BRETON FOLKLORE AND ARTHURIAN ROMANCE*

IN 1880 the eminent Breton folklorist Luzel wrote as follows in the
Revue Celtique :[1] "Il nous a paru digne de remarque qu'on ne trouve
le nom d'aucun des héros de la Table Ronde dans la bouche de nos conteurs populaires, pas plus dans la basse que la haute Bretagne, pas
même le nom d'Arthur, et qu'on ne rencontre aussi aucun souvenir des
aventures et des exploits qui, quoique imaginaires presque tous, les ren-
daient fameux." To be sure, Luzel conceded that there were some commonplace features of romantic fiction—rescues of princesses, giants,
fays, dwarfs, and so forth—to be found both in the mediaeval romances
and in the modern tales of the Breton peasantry, but he went no further
than to say that "une partie de tout cela peut bien être de source celtique
... et nous venir du cycle d'Arthur, bien que nous soyons enclin à croire
à une source antérieure et à une autre provenance."

This pronouncement of Luzel's represents a natural reaction against
the suspicious procedures and large claims of Vicomte Hersart de la
Villemarqué,[2] but also reveals a lack of familarity with the romances of
the Round Table. Rendered overcautious by the fabrications and the
fantasies of his compatriot, knowing too little of the history and the details of the *Matière de Bretagne*, Luzel failed to recognize in the folk
tales which he collected the significant affinities between the mediaeval
and the modern traditions.

We possess, of course, abundant evidence that in the twelfth century

---

* A French translation has been published in the *Annales de Bretagne*.
[1] *Rev. Celt.*, IV (1880), 433.
[2] F. M. Luzel, *De l'authenticité des chants du Barzaz-Breiz* (Paris, 1872).

the Bretons were familiar with the legends of Arthur and contributed to their formation. Abbé de la Rue, Stephens, Zimmer, and Brugger have established the point beyond the possibility of doubt.[3] Gaston Paris declared:[4] "C'est par les chanteurs et conteurs bretons ... que les fictions celtiques, dépouillées en général du caractère national que la plupart d'entre elles avaient eu autrefois, pénétrèrent dans le monde roman." Bédier also, in his famous study of the Tristan legend,[5] arrived at the same conclusion: "La matière de Bretagne est le produit de la fusion des légendes armoricaines et des légendes galloises." The Modena sculpture, William of Malmesbury, Wace, and Giraldus Cambrensis combine to assure us that the diffusion of the Round Table cycle was due first of all to the professional Breton story tellers.[6]

It would be strange indeed if the traditions and tales which the Breton *conteurs* made famous in the twelfth century had left no trace in their homeland. It will be the purpose of this article to pass in review certain motifs and episodes which survive in the Arthurian manuscripts of the Middle Ages and which also survived almost to our own time among the peasants and fisherfolk of Armorica, and to determine, if possible, the nature of the relationship between the two traditions.

Of these parallels between mediaeval chivalric fiction and modern folk tales many were discovered by the great scholars of an earlier day. But I trust that I have been able to add a few others which have not been noted before, and that the sum total will be imposing.

No Breton romance made a deeper or more lasting impression on the imagination of Europe than the love story of Tristan and Iseut,[7] and it is natural that we should find reminiscences of it or even sources of it in Brittany. Near Douarnenez lies an island which since the year 1368 and perhaps earlier has borne the name of Ile Tristan.[8] Near Douarnenez also is the village of Ploumarch, and there in 1794 the following tale was told:[9]

Le roi Portzmarch faisait mourir tous ses barbiers, de peur qu'ils racontassent au public qu'il avait des oreilles de cheval. L'intime ami du roi venait le raser; il

[3] Abbé de la Rue, *Essais historiques sur les bardes, les jongleurs, et les trouvères* (Caen, 1834), I, 64-99; T. Stephens, *Literature of the Kymry* (Landovery, 1849), pp. 418-423; *Zts. f. franz. Sprache u. Lit.*, XIII (1891), 86-105; *ibid.*, XX[1] (1898), 79 ff.; *ibid.*, XLIV[2] (1922), 78 ff.

[4] G. Paris, *Littérature française au moyen âge*, 4th ed. (Paris, 1909), p. 97.

[5] Thomas, *Tristan*, ed. J. Bédier, II (Paris, 1905), 127.

[6] *Romanic Review*, XXXII (1941), 7-9, 22-28; R. S. and L. H. Loomis, *Arthurian Legends in Medieval Art* (New York, 1938), pp. 32-35; R. S. Loomis, *Arthurian Tradition and Chrétien de Troyes* (New York, 1949), pp. 15-20; *Mod. Phil.*, XXXIII (1936), 233-235; Wace, *Roman de Brut*, ed. I. Arnold (SATF), II, vv. 9752-53; E. K. Chambers, *Arthur of Britain* (London, 1927), pp. 102, 272.

[7] R. S. and L. H. Loomis, *op. cit.*, pp. 26, 42.

[8] *Romania*, XLVI, 39 f.

[9] F. Cambry, *Voyage dans le Finistère en 1749* (Paris), II, 287.

avait juré de ne pas dire ce qu'il savait; mais ne pouvant résister à la rage de raconter ce fait, par le conseil d'un sage, il fut le dire aux sables du rivage. Trois roseaux naissent dans le lieu, les bardes en firent des hanches de haut-bois qui répétaient: Portzmarch, le roi Portzmarch a des oreilles de cheval.

Sébillot gathered two more recent versions of the same anecdote, one of which was current at Quimper, and pointed out that a stone sculpture, representing a human head with horse's ears, is preserved in the local museum.[10] This head before its removal to its present place was called by the people of the quarter "la Tête du roi March." For over a century and a half, then, the legend of King Mark and his ears has been familiar in this part of Finistère.

It is well known, of course, that Béroul, late in the twelfth century, told a similar tale of the uncle of Tristan.[11] A dwarf who is on confidential terms with Mark knows his secret, but refuses to divulge it to three inquisitive barons. He leads them, however, to a thornbush and tells the the tree that Mark has "oreilles de cheval." The barons later inform the king that his secret has leaked out, and in a rage he decapitates the culprit.

As Miss Schoepperle made clear in her classic study of the Tristan legend,[12] Béroul could not have been the source of the Breton folk tradition. A Welsh variant, quite similar to the Breton, and also attached to King Mark, was current in Carnarvonshire as early as 1693.[13] It is incredible that the Bretons and the Welsh should both have singled out this episode from Béroul and should both have added the detail that a flute made from reeds revealed the secret of King Mark's ears. Essentially the same story, moreover, is found in an Irish saga of the tenth century.[14] Though doubtless influenced, if not inspired, by the classical story of Midas, the legend of the king with horse's ears must have been current on Celtic soil and become attached to King Mark because his name meant horse. Offshoots from this legend were preserved by Béroul about 1200 and by Breton peasants as late as 1850.

It has been recognized for some fifty years that the historic original of Tristan was a certain Drust who reigned over the Picts about 780.[15] Deutschbein proved that at a very early stage a version of the widespread Perseus and Andromeda story attached itself to Drust and fur-

---

[10] *Revue des traditions populaires*, VII (1892), 356-359.

[11] Béroul, *Tristan*, vv. 1306-51.

[12] G. Schoepperle, *Tristan and Isolt* (London, Frankfort, 1913), II, 269-271.

[13] J. Rhys, *Celtic Folklore, Welsh and Manx* (Oxford, 1901), I, 233-234; II, 572-573.

[14] *Ibid.*, II, 573-574; *Rev. Celt.*, II (1874), 197-199; G. Keating, *History of Ireland*, ed. Dineen, II (Irish Texts Soc., VIII), 173-175; *ibid.*, IV (I.T.S., XV), 340.

[15] Thomas, *Tristan*, ed. Bédier, II, 105-108; *Zts. f. franz. Sprache u. Lit.*, XIII¹ (1891), 69; *Comptes Rendus de l'Ac. des Inscr. et Belles Lettres* (1924), p. 128.

nished two episodes to the romances of Tristan.[16] These were, first, Tristan's victory over the champion from Ireland who demanded a human tribute, and his wounding in the fight; second, the recognition of Tristan in the bath by a foreign princess and the discomfiture of a false claimant to the hand of the princess. Thus what had been a single episode in the original story of Drust was split and elaborated as two adventures of Tristan.

The great folklorist, Sidney Hartland, showed that the Perseus and Andromeda story survived as folk tales scattered throughout Europe, and noted several versions collected in Brittany in modern times.[17] One of these Breton tales, discussed by the late Professor Van Hamel in the *Revue Celtique*,[18] may be summarized briefly as follows:

> A princess is to be sacrificed to a dragon with six heads. A boy hero undertakes to deliver her, and her father promises to give her to him if he should succeed. With the help of his horse, his dog, and a helmet, the boy severs the dragon's heads. He cuts out the tongues but leaves the heads on the spot. While he is preparing to go before the king, a hideous dwarf takes the heads and presents himself to the king as the dragon slayer and claims the princess. By the dwarf's orders the hero is refused admittance to the palace, but finally he wins the chance to present his claims. He produces the six tongues of the dragon and so wins the lady. The dwarf is hanged.

Two points are important for determining the relationship of this folk tale to the Tristan romances. We have here not two separate episodes as in the romances, but a single story. There is no trace of the recognition of the hero in the bath. These two facts render it highly improbable, if not impossible, that the Breton folk tale is derived from the Tristan romances. On the other hand, it is obvious that the romances have been influenced at some stage by the popular formula, for in the original story of Drust there was no dragon combat and no severed tongues. Just when and where these additions and alterations were made in conformity with the folk-tale formula, I am unable to say. But it may well have been in Brittany, where we have evidence that the Tristan legend had attained a vogue as early as 1000,[19] and where it certainly underwent considerable development in the next century.

Van Hamel, therefore, was right in maintaining that the modern Breton folk tales of this type were not offshoots from the Tristan romance, but on the contrary the ancestors of the folk tales had contributed at an early period to the formation of the romance. Thus, as with the tale of Mark's ears, the mediaeval courtly versions and the modern

---

[16] *Beiblatt zur Anglia*, XV (1904), 16-21.

[17] S. Hartland, *Legend of Perseus* (London, 1894-96), III.

[18] *Rev. Celt.*, XLI (1924), 331-349.

[19] *Mod. Lang. Notes*, XXXIX (1924), 326-327; Pierre le Baud, *Chroniques de Vitré* (Paris, 1638), p. 5; H. Morice, *Mémoires pour servir de preuves à l'histoire de Bretagne* (Paris, 1742), I, 370, 372, 382, 386, 387, 408.

popular versions are cognates, both descended from or affected by narrative formulae current in Celtic territory at least as early as the twelfth century.

The motif of the black and white sails presents a more complicated problem. It is present in the classical legend of Theseus and in folk tales from Ireland, Celtic Scotland, and Brittany. *A priori,* it is unlikely that a version of the Theseus legend, accessible only in the scholiast Servius,[20] should have been incorporated in the Tristan romances; moreover, the parallel is far from close. The Irish versions also present quite a different situation from that in the romances.[21] The Scottish folk tale, as Miss Schoepperle and Dr. Brugger recognized,[22] offers more striking similarities to the Tristan story, but again the resemblance is not very strong, nor do we find instances where the Scots of the Highlands or the Hebrides derived material from Arthurian romance or contributed to it. It is the Breton version which, on the grounds of antecedent probability, is most likely to be related to the mediaeval texts. Let us turn to the *Tristrant* of Eilhart von Oberg and see how he treats the tragic conclusion.[23]

In his Breton castle, the wounded lover sends a damsel daily to the shore to watch for the coming of Iseut's ship and to report whether the sail is white or black, knowing that if it is black Iseut has not come. Tristan's jealous wife, Iseut of Brittany, learns of the scheme and persuades the girl to give her the news first. When at last Iseut's ship is sighted with a white sail, Tristan's wife lies and tells him that it is black. The sick man dies, and Iseut on her arrival expires on the body of her lover.

Compare this with the Breton tale which was current on the islands of Molène and Ouessant fifty years ago. In the words of the reporter, M. Cuillandre:[24]

Il s'agissait d'un voyage d'épreuve en pays lointain; le héros devait en revenir vainqueur avant d'épouser la fille du roi dont il était épris et qui l'aimait elle aussi. Il fut convenu entre les deux jeunes gens que si l'entreprise réussissait, le vaisseau qui ramènerait le héros porterait une voile blanche; dans le cas contraire, ce serait une voile noire. L'attente fut longue, semble-t-il. La jeune princesse languit et tomba gravement malade. Elle envoyait souvent une compagne au sommet d'une tour pour voir si quelque voile n'apparaissait pas à l'horison. Un matin une voile se montra. La malade demanda: "Noires ou blanches sont les voiles du bateau?" Sa compagne répondit que la voile était sombre comme la nuit. Et la fille du roi mourut, désespérée. Ce fut le châtiment du père qui détestait le héros et qui avait dicté la réponse à la compagne de sa fille.

---

20 Thomas, *Tristan*, ed. Bédier, II, 137-140.

21 Schoepperle, *op. cit.*, II; 438; *Rev. Celt.*, XXXII (1911), 184-193.

22 Schoepperle, *op. cit.*, II, 438, note 2; *Archiv f. d. Studium d. Neueren Sprachen*, CXXX (1913), 132-136.

23 Schoepperle, *op. cit.*, I, 62-63; Eilhart von Oberge, ed. F. Lichtenstein, *Quellen u. Forschungen*, XIX (1877), vv. 9256-391.

24 *Rev. Celt.*, XXXVII (1917-19), 323.

.There is, of course, one marked difference between this tale and
Eilhart's narrative. It is a woman, not a man, who meets her death
on hearing of the black sail. Otherwise this is the closest analogue we
have to the tragic ending of Tristan—the colors of the sails, the woman
sent to report the arrival of the ship, the hatred which inspired her
lie, all these features correspond. Moreover, this tale was current on
islands not far from the Ile Tristan; and the islands are too remote from
bookish centers to have derived their traditions from mediaeval romances. Are we not justified in concluding either that this folk tale
of the black and white sails was current independently on Breton soil
as early as the twelfth century and was used by Breton *conteurs* to
furnish a dramatic ending to the love story, or that it is a fragmentary
and distorted survival of the *conteurs'* story? At any rate, it could not
have been derived from the French source of Eilhart.

To recapitulate, three elements in the history of Tristan are paralleled in the folklore of Lower Brittany, two of them being popular
on the west coast not far from the Ile Tristan, and one of these being
attached to King Mark. There can be no doubt that there is a relationship between the mediaeval literary forms and the modern oral forms.
But it has been demonstrated that the folk-tale versions of Mark's ears
and of the dragon slayer could not have been extracted from any extant version of the Tristan romance, and it is not very likely that this
was the case with the formula of the black and white sails. The only
reasonable inference is, then, that the folk tales are derived from lost
oral forms of the romance, or that the Breton reciters of the eleventh
and twelfth centuries wove piquant and dramatic situations from current popular fiction into their longer narratives. When we realize that
all three of these formulae have their analogues in famous legends of
antiquity, in the stories of Midas, Perseus, and Theseus, it does not
seem astonishing that they should have lived on the lips of Breton
peasants and fishermen for eight or nine hundred years.

Since we have observed that the motif of the black and white sails
was well known in the islands of Molène and Ouessant two generations
ago, let us turn our attention to a belief which dominated the imagination of their inhabitants, a belief in sea fairies known as Morgans. The
following legend, reported by M. Cuillandre from the Ile Molène early
in this century, has been translated into English:[25]

The Morgan is a fairy eternally young, a virgin seductress whose passion, never
satisfied, drives her to despair. Her place of abode is beneath the sea; there she
possesses marvellous palaces where gold and diamonds glimmer. Accompanied by
other fairies, of whom she is in some respects the queen, she rises to the surface

25 W.Y.E. Wentz, *Fairy-Faith in Celtic Countries* (Oxford, 1911), pp. 200-
201; see *Annales de Bretagne*, XXXV (1921-23), 634.

of the waters in the splendor of her unveiled beauty . . . By moonlight she moans as she combs her fair hair with a comb of fine gold, and she sings in a harmonious voice a plaintive melody whose charm is irresistible. The sailor who listens to it feels himself drawn toward her . . . But the arms of the fairy clasp only a corpse; for at her touch men die, and it is this which causes the despair of the amorous and inviolate Morgan.

Since the name Morgan is properly masculine, the name Mari is often prefixed to indicate the sex of these fairies. Sébillot wrote in 1905:[26]

Lorsque les marins de Basse-Bretagne avaient cédé à la séduction des Mari Morgan, ils arrivaient aussi dans un palais de nacre et de cristal, où les attendaient des plaisirs de toutes sortes. Ils épousaient la Mari Morgan qui les avait enlevés, et si l'espoir de reprendre leur place parmi les hommes leur était interdit, ils finissaient par ne pas trop s'en plaindre. Riches, choyés, servis à souhait, ils vivaient heureux, grassement, et avaient beaucoup d'enfants.

Souvestre gave over a hundred years ago a similar account of a Mari Morgan who haunted, not the seashore, but a pond near Vannes:[27]

Une mary-morgan habite l'étang du duc, près de Vannes, elle en sort quelquefois pour tresser au soleil ses cheveux verts. Un soldat l'a surprise un jour sur son rocher, et, attiré par sa beauté, il s'approcha d'elle; mais la mary-morgan l'enlaça de ses bras et l'entraîna au fond de l'étang.

Though Souvestre does not say so, the soldier doubtless lived with his fairy mistress in her watery home. We shall later have reason to question the good faith of Souvestre as a reporter of folk tales, but in this instance his testimony is supported by too many other witnesses to be put aside.

The Morgans, then, possess two constant characteristics—their aquatic abode, whether salt water or fresh, and their amorous propensities. It can hardly be a coincidence that these are precisely the two outstanding characteristics of Morgain la Fée in mediaeval literature. Geoffrey of Monmouth and Etienne de Rouen both call her a *nympha*;[28] in *Floriant et Florete* she is one of "trois fées de la mer salée";[29] Hartmann von Aue says she could live above and under the waves;[30] the Provençal romance of *Jaufré* relates that the hero was pushed into a spring by a maiden who leapt in after him, clasped him to her, and the two descended to her lovely land at the bottom.[31]

It is obvious that Jaufré and the soldier of Vannes had the same

[26] P. Sébillot, *Folk-lore de France* (Paris) II, 36.

[27] E. Souvestre, *Les derniers Bretons* (1843), p. 111.

[28] E. Faral, *Légende arthurienne* (Paris, 1929), p. 340, v. 1124; p. 334, vv. 916-31; *Mod. Phil.*, XXXVIII (1941), 290.

[29] *Floriant et Florete*, ed. F. Michel (Edinburgh, 1873) ; ed. Harry F. Williams (Ann Arbor, 1947), vv. 549-53.

[30] Hartmann von Aue, *Erek²*, ed. M. Haupt (Leipzig, 1871), vv. 5177-9.

[31] *Jaufré*, ed. H. Breuer (Göttingen, 1925), vv. 8378-435, 8743-6.

supernatural experience with the same supernatural female. One was drawn to the bottom of a spring in the arms of "la fada del Gibel," that is, Morgain la Fée.[32] The other was drawn to the bottom of a pool in the arms of a fay, Mary Morgan. Here, then, is one marked correspondence between the sirens of Breton folklore and the notorious enchantress of the *matière de Bretagne*.

Another marked similarity lies in their amorous natures. Morgain la Fée had a number of lovers: Guiomar, Floriant, Ogier le Danois, Renoart, Breus.[33] She also offered her favors, in vain, to Lancelot, Alisandre l'Orphelin, Tristan, and Hector of Troy![34] Here we have a second trait common to a fairy queen of Arthurian romance and the Morgans of modern Brittany. Thus the curiously masculine name, the sex, the haunting of waters both salt and fresh, the land beneath the waves, the seduction of human lovers—all tend to assert the original identity of Morgain la Fée with the fairies of yesterday. And, in view of its inherent probability, the hypothesis may well be accepted.

One may also recognize the humble relations of the mediaeval Morgain in the fairies of the Côtes-du-Nord who dwell in caverns by the sea or in rock shelters near a pond or stream. They are called Margot la Fée, apparently because the female name Margot seemed more appropriate than the masculine Morgan. Their relationship to the fairy queen of the romances is rendered probable by the remarkable parallel between a folk tale about Margot la Fée, published by Sébillot in 1882,[35] and an Arthurian story—a parallel to which Miss Paton drew attention almost fifty years ago.[36]

Une Margot la Fée, dont la fille est à un certain jour de l'année metamorphosée en couleuvre, prie un paysan d'aller sur la route et de couvrir avec un bassin la couleuvre qu'il trouvera, à l'endroit désigné; il y va et reste assis sur le bassin jusqu'au soir; alors il le lève, et au lieu d'une couleuvre, il voit une belle jeune fille qui le récompense magnifiquement.

As Miss Paton pointed out, a similar story is told in an Italian *cantare* of the fourteenth century, *La Pulzella Gaia*.[37]

Galvano (i.e. Gawain) was worsted in a fight with a horrible serpent, but when he revealed his name, the serpent turned into a beautiful maiden. She said that she was the daughter of la Fata Morgana, and had long desired him for her lover. To this proposal Galvano consented and received from his faery mistress a ring which

[32] *Ibid.*, vv. 10651-4; L. A. Paton, *Fairy Mythology of Arthurian Romance* (Boston, 1903), p. 150.

[33] Paton, *op. cit.*, pp. 50, 61-62, 74-80; *Floriant et Florete*, vv. 2523-4; E. Löseth, *Roman de Tristan en prose* (Páris, 1891), par. 118, 291a, 292a, 611.

[34] *Speculum*, XX (1945), 183-186; Löseth, *op. cit.*, par. 190-192.

[35] Sébillot, *Traditions et superstitions de la Haute Bretagne* (Paris, 1882), p. 109.

[36] Paton, *op. cit.*, p. 100, note 7.

[37] Ezio Levi, *Fiore di leggende* (Bari, 1914), pp. 31-58.

brought him whatever he wished. But after a while he disobeyed her command, and she returned to her mother, Morgana, who transformed her from the waist down into a fish and placed her in a tower, waist-high in water. Galvano, after a long search, obtained access to the tower, delivered his mistress from her aqueous fate, and substituted Morgan in her place. The lovers then returned happily to Camelot.

It cannot be mere coincidence that in the Breton tale we have the daughter of Margot la Fée, transformed into serpent shape and delivered by a man who was well rewarded for his deed, while in the Arthurian poem we have a daughter of Morgain la Fée, transformed into a serpent and delivered by a knight who received from her a wishing ring. If it be suspected that the Italian story is a mere invention, the contrary is proved by the fact that the elements are found, somewhat distorted and reshuffled, in the *Vulgate Lancelot*.[38] There we read that Gauvain came to a tower, entered, and discovered a maiden suffering great anguish in a marble vat of scalding water. He failed in his effort to lift her out and departed. Later Lancelot came to the same tower and succeeded in releasing her from her enchantment. It is at least a startling fact that Malory in retelling Lancelot's feat (as incorporated in certain manuscripts of the *Prose Tristan*) states that the enchantment was the work of Morgain la Fée.[39] Both the French and the English versions go on to say that, immediately after the exploit, Lancelot lifted the lid of a tomb and killed a serpent which issued from it.

In this whole group of stories recorded in the thirteenth, fourteenth, fifteenth, and nineteenth centuries, we have a medley of several of the same elements: Morgain or Margot, fay or enchantress; her daughter metamorphosed into a serpent; the combat of a hero with a serpent; the deliverance of the daughter of Morgain or Margot. It is an odd fact that the Breton version of the nineteenth century comes closer to the Italian version of the fourteenth than to any other.

This connection between the mediaeval and modern fays finds still another support. One François Mallet of Gouray told Sébillot in 1880 that the Margots were wont to give names to infants, especially those of noble houses, bestowed gifts on them, and predicted what they would become.[40] This is exactly the same power which the mediaeval texts attribute to Morgain la Fée. At midnight, after the birth of Floriant, three fays of the salt sea arrived, the mistress of whom was the renowned sister of Arthur.[41] She proclaimed that the child would be "a good knight, the boldest, fiercest, wisest, and best mannered." She and

---

[38] H. O. Sommer, *Vulgate Version of the Arthurian Romances*, IV, 342; V, 106.
[39] T. Malory, *Works*, ed. E. Vinaver (Oxford, 1947), II, 791-793.
[40] Sébillot, *Traditions et superstitions*, p. 110.
[41] See *supra*, note 29.

her companions then transported him to her abode of Mongibel. Likewise, according to a romance of the fourteenth century, six fays appeared at the birth of Ogier le Danois and conferred various gifts on him.[42] Morgain, the last, foretold that, after a long and glorious career, the hero would come to dwell with her in Avalon. A similar account of Arthur himself is furnished by the English poet Layamon about 1200; and, though Morgain herself is not named at this point, we read later of a fay, Argane or Argante, who conveyed the wounded Arthur to Avalon.[43] Furthermore, it is a significant fact that Layamon implies clearly that the king's youth was passed in Little Britain,[44] the land of the Morgans.

The influence of the Breton fancy on the fairy world of the Arthurian romances can also be traced in the episode of the illuminated tree, related by Wauchier de Denain in his continuation of the *Conte del Graal*.[45]

After Perceval's adventure at the Mont Douloureux, he rode all afternoon in a tempest of thunder and lightning. But, when night came on, the weather cleared and the moon and stars glittered in the sky. He saw before him a large tree, covered with a thousand candles. As he drew near, the tree seemed to catch fire. But suddenly the candles and the tree were extinguished and darkness reigned. When he came to the spot, he found no candle, light, or living thing.

Wauchier himself offers no explanation of this marvel; but in Manessier's continuation the Fisher King declares that it is the tree of enchantment, where fays gathered, that Perceval's approach had put them to flight forever, and that neither tree nor candles would ever be seen again.[46] The analogous incident in *Durmart le Gallois* is contaminated by a foreign element, the mysterious child in the tree, and the adventure receives a theological interpretation.[47] Wauchier's version is surely the more natural and primitive.

Miss Weston, Professor Peebles, and Dr. Brugger have discussed these episodes,[48] and Professor Panzer has more recently pointed out

---

[42] Le Roux de Lincy, *Livre des légendes* (Paris, 1836), pp. 178-179.

[43] Layamon, *Brut*, ed. F. Madden (London, 1847), II, 384, 546; III, 144. See C. Potvin, *Perceval le Gallois* (Mons, 1866-71), V, 123-124; *Mervelles de Rigomer*, ed. W. Foerster, H. Breuer (Dresden, 1908), vv. 9403-6; *History of the Valiant Knight Arthur of Little Britain*, ed. E. V. Utterson (London, 1814), pp. 44-47; Raynouard, *Lexique roman* (Paris, 1840), III, 282a; L. Gautier, *Epopée française*, IV, 111; Robert of Brunne, *Handlyng Synne*, ed. Furnivall (London, 1901), I, 21; R. Pecock, *Repressor of Over Much Blaming of Clergy*, ed. C. Babington (London, 1860), p. 155; *Germanic Review*, XIX (1944), 128-129.

[44] Layamon, *Brut*, II, 408-412.

[45] Potvin, *Perceval le Gallois*, IV, vv. 34414-32.

[46] *Ibid.*, IV, vv. 35366-87.

[47] *Durmart*, ed. E. Stengel (Tübingen, 1873), vv. 15559 ff., 15817 ff.; E. Brugger, *Illuminated Tree in Two Arthurian Romances* (New York, 1929), pp. 19-24.

[48] Brugger, *op. cit.*; *Bulletin of the John Rylands Library*, IX (1925); *Medieval Studies in Memory of G. Schoepperle Loomis* (New York, Paris, 1927), pp. 285-299.

the right solution.[49] The quest leads us, this once, not to a modern analogue but to a natural phenomenon which has been observed in Brittany in modern times and which, of course, could have been observed there in any age. *La Grande Encyclopédie* asserts that "le feu de Saint Elme se manifeste souvent ailleurs que sur mer, par exemple aux sommets des toits and des arbres."[50] Canon Mahé wrote in his *Essais sur les Antiquités de Morbihan* :[51] "Tantôt les arbres, tout en feu au milieu de la nuit paraissaient former un vaste incendie, et à cet éclat fantastique succédait une obscurité profonde qui faisait frissonner." Especially interesting and pertinent is the testimony of Miorcec de Kerdanet, writing in 1837 :[52] ". . . de ces solitudes impénétrables, la nuit fuyait et, sans se consumer, les arbres devenaient autant de flambeaux . . .; mais bientôt tout s'éteignait, et une obscurité plus terrible encore ressaisissait la forêt mystérieuse."

Here is an experience almost identical with that of Perceval. Naturally the peasants of the Middle Ages interpreted it as the work of fays, just as the Fisher King does. Once more it seems that a romantic scene of the Arthurian cycle found its inspiration in the fantasies of the mediaeval Bretons.

Long-recognized and incontestable connection between the mediaeval cycle and the customs formerly prevailing among the Armorican peasantry is to be found in the famous series of scenes at the storm-making fountain which Chrétien describes in *Yvain*. It is needless to recall the details. Suffice it to say that first Calogrenant, then Yvain, and still later Arthur approached the spring beneath the pine in the forest of Broceliande, poured water upon a block of stone near by, and produced at once a heavy storm of rain. Chrétien's contemporary, Wace, is the first witness to the general belief in the magic virtues of this spring, telling us in his *Roman de Rou* (1160-74) how huntsmen in time of drought used to visit the fountain of Berenton, dip up water from it in their horns, wet the stone near by, and so bring on rain.[53] We have unimpeachable testimony to the practice in a series of mediaeval writers, Giraldus Cambrensis, Guillaume le Breton, Thomas of Cantimpré, and a document of 1467 describing the customs of the forest of Broceliande.[54] Finally we have a record that in 1835 after a

---

[49] *Sitzungsberichte d. Heidelberger Akad. d. Wissenschaften*, ph.-hist. Kl. (1940), pp. 29-30.

[50] *Grande Encyclopédie*, XVII, 366b.

[51] J. Mahé, *Essais sur les antiquités de Morbihan* (Vannes, 1825), p. 426.

[52] D. Miorec de Kerdanet, ed., *Vies des saints de la Bretagne armorique*, par Fr. Albert Le Grand (Brest, 1837), "Vie de S. Salomon," p. 360. See F. Bellamy, *La Forêt de Bréchéliant* (Rennes, 1896), pp. 47-48.

[53] Wace, *Roman de Rou*, ed. H. Andresen (Heilbronn, 1879), II, 283-284.

[54] *Beihefte zur Zts. f. romanische Phil.*, LXX (1921), 139-142; W. Foerster, *Kristian von Troyes, Wörterbuch* (Halle, 1914), 99*-103*.

long drought a curé of Concoret led a procession to the spring, dipped an aspergill in the water, and sprinkled the *perron*.[55]

Can anyone seriously believe that it was Chrétien's poem which gave rise to this popular custom of seeking relief from drought at the fountain? That would be the reverse of the common relationship. Frequently in literary history a Theocritus, a Virgil, a Shakespeare draws his materials from folk ritual or folk custom. Never, unless I am much mistaken, does a literary genius imagine such a practice and succeed in imposing it on country people who cannot read. Wace himself affirmed that the forest of Broceliande furnished the subject of Breton tales,[56] and doubtless there was a tradition of the rain-making spring of Berenton. Once more, then, we find a Breton legend of local currency, incorporated in a twelfth-century romance, which has survived independently into the nineteenth among the peasantry.

Let us continue our comparisons. Luzel collected a folk tale in 1874 which tells how a young man crossed the sea, arrived at an island where orange trees abounded, and in this evidently southern land came upon a dwarf and his two giant brothers, who dwelt in a crystal palace.[57] One cannot but be reminded that Chrétien introduces us in *Erec* to the dwarf Bilis, king of the Antipodes, and to his brother, the giant Brien.[58] This pair, Bilis and Brien, appear somewhat disguised throughout the Round Table cycle[59]—and here is another appearance in a modern Breton fairy tale.

From Carnac there comes a macabre story of a seamstress who, passing one evening through a cemetery, saw on a grave a new white cloth.[60] Yielding to temptation, she cut off a piece, returned home, and on the following night was working on the stolen cloth when a spectral man entered and threatened her with death unless she replaced it. She hurried back to the cemetery and sewed the stolen piece of cloth to the remaining portion. As soon as she had done this, the whole was whisked away and disappeared into the night.

Every student of Arthurian romance must have been struck by the considerable number of scenes laid in cemeteries; Mrs. Laura Hibbard Loomis has shown that one of them was of Irish origin.[61] Several deal with the theme of a woman who enters a perilous cemetery and brings

---

[55] Hersart de la Villemarqué, *Romans de la Table Ronde*, 3rd ed. (Paris, 1860), p. 235.

[56] Wace, *op, cit.*, II, vv. 6395-6.

[57] F. M. Luzel, *Contes populaires de Basse-Bretagne* (Paris, 1887), I, 244-245.

[58] *Erec*, vv. 1993-9.

[59] *PMLA*, LVI (1941), 920-924; R. S. Loomis, *Arthurian Tradition and Chrétien de Troyes*, chap. XX, LX, LXXV; H. Newstead, *Bran the Blessed in Arthurian Romance* (New York, 1939), pp. 75-76, 164-167.

[60] W. B. Johnson, *Folktales of Brittany* (London, 1927), pp. 133-134.

[61] *Mod. Lang. Rev.*, XXVI (1931), 408-426.

away a cloth. Two versions are found in *Perlesvaus* and *Le Chevalier aux Deux Epées*; both form no integral part of the plot, and the motivation of the characters is fantastic, even absurd. The *Perlesvaus* incident runs as follows :[62]

The sister of the hero made a vow to obtain from "l'Aitre Périlleus" a piece of the cloth in which Christ's body was wrapped for burial. Riding a mule, she entered the cemetery after dark alone. The graveyard was hallowed, but outside the ghosts of knights who had been buried outside the sacred precincts fought with each other and made a great uproar. The damsel came to a chapel, alighted, and found the most holy cloth above the altar; but when she was about to take it, it rose into the air. When she had prayed, the cloth descended upon the altar and a part of it separated itself, and this she placed in her bosom. At dawn the damsel departed from the burial ground, and on returning to her mother's castle, gave the holy cloth to her brother Perlesvaus to aid him in recovering his patrimony.

The irrationality of this adventure is patent. The explanations explain nothing. Why is the holy shroud found in a remote and mysterious chapel in Britain? Why should it serve the territorial pretensions, however just, of a Welsh prince? Why does the dangerous task of procuring it devolve on a maiden? It is obvious that the motivation is artificial, superimposed on a pre-existing narrative. This conclusion is supported by the fact that the parallel episode in *Le Chevalier aux Deux Epées* furnishes an entirely different motivation but equally irrational and forced.[63] In this poem it is the Lady of Caradigan who was obliged to seek in a waste chapel a part of a surcoat which the king of Outre-Ombre had left on the altar. It seems clear, then, that we have to do with a formula of which the original meaning has been lost. Nevertheless, the situation was thrilling and dramatic. The mediaeval author, like the peasant of yesterday, could inject into it such sense as he pleased, and the sense did not need to be very realistic, considering that the events were laid in the notoriously fantastic days of King Arthur. The tale of the seamstress of Carnac is but the most recent offshoot of the old wild *conte* which was employed by the romancers.

Let us observe that, in all the cases we have considered, the modern folk tale is not linked to personages of the Arthurian circle—except those which are concerned with the Morgans or King Mark, and even these are not derived from the mediaeval versions. All the evidence shows that the mediaeval Breton *conteurs* drew from the great reservoir of contemporary popular traditions many of the most striking elements of their narrative repertory. This is the reason that one could hear in the last century from the lips of rustics and fishermen essentially the same tales which one can read in the French and Anglo-Norman texts of the Middle Ages.

---

[62] *Perlesvaus*, ed. W. A. Nitze and T. A. Jenkins (Chicago, 1932-37), I, 220-233. See *ibid.*, II, 306-309; Malory, *Works*, ed. Vinaver, I, 279-282; III, 1414-5.
[63] *Chevaliers as Deus Espees*, ed. W. Foerster (Halle, 1877), vv. 441-993.

But there is a fairy tale, told to Luzel in 1855, which contains a situation which, so far as I am aware, does not belong to the common stock of European folklore and which cannot be traced to any other source than to a developed romance of the Grail. The hero of this tale by chance encounters an old man, his uncle, who dwells in the depths of a forest and who has subsisted for twenty years on a crust of bread.[64] One inevitably recalls the famous scene described by Chrétien where Perceval comes by chance to the hermitage of his uncle, who informs him that another uncle of his, the unseen invalid of the Grail Castle, has subsisted for twenty years (the number is supplied by four manuscripts) on the eucharistic bread.[65] I have attempted in my book, *Arthurian Tradition and Chrétien de Troyes*,[66] to show that this scene represents a fairly complicated and late development in the ancient legend of the Grail. Unless I am mistaken, therefore, this meager detail in the modern story is the only certain example in Breton folklore of a borrowing from the vast literature of Arthur.

But it may be objected that the tale of *Perronik*, which Souvestre published in 1845, professedly from the recitation of a maker of sabots in the neighborhood of Vannes, presents a much more striking and extended parallel to Chrétien's poem. Unfortunately the authenticity of *Perronik* is suspect and scholars have debated at intervals over a century the problem of its nature. Is it a true descendant by oral transmission of a Celtic tale of Perceval, as Souvestre maintained, or is it an artificial concoction by Souvestre himself? Let me summarize the story, which occupies thirty-four pages.[67]

Perronik was one of those poor halfwits for whom the charity of Christians takes the place of father and mother. One day, coming to a farmhouse, he found the housewife alone and asked for food. He persuaded her by his flatteries to give him an ample meal. A horseman approached and inquired the road which led to the castle of Kerglas, where the *bassin* of gold and the diamond lance were kept at the bottom of a vault. "The *bassin* of gold," he said, "produces at once the food and the wealth one desires; one has only to drink to be healed of one's ills; and even the dead come to life if it touches their lips. The diamond lance kills and breaks whatever it strikes." The farm woman warned the cavalier that more than a hundred other gentlemen had already passed in search of the *bassin* and the lance, but none had returned. The cavalier, however, continued on his way; and Perronik, for his part, was employed at the farm as a herdboy. In the course of time many cavaliers passed in quest of the castle of Kerglas, but none came back. One evening an old, white-bearded man came out from a forest, approached Perronik, and revealed he was a sorcerer of the giant Rogéar, who possessed the *bassin* and lance. From this ancient Perronik learned the charm by which he

---

[64] Luzel, *Contes populaires de Basse-Bretagne*, I, 179.

[65] *Percevalroman*, ed. A. Hilka (Halle, 1932), vv. 6338-431.

[66] *Arthurian Tradition and Chrétien de Troyes*, chap. LXXV.

[67] E. Souvestre, *Le Foyer breton* (Paris, 1864), pp. 137-170; *ibid.* (Paris, 1947), pp. 257-274.

could catch a colt belonging to Rogéar. So, one day, mounted on this colt, the herdboy set out for the giant's castle and succeeded by his smartness in overcoming the perils of the journey. These perils included trees which seemed to blaze, a garden watched by a ferocious lion, a lake of dragons, and a valley guarded by a black man. When Perronik came in sight of Kerglas, he met, seated near a ford, a woman in a black robe with a body yellow as that of a Moor. He set her on the crupper of his colt, crossed the ford, and, following her instructions, entered the castle, killed Rogéar, and won the *bassin* and lance. Then he went to the court of the king of Brittany at Nantes, defeated the French, and revived the dead Breton soldiers by touching their lips with the *bassin*. After conquering the rest of France, he journeyed to the Holy Land, forced the emperor of the Saracens to be baptized, and married his daughter.

Let us see, now, what Souvestre wrote concerning the relation of this naive tale to the mediaeval Perceval and Peredur romances.[68]

Les rapports d'origine qui existent entre ce poème [the *Conté del Graal*] et le conte breton ne sont point, à ce qu'il nous semble, difficiles à saisir. Dans les deux récits il s'agit de la conquête d'un bassin et d'une lance dont la possession assure des avantages du même genre; les héros de la version française et de la version armoricaine sont soumis à des dangers, à des tentations, et la réussite leur assure à tous deux la couronne. On pourrait même peut-être trouver quelques rapports de personnage entre l'idiot Perronik allant devant lui sans savoir où, et arrachant à la fermière son pain de méteil, son beurre frais baratté, son lard de dimanche, et ce Perceval simple, ignorant, grossier, qui débute par dévorer deux pâtés de chevreuil et boire un grand pot de vin. A la vérité, les détails diffèrent et les épreuves subies par Perronik ne ressemblent point, en général, aux épreuves imposées à Perceval; mais, en revanche, elles rappellent, de fort près, celles que surmonte Peredur, le héros de la tradition galloise. Il semble donc que le conte armoricain a puisé successivement aux deux sources française et bretonne. Né de la tradition galloise, modifié par la version française, et enfin approprié au génie populaire de notre province, il est devenu, en s'altérant par une suite de transmissions, ce que nous le voyons aujourd'hui.

What are the arguments in favor of the authenticity of *Perronik?* First, the story has a completely rustic flavor; it seems to be the creation of the folk imagination, not an artificial product of the age of Louis-Philippe. Second, if it is a forgery, the author must have been inconceivably clever in restricting or disguising his borrowings from the mediaeval romances. Except for Perronik-Perceval, the proper names bear no resemblance to each other. The sacred associations of the Grail and the lance which are emphasized in the French poem are totally absent from *Perronik*. The Fisher King and the giant Rogéar have nothing in common except the possession of the vessel and lance. Third—and this is an argument which weighed heavily with me—the properties of the two talismans possessed by Rogéar are not at all those attributed to the objects guarded by the Fisher King nor those of the dish and lance in *Peredur*; but they are almost identical with the properties attached in a Welsh list of the fifteenth century to the vessel and the sword of Rhyd-

---

[68] Souvestre, *Foyer breton* (1864), p. 177; (1947), p. 279.

derch. The *bassin* of gold described by Souvestre "produces at once the food and the wealth one desires." As for the dish (*dysgl*) of Rhydderch in the Welsh list, "whatever food was wished thereon was instantly obtained."[69] The diamond lance described by Souvestre "shone like a flame." In the Welsh list there is no lance, indeed, but the sword of Rhydderch; "if anyone except its owner drew it from the sheath, the sword seemed like a flame in his hand."[70] If Souvestre did not know this Welsh document, how can one account for the correspondence with *Perronik* except through a traditional link? Such a parallelism can hardly be fortuitous. These three considerations seem to assure the authenticity of *Perronik*.

On the other hand, there are certain facts which warrant suspicion. If Souvestre had wished to fabricate a Breton folk tale, he had the necessary qualifications to write a good imitation. *Les Derniers Bretons*, which he had published in 1835, demonstrates his remarkable familiarity with the traditions current among the country folk of his time; his vast production of novels and plays demonstrates his talent for shaping the materials provided by what he had seen and heard. Moreover, it is embarrassing that no one but Souvestre seems to have heard from the lips of the humble a word about Perronik "l'idiot," or the *bassin* of gold, or the diamond lance.

The most formidable argument against the genuineness of the tale is the fact that we can discover in *Les Contes populaires des anciens Bretons* by Vicomte Hersart de la Villemarqué a considerable number of the special features of the suspect narrative, some of which indeed cannot be explained otherwise than as borrowings from this book. Villemarqué published his work in 1842, and Souvestre cited it as the source of his summary of the *Conte del Graal*. It was also an obvious source for his knowledge of *Peredur*. Now it is a striking fact that the *bassin* of gold, which has never been met with in the genuine popular traditions of Brittany and which does not occur in the *Conte del Graal* or *Peredur* (the words *graal* and *dyscyl* both meaning "dish," not "basin"), is to be found in the résumé which Villemarqué gives of the French poem:[71] "deux demoiselles, l'une avec un *tailleor* ou couteau[72] [*sic*] d'argent, l'autre avec un *graal* ou bassin d'or pur émaillé." In fact, Villemarqué uses the word *bassin* to translate not only *graal* but also the Welsh words *dyscyl* and *peir* (caldron).[73] He insists on the word, giving *Peredur* the alternative title, *Le Bassin magique*.[74] It

---

[69] Edward Jones, *Bardic Museum* (London, 1802), p. 48.

[70] *Ibid.*, p. 47.

[71] Villemarqué, *op. cit.*, p. 136.

[72] *Tailleor* means a "carving platter," almost a synonym of *graal*.

[73] Villemarqué, *op. cit.*, pp. 337, 143. See J. Gwenogvryn Evans, *White Book Mabinogion* (Pwllheli, 1907), col. 130, 44.

[74] Villemarqué, *op. cit.*, p. 321.

would be extremely strange if Souvestre had met in a folk tale a descendant or counterpart of the Grail in the form of a basin, which is
never found in the mediaeval texts but only in the summary of these
texts which had appeared three years before the publication of *Perronik* and which he certainly had read. Besides, Souvestre assigns to the
bassin, as we have seen, the power of reviving the dead, a power which
is never, so far as I am aware, attributed to the Grail in the mediaeval
romances—but which is twice mentioned by Villemarqué as a property
of the *bassin* sought by Perceval and is once mentioned by him as a
property of the *bassin* of Bran the Blessed, Welsh prototype of Bron,
guardian of the Grail.[75] Here is another reason for questioning the
good faith of Souvestre.

Villemarqué's book supplies an explanation of other details in *Perronik*. It informs us that "Taliésin place le bassin bardique dans la grotte
d'une magicienne."[76] This reminds us of the fact that the *bassin* of the
magician Rogéar was kept at the bottom of a vault. From Villemarqué
might have come the genuinely traditional concept of the venerable man
who was the brother of the owner of the *bassin* and who gave the hero
good counsel.[77] So too with the damsel clad in black.[78] As for the dangers
which Perronik surmounts and which Souvestre himself compares to
those encountered by Peredur, could they not have been suggested by
Villemarqué's statement that the author of *Peredur* involves his hero in
contests "non-seulement avec des géants comme d'autres guerriers, mais
encore avec des lions, des serpents, des dragons, des monstres marins
. . . "?[79] The black man with six eyes, described by Souvestre, may have
some connection with the one-eyed black man in *Peredur*.[80] To be sure,
the details differ considerably in all these adventures, but an astute
counterfeiter does not reveal too clearly his procedure.

Only the resemblance between the flaming lance of Rogéar and the
blazing sword of Rhydderch remains to be explained; it is the one apparently primitive feature which does not have a plausible source in
Villemarqué's book. I have not succeeded in discovering exactly where
Souvestre might have come across the list of the Thirteen Treasures of
the Isle of Britain, but there were certainly more books than one which
contained it and which a man whose curiosity was aroused might have
consulted. Already in 1802 the list had been published in English translation;[81] in 1819 it was known in Austria and the *dysgl* of Rhydderch had
been recognized as a counterpart of the Grail;[82] Villemarqué himself

---

[75] *Ibid.,* pp. 139, 143.
[76] *Ibid.,* p. 142.
[77] *Ibid.,* p. 137.
[78] *Ibid.*
[79] *Ibid.,* p. 145.
[80] *Ibid.,* pp. 362-365.
[81] See *supra,* note 69.
[82] *Jahrbücher der Literatur,* V (Wien, 1819), 42-43.

mentioned the thirteen wonderful objects in discussing the Celtic *bassin*,[83] though he did not name them. It is possible, therefore, that Souvestre knew the blazing sword of Rhydderch, deliberately blended it with the bleeding lance of the Grail romances, and so created the flaming lance of Rogéar.

We cannot, it seems, grant to Souvestre the title of a scrupulous, scientific, honest folklorist, but rather that of an extremely clever and artistic manipulator. *Perronik* is a Breton counterpart of the Ossianic poems of Macpherson.

Though convinced until recently of its genuineness by the arguments of Junk[84] and the considerations set forth above, I am now to be counted among the skeptics. Such disillusionment, however, should not diminish our confidence in the other results obtained in this study. No one has ever challenged the authenticity of the materials gathered by Luzel, Sébillot, and M. Cuillandre. As for the other parallels, it is impossible to regard the Breton versions as concocted on the basis of the romances— either internal evidence proves them to be independent or it can be shown that their authors did not have access to the mediaeval texts.

I do not pretend to have exhausted the subject of the relations between Breton folklore and the romances of the Round Table. Breton scholars may be able to point out other significant analogies.[85] But, in any case, the number of parallels which I have presented is large enough, I trust, to demonstrate that, in addition to the numerous Irish and Welsh elements which scholars have obliged us to recognize, there are others contributed by Little Britain—some of the most important and charming, indeed, in the *matière de Bretagne*.

---

[83] Villemarqué, *op. cit.*, p. 144.

[84] *Sitzungsberichte d. Kaiserlichen Akad. d. Wissenschaften in Wien*, ph.-hist. Kl., Bd. 168, Abh. 4.

[85] I have omitted some folklore commonplaces common to both bodies of fiction, for instance: disenchantment by a kiss, fairyland at the bottom of a well, banquet set out in an uninhabited castle. See Luzel, *Contes populaires de Basse-Bretagne*, I, 55 f., 246, 267 f. On legends of Merlin, see *Mélanges bretons et celtiques offerts à M. J. Loth* (Rennes, Paris, 1927), pp. 349-363.

The Strange History
of
Caradoc of Vannes

(<u>Franciplegius</u> pp. 232-39)

The Strange History of Caradoc of Vannes

IN ALL THE Arthurian cycle it would be difficult to find a narrative more bizarre and barbaric than that incorporated in the First Continuation of Chrétien's *Perceval* and often referred to as the *Livre de Caradoc*.[1]

We are told that King Caradoc of Vannes[2]—not the hero, but his putative father—married Isaive of Carhaix, a niece of Arthur's. But the new queen's paramour, the enchanter Eliavres, contrived on three successive nights to place in the king's bed, instead of the queen, a greyhound bitch, a sow, and a mare, each metamorphosed by magic into the shape of the bride. Eliavres himself took advantage of the opportunity to lie thrice with the queen and begot on her a son, who received at birth the name of his supposed father, Caradoc. Young Caradoc's first exploit was the successful passing of the so-called Beheading Test, familiar to readers of *Gawain and the Green Knight* as the major theme of the English masterpiece.[3] In fact, as Laura Hibbard Loomis[4] and others have noted, there are marked resemblances between the French and the English versions. But the Caradoc version ends quite differently, for the challenger revealed himself to the young hero as his true father, Eliavres. Young Caradoc then hastened to Vannes and told the king of the deception practiced upon him. Whereupon King Caradoc imprisoned his adulterous wife, and forced the adulterer, Eliavres, to lie successively with a bitch, a sow, and a mare, thus fitting the punishment to the crime. From these monstrous unions were born three animals, of which the boar was named Tortain[5] and the colt, Levagor or Loriagor.[6]

To avenge herself and her paramour, the queen concealed a snake in a cupboard and bade her son open it. The serpent leaped out, fastened itself on Caradoc's arm, and began gradually to suck out his life. A friend, learning of his plight, forced the treacherous queen to disclose a remedy. Caradoc, accordingly, took his place in a vat filled with vinegar. Beside it was set a vat of milk, in which stood a pure maiden who had volunteered to save Caradoc's life. When she exposed her breast

91

above the rim of the vat, the snake released Caradoc's arm and sprang toward her. Caradoc slashed at the reptile with a sword, but, alas, cut off the maiden's nipple. The wound, however, promptly healed, and when, soon after, King Caradoc died, young Caradoc, on succeeding to the throne, married his beloved benefactress. However, his arm had shrunk and hence he was called Caradoc Briebras[7]—a cognomen meaning, of course, "Short Arm"; and his wife's breast lacked the nipple. When, after the lapse of some time, he received as a gift the golden boss of a shield endowed with marvelous curative virtues, he applied the golden boss to his wife's breast and it adhered to the flesh, replacing the missing nipple.

The last episode in the *Livre de Caradoc* is concerned with the somewhat farcical theme of the chastity-testing horn.[8] When on a visit to Arthur's court, Caradoc, because of his wife's perfect fidelity, was able, alone of all the husbands there present, to drink from the horn without spilling a drop. Fearing Guenevere's hatred, he dispatched his paragon of a spouse for safety's sake back to Vannes.

This sensational and somewhat scabrous history, particularly the portion relating to the snake, the short arm, and the golden breast, was in 1899 the subject of two articles in *Romania*, by Gaston Paris and Ferdinand Lot, respectively (XXVIII, 214–31 and 568–78). They offered different solutions to the genetic problem and the subsequent migration of this complex of adventures, but, with all due deference to their erudition, a better hypothesis may, I believe, be found. So, after the lapse of sixty-six years, let me undertake the untangling of the threads of a fascinating story.

To Paris goes the credit of first assembling all, or nearly all, the pertinent evidence. It is also to his credit that he claimed no more for his conjectures about the transmission of the story than a measure of plausibility; for, under critical examination, these conjectures prove to be mainly mistaken. He suggested Irish origin for the story of the serpent, the self-sacrificing maiden, and the golden breast, perhaps because he had previously discovered the Irish origin of the Beheading Test (*Histoire littéraire de la France*, XXX, 71–78). But there are no Irish analogues for the serpent story. Paris argued further that the tradition crossed at a remote period from Ireland to Scotland (*Romania*, XXVIII, 227), but though there are two clear Scottish analogues (of which more later), neither is recorded until the nineteenth century. There is, therefore, no evidence that anything like the story of Caradoc and his deliverance from the snake by his self-sacrificing wife-to-be existed in Ireland at any period, or in Scotland till modern times.

Paris also surmised that another branch of the tradition passed from Ireland directly to Brittany. This hypothesis was properly criticized by

Lot in his *Romania* article, but the critic offered an equally baseless proposal – namely, that the serpent story and its sequel, originating in Scotland, passed thence to Wales. But Caradoc, the protagonist, was not, as Lot asserted (p. 576), renowned in the North,[9] and it is only when we look to Wales that we find any traces of him in the early Middle Ages. A manuscript in the British Museum,[10] dated c. 1200, contains a Latin life of the historic St. Paternus, bishop and founder of the church of Llanbadarn Fawr near Aberystwyth in the first half of the sixth century. This *Vita*, according to Tatlock (*Speculum*, XIV [1939], 349), must have been composed before 1136; it celebrates Caradoc Brec[h]bras (Armstrong) as a generous benefactor of the saint.

The hero of the *Livre de Caradoc*, then, was a historic personage of Wales, and it is in Wales that we find certain elements of his legend. His wife, Tegau, was famed for her chastity. Her mantle was listed among the Thirteen Treasures of Britain:[11]

> It would not serve anyone who had violated her marriage or her virginity. For the woman who remained true to her husband it would reach to the ground, and to the one who had violated her marriage it would not reach to her lap, and for this reason there was envy against Tegau Eurvron.[12]

Though the description of the mantle is found in no manuscript antedating the sixteenth century, an English poem, *Annot and Johon*,[13] proves that even as early as the thirteenth century Tegau's reputation for truth had spread across the border to England.

The nickname or epithet attached to Caradoc's wife, Eurvron, signifies "Golden-breast," but it is doubtful whether this means that she was supposed to have a breast made of the precious metal. For *aur* in Welsh usage, as well as the word meaning "golden" in other languages, was often used metaphorically as a complimentary term.[14] In a sixteenth-century tale, *Ystoria Trystan*, Essyllt refers to her handmaid as a "golden mistress," *gordderch aur*,[15] which certainly does not mean that the maid was an image cast in gold. Presumably, then, Tegau was renowned not only for her virtue but also for her physical charms.

Not only did the Welsh Caradoc possess a paragon in his wife but a Welsh manuscript of the late twelfth century, the Black Book of Carmarthen, attests the excellence of his horse: among the three bestowed coursers of the Isle of Britain was Lluagor, the steed of Caradoc Breichbras.[16]

That this Caradoc of Welsh tradition is identical with the hero of the French *Livre de Caradoc* is obvious. The former acquired an epithet Brech-Bras and possessed a wife (nicknamed "Golden-breast") famed for her fidelity, and·a horse named Lluagor. The latter, hero of the

Livre de Caradoc, acquired an epithet Briebras, possessed a wife famed for her fidelity, and had for a half-brother a horse named Levagor or Loriagor.

How did this Welsh Caradoc Brechbras become the Caradoc Briebras of Vannes? To this question Lot provided the answer in his *Romania* article of 1899. Correcting Paris's wild hypothesis that the legend had come from Ireland via Brittany to Wales, Lot showed how the legend had been transmitted from Wales to Brittany. It appears that three saints of the Dark Ages were named Paternus.[17] One was appointed Bishop of Vannes c. 465. Of him nothing more is really known, but in the Middle Ages ignorance seldom prevented the growth of a saint's legend. Today a church dedicated to St. Paternus stands in a suburb of Vannes, and there his relics were formerly venerated.[18]

The second Paternus was a historic bishop of Avranches in Normandy (562–65). The third has been mentioned above as the founder of the church of Llanbadarn Fawr. About this Welsh Paternus, as already stated, was composed a typical *Vita*, recounting his missionary labors and telling how he found a patron in King Caradoc Brec[h]bras, who made large grants of land to the church of Llanbadarn.

In this *Vita* of the Welsh Paternus Lot recognized an interpolation, composed in Brittany by a Breton author, who confused the Welsh St. Paternus with Paternus, Bishop of Vannes (*Romania*, XXVIII, 571). In this interpolation we read that Caradoc, surnamed Brec[h]bras, enlarged his dominions even beyond the borders of Britain. Coming to Letavia (that is, Armorica), Caradoc brought it under his sway. It was this Caradoc who, if we may believe the *Vita*, persuaded Paternus to leave Wales for Brittany, and it was Vannes which the saint chose for his episcopal see. At Vannes too, according to the *Vita*, Caradoc built a palace.

So much for the interpolation. Lot's comment is as follows:

> L'auteur a lu dans la Vie insulaire que Caradoc Brechbras avait fait de grandes donations à Saint Padarn et à son église. Ne sachant rien de l'histoire du Vannetais au Ve siècle et voulant à tout prix s'expliquer l'origine de l'église de Vannes dont il croyait Patern le fondateur, il a inventé de toutes pièces ce gauche roman du roi Caradoc étendant son pouvoir au delà de la Manche, sur la Letavia et la ville de Vannes, où il possède un palais. [*Romania*, XXVIII, 574]

There can be little doubt that Lot was right, and that because of a mistaken identification of the two saints who bore the name Paternus, the benefactor of the one was assumed to be the benefactor of the other, and so Caradoc Brechbras came to be regarded as a king of Vannes. This bit of pseudohistory was soon accepted as fact, and a Latin sermon on the subject of the relics of St. Paternus at Vannes refers to the palace of Caradawc, *cognomento* Brech Bras, and to the church which Caradawc had built at his own expense.[19]

It was not only the name of Caradoc Brechbras and his reputation for liberality toward the clergy which were transferred to Brittany. As we have seen, there came with him his epithet, his wife's renown for fidelity, and the name of his horse, Lluagor. There were other traditions, hundreds of them, which are known to have crossed the Channel from Wales to Brittany, among them the tale of Twrch Trwyth, the boar son of a prince, whose ravages are narrated in *Culhwch and Olwen*, and who is recognizable in the *Livre de Caradoc* as the boar Tortain, son of Eliavres (*Romania*, xxviii, 217, 578). All these Welsh tales about Caradoc were evidently adopted by the people of Vannes as a part of their earliest local history; and coming to the attention of the professional *conteurs* excited their imagination and their ingenuity.

How much of the scabrous tale about the begetting of the three animals by the enchanter Eliavres rests on an earlier Welsh tradition, how much was invention, it seems impossible to say. But the episodes connected with the serpent seem to be a deliberate invention, demanded by the curiosity of French audiences. The *conteurs* who exploited these traditions for profit were mainly bilingual; and so presumably were most of their patrons, the aristocracy. But as years passed, fewer understood or spoke Breton. *Brechbras* became a meaningless epithet. Could it not have been *Briebras*, French words meaning "short arm"?[20] This is the substitution we find in Chrétien's *Erec*, where Caradoc is mentioned among the knights of the Round Table (ed. W. Foerster, vs. 1719). Once *Briebras* came into vogue in place of *Brechbras*, questions arose. Why did Caradoc have a short arm? Likewise, the epithet of Caradoc's wife, translated into French and interpreted literally as "Golden-breast," called for an explanation. How did she come to have a breast of gold?

Faced with the problem of accounting for Caradoc's short arm and his wife's golden breast, a Breton storyteller, we may assume, drew on his imagination and invented the tale of Caradoc's vengeful mother, the snake, the vats of vinegar and milk, the self-sacrificing maiden, and the golden boss which took the place of her nipple. Thus ingeniously the descriptive epithets of Caradoc and his wife were explained, and the narrative was thus neatly adapted to the tradition that Caradoc's wife was a nonpareil of connubial devotion.

This entertaining tale passed, as we know, into the *Livre de Caradoc*, and was incorporated in the compilation which formed the First Continuation of Chrétien's *Perceval*. The same tale appears in a late Breton life of St. Budoc.[21] Here it is the saint's mother who displayed her filial piety by releasing her father from a serpent which had fastened itself on his arm, and it was God who rewarded her sacrifice by giving her a golden breast. This borrowing of the serpent story and its sequel by the author of the *Life of St. Budoc* seems to show that it continued to enjoy a vogue in Brittany for some time.

But what is one to make of the fact that a tale tied, as we have seen, to Vannes and originating in the attempt to explain the epithet *Briebras* to French auditors, turns up in nineteenth-century Scotland, first as the conclusion to a ballad entitled the *Queen of Scotland* and localized at Edinburgh,[22] and secondly in the repertoire of a Gaelic-speaking tinker (*Romania*, xxviii, 219 f.)? It was doubtless this fact (first pointed out by the American scholar Carrie Harper, see *MLN*, xiii [1898], 417 ff.) which led Lot to postulate a Scottish legend of Caradoc Vreichvras and the serpent anteceding the Welsh and Breton traditions of the same hero. But there is no reason to believe that our Caradoc was ever a Scottish hero, and the explanation of his short arm by the story of the snake could only have been devised after he had come to be known to the French as *Briebras*.

How account for the transference of the serpent story with its sequel concerning the golden breast to Scotland from Brittany? The answer is not difficult. Though few Arthurian scholars have recognized the fact, there is ample evidence that Breton *conteurs* were welcomed in southern Scotland as early as the reign of David i, who ascended the throne in 1124.[23] We possess three Breton *lais*: *Doon*, *Desiré*, and *Gurun* (the last preserved in Norse translation), which evince some knowledge of Scottish geography. We have testimony that *histriones* were telling stories of Ewen, son of Urien, in twelfth-century Scotland.[24] This Ewen is, of course, identical with Chrétien's Ivain, son of Urien, who married the daughter of Duke Laudunet, that is, Lothian.[25] In fact, the ballad of the *Queen of Scotland* furnishes its own proof that it was derived from Arthurian traditions of the twelfth century. It not only concludes, as scholars seem to agree, with what is substantially the tale of Caradoc and the serpent (though the name of the hero has been changed) but it also opens with an incident drawn from sources close to the Vulgate cycle.[26] The queen of Scotland had a painted chamber in Edinburgh castle. It was the scene of a vain attempt on her part to seduce the young hero. Turning to the Prose *Lancelot* we read that Queen Morgain la Fée vainly attempted to seduce young Lancelot in her castle.[27] In the *Mort Artu* we learn that her castle, the scene of her attempt, was not far from Edinburgh and was adorned with mural paintings.[28]

We are justified, then, in concluding that the two Scottish analogues to the story of Caradoc and the serpent were not indigenous to Scotland and do not represent the sources of the French romance. They are, on the contrary, the late survivors of a Breton tradition transmitted to Scotland in the twelfth or thirteenth century by the French-speaking *conteurs*.

Is it necessary to stress the important part which misinterpretation and mistaken ingenuity have played in the development of this legend of Caradoc, his shrunken arm, and his wife's golden breast? At any rate, it is surely relevant to recall that precisely the same factors, misinterpretation and mistaken ingenuity, best account for the sanctification of the originally heathen Grail legends, for the conversion of Bran's drinking horn, which provided the drink and the food one desired, into the Corpus Christi, the Body of Christ.[29]

To summarize: The strange history of Caradoc of Vannes had its origin not in Ireland or Scotland but in Wales. There in the sixth century flourished a chief Caradoc, surnamed Brechbras, "Arm-strong." He was a benefactor of St. Padarn or Paternus. His wife Tegau came to be renowned as a model of fidelity, and also, it would seem, for the beauty of her figure; hence her nickname, meaning "Golden-breast." Because of a confusion between St. Padarn of Wales and St. Paternus of Vannes, the Bretons adopted Caradoc as the traditional benefactor of their own saint, hence, as a former ruler of Vannes. The French *Livre de Caradoc* retains certain Welsh elements, such as a corrupt form of the name Lluagor, which belonged to Caradoc's horse; a French misinterpretation of the surname Brechbras as meaning "Short-arm"; the concept of Caradoc's wife as a nonpareil of fidelity. The tale of the serpent represents an ingenious attempt to combine this last tradition with incidents explaining why Caradoc was called Briebras, and how his wife came to have a golden breast. This combination could hardly have crystallized before the twelfth century; and either in the same or the next century Breton *conteurs* transmitted it, along with other stories of the Arthurian cycle, to Scotland. There as an oral tradition it lingered on into the nineteenth century in both Gaelic and English forms.

NOTES

1. It is found in all three versions, ed. W. Roach (Philadelphia, 1949–55). The following résumé is based on MS. L (Brit. Mus. Add. 36, 614), which seems closest to the original. See Roach's edition, III: I, 130–204. Professor Hélaine Newstead most obligingly read an earlier version of this paper as my proxy at the Vannes Congress in 1960.

2. Some MSS. substitute *Nantes* for *Vannes*.

3. See G. L. Kittredge's *A Study of Gawain and the Green Knight* (Cambridge, Mass., 1916).

4. *Arthurian Literature in the Middle Ages*, ed. R. S. Loomis (Oxford, 1959), p. 531.

5. This form occurs in MSS. T, V, D of the Long Version and MS. E of the Mixed Version.

6. These are the forms given respectively by MS. L and the printed text of 1516. Variants include *Lorigal*, *Loriagort*, and *Lorzagor*.

7. Other forms of the epithet are given by Gaston Paris in *Romania*, XXVIII (1900), 222 f.

8. On the horn test, see T. P. Cross in *MP*, X (1913), 289–99; O. Warnatsch, *Der Mantel* (Breslau, 1883); *Speculum*, IX (1934), 38–50.

9. A Caradoc, to be sure, is mentioned several times in the *Gododdin*, a lament (composed c. 600) for the warriors of British stock who fell in

the Battle of Cattraeth. But Caradoc was a fairly common name among Britons, and there is no reason to identify the northern Caradoc with Caradoc Breich Bras.

10. Vespasian A. xiv; ed. A. W. Wade-Evans in *Vitae Sanctorum Britanniae et Genealogiae* (Cardiff, 1944). See *Studies in the Early British Church*, ed. N. K. Chadwick (Cambridge, 1958), pp. 157–59, 183–200.

11. See R. S. Loomis, *Wales and the Arthurian Legend* (Cardiff, 1956), pp. 158–61, and Rachel Bromwich, *Trioedd Ynys Prydein* (Cardiff, 1961), pp. cxxx–cxxxv, 240–49.

12. Trans. F. N. Robinson in *Lyrics of the Thirteenth Century*, ed. Carleton Brown (Oxford, 1933), p. 226.

13. Robinson, p. 138.

14. D. Silvan Evans, *Geiriadur Cymraeg*, I, 409: "As a prefix in composition, *aur* signifies (a) *gold, golden*; and (b) *precious* as *gold . . . splendid, brilliant, illustrious.*"

15. T. P. Cross, "A Welsh Tristan Episode," *Studies in Philology*, XVII (1920), 97, 106.

16. Bromwich, pp. ciii–civ, cvi, 97 f. In the Black Book, *Breichbras*, not spelled out, is implied by initial *B*.

17. S. Baring-Gould and J. Fisher, *Lives of the British Saints* (London, 1907), IV, p. 43.

18. G. H. Doble, *Saint Patern* (Long Compton, 1940), p. 31.

19. A. le Moyne de La Borderie, *Histoire de Bretagne* (Rennes-Paris, 1896), I, p. 307 n.

20. In *Rev. Celt.*, XIII (1892), 494, J. Loth maintained that Fr. *Briebras* could have arisen only as the result of misunderstanding a written, not an oral, version of the legend, since

in Wales the cognomen *Breichbras* had long ceased to be pronounced as such, mutation having substituted *v* for *b*. H. Zimmer, the Celtist, though admitting that this is true if the misinterpretation took place in Basse-Bretagne in the twelfth century, argued that in Haute-Bretagne the mutation must have occurred after the story of Caradoc Brech Bras had been transmitted to the French; see Chrétien's *Karrenritter*, ed. W. Foerster (Halle, 1899), p. cxxiv.

21. G. H. Doble, *Saint Budoc*, 2d ed. (Long Compton, 1937), pp. 1, 2; Baring-Gould and Fisher, IV, p. 331.

22. F. J. Child, *English and Scottish Popular Ballads* (Boston, 1883–98; repr. New York, 1956), v, pp. 176–78. First published by P. Buchan, *Ancient Ballads and Songs of the North of Scotland* (Edinburgh, 1828), I, pp. 46–49.

23. R. S. Loomis, *Arthurian Tradition and Chrétien de Troyes* (New York, 1949), pp. 17, 109–14, 272, 301–305.

24. *Studies in the Early British Church*, ed. N. K. Chadwick, pp. 281–84.

25. Loomis, *Arthurian Tradition*, pp. 302 f.

26. *Proceedings of the Society of Antiquaries of Scotland*, 1955–56, pp. 9 f.

27. H. O. Sommer, *Vulgate Version of the Arthurian Romances* (Washington, 1909–13), IV, pp. 123–28; v, pp. 91–93, 215–18.

28. *Ibid.*, VI, 234–35.

29. Loomis, *Arthurian Tradition*, pp. 170–75; *The Grail, From Celtic Myth to Christian Symbol* (Cardiff-New York, 1963), pp. 25 f., 59–61.

The Visit to the Perilous Castle

(Publications of the Modern Language Association of America Vol. XLVIII, No. 4, pp. 1000-35)

THE VISIT TO THE PERILOUS CASTLE: A STUDY OF THE ARTHURIAN MODIFICATIONS OF AN IRISH THEME

DISCUSSION of the Homeric question, the Carolingian epic, the ballads, and Arthurian romance remains, and seems destined to remain for some time a conflict between two hypotheses. One may be called the traditionalist hypothesis; for it emphasizes the origins of narrative themes in oral traditions more or less remote from the first recorded versions, and attempts to trace genetic relations between the surviving versions and to explain differences between them on the assumption that originals or intermediate stages or both are lost. The second hypothesis may be called that of literary craftsmanship, for it minimizes or denies the existence of any oral tradition, finds the source of our surviving texts either in other written texts or in the creative imagination of the author, and attempts to explain the differences between one version and another by some artistic or rational motive controlling the later author. A classic of the traditionalist school is Professor Gilbert Murray's *Rise of the Greek Epic;* a classic of the contrary school is M. Bédier's *Légendes Épiques.* The traditionalist hypothesis emphasizes the genetic relationship of story-patterns to their sources; the hypothesis of literary craftsmanship emphasizes the intellectual and artistic processes which create or modify story-patterns.

Viewed simply as methods of approach, these two hypotheses are by no means mutually exclusive or irreconcilable. There is not a traditionalist who denies that tradition is constantly affected by the individual author, by his memory, his selective and organizing ability, his artistic power, his moral, social, and religious standards. There is not, on the other hand, any upholder of the importance of literary craftsmanship so extreme as to assert that the surviving texts of a cycle owe nothing to stories of an earlier age. It is as false to charge adherents of the traditionalist school with ignoring the part played by the individual author's equipment in the development of tradition as it is to charge the champions of literary craftsmanship with denying altogether the existence of lost sources. It is rather a question of emphasis, of degree; and the real issue is: Which emphasis is justified by the evidence?

If we limit ourselves to the Arthurian field and study there a particular group of stories with the aim of finding an answer to this question of emphasis, it would be well to take a group thoroughly represented in texts of various periods and languages and for which a remote origin in oral tradition has been claimed. Then if literary craftsmanship be the main factor in the origin and development of the stories, we should be able to make a list of the stories in the order of their composition, with Crestien de Troyes at the head; to show that Crestien owed little to antecedent tradition, oral or otherwise; to explain every other form of the story as the product of the author's intelligence and artistry acting upon one or more antecedent written texts. This I believe to be a fair statement of the hypothesis of Arthurian evolution as illustrated by Bruce in his *Evolution of Arthurian Romance*, Professor Golther in his *Parzival und der Gral*, and M. Faral in his *Légende Arthurienne*—except, of course, that the last is concerned with an earlier period than Crestien's. If, however, the traditionalist view be correct, then we should expect to find quite a different situation. We should expect to find a remote source, Celtic or otherwise, for the whole group, or at least find reason for postulating such a source. We should not expect to find the most faithful and complete Arthurian representative of that source, unless by sheer accident, in Crestien de Troyes. On the contrary, since it is a well-recognized phenomenon, admitted even by Bruce, that "in Arthurian romance, as in other forms of literature, older traditions about any given character often survive by the side of those of later origin," more faithful and complete versions may first be recorded in the fifteenth century, while fragmentary and altered versions may find their way into literature as early as the twelfth. In fact, the chronological sequence of the surviving literary forms will fail to account for their variations except in a few cases of literary borrowing, such as the *Vulgate Lancelot's* use of Crestien's *Charrette*, or of translation, such as Gottfried von Strassburg's use of Thomas and Eilhart. We shall nevertheless see, in addition to the meaningless alterations of the original source, due merely to the lapse of memory, other significant alterations showing the efforts of individual *conteurs* and romancers to adapt the tradition to their standards of coherence, rationality, manners, and morality. We shall expect to find other normal phenomena of tradition, such as conflate versions where two forms of the same story have been combined so that they present duplicate developments from the same original feature, conflate versions where two inconsistent versions of the same story have been unskillfully patched together, and contaminated versions where extraneous story elements have intruded. If the story chosen furnish a thorough illustration of the possibilities of traditional development, we shall find versions that superficial examination would reject at once as totally unrelated to the ultimate source, but whose relationship to that source can be demonstrated by their affinity to intermediate forms which exhibit clear traces of their origin. There will, I believe, be no dispute that if the traditionalist hypothesis be true, such should be the posture of affairs.

In the following study I have attempted to examine a group of Arthurian stories, which for convenience let us call the Visit to the Perilous Castle, though it is understood that the group does not include every visit to a perilous castle in the Round Table cycle, but only those whose affinity to the visit of Cuchulinn to Curoi's fortress can be established. They seem to me to fit in perfectly with the requirements of the traditional hypothesis, as I shall try to show. By no effort of the imagination can I derive all, or most of them, from Crestien, as should be possible on the hypothesis which emphasizes literary craftsmanship. And if the fact that I am deeply committed to the traditionalist hypothesis disqualifies me as a judge of evidence, let me invite my readers to offer a satisfactory explanation of the fifteen Arthurian tales submitted below, relying mainly on Crestien as a source, accounting for the divergences from Crestien by the operation of the taste and intelligence of their respective authors, and showing how the chronological order of the tales corresponds in a general way to the stages of their development. If a satisfactory interpretation of the evidence can be made on these, the avowed principles of Bruce and Golther, I will cheerfully abandon my creed and subscribe to theirs.

My choice of the Visit to the Perilous Castle as a test case is based on the following reasons:

1. The supposed Celtic source is of undoubted antiquity. Professor Thurneysen, the most eminent authority, assigns the two stories from *Bricriu's Feast* to the eighth century,[1] and the mythological elements which they contain indicate that they are even older in content.[2]

2. The supposed Irish source belongs to a cycle concerned with Curoi, Cuchulinn, and Blathnat, which had a profound influence on Welsh literature. Blathnat's betrayal of Curoi is the source of the treachery of Blodeuwedd in *Math Vab Mathonwy;*[3] Curoi, Conchobar, Conall, and Loegaire, though their names are corrupted, appear among Arthur's warriors in *Kilhwch and Olwen;*[4] there is a Welsh poem on the death of Curoi;[5] and Melwas' abduction of Guinevere in the *Vita Gildae* is reminiscent of Curoi's abduction of Blathnat.[6]

---

[1] R. Thurneysen, *Irische Helden- und Königsage* (Halle, 1921), p. 449.

[2] R. S. Loomis, *Celtic Myth and Arthurian Romance* (New York, 1927), pp. 47–50, 68 f.; *Studi Medievali, Nuova Serie*, III, 291–294; *Celtic Review*, x (1915), 265; *Proc. of Roy. Ir. Acad.*, XXXIV, c, 138.

[3] W. J. Gruffydd, *Math Vab Mathonwy* (Cardiff, 1928), 265–270.

[4] J. Loth, *Mabinogion* (Paris, 1913), I, 261 f.; *Rev. Celt.*, XLI, 489.

[5] W. F. Skene, *Four Ancient Books* (1868), I, 254; II, 198.—Cf. T. P. Cross, W. A. Nitze, *Lancelot and Guenevere* (Chicago, 1930), p. 41 n. 2.

3. Strong evidence has already accumulated that parts of this Curoi cycle penetrated deep into Arthurian romance. It is generally known that there are seven variants of the Beheading Test in Arthurian literature, obviously derived from the eighth-century version in *Bricriu's Feast*.[7] Curoi's abduction of Blathnat seems not only to have influenced the *Vita Gildae* but also Carado's abduction of a damsel in the *Vulgate Lancelot*, Milocrates' abduction of a damsel in the *De Ortu Walwanii*, and Escanor's abduction of a damsel in *L'Atre Perillos*.[8] And the story we offer as a main source has already been put forward as the original of the *Lit Périlleux* episodes in Crestien's *Conte del Graal*, Wolfram's *Parzival*, Heinrich von dem Türlin's *Krone*, the *Vulgate Lancelot*, and *Artus de la Petite Bretagne*.[9] We have an opportunity, then, to test more or less directly these claims for the extraordinary influence of the Curoi cycle on Arthurian romance.

4. The development of the Irish theme of the Visit to the Perilous Castle, as we shall attempt to trace it, furnishes not only illustration of those processes which the traditionalist emphasizes, such as conflation, contamination, and meaningless omissions and alterations due to defects of memory, but also striking illustration of those processes which preoccupy the student of literary craftsmanship. If the present study has any cogency and value, it will serve not only to confirm the traditionalist hypothesis but also to underline the part played by the intelligence of numerous anonymous transmitters and moulders of tradition, to stress the rôle of reason in the evolution of romance.

All the Irish material on the Curoi cycle is brought together, summarized, and carefully analyzed by Professor Thurneysen in his *Irische Helden- und Königsage*, pp. 451–466. Except for his tendency to regard the cycle as merely a literary product and to see the influence of MS. rather than oral tradition at work, his discussion may be regarded as authoritative. The line of development we are to follow springs from two episodes in *Bricriu's Feast*, both forming part of the eighth-century text, and to be found with translation on pp. 101–129 of G. Henderson's edition. The more important episode recounts the visit of Cuchulinn and his two rivals to Curoi's fortress, and the tests to which they are there subjected. The other episode is the so-called Champion's Bargain, and relates the testing of the rivals conducted at the court of Ulster by Curoi in the

---

[6] *Mon. Germ. Hist.*, XIII (1894), 107. Cf. Cross and Nitze, *op. cit.*, 21.—Note the one-year search common to both the Curoi and the Melwas abduction.

[7] R. S. Loomis, *op. cit.*, p. 59.   [8] *Ibid.*, pp. 7, 15, 21, 22 n. 36.

[9] *Ibid.*, pp. 159–175.—The Galaphes version on p. 162 may be a story not of Curoi's castle, but of Bran's. Cf. *Miscellany of Studies Presented to L. E. Kastner* (Cambridge, 1932), pp. 347 f.

guise of a churl in a gray mantle bearing an ax. The ramifications of this latter story have been subjected to close and learned scrutiny by Professor Kittredge in his *Study of Gawain and the Green Knight;* and his examination in the same book of many analogs to the temptation of Gawain by Bercilak's wife led him to include several other stories which we shall discuss. But he made, as it seems to me, the unfortunate mistake of regarding *Gawain and the Green Knight* as the ultimate flowering of a single version of a single episode of the Curoi cycle, which had become accidentally transplanted to England, instead of seeing the romance as but one blossom in a thicket which had its roots in the whole Curoi cycle, including the Visit to Curoi's Fortress; and he missed the implications of that visit which brought together the famous lovers, Cuchulinn and Curoi's wife, Blathnat. Yet the range of Professor Kittredge's Arthurian studies and his perspicacity are amply demonstrated by the fact that he assembled so large a group of parallels to the temptation of Gawain and realized that somehow they were significant. My own borrowings from his storehouse of materials must be manifest and should not go unacknowledged.

Let us now examine the two episodes from the Curoi cycle which form as it were the roots of the tree. And first let me give a summary of what is for our purpose the less important episode, the Champion's Bargain.[10]

I. The Champion's Bargain

There entered the royal court of Ulster a *bachlach,* or churl, of gigantic size; "as thick as the wrist of any other man each one of his fingers." He was clad in a hide and a *brat lachtna,* or gray mantle. In his hand was a great ax. His boast, "Whatever be my height, the whole household shall have light, and yet the house shall not be burned," is simply fatuous unless, taken in conjunction with other features, it is interpreted as an allusion to his solar functions. The writer of *Bricriu's Feast* does not say that the churl's face shed radiance; he takes it for granted. Exempting the king, the churl issued a challenge to the warriors of Ulster to exchange blows with the ax: "Come whosoever of you that may venture that I may cut off his head tonight, he mine tomorrow night." In response to these taunts, Munremar accepted the challenge, but insisted that the order be reversed. The *bachlach* agreed, submitted to decapitation, picked up his head, and departed. But the next day when the giant, his head restored, returned to complete the bargain, Munremar was absent. Loegaire and Conall in turn likewise failed to carry out the pact with the churl. Finally, the churl came in a fury and cried, "Ye men of Ulster, your valor and your prowess are gone. . . . Where is that wretched creature that is called Cuchulinn?" Cuchulinn then rose and struck off the giant's head and split it into fragments. When the giant returned

---

[10] *Feast of Bricriu,* ed. G. Henderson, Ir. Texts Soc., ɪɪ (London, 1899), 117; G. L. Kittredge, *Study of Gawain and the Green Knight* (Cambridge, Mass., 1916), p. 10; Thurneysen, *op. cit.,* p. 460.

the next day and found Cuchulinn faithful to the bargain, he awarded him the sovranty of the warriors of Ireland. "Of the warriors of Ulster and Ireland none is to be compared with thee in valor, bravery, and truthfulness." The churl then departed and we are told, as doubtless an Irish audience of the eighth century would already have detected from the famous gray mantle, which Curoi wears in several other tales,[11] that the stranger was Curoi.

The second, and for us the more important, episode is the visit of Cuchulinn and his two rivals to Curoi's fortress, which may be summarized thus.[12]

II. The Visit to Curoi's Fortress

Cuchulinn, Loegaire, and Conall went to Curoi's fortress that Curoi might judge which of them best deserved the sovranty among the heroes of Ireland. When they arrived at night, Curoi had departed, but knowing they would come, he had counseled his wife regarding the heroes, and she acted according to his wish, providing them with refreshing drinks and excellent beds. She told them also that each was to take his turn watching the fortress by night till Curoi returned. Every night the fortress revolved. (The mythic meaning of this phenomenon, which I asserted in *Celtic Myth*, pp. 49 f, has been independently discovered by Johannes Hertel in Vedic texts. Cf. Hertel, *Die Himmelstore*, pp. 41–44.) Cuchulinn's rivals took the seat of watch for two successive nights. Each was attacked by a giant hurling stakes, and was thrown out of the fortress. Finally Cuchulinn took the seat, was attacked in turn by three troops of nine foes and by a huge monster, and slew them all. The giant then approached and hurled his stakes; Cuchulinn flung his spear but did not touch the giant. At last with his sword he forced the giant to surrender and to grant him the sovranty of Ireland's heroes. Exultant, Cuchulinn then executed leaps of triumph out of the fortress and back into it. Blathnat, Curoi's wife, had known full well of his plight and recognized his sigh of triumph. Soon Curoi returned and accorded to Cuchulinn the sovranty of Ireland's heroes in almost the same terms the giant had used. The three rivals then left Curoi's fortress.

Three points are worth noting in regard to this narrative. First, the name of the hostess who shows such sympathy for the hero is Blathnat, meaning "Little Flower," and her floral nature is emphasized in the description of her Welsh counterpart Blodeuwedd, who was created out of the blossoms of the oak, the broom, and the meadowsweet.[13] Second, the

---

[11] *Feast of Bricriu*, p. 46, l. 5, Curoi wears an *arit odor*, "gray covering"; on the same page (Egerton MS.) he wears an *arait breclachtna*, "speckled gray covering." Cf. also Thurneysen, *op. cit.*, pp. 441, 443, 445.   [12] *Feast of Bricriu*, pp. 101–115.

[13] W. J. Gruffydd, *Math Vab Mathonwy*, 27, 263 ff.—It seems to me quite unnecessary to postulate an intermediate form Blodened, since the name Blodeuwedd seems to have had an independent origin in a nickname for the owl (cf. Gruffydd, p. 256) and would easily have been substituted by the Welsh for Blathnat because of the common element meaning "flower."

giant who fights Cuchulinn and grants him the sovranty, as Professor A. C. L. Brown long since pointed out,[14] is surely the giant Curoi himself, to whom the heroes have been sent to decide the question of sovranty and who later declares the same decision in terms almost identical with those the testing giant had used. Third, Zimmer, without any thought of the Arthurian problems involved, pointed out that, Blathnat and Cuchulinn being famous lovers, there was strong reason to suspect that they would take advantage of Curoi's absence to indulge their passion, and that such an amorous passage had stood in the original form of the Visit to Curoi's Fortress.[15] Miss Buchanan in a recent article[16] has shown how this strong suspicion may legitimately become certainty because of the support which it receives from *Gawain and the Green Knight* and the *Carl of Carlisle*, in both of which Gawain has a love affair with his host's wife with the connivance of the host. And the evidence yet to be presented in this article leaves no room for doubt: an amorous interlude between Cuchulinn and Blathnat, connived at by Curoi, once formed an important part of the Visit to Curoi's Castle.

Miss Buchanan has also made it clear that this story, both as it stands in *Bricriu's Feast* and as we are obliged to reconstitute it, contains certain puzzling features. Since it is not explicitly stated that the attacking giant was Curoi and since it is explicitly stated that Curoi departed before the heroes' arrival and returned three days later, the way was left open for various answers to the question whether he was absent or present during Cuchulinn's visit. Again, Curoi had been solicitous about Cuchulinn's reception and instructed Blathnat to show him all hospitality, and yet he had apparently been the instigator of several attacks upon his guest, and had himself been the most formidable of the antagonists, only to return and in friendly fashion proclaim his guest's prowess. Was Curoi friend or foe? Thirdly, what was his attitude toward the love of Cuchulinn for his wife? Did his instructions to Blathnat show, as they seemed to do, that he connived at and actually encouraged the affair? Or did the night attack upon his guest reveal a disposition to interfere? The Irish story must have presented these three mystifying elements, and the Irish *filid*, the Welsh *cyfarwyddon*, and the Breton *conteurs* who carried on the tradition exercised their wits on three questions: 1. Was the host present or absent during the hero's visit, and if absent, what was his share in the attack? 2. How was the friendliness and hospitality displayed by the host himself or by his orders to be reconciled, if at all, with the murderous attack which he connived at or made

[14] *Studies and Notes in Philology and Literature*, VIII (Boston, 1903), 55 n.
[15] *Sitzungsberichte der königlichen preussischen Akademie der Wissenschaften, phil. hist. Kl.*, IX (1911), 174.   [16] *PMLA*, XLVII, 2 (June, 1932), 315–338.

himself? 3. What was the meaning of the host's encouragement of the embraces of his wife and his guest? Obviously such a thoroughly ambiguous situation as this offered ample scope for the ingenuity of the storyteller, and we must expect the answers given to the three questions to be very different. In fact, one of the chief interests of this study lies in the clarity with which we can discern what the problems were which faced the redactors of this story, and the clarity with which we can see their ingenuity at work on those problems.

III. *The Carl of Carlisle*

Some seven centuries later than the composition of *Bricriu's Feast* the romance of the *Carl of Carlisle*, as preserved in the Porkington MS., was composed.[17] Like all other Middle English romances of the Round Table cycle, it is derived more or less immediately from the French, and doubtless the tradition had reached the French through the regular channels from Brittany and Wales. Let us note the correspondences with our two Irish sources as we proceed through this résumé.

Three barons of Arthur's court, Gawain, Kay, and Baldwin, needing shelter after a day's hunting, decide to repair to the castle of the Carl of Carlisle, though Baldwin warns them no baron hitherto has escaped thence without a beating, and only by God's grace has any escaped alive. When they enter, a lion and three other beasts threaten to attack them, but retire at the Carl's command. This Carl or churl is a gray-bearded giant, whose finger is as large "as any leg that we bear." After drinking, Baldwin rises to tend his horse and incidentally mistreats the Carl's foal. Suddenly the Carl appears and floors the offender. Kay does the same thing and receives a similar buffet. Gawain, however, behaves courteously and receives the host's thanks. He is then instructed to hurl a spear at the host, but the giant dodges and congratulates Gawain on the force of the blow. He then seats Gawain at table opposite his beautiful wife, and Gawain is greatly smitten so that he eats no supper. The Carl rebukes his guest and asks his daughter to play her harp. After supper, Gawain is led to the Carl's bed and bidden to take the Carl's wife in his arms and kiss her. Gawain, always obedient, does so, but when he would have grown bolder, his host calls a halt, sends his daughter to Gawain's bed, and leaves them to play all night. The next day Gawain is shown a heap of bones, which the Carl tells him are the remains of all previous guests at the castle, for all had failed to do as he had bidden and had been slain by the Carl or his beasts. (According to the late version preserved in the Percy Folio, the Carl now commands Gawain to cut off his head, with a threat that if he does not do so, the Carl will cut off Gawain's. Gawain again obeys, and the Carl is promptly transformed into a knight of normal size.) The

---

[17] F. Madden, *Syr Gawayne*, Bannatyne Club (London, 1839), 187.—The later Percy Folio version is on p. 239. Cf. Kittredge, *Study of Gawain and the Green Knight*, pp. 85–89, 301 f.

Carl now vows reformation, dismisses Gawain, Kay, and Baldwin with gifts, invites Arthur to his castle, feasts him, and is invested with the lordship of the country of Carlisle. Arthur gives him the name Karlyle, which in the French original would be Cardoil. His daughter weds Gawain.

It is easy to recognize here several correspondences with the Irish: the three heroes who arrive at a castle and are tested; the gigantic churl who is their host; the huge fingers; the monsters who attack the guests; the rough handling to which two of the heroes are subjected; the hurling of a spear at the giant, which does not touch him; the love affair between the hero and the host's wife, actually instigated by the host to the point where they lie in bed and kiss; the hero's decapitation of the churl; the churl's pronouncement of the hero's superior prowess; the departure of the three heroes. As we shall see later, it is even possible that the Carl's gray beard is indirectly derived from Curoi's famous gray mantle, for we find that in a story, clearly related to the *Carl*, the giant host is called ambiguously "the gray man."

A matter of even greater interest is to see how in the process of transmission the three mysteries of the original Irish tradition have been cleared up. To the question whether the Carl was present or not during the various tests applied to the barons, the answer is an unequivocal yes. He is not only cognizant of every trial but takes an active share in it. The question of his attitude is answered by the supposition that, though he bore his guests no ill will, he was accustomed (as a result of enchantment, according to the Percy version) to submit each of them to a trial of courteous submission to himself as host, with fatal consequences if they failed. This moral was apparently considered so edifying by medieval homilists that a group of exempla came into existence, based on some version closely akin to the *Carl*, and setting up the obedient Gawain as the paragon of guests.[18] The third puzzle is ingeniously solved by making the embraces of Gawain and the Carl's wife a supreme test of obedience: Gawain is obliged to refrain when his passions are roused. Thus also the Carl is saved from being his wife's pander. The chief difficulties in the original story are thus eliminated.

Despite its marked resemblance to the Irish stories, however, the *Carl of Carlisle* does not seem to be the result of a simple process of derivation, but rather represents the intertwining of several derivates. It seems to combine a version where three heroes are tested, with another version where only one hero was tested; for Baldwin and Kay are not subjected at all to the spear-hurling test and the beheading test. It seems to combine a version where the successive combats of the three Irish heroes with

18 Kittredge, *op. cit.*, pp. 93–103.

the giant are represented by the foal test, and another version where Cuchulinn's combat with the giant is represented by the spear-flinging test. It seems to combine two versions of the love affair, one a temptation by the host's wife, and another in which there is no temptation, but mutual complaisance, and the wife for obvious reasons has been replaced by a daughter. As we proceed, we shall be able to verify the first and third of these suppositions by the discovery of derivates from the Visit to Curoi's Fortress where there is only one hero and where the only "lady in the case" is the host's daughter. Everything points to the *Carl* as an excellent illustration of the traditionalist hypothesis, and also of the shaping of tradition by individual intelligence.

IV. The Galagandreis episode in *Lanzelet*

The German romance of *Lanzelet* was translated by the Swiss Ulrich von Zatzikhoven about 1195 from a French original, and deserves far more exhaustive study than it has received so far.[19] Like *Peredur*, it is an obvious conglomeration of traditional adventures which the author has taken little or no pains to harmonize. The episode that interests us occurs early in the poem.[20]

Lanzelet meets two knights, Kuraus and Orphilet, and the three decide to seek harborage in the castle of a rich forester named Galagandreis. Kuraus says that the castellan has a most beautiful daughter, but a guest may easily lose his life there, because the host will not allow the slightest breach of manners to go unpunished. The three knights are welcomed hospitably and watch their behavior. Lanzelet is ushered by Galagandreis himself into the presence of his daughter and proves himself a most agreeable table-companion to her. All three knights are led by the host to their beds. The beautiful daughter then appears and offers her love first to Orphilet, but he refuses from dread of her father. She is also repulsed by Kuraus. Lanzelet, without waiting for an invitation, enjoys her love. In the morning Galagandreis angrily knocks at the door. He brings two knives and bucklers, commands Lanzelet to stand by one wall while he himself stands at the other, and gives Lanzelet knife, buckler, and the choice of the first throw. Though Lanzelet yields this advantage to his host, he survives and kills his adversary. Galagandreis' daughter is now in great perplexity, but she summons her best knights, shows that no blame falls on the young hero, and with their consent marries him. Kuraus and Orphilet depart for Arthur's court.

It is unnecessary to labor the similarity of this tale to the *Carl of Carlisle*. It offers much the same answer to the first two ambiguities of the Irish tradition, but regarding the love affair, it diverges sharply. Instead of commanding the hero to lie with his wife and daughter in succession as the Carl does, Galagandreis has no wife, is watchful of his

---

[19] Cf. Webster in *M.L.R.*, XXVI, 71.

[20] P. Piper, *Das Höfische Epik* (Stuttgart), II, 173–175. Cf. Kittredge, *op. cit.*, pp. 219, 262.

daughter's honor, and proposes the duel with Lanzelet to avenge its violation. This solution of the third difficulty, therefore, abandons the traditional complicity of the host in the hero's amour, and by substituting the host's daughter for his wife, renders the whole story more natural and less repulsive to the pious public. Noteworthy is the coalescence here of the two encounters of Cuchulinn with Curoi, the motif of the alternating blows in the Champion's Bargain having influenced the motif of the duel with missile weapons in the Visit to Curoi's Fortress.

V. The Belian Episode in *Wolfdietrich*

Wolfdietrich, one of the *Heldensagen*, exists in a number of versions, of which version A, here followed, is regarded as the most authentic.[21] Only the name Belian, found in D[22] and possibly a survival from the *Ur-Wolfdietrich*, is here applied to the anonymous host of A. The episode we are about to consider has been touched by Crusading literature, but both Professor Kittredge and Professor Schneider have recognized its affinity to the Galagandreis adventure.[23]

Wolfdietrich is entertained by a dwarf and is warned that the land belongs to a paynim, Belian, who forces all Christians to a duel of knife-throwing and thus has slain many. The hero arrives before a magic castle, on the battlements of which are mounted the heads of many of Belian's victims. Belian and his daughter see Wolfdietrich approaching and at her desire five hundred retainers sally forth to welcome him. When he refuses to disclose his name, the Saracen flies into a rage, but is quickly mollified by his daughter and offers her to the stranger. The damsel takes the knight into the hall and seeks to learn his name, for her gods have prophesied that a Greek named Wolfdietrich will survive her father's missiles. The stranger evades the question and sits down with her and her father to the best of viands. She looks upon Wolfdietrich with longing, but Belian declares that his head shall yet adorn the battlements. Once more he relents and offers his guest a castle if he will marry the maid. But Wolfdietrich spurns all blandishments; even though he lies with the damsel all night and she offers him twelve kingdoms, he will not unite with her. In the morning Belian returns and rages because his daughter has been scorned and proclaims a judicial combat. Knives and bucklers are provided. With the first three throws Belian tries to kill Wolfdietrich, but in vain, and is himself killed. When the hero tries to depart, the princess causes the castle to revolve under him like a wheel, but one after another he surmounts her enchantments and escapes.

That this story is related to the Galagandreis episode cannot be denied, though it is not, as Schneider supposed, a direct borrowing. It is inter-

---

[21] *Deutsches Heldenbuch*, ed. A. Amelung, O. Jänicke (Berlin, 1871), III, 154–157; H. Schneider, *Deutsche Heldensage* (1930), 136 f.

[22] *Deutsches Heldenbuch*, IV, 74.

[23] Kittredge, *op. cit.*, p. 219; H. Schneider, *Die Gedichte und die Sage von Wolfdietrich* (München, 1913), p. 261 ff.

esting to note that here as in many other variants of the visit to the Perilous Castle, the original feature of the three guests has vanished, but another Irish feature, the revolving castle, absent from the *Carl* and *Lanzelet*, has survived here, and we shall meet it again. The question of the host's presence is once more answered definitely in the affirmative, but his attitude toward his guests is ambiguous as in the Irish; now he breathes out barbaric threats, now he offers his daughter and castle. This unexplained variability of temper may well be a reflection of the original uncertainty of Curoi's attitude to Cuchulinn. There is humor in the changes made in the love-scene and its consequences. The host and his daughter having been converted into Saracens, Wolfdietrich's religious scruples will not permit him to take advantage of her favors, as Gawain and Lanzelet have availed themselves of the favors of less heathenish damsels. Accordingly when Belian makes his morning visit to his daughter's bed, he cannot, like Galagandreis, take umbrage at her lost maidenhood; his ire must therefore find its justification in the slight put upon her charms. The motivation of the missile combat between host and guest differs from the motivation of the spear-hurling in the *Carl* and the knife-throwing in *Lanzelet*, and thus shows once more how the same traditional theme undergoes perpetual modification from the intelligent craftsmanship of the redactors.

VI. The *Chevalier à l'Espée*

The *Chevalier à l'Espée*[24] was composed by an unknown author of the Isle de France, and is of uncertain date. Professor Armstrong's attempt to date it before 1210[25] seems based on two dubious considerations: one the doubtful dating of Heinrich von dem Türlin's *Krone*, which its editor places about 1220, rather than 1210; the other the fallacy which vitiates so much of the dating of Arthurian literature, namely, that if two romances contain similar incidents, they are to be regarded, in the absence of contrary evidence, as standing in the relation of source and derivate. Heinrich's poem does contain an incident strongly reminiscent of the episode we are about to study;[26] but as we have seen before and shall see over and over again, parallels are not necessarily so related; they may be cognates, and then one is entirely valueless as an indication of the date of the other. The date of the *Chevalier* is therefore unsettled. Two-thirds of this short poem is occupied by the episode now to be summarized.

[24] *Le Chevalier à l'Epée*, ed. E. C. Armstrong (Baltimore, 1897), p. 50 f.—Cf. Kittredge, *op. cit.*, pp. 89–93, 302 f.　　　　　　　[25] *Chevalier à l'Epée*, pp. 51, 61

[26] Heinrich von dem Türlin, *Krone*, ed. G. H. F. Scholl (Stuttgart, 1852), pp. 100–106. Cf. Kittredge, *op. cit.*, p. 253.

Lost in a forest, Gawain discovers a hospitable knight, who invites him to his castle, and goes ahead to prepare for his coming. As Gawain approaches the castle, sheperds warn him that his host is wont to put to death all who do not obey him, and that none have ever returned from his castle. Despite the warning, Gawain rides on, is welcomed by the lord of the castle, and is promptly introduced to his beautiful daughter. The host pointedly remarks that he will have no objection if she falls in love with the stranger and instructs her to deny him nothing. He then leaves the two by themselves for awhile, and they are promptly seized with desire. She discourages his advances, however, and warns him to obey her father's commands on peril of his life. The host returns, dinner is served, and once more he recommends Gawain to his daughter as a lover. He departs, this time to view his forests, leaving instructions with his retainers to seize Gawain if he should try to escape. Once more the damsel warns Gawain not to be deceived by her father's gracious manner. When towards evening the *chevalier* returns, they sup; then the host brings his guest and his daughter to his own bed and bids them lie in it. He leaves them and Gawain would satisfy his desire, but the damsel warns him that if he does so, a sword hanging near by will fly from its scabbard and wound him. Nevertheless, he twice approaches her, only to be thwarted and wounded by the flying sword. In the morning the castellan enters the chamber and is disappointed to find his guest alive. He discovers some blood from Gawain's wound, but when Gawain frankly acknowledges his boldness during the night, the *chevalier* declares that all will be well if Gawain will declare his name and country. On hearing the name of his guest, the *chevalier* pronounces him peerless in all the land of Logres, and relates how the sword which has slain all previous visitors was endowed with the faculty of choosing the best. He bestows his daughter on the hero, and the following night the lovers spend in the same bed without interference from the sword.

There is an obvious relation to the *Carl of Carlisle* displayed in the insistence upon Gawain's obedience to the host and in the love affair with the daughter. But as Kittredge pointed out,[27] the author of the *Chevalier à l'Espée* bungled his theme badly, failed to bring out sharply the various tests of obedience, and what seems to be the supreme test, the chastity of the damsel, is not even the subject of a command. Indeed the *chevalier* seems to have encouraged rather than forbidden Gawain's attack upon her. It is probable that the author has attempted to conflate a version emphasizing the duty of obedience, such as the *Carl*, with a version like the Galagandreis episode, emphasizing respect for the lady's honor. The host's return in the morning and the proclamation of Gawain's supremacy are precise parallels to the original Irish tradition. The departure of the host to view his forests seems to link the poem with the group of cognates, to be examined later, in which the host goes out hunting. Perhaps most interesting is the way in which the author has sought to combine the temptation episode as we have

[27] Kittredge, *Study of Gawain and the Green Knight*, pp. 90 f.

seen it in the *Lanzelet* and *Wolfdietrich*, in which there is no intrusion on the lovers' privacy, with another group of cognates in which the hero lies down on a bed only to be assailed by a shower of missiles, the *Lit Périlleux* group. In fact, the *Chevalier à l'Espée* is only comprehensible as an unfortunate attempt to conflate wide variants of the same story.

If we look at the author's solution of the three original difficulties, we shall see that one of them has not been met successfully. The host is continually coming and going, and one explanation for his absence, as Kittredge pointed out, is a lame one, the provision for the dinner, since he had already ridden ahead expressly to make arrangements for the entertainment of his guest. His attitude toward his guest, however, is rational enough. He is, though superficially gracious, really malicious, until the sword test proves Gawain to be the peerless knight. And he encourages Gawain's passion for his daughter in order that, unless Gawain is the peerless knight, he may be trapped to his destruction.

It is interesting to note at this point that every one of the four romances has given a different explanation of the host's attitude toward the bedroom adventure: in the *Carl* the incident is a supreme trial of the hero's obedience to his host; in the Galagandreis episode a trial of his respect for the proprieties; in *Wolfdietrich* a trial of his Christian faith; in the *Chevalier* a somewhat muddled trial both of his self-control and of his prowess, due to the fusion of the temptation and the missile test.

The next two episodes belong to the *Lit Périlleux* group, which I have discussed elsewhere.[28] Here our concern is to observe how this theme of the Perilous Bed connects on the one hand with the *Chevalier à l'Espée* and on the other with the Visit to Curoi's Fortress.

VII. The Karadas Episode in *Diu Krone*

Diu Krone is a long episodic romance, whose chief hero is Gawain, composed about 1220 by Heinrich von dem Türlin. Miss Weston more than any other scholar seems to have realized its importance as a storehouse of tradition independent of Crestien.[29] Here follows a summary of Gawain's adventures at Schastel Mervillos.[30]

The hero is entertained by a knight, Karadas, in his house and is told of an en-

---

[28] R. S. Loomis, *Celtic Myth and Arthurian Romance*, pp. 159–176, 223 f. Cf. also *Le Chevalier à l'Epée*, pp. 59–62.

[29] J. L. Weston, *Legend of Sir Gawain* (London, 1897), cf. Index, *sub Diu Krone*. Weston, *Sir Gawain at the Grail Castle* (London, 1903), viii ff. Cf. also *Romania*, XII, 506; *Englische Studien*, XXXVI, 346; G. Schoepperle, *Tristan and Isolt* (London, Frankfort, 1913), II, 534 ff. *La Damoisele à la Mule*, ed. B. Orlowski (Paris, 1911), pp. 62 f.; Warnatsch, *Der Mantel* (Breslau, 1883), pp. 118 ff.; R.S. Loomis, *op. cit.*, cf. Index *sub Heinrich;* L. L. Boll, *Relation of Diu Krone to La Mule sanz Frain* (Washington, 1929).

[30] Ed. Scholl, ll. 20346 ff.

chanted castle near by, where many knights have lost their lives. But if any knight be found so stout of heart as to spend a night in the castle without scathe, he will be given the castle and a lovely maiden to wife. In spite of his host's dissuasion Gawain insists on being guided to the castle. Accordingly Karadas and Gawain ride thither and are entertained by a lovely maiden, who with the aid of her squires serves them with a plentiful supper, as one would "a dear guest." Afterwards Karadas takes his leave, with a warning against the Perilous Bed and a promise to return in the morning. The damsel too leaves with mournful eyes, knowing that death has overtaken many who have preceded her guest in the adventure, and little does she sleep. As soon as Gawain lies down in the bed, it begins to move, windows slam, and arbalests and bows shoot down five hundred bolts. Gawain hears the wailing of the women, but unharmed he goes to sleep. In the morning the maiden and her squires find Gawain none the worse and inform the queen of the castle, Igern. Karadas, too, arrives in great anxiety, wakes the hero, and promptly arms him against a new peril. A lion is loosed against him, and when Gawain has slain it, Karadas gives thanks and praise for the victory. The queen with all her folk then appears and presently announces that by reason of his services, the unknown hero shall be lord of the castle and shall have his choice of the lady Clarissans or her mother as his *amie*. Gawain, who now suddenly learns that the ladies of the castle who are offered him are his sister and mother, does not reveal his identity, takes refuge in delay, and escapes.

Such a conclusion betrays at once the hand of a bungling redactor. Even in the romances, it is unnatural for a knight to come to the dwelling of his mother and sister without realizing it, and when he does realize it, to depart without making himself known. For one thing, there has been contamination here. The multiplication of ladies is, as I have indicated elsewhere,[31] due to the luckless attempt—made long before Heinrich's time since we have the same combination in Crestien and Wolfram—to fit the tradition of the night in Curoi's fortress into the entirely independent Irish legend of Bran's voyage to the Isle of Maidens. The queen Igern and Gawain's mother and sister are therefore extraneous elements. The natural and traditional ending of the story was Gawain's union with the lovely damsel who tended him as a dear guest; she was his true *amie*. This is what we have in the *Carl, Lanzelet,* and the *Chevalier*. It is therefore not without significance that elsewhere Heinrich discloses the name of Gawain's love, Flori,[32] just as Cuchulinn's hostess was called "Little Flower." Nor should it escape us that in the French original of the *Carl* the host presumably received the name of Cardoil, and that it suggests comparison with the name of the host in *Diu Krone*, Karadas. This is by no means the last evidence we shall encounter that the names, as well as the incidents, are traditional.

[31] Loomis, *op. cit.*, pp. 177–179.
[32] Ll. 1294 f.

The *Lit Périlleux* links this tale to the *Chevalier;* the lion to the *Carl*. But there are elements also which bear direct comparison with the Visit to Curoi's Fortress. Karadas' departure at night, his return in the morning, his proclamation of Gawain's valor, the service of the damsel and her solicitude over Gawain's fate are strongly reminiscent of the behavior of Curoi and Blathnat respectively; and the shower of bolts which Gawain endures recalls the rain of oak branches which the Irish heroes had to endure in Curoi's fortress. Even the *Lit Périlleux* is a development from the "seat of watch," which it is easy to account for since the Irish seat was an *imda* or couch.[33] Though the agreement between *Bricriu's Feast* and *Diu Krone* may be fortuitous on one point, the absence of a temptation, the other correspondences are hardly capable of such an explanation.

The Karadas episode contains a satisfactory solution of the three bewildering points in the Visit to Curoi's Fortress. The question of the host's presence is met by a compromise: he is present when the hero arrives at the testing castle and during his fight with the monster, but absent during the shower of missiles. The difficulty of his attitude toward the hero is largely removed by the novel idea that he is not lord of the castle where the tests occur and does his best to warn Gawain against the bed and to arm him against the lion. Indubitably he is the hero's friend. And his attitude toward the love affair occasions no perplexity, because there is no love affair—a different solution of the problem from any of the four preceding.

VIII. The Porte Noire Episode in *Artus de la Petite Bretagne*

This is another neglected romance. Composed in the fourteenth century, it contains much late material, and has therefore been ignored. Its hero is ostensibly a Breton knight of much later date than the traditional king Arthur, but there is reason to suspect that parts of his story were originally told of his renowned namesake. Like him he has a sword Clarent or Clarence, and was reared in Brittany.[34] At any rate, it is clear that the following episode is altogether derived from the Arthurian cycle.[35]

The princess Florence had in her service a clerk of royal lineage, who was learned

[33] R. Thurneysen, *Sagen aus dem alten Irland* (Berlin, 1901), p. 26.

[34] Loomis, *op. cit.*, p. 172.

[35] The following summary is based on the MS., *Livre du Petit Artus,* now in the New York Public Library, of which a full description with half-tones of five illuminated pages was published by the Library in 1928. The one opposite p. 6 illustrates the Porte Noire adventure. Lord Berners' English translation was published in 1550 and reprinted by Utterson in 1814. The material for this summary is drawn from folios 18ʳ, 21ᵛ, 50ʳ, 52ᵛ–61ᵛ.

in astronomy and magic, and who loved and served her loyally. She was mistress of a perilous castle called the Porte Noire, built by enchantment, but she prudently did not reside there. The magician, Estienne, knew by his arts that a certain knight was destined to come, endure the perils of the Porte Noire, and win its mistress. Florence promptly fell in love with the destined knight and sent Estienne to the castle to await his coming. Artus, accompanied by his squire Baudoin, meanwhile set out for the Porte Noire, was harbored on the way by a lord who warned him that no one who took the road to the right ever returned. Artus, undeterred, took this road, and slaying twelve knights who opposed his entrance, forced his way into the castle, where Estienne was watching his progress from the battlements. Artus left Baudoin in the court, entered the Palais Aventureux, discovered a rich chamber containing a marvelously rich bed. At the head of the bed was an image bearing a bow and arrow and inscribed with a warning that the bed was fatal to all but the destined knight. A great, horrible voice cried: "Here is the end." Estienne then knew that Artus had entered the palace. There was a clapping-to of windows and a great noise; the building trembled. Once more the great voice was heard. Two lions attacked Artus in succession and were slain. Artus had next to deal with a giant, clad in a serpent's hide, carrying an ax, raging at the slaughter of his lions, and killed him also. Again the great voice proclaimed the end. Weary from his wounds, Artus lay on the bed; the image loosed the arrow; it struck and opened a window, whence issued smoke and stench. Swords flew about like rain. A lance of fire struck the bed, but Artus leapt aside. The palace began to turn like a wheel, but Artus clung to the image, which did not move. When the motion stopped and all was light and quiet again, he sank exhausted on the bed. A voice announced: "It is finished!" Baudoin then joined his master and dressed his wounds. Artus released two prisoners and was served a good dinner by the cook of the castle. After still another combat, Artus was led to an orchard, where Estienne greeted him as the sovereign knight of the world, for no other had emerged from the Palais Aventureux. To the perilous chamber Artus returned with Estienne and supped as luxuriously as if he had been in the abode of Florence herself, and though she was not present, she paid all the expenses. Estienne departed, charging Artus to sleep in the bed of his former adventure. Artus did so and woke at midnight to see a crowned woman, the most beautiful ever seen, standing before him. She announced further adventures and vanished. The next morning Estienne returned, showed Artus an image, and declared that it was the exact counterpart of Florence and of his visitor of the night before, the fairy Proserpine. Needless to say, Artus performed all the necessary exploits and won Florence at last.

The resemblances to the stories we have already examined are overwhelming. Baudoin, who plays a subordinate rôle to Artus, suggests the Baldwin who plays a subordinate rôle to Gawain in the *Carl*. The knowledge on the part of Estienne and Florence of the coming of a destined knight and the turning castle offer definite links with the Belian adventure in *Wolfdietrich*. The magic bed and the flying swords recall the *Chevalier à l'Espée*. The absent but solicitous host, the bed that moves, the slamming windows, the rain of missiles, the lion combat, the congratulations of the host, are paralleled in *Diu Krone*. Most interesting is the treatment of the hostess. Two reasons seem to have kept the the originator of this version of the story from bringing Florence in person into her own castle; he wished to avoid imputing to his heroine the questionable conduct ascribed to her by tradition; he regarded so dangerous a castle as no fit abode for her; he therefore resolved to adopt the familiar motif of the *princesse lointaine*, loved before she was seen. So while he concedes to tradition the fact that the castle belonged to Florence and that she was responsible for the hospitality which the hero enjoyed there, the story-designer expressly denied the natural supposition that she was herself present. "Si furent seruis trop richement comme en lostel de la haulte florence, et non obstant quelle ny fut pas, si paia elle les despens."[36] Could there be a neater instance of the medieval author's respect for tradition even when he contradicted it? Nor should one overlook the appearance of Florence's exact counterpart at the bedside of Artus. We have seen in the Galagandreis story and shall see in several other versions that a nocturnal visit by the heroine to the hero's chamber was one form which Blathnat's intrigue with Cuchulinn took in Arthurian tradition. It would seem as if the originator of the Porte Noire version has once more been unwilling to depart wholly from his sources but has avoided all scandal by bringing to Artus' bedside not Florence but her double, and making her errand there merely prophetic.

That the Porte Noire tale is a conflation of variant versions of the Visit to the Perilous Castle seems clear. For instance, the flying swords, the figure shooting an arrow, and the lance of fire seem to be three developments from the same original concept of the missile weapons which we find in the Visit to Curoi's Fortress. The image shooting an arrow betrays contamination by such non-Celtic stories as that told of Pope Gerbert by William of Malmesbury;[37] and there is probably some connection with the Melusine tradition. We shall see, moreover, as we proceed, that the Porte Noire episode contains features that appear in other variants of the Visit to the Perilous Castle. But even though it be certain that the Porte Noire is to some extent a composite version, it is hard to explain it altogether as a mosaic made up at random from a group of similar but not cognate tales. It must represent in the main a genuine outgrowth from the two Irish stories of Curoi and Cuchulinn with which our study started. Even the evidence of conflation would indicate that

[36] Fol. 57b v.
[37] *Gesta Romanorum*, tr. C. Swan, Tale cvii, Note 10.

the redactor realized that he was attempting to harmonize the variants of the same story. Otherwise, it is hard to conceive that by a fortuitous selection he should have brought together thirteen features derived from our Irish sources, namely: the enchanter's foreknowledge of and solicitude concerning the hero's coming; his absence from the scene of testing; his knowledge, despite his absence, of the hero's victory; the turning castle; the hero's taking the seat of watch; the flying shafts; the combat with monsters; the combat with Curoi himself, described, as in the Champion's Bargain, as wearing a hide and carrying an ax; the enchanter's declaration of the hero's sovranty in prowess; the interest of the lady of the castle in the hero's fate; her provision for his entertainment; the suggestion of a nocturnal visit to the hero's bed; her name Florence. It is the strongest possible support for the traditional origin of the Porte Noire tale that not only does it offer a greater number of correspondences to the Irish than does the *Carl of Carlisle*, but only two of the correspondences are identical with those in the *Carl*.

The three ambiguities of the Irish tradition are met as follows: The question of Curoi's presence or absence has resulted in the splitting of Curoi into two figures, the enchanter who is absent from the scene of test but cognizant of all that goes on there, and the attacking giant. The question of Curoi's attitude toward the hero is thus solved also; Estienne is consistently friendly and, like Karadas, bears no responsibility for the attacks on the hero. The third question likewise is solved much as in the Karadas story; for neither Karadas nor Estienne has any title to be jealous of the heroine's affection for the hero, nor is there any display of that affection sufficient to arouse jealousy.

IX. The Roaz Episode in *Wigalois*

Wigalois was composed about 1205 by Wirnt von Gravenberg. It was his first work and according to his assertion was based on a narrative told him by a squire. In fact, it is a German version of the romance of Gawain's son Guiglain, of which Renaud de Beaujeu's *Bel Inconnu* (ca 1200) and *Libeaus Desconus* (ca 1350) are the extant French and English versions.[38] It resembles, moreover, so strikingly the fourteenth-century romance, *Le Chevalier du Papegau*, that a common source for the two in the twelfth century has been demonstrated by Heuckenkamp.[39] The Roaz episode is the climax of the German romance.[40]

---

[38] W. H. Schofield, "Studies in the Libeaus Desconus," *Studies and Notes in Philology and Literature*, IV (Boston, 1895).

[39] *Le Chevalier du Papegau*, ed. F. Heuckenkamp (Halle, 1896), p. liv.

[40] Wirnt von Gravenberg, *Wigalois*, ed. Kapteyn, *Rheinische Beiträge*, IX (1926), ll. 6770–8565.

Wigalois, son of Gawain, was summoned to rescue Larie, the loveliest lady in the world, from the encroachments made on her domain by the heathen enchanter Roaz since the death of her father Belnain. The young hero is graciously received by Larie and her mother in their castle of Roymunt and falls a complete victim to Larie's charms. To win her hand, he sets out for the enchanter's castle, Glois. Crossing a moor near the castle, he is overtaken by a great mist. Then he finds his road blocked by a gateway in which an iron water wheel, fitted with swords and clubs, revolves,—a villainous contrivance of the magician's. In answer to prayer the mist vanishes, the wheel stops, Wigalois inserts a bar in the mechanism, and passes the gateway. A voice rings out threatening him with death. But he manages to overcome a monster, half-horse, half-dog, flinging fire. A voice announces in the castle of Roaz the fate of the monster and the imminent doom of Roaz himself. Wigalois arrives before the castle, which is richly adorned with marble and gold. When two gray-haired knights drive him from the gate, he slays one and spares the other. After resting, he enters the castle and finds great riches. There comes a flash of lightning. Then Roaz issues from a door, hidden behind a cloud, but when Wigalois makes the sign of the cross, he stands revealed. Roaz' wife and twelve maidens enter bearing tapers and remain to watch. When Wigalois is attacked by the powerful giant, the lady mourns his desperate case. The combat lasts all night till Roaz falls. His wife, whose sympathies have shifted back to her husband, dies of grief. When day breaks, there comes in an old earl, reduced by Roaz to serve as porter, who brings the exhausted hero back to life, and offers his allegiance. The heathen inmates of the castle surrender and are baptized, and the earl is put in charge of the treasure. Wigalois, feeling greatly refreshed after he has been washed and fed, mounts a horse, rides out, caracoles about, and returns. He stops the revolving wheel, and sets out for another castle, where he awaits Larie and her mother.

The first point to be noted is the contamination of the tradition and the source of that contamination. It is impossible to bring all the evidence together here. Some of it I have assembled elsewhere,[41] and may be consulted by the curious. I hope, however, that anyone familiar with the characteristics of the Visit to the Perilous Castle as we have observed them, reading the nocturnal adventures of Gawain in the Castle of Corbenic as related in the *Vulgate Lancelot*[42] and the adventures of the same hero in the castle of Bran de Lis as told by Pseudo-Wauchier,[43] will recognize there the familiar pattern, contaminated in somewhat the same way as are the nocturnal adventures in the castle Glois. A little investigation will reveal the source of, and the reason for, that contamination. The Welsh Bran presented a general resemblance as a giant of supernatural powers to Curoi. There seems to have been a more specific resemblance in a local tradition that Bran's castle was the scene of

---

[41] *Kastner Miscellany* (Cambridge, 1932), pp. 347 f.

[42] H. O. Sommer, *Vulgate Version of the Arthurian Romances*, IV, 343–347.

[43] *Perceval le Gallois*, ed. C. Potvin, III (Mons, 1866), 284–300.

uncanny nocturnal combats like those in Curoi's fortress.[44] The result was a number of stories where the two sets of nocturnal adventures are combined and other stories in which Bran has taken over Curoi's role as closely related to Gawain's (or Bohors') leman[45] and as Gawain's mortal foe. Since we find Bran's name corrupted as Brauz and initial letters are often omitted by scribes,[46] it is highly probable that we have in these facts the explanation of the name Roaz. The specific evidence for this belief lies in detailed similarities between the adventure in Roaz' castle and those in the castles of Bran, of Bran de Lis, and of Corbenic (= Cor Beneit, Bran's horn of plenty). A notable feature of the combat in Chastel Bran, related in *Fouke Fitz Warin*, is the power of the cross which the hero exercises against his adversary. The fight in the castle of Bran de Lis is distinguished by the bringing of candles and torches and by the presence of a lady whose sympathies are divided between the two combatants. Gawain's fight in Corbenic is preceded by the entrance of twelve maidens. All these features are present in the account of the combat with Roaz, and tend to show that the contamination of the Curoi tradition in this episode is due to the influence of the nocturnal combat in Bran's castle.

The second point to be noted is that we can fill out or check the adventures of Wigalois by those of Arthur in the *Chevalier du Papegau*, a fourteenth-century prose romance, recognized by Heuckenkamp as a close cognate of Wirnt's poem. In the *Chevalier* the heroine's name is Flor,[47] not Larie; doubtless the common source gave Florie. The turning wheel is placed in a bridge directly before the castle.[48] After the hero's triumph he rides to the castle where Flor and her mother dwell.[49] These features were probably present in the common source of *Wigalois* and the *Chevalier du Papegau*, which we shall call WP.

We are now in a position to note the correspondences between WP and *Artus* and the indebtedness of WP to the Curoi-Blathnat complex. WP shared with *Artus* the periodic announcements of the mysterious voice; the combats with the defenders of the gate, the monster, and the giant; a lightning flash; the arrival of a man who tends the hero's wounds; the delivery of captives; the name of the lady for whom the deeds were done, Florence or Florie. More significant are the connections with the Irish tradition. For the name Wigalois is obviously the German version of Guiglains, which the French themselves turned into Gliglois and which

---

[44] *Fouke FitzWarin*, ed. L. Brandin (Paris, 1930), pp. 3–5.

[45] For Pseudo-Wauchier Gawain's *amie* is sister of Bran de Lis; in the *Vulgate Lancelot* Bohors' one love-affair is with Brangor's daughter.

[46] Loomis, *op. cit.*, p. 145 f., *MLN*, xxvi, 66 f.

[47] P. 25.   [48] P. 72.   [49] P. 76.

is etymologized by Wirnt as Gwi von Galois.[50] The element *galois* is simply the adjective meaning "Welsh" introduced through this mistaken effort at etymology. And Guiglain offers to the most casual eye a suspicious likeness to the correct Irish form Cuchulainn. The names Larie and Flor must be traditional and are accounted for as translations of Blathnat, just as the Arthurian Lion and Lac are translations of Welsh Llew and Llwch.[51] The magic wheel corresponds strikingly to the wheel which was in motion at the door of a fortress attacked by Cuchulinn and which had to be stopped before he could enter and carry off Blathnat, as told by Keating.[52] Probably, the concept of Curoi's revolving castle, which is described both in *Wolfdietrich* and *Artus*, as revolving like a wheel, had been rationalized very early among the Irish as a wheel revolving before the castle to bar ingress, and this version descended both to Keating and to WP. Another peculiar trait of *Wigalois* is the hero's sudden whimsical sortie from the castle to take a turn on horseback. What can this rather strange and pointless incident be but the survival of Cuchulinn's preternatural leaps of triumph which carried him out of the castle and back into it again?

The three puzzles in the visit to Curoi's castle are answered satisfactorily. The enchanter who plays Curoi's rôle is unmistakably present and unmistakably hostile. As regards the heroine, the representative of Curoi has taken up an entirely different relationship from any we have encountered so far. He is her enemy, who has attacked her castle and kept her confined to it, while he himself lives in another. According to the *Chevalier du Papegau* he wishes to seize her for his wife.[53] Curiously enough, however, WP preserves side by side with this new development the old tradition that Curoi's wife was present in the fortress and showed sympathy for the hero, for, as we have seen, in *Wigalois* the enchanter has a wife who witnesses the combat, and mourns at first the plight of the young hero. It is clear that WP conflated two versions of the situation and rôle of Blathnat. The new version which represents her as the heiress of a castle, where she is being hard pressed by the attacks of an unwelcome suitor, we shall meet again in purer form later.

X. The Gringamore Episode in Malory

The romance of Gareth occupying the seventh book of Malory's *Morte d'Arthur*, completed in 1469, represents a lost French text of a highly composite nature. It approximates the *Bel Inconnu* group most closely, but it has absorbed details from many early romances, of which Gareth's

---

[50] L. 1574.

[51] *PMLA*, xlv (1930), 432–438. *M.L.R.*, xxiv (1929), 425–427.

[52] Keating, *History of Ireland*, Irish Texts Soc., viii, 223.   [53] P. 26.

assignation with Lyones in Gringamore's castle interests us as a patent survival of certain details from the Champion's Bargain. Gareth is, of course, Gawain's brother Gaheriet or Gaheris, and as I have shown elsewhere, was originally identical with Gawain.[54]

Gareth has been summoned to the rescue of a besieged lady, but after accomplishing the feat of overcoming a series of her besiegers, he arrives at the castle only to be sent off for a twelvemonth ere he can win her. However, the lady Lyones promptly repents and sends her brother Gringamore, lord of the Castle Perilous beside the Isle of Avilion, to bring him back. This Gringamore does by the unusual expedient of sneaking up and carrying off Gareth's attendant dwarf. When Gareth pursues and asks a poor man if he has seen a black knight on a black horse, he is warned not to follow, for Gringamore is one of the "periloust" knights of the world. However, he persists and presently comes before the Castle Perilous, whither Lyones and her sister meantime have arrived. After some high words, he is admitted, given back his dwarf, and welcomed by Gringamore and his sister. Though Gareth is not aware of her identity, by supper time he is far gone in love and can not eat. Gringamore, seeing this, encourages the affair, commends Gareth to his sister and declares to him that the lady is his at all times, "her worship saved." Before night comes, she reveals her identity, and the lovers arrange an assignation in the hall where Gareth has his bed. Lynete, the sister, however, is aware of what is going on and takes steps to prevent its consummation. At midnight Lyones comes wrapped in a mantle and lies beside Gareth. Suddenly he sees a knight enter with a long ax in his hand and many lights about him. Gareth leaps for his sword, overcomes the intruder, and smites off his head. Dame Lyones' cries bring Gringamore, and he expresses indignation at the injury done to his guest, but none whatsoever at his sister's open avowal of her passion for Gareth. Lynete then enters, puts the decapitated knight together again, and he walks off whole, much to the surprise of them all. Ten nights later these events repeat themselves. There is a great light as it were the number of twenty torches both before and behind the intruder. Gareth takes the precaution to cut his head into a hundred pieces this time, but again through the agency of Lynete, he departs whole. This is the last we hear of him. After many more adventures Gareth weds Lyones, who is herself called the Lady of the Castle Perilous.[55]

It is easy to see the similarity of this episode to the *Chevalier à l'Espée* in the warning of the poor man, the prompt infatuation of the hero and the host's sister with each other, the encouragement offered by the host, the interruption of the lovers in bed, and the entrance of the host. But instead of the flying sword, we have as the perilous element the knight with an ax, a feature which relates the story to the Porte Noire episode and of course to the Champion's Bargain. It is astonishing what authen-

[54] R. S. Loomis, *Celtic Myth and Arthurian Romance*, p. 84; *PMLA*, XLIII (1928), 386 ff.

[55] On this nocturnal adventure cf. Kittredge, *op. cit.*, pp. 265 f. On Book VII cf. Vinaver in *Medium Aevum*, I (1932), 157.

tic details seem to have survived from the Irish. Not only does the head of the ax-bearing intruder fit on again, not only does he walk off whole, but he does it after his head has been split into fragments, just as in the Champion's Bargain. Moreover, the lights about this ax-bearing giant explain the mysterious taunt hurled at the other ax-bearing giant, Curoi, and his reply that he brings light to the household but not burning. This bit of evidence seems to me to clinch the hypothesis on which we have been working—that Curoi, in spite of his departure from his fortress, was inconsistently recognized by the Irish story-tellers as the giant who attacked Cuchulinn. In the version which has survived in the Gringamore episode some Irishman who knew what he was doing must have made the identification of the attacker clear by giving him the peculiar characteristics of Curoi in the Champion's Bargain.

The names of Lyones, Lynete, and Gringamore are, of course, intrusive, though Lunete, according to Crestien, was the name of one of Gawain's loves.[56] Gringamore is obviously the same figure as the "Guigomars . . . de l'isle d'Avalon fu sire," whom Crestien mentions in *Erec*, though his name is closer in form to the hero of the lai *Guingamor*.[57] The tampering with the original plot is not always felicitous. The relation of Lynete to the ax-bearing knight is never accounted for. We are prepared by Gringamore's black arms, black horse, and his reputation as one of the "periloust" knights of the world, to find him a black-hearted villain. Quite the contrary; after his initial prank of absconding with Gareth's dwarf, he is the courteous and friendly host. Charming as the Gareth story is, it is patently a pastiche.

Its solution of the puzzles which the Visit to Curoi's Fortress presents are, however, plausible. The host is absent during the attack and disclaims responsibility for it. After he learns of Gareth's high birth, he is a consistent tuft-hunter. Toward his sister's amour he is consistently blasé.

XI. *Gawain and the Green Knight*

This, the finest of Middle English romances, was composed by an anonymous author in Cheshire or Lancashire about 1375.[58] Its indebtedness to the Champion's Bargain has been amply demonstrated by Professor Kittredge, its indebtedness to other parts of the Curoi cycle by Miss Buchanan.[59] In order that its connection with the Irish saga and the stories which we shall examine later may be clear, it is necessary to start our summary at an early point in the narrative.

[56] *Ivain*, l. 2415 ff.

[57] On this name cf. Brugger in *Zeits. f. franz. Spr. u. Lit.*, XLIX (1927), 206–216, Zimmer, *ibid.*, XIII (1891), 7 ff., and Freymond, *ibid.*, XVII (1895), 17 ff.

[58] Ed. J. R. R. Tolkien, E. V. Gordon (Oxford, 1925), p. xxi f.   [59] See note 16

Before Arthur's court assembled at New Year's there enters a haughty knight, green all over, mounted on a green horse. He is richly clad and bears an ax. He asks for the governor of the company, and all are silent in wonder, till Arthur speaks. The giant knight then challenges anyone to an alternate head-cutting. When no response comes, he derides the fame of Arthur's house and declares it overthrown. Arthur accepts the challenge, but Gawain takes his place and actually cuts off the Green Knight's head. He undertakes to meet his adversary a year hence at the Green Chapel. When the appointed time approaches, the courtiers lament, but he sets out for his rendezvous. He comes to a castle, is welcomed by its lord, a tall knight with "a face fierce as fire," and in the evening he meets the lord's beautiful wife and an ancient dame. Before long he asks to be the fair lady's servant, and the next day they sit together at meals and take much comfort from the dalliance of private speech. During the Christmastide Gawain is hospitably entertained, and then for three days his host absents himself to hunt, recommending his guest to his wife's company. Each successive morning the lady comes to Gawain's bed and tempts him, but he courteously declines her offers, except for the love-token of a girdle. He keeps his tryst with the Green Knight, who declares him a pearl among white peas, reveals his own name, Bercilak, and his identity with his late host. He has connived at his wife's advances and knows all that went on in his absence.

It would be supererogatory to discuss here the Irish connections of this romance, so fully treated by Kittredge and Miss Buchanan, and the ingenuity with which the various Irish strands have been combined into a coherent plot. It is scarcely necessary to point out that the Gringamore episode, just examined, offers a different combination of some of the same elements. But it is important to realize that the name Bercilak is traditional, going back to the Irish noun *bachlach*, a "herdsman," by which Curoi is regularly designated in the Champion's Bargain.

XII. The Guingambresil Episode in the *Conte del Graal*

Just about two centuries earlier than *Gawain and the Green Knight* was written, Crestien de Troyes began and left unfinished the *Conte del Graal*. Though Perceval is the ostensible hero of the poem, Gawain takes the center of the stage a good part of the time, and one of his adventures is concerned with a certain Guingambresil.[60] That this personage was already known to Crestien's readers is evident from the way in which he is introduced: "Atant ez uos que venir voient Guinganbresil parmi la porte De la sale." Apparently no identification of the knight seems to have been required. Here is a résumé of the adventure.

Before Arthur's court there enters Guingambresil. He greets the king, but charges Gawain with slaying his lord. Gawain takes up the gage, and Guingam-

[60] Ed. Baist (Freiburg-in-Breisgau), ll. 4709–4775, 5665–6177. Ed. Hilka (Halle, 1932), ll. 4747–4814, 5703–6215.

bresil challenges him to combat before his lord's son, the King of Cavalon, forty days later. Gawain accepts, the newcomer departs, and Gawain in turn amid the laments of the courtiers sets out to keep his rendezvous. After an irrelevant affair he meets a tall youth setting out on a hunt, who turns out to be, though the author does not inform us, the King of Cavalon. Apparently he does not know Gawain by sight, for he at once insists on his harboring in his own castle, and sends a messenger to his sister most emphatically charging her to love and cherish his unknown guest till his return from the hunt. She seats Gawain beside her; he offers to become her knight; and presently both are kissing and making great joy. Suddenly a vavasour enters, recognizes Gawain as the reputed murderer of his former lord, reproaches the damsel, and rouses the town. Some of the commons seize axes, others whatever they can pick up. Gawain and the lady defend themselves. The king returns, and immediately after him Guingambresil. The latter at once declares to the king that this attack by his subjects upon his guest does him great dishonor. The king agrees and disperses the commons, and Gawain swears to return after a year for another rendezvous with Guingambresil.

If Crestien originated and took much interest in this story, all signs fail. He leaves us to discover that Gawain had reached Cavalon and that his host was king of that land. Guingambresil's challenge is told in most summary fashion, and we have already remarked on the way in which he is introduced. And there are other reasons for supposing the story traditional.

When we look at the name Guingambresil, it looks suspiciously like a portmanteau word based on Guingamor and Bercilak, names of the hosts in our last two tales. Our suspicion is confirmed by the way in which the Gringamore and Bercilak stories supply the elements of the Guingambresil story. The former supplies the lord of (C)Avalon, who recommends a guest to his sister's love, a violent love affair, an interruption, and an attack by men with axes. The latter supplements these elements by a challenge at Arthur's court, its acceptance by Gawain, the rendezvous for a later date in another place, the absence of the host on a hunt during the love affair. This is a fairly clear case of conflating two derivatives from the same ultimate source. If any doubt remain as to this analysis of the Guingambresil story, let us consult Wolfram von Eschenbach's version of the same episode.

XIII. The Vergulaht Episode in Wolfram's *Parzival*

This romance was composed about 1205, and its relation to the *Conte del Graal* has been the subject of infinite controversy. Wolfram avers that he follows in preference to Crestien a certain Kyot, and the odds now seem decidedly in favor of the existence of an eminent poet Guiot[61] and

---

[61] M. Wilmotte, *Le Poème du Graal et Ses Auteurs* (Paris, 1930), p. 17,

of Wolfram's large dependence on him.[62] A comparison of Wolfram's treatment of the Guingambresil episode sheds a good deal of light on the subject.[63]

Into Arthur's court rides a haughty knight, richly clad, bearing a sheathed sword. He asks for Arthur and Gawain, salutes the king, and defies Gawain to single combat forty days later before the king of Askalon. If a false knight sit at the Round Table, its fame is gone. The king is sad and silent but at last he speaks, and says he would take the challenge, were Gawain dead. But Gawain takes it; the stranger announces his name as Kingrimursel and his country as Askalon, and departs. The courtiers fear for Gawain's fate, but he sets out and after irrelevant adventures comes to the land of Askalon. He meets the King Vergulaht and five hundred knights out hawking. The king's glance is like daylight at night, and he is of fairy race. He sends Gawain to his castle with a messenger telling his sister to entertain him. The lady is beautiful, of course; they kiss and sit side by side, and things might have come to a pass if they had not been interrupted. A knight recognizes Gawain as the supposed slayer of his king, and rouses the town. Gawain and the lady defend themselves. Vergulaht returns. Kingrimursel also arrives and since he has promised Gawain safe-conduct, joins him against the townsfolk. Vergulaht, however, is about to lead them against his guest when he is induced by a vassal to make a truce. After an angry council, Gawain is permitted to depart on condition that he return a year hence for the fight with Kingrimursel.

First, it should be observed that the name Kingrimursel is obviously an attempt to pronounce Guingambresil. Second, Kingrimursel's challenge is told in greater detail than Guingambresil's, and the additional details find several parallels in *Gawain and the Green Knight:* for example, the richness of the stranger's equipment, the weapon in his hand, Arthur's chagrin, the taunt directed at the Round Table, Arthur's conditional acceptance of the challenge. In fact, it seems odd that no commentator, so far as I am aware, has noted the resemblance. Third, the name Vergulaht for the lord of the castle seems to be, like Bercilak, derived from *bachlach*, which was pronounced in Irish as a trisyllable. But it must represent a different branch of the tradition from the -bresil of Guingambresil since it contains the original palatal sound in the middle of the word instead of shifting to a sibilant. Two *bachlach* stories, then, seem to have contributed to Wolfram's version: in one the lord of the castle was called Bresilak, in the other Vergulaht. The Bresilak version would have resembled *Gawain and the Green Knight*, where the lord of the castle is called Bercilak, containing the challenge, the host's hunting, amorous

[62] Mary Williams, *Essai sur la Composition du Roman Gallois de Peredur* (Paris, 1909), pp. 81–95; Zenker in *Romanische Forschungen*, XL, 256 ff.; Nitze in *Studies in Honor of A. M. Elliott*, (Baltimore, 1911), I, 19 ff.; R. S. Loomis, *Celtic Myth and Arthurian Romance*, pp. 166, 223 f.

[63] Wolfram von Eschenbach, ed. E. Martin (Halle, 1900), 318, 20–325, 17; 399, 1–432, 30.

scenes, and the arrangement of a second rendezvous. It was telescoped with a Gringamore version, containing similar scenes at the castle, but adding the localization at Cavalon, the relationship of brother and sister, and the attack on Gawain by ax-bearers. It is probable that in this composite version Guingambresil was both challenger and lord of the castle. This version in turn absorbed what was probably a story of the *Chevalier à l'Espée* type, where there was no challenge, where the lord of the castle was met by the hero in the forest, vigorously encouraged the hero's amour, absented himself in the forest, and was named Vergulaht or something like it. This new figure usurped the rôle of lord of the castle, and Guingambresil was demoted to the position of the lord's kinsman. No finality can be attached to such a solution of the problems presented by a highly composite narrative, but this explanation seems to have the evidence in its favor. It suggests how complex had been the history of these tales before Crestien and Guiot put them into verse.

The combiner's solution of the problems presented by conflicting traditions, if not always happy, is novel. He successfully reconciles the host's absence with his instructions to his sister by the device of a messenger. He is not so successful in harmonizing the delivery of Guingambresil's challenge with his absence during the love scene and attack on Gawain, for the challenger, who had left Arthur's court sooner than Gawain and presumably had no distractions on the way, should have reached Cavalon before him. The combiner's explanation of the attack on Gawain in the castle of a most friendly host is new and ingenious, but it contains one improbability—that Gawain should not have been recognized, or should not have revealed his name and errand, sooner. Guingambresil's attitude toward Gawain, of hostility combined with magnanimity, is consistent and honorable throughout. Vergulaht's conduct toward Gawain represents a less successful attempt to rationalize the original ambiguity of Curoi's conduct to Cuchulinn. It veers from extreme hospitality to nascent hostility, and involves an unpardonable breach both of his obligations as host and of Kingrimursel's promise of safe conduct. Wolfram, doubtless following his source, starts with a panegyric of Vergulaht, but as the story proceeds, his keen moral sense is shocked by Vergulaht's treachery and he cannot find words too strong for his condemnation. The postponement of the judicial combat for another year, which is doubtless a survival of the traditional feature, found in *Gawain and the Green Knight* and originating in the Yellow and Terror version of the beheading test, that the hero's visit to the challenger's abode led to another rendezvous,[64] is inadequately motivated both by Crestien and Wolfram.

[64] R. S. Loomis, *op. cit.*, p. 68 f.

XIV. The Outraged King Episode in *Peredur*

One of the extraordinary developments of the Visit to Curoi's Fortress in Arthurian romance was the tendency to inject greater realism and familiarity by the expedient of substituting for the uncanny nocturnal happenings in the Castle Perilous, banal combats in the field in broad daylight. It was obviously a change for the worse, and has rendered the stories where it has been applied so commonplace that their true origin has never been suspected. Yet the rest of the pattern has been left so far intact that there can be little doubt of its relationship to the Irish source. Oddly enough, three of these versions survive in the Welsh romance of *Peredur*, and to them we shall direct our attention. *Peredur*, it may be remarked, is by general consent admitted to be based in large measure on a French original. There is no general agreement as to its relation to the *Conte del Graal*, with which it runs parallel in many episodes, containing, for instance, the Guingambresil tale in a condensed form. But Professor Zenker in an admirable article,[65] not to mention the work of others, has proved that *Peredur* and the *Conte del Graal* owe their similarity to common sources, probably removed by several steps. It is but one more exposure of the popular fallacy that every analog of Crestien's in the Arthurian cycle is a derivative. A résumé of the first episode follows.[66]

Peredur met a party of huntsmen, and the leader, a king, invited him to his palace, and despatched a page to bid his daughter entertain the knight till his return. Peredur was greeted joyfully by the princess and seated beside her at their repast. She laughed loudly at all his remarks, with the curious result that the page went back to the king to tell him that the youth seemed to be already the damsel's husband, or if not, would be so before long. The king thereupon set strong men upon Peredur and cast him into prison. His daughter, however, seems to have had free access to the dungeons and furnished her lover with the best of everything and even had her own couch brought in that she and Peredur might converse during the night. The next day when he learned that there was to be a battle between the king and his enemy, an earl, he begged her to provide horse and armor and promised to return that evening. Accordingly for three days Peredur issued forth incognito in a red surcoat and slew the men of the earl, and returned each night to his prison and the damsel. The fourth day he slew the earl himself. The princess then revealed the identity of the victor to her father, and the king offered Peredur his daughter in marriage and half his kingdom. She herself told the youth of her love, but he insisted on leaving her to seek the Castle of Wonders.

This episode is so obviously a compound of the Guingambresil formula

---

[65] *Romanische Forschungen*, XL, 251 ff.—Cf. *Rev. Celt.*, XLVII (1930), 39.

[66] J. Loth, *Mabinogion* (1913), II, 111–114.

and the three days tournament that it hardly needs discussion. Though the three days combat is an old folklore motif of quite independent origin,[67] its insertion here in place of the nocturnal attack was probably suggested by something in the tradition which neither the Guingambresil nor the Vergulaht version supplies. The idea of three successive combats has probably come down from Curoi's fight with the three heroes, Conall, Loegaire, and Cuchulinn, on three successive nights—a tradition which seems to survive in the three throws in *Wolfdietrich* and the three days temptation in *Gawain and the Green Knight*. Whether this conjecture be correct or not, there can be little doubt of the incorporation of the three-days tournament in a story of the Guingambresil type, derived from the Curoi cycle. The next tale from *Peredur* shows the intrusion of the same element into a story of the *Carl of Carlisle* type.

XV. The Gray Man Episode in *Peredur*

Professor Kittredge observed the marked similarity of detail between the *Carl* and this episode in *Peredur*, and hazarded the suggestion of a common French source.[68] There is nothing, of course, improbable in the view, though the source could not have been an immediate one.[69]

Peredur in the course of miscellaneous adventures finds his road blocked by a chained lion, sleeping beside a pit full of the bones of men and animals. He kills the lion and approaches a castle. Before it sits a huge, gray man, who expresses anger that his "porter," the lion, has not done his duty. Nevertheless, he and his sons escort Peredur into the castle, where the tables are laid with food and liquor. An old and a young woman of great size enter. Peredur is seated next the damsel, and during the meal she looks at him and grows sad. She declares her love and warns him that the next day he will have to fight the vassals of her father, the gray man, who are all giants. Peredur implores her to have his horse and arms placed in his lodging that night, and she arranges it. The next morning the wife and daughter of the gray man urge him to spare the youth from the approaching battle, but in vain. By evening, however, Peredur has killed a third of the giants. Again the women intercede with the gray man in vain. The battle is resumed and Peredur kills one of the gray man's sons. Once more the women, who are watching from the battlements, ask for peace. Peredur now kills the second son, and the gray man is persuaded to surrender. He declares that Peredur is the first Christian to escape from the valley alive. Peredur has him baptized and sends him to do homage to Arthur, and Arthur bestows on him the lordship of the valley.

The points of contact with the *Carl of Carlisle* are striking: the lion, the heap of bones, the fact that no previous visitor has escaped alive,

---

[67] *Haverford Essays* (Haverford, Pa., 1909), p. 248 ff.

[68] Kittredge, *op. cit.*, p. 260 ff.

[69] Loth, *Mabinogion*, II, 83–87.—The translation of *llwyt*, "gray," by "aux cheveux gris" is probably a mistake.

the giant host, his wife and daughter, the amorous developments at dinner, the submission of the giant to Arthur, and his obtaining the confirmation of his lordship. The bizarre love affairs of Gawain in the Carl's castle, however, have been reduced to a very simple and conventional form. The hero cherishes no adulterous passion for his host's wife; the daughter's passion for the hero leads only to laudable efforts to save his life. Equally significant is the substitution for the grotesque beatings and spear-throwings in the *Carl* of a daytime fight, divided into three stages. To be sure, there may be a vestige of a nocturnal combat in Peredur's request to have his arms placed in his lodging that night. But the actual test of the hero's valor is a three-days combat, as is clearly implied by the statement that by the evening of the first day Peredur had killed a third of the giants. The obvious analogies which the episode offers to the previous one leave no doubt on the matter. Once more we have a clear instance where one of the familiar patterns derived from the Visit to Curoi's Fortress has been contaminated by the extraneous motif of the three-days combat in lieu of the more grotesque or savage ordeals of the original. Indeed the Gray Man story, though it retains some of the savagery of its sources, has lost all trace of their inconsistency. There is no question regarding the host's presence, or his attitude toward the hero, or his feeling toward his daughter's little romance.

The adjective applied to the giant host, *llwyt*, meaning "gray,"[70] is ambiguous, since it may refer, like the adjective *melyn*, "yellow," applied to Kynon's host in *Owain*,[71] either to his clothing or to his hair. It would seem to be traditional since it fits the theory that Curoi, the host, famous as "the man in the gray mantle," reappears in *Peredur* as the "gray man," and in the *Carl* as gray-bearded. At this point it may not be irrelevant to note that the greenness of Bercilak has a very simple origin in the ambiguity of another word. Both in Irish and in Welsh, *glas* may mean either "gray" or "green." What neater explanation could there be for the fact that Curoi, the "man in the gray mantle," is represented in Arthurian legend by the Gray Man and the Green Knight?

XVI. The Besieged Lady in *Peredur*

Here once more the three-days combat appears in conjunction with a familiar form of the tradition we have been studying, this time with the *Chevalier à l'Espée* pattern.[72]

Passing through a devastated land Peredur arrived at a castle and was disarmed by eighteen lean youths. Their sister entered, the fairest lady ever seen. She welcomed Peredur, seated him at her side, and at supper favored him above all

---

[70] J. G. Evans, *White Book Mabinogion* (Pwllheli, 1907), col. 146.

[71] *Ibid.*, col. 225, 234 f.   [72] Loth, *Mabinogion*, II, 67–73.

others in the distribution of the meagre repast. When the hero had gone to his chamber, the youths commanded their sister to go to his bedside and offer herself to him as wife or *amie*. Terrified by their threats, she obeyed, and entered Peredur's chamber weeping. He awoke and learned that she was the lady of the castle, was sought in marriage by an earl whom she hated, and was being besieged by him till all her retainers were half-starved. The next day, indeed, she was expecting an attack by the earl's troops. She was ready to give herself to Peredur in return for his aid. Peredur magnanimously refused to take advantage of her offer until he had shown himself worthy of it by his deeds. The next morning he sallied forth alone to battle, and the evening of that day he overthrew the master of the earl's household and forced him to supply the castle with food and drink, and to return a third of the damsel's lands. The damsel was joyous that night. The second day was like the first: at the end of it the steward surrendered a third of the damsel's lands, and replenished her supplies. At the end of the third day the earl himself was vanquished, and Peredur remained three weeks with the lady to see that all the realm was restored to her. It was not till he departed that he declared his name and promised her his service.

Readily let it be confessed that this might seem to be but a patchwork of romantic commonplaces. Even the feature which we have found so characteristic of the tradition—the men of the castle sending their sister to be the mistress of a stranger knight—has been given a new interpretation, and there are none of the peculiar details that appear in the previous stories. Nevertheless, we have seen already two cases of the three-day combat as a development of the attack on Curoi's guests. And when it is combined with so familiar a development of the amours of Cuchulinn and Blathnat as the lady sent by her brother or father to a stranger knight's bed, the combination is hardly to be ascribed to coincidence. New rationalizations of the old patterns are precisely what our study has led us to expect. Here the most significant departure is the natural one of arguing that if the lord and lady of the castle are friendly to the hero, and if he for three days or nights fights with hostile forces, these forces must be the enemies of the lord and lady of the castle, not the lord or his subjects. This conclusion abolishes at a stroke the old difficulties about the presence of the host during the attack on the guest and his responsibility for it, and it furnishes a most plausible explanation for the nocturnal visit of the hostess to the hero's chamber. We shall now see that Crestien's version of this same story supplements the evidence of traditional origin.

XVII. The Clamadeus and Guingeron Episode in the *Conte del Graal*

This is one of the famous stories related by Crestien—Perceval's arrival at Belrepaire and his romantic championship of the chatelaine,

Blancheflor.[73] It hardly seems necessary to summarize it, for in general it corresponds to the preceding tale from *Peredur*. The differences that concern us are these: the lady acts on her own initiative in seeking Perceval's chamber; Perceval does not chastely send her away but demands her *druerie* as the immediate condition of his aid, and spends the night with her, mouth to mouth; the lady is named Blancheflor, her suitor Clamadeus, his seneschal Guingueron.[74]

Except for the first, these seem to be primitive features. It is an eloquent commentary on the theory that Crestien intended his Grail from the outset to be a holy Christian relic, that his hero is prepared for the vision of it by several days of indulgence in the cardinal sin of *luxuria*. More remarkable still, no reproach is ever addressed to him on the subject of his lechery; and his failure to meet the Grail test is attributed explicitly to another cause. Indeed the Blancheflor liaison has all the pagan atmosphere of the *Carl* and the Galagandreis episode.

We have already seen the lady Flor de Mont in a predicament very similar to Blancheflor's, and we saw that her name was traditional. It seems reasonable to conclude that Blancheflor is a mere embellishment on the traditional name, due to the influence of the popular romance of *Flores et Blanchefleur*. We have seen also in two stories from *Peredur* that the host, originally the attacker of the hero, has been converted into the besieger of the castle. Two of the hosts we have studied have been named Cardoil and Caṛadas, and one Gringamore. The relation of the last name to Guingueron may remain problematical, but the relation of Cardoil and Caradas to Clamadeus seems to me probable. For there is not a little converging evidence that, just as the common noun *bachlach* applied to Curoi reappears in several forms in Arthurian romance, the name Curoi itself was at some stage confused with the Welsh name Caradoc and so survived in all manner of corruptions.[75] One clear case is in the *Vulgate Lancelot* where we learn that a giant, Carados, carried off a woman from her lover, brought her to his castle, fought with Lancelot, who pursued him to his lair, was betrayed by the damsel, who gave his sword, with which alone he could be slain, to Lancelot, and that he died crying out against her treachery.[76] This is, of course, in outline the story of Curoi's abduction of Blathnat and her rescue by Cuchulinn,[77] and here we have Curoi under the name Carados. When, therefore, we find that in two separate derivates from the Visit to Curoi's Fortress the host

[73] Crestien de Troyes, *Conte del Graal*, ed. Baist, 1682–2695. Ed. Hilka, ll. 1706–2703.

[74] This form is given by MS. B.N. fr. 12577, and is supported by Wolfram's Kingrun. Cf. C. Potvin, *Perceval le Gallois*, II, 113.   [75] *PMLA*, XLV (1930), 431.

[76] H. O. Sommer, *Vulgate Version of the Arthurian Romances*, IV, 114–137.

[77] Thurneysen, *Irische Helden- und Kŏnigsage*, p. 434. Loomis, *op. cit.*, pp. 13–15.

is called Cardoil and Karadas, the case becomes impressive. Moreover we get in the *Vulgate Lancelot* a certain Claudas, "qui estoit li hons el monde qui plus amoit hache en grant melee, & bien sen sot aidier a grans cous doner,"[78] and whose portrait is said explicitly to be based on tradition.[79] "Li contes dist quil auoit bien. ix. pies de lonc a le mesure des pies de lors. Si auoit le viaire noir & gros. & les sorchiex velus & les iex gros & noirs, lun loing del autre. Il auoit le neis court & reskignies & le barbe rousse." Compare the portrait of Curoi: "A big, very ugly churl. . . There was not among the Ulstermen a hero who would reach half his size. . . Each of those two eyes standing out of his head as big as a caldron. . In his right hand an ax." And let us remember Sir Bercilak's reddish brown beard.[80] Carados, Cardoil, and Claudas are all giants hostile to Arthur and his knights, and all, together with Karadas, bear marked resemblances to Curoi. I do not believe, therefore, that in a story where Blancheflor plays the part of the "Little Flower," it is pure coincidence that the rôle of the hostile champion with whom the hero has to contend is taken by Clamadeus. It goes to show, as we have seen over and over again, that not only are the story patterns traditional, but also in many cases the names.

If the argument in regard to the Clamadeus and the Guingambresil episodes in the *Conte del Graal* holds water, we can then add these two elements to the others in Crestien's poem for which a Celtic descent has been shown. The Perceval *enfances* have been clearly related to those of Finn by Nutt and Pace.[81] The blood-drops in the snow have been derived from the same feature in the love-story of Deirdre by Zimmer and Professor Zenker.[82] The strange similarity between the interior of the Grail King's palace and that of King Conchobar has been brought out by Professor Nitze.[83] The joining of the sword in the Grail castle has been elucidated by an Irish parallel suggested by Professor Pennington.[84] Certain points of resemblance between the Chateau Merveil adventure and the *Voyage of Bran* were detected by Miss Weston.[85] The *eschacier* and the *Lit Périlleux* I first connected with the *Dream of Maxen* and the Visit to Curoi's Fortress.[86] The Grail itself and the scene in the Grail

---

[78] Sommer, *op. cit.*, III, 61.

[79] *Ibid.*, 26.

[80] *Gawain and the Green Knight*, ed. Tolkien and Gordon, l. 845: "al beuer-hwed."

[81] *Folklore Record*, IV (1881), 1 ff. *PMLA*, XXXII (1917), 598 ff.

[82] H. Zimmer, *Keltische Studien* (Berlin, 1884), II, 201 ff. *Rom. Forsch.*, XL (1926), 314–322.

[83] *Studies in Honor of A. M. Elliott* (Baltimore, 1911), I, 19 ff.

[84] *MLN*, XLII (1928), 534–536.

[85] J. L. Weston, *Legend of Sir Gawain*, p. 36 ff.

[86] *Celtic Myth and Arthurian Romance*, pp. 165–170.

castle I have endeavored to interpret in the light of many texts discovered by my predecessors.[87] What consistent hypothesis but the
Celtic can account both for large patterns and small details from the beginning to the end of Crestien's poem, and for much in the continuators
besides?

The presentation of my case regarding the Visit to the Perilous Castle
is concluded, at least for the nonce. If the argument from parallelism has
any validity at all, the derivation of the *Carl of Carlisle*, the Porte Noire
episode, *Gawain and the Green Knight*, and the Vergulaht episode, from
Irish traditions of the eighth century seems to me established. The remainder of the fifteen stories can easily be fitted into the genealogical
scheme. We find both conflation and contamination. We find both
meaningless, pointless variations such as occur through failings of
memory, by the side of purposeful variations which show the intelligence of the redactors operating through the centuries to rationalize the
apparent inconsistencies of the original Irish story. The notion of a
special creation of Arthurian romance between the years 1160 and 1180
does not seem to fit the facts.

No Arthurian scholar needs to be reminded that if the derivation I
have set forth is correct, it involves much more than the fifteen derivates
examined. For these in turn are obviously the cognates of many more
tales of the Round Table cycle. If the fifteen are descended from the
two Irish tales concerning Curoi and Cuchulinn, so must be a large
number of other tales of the Visit to the Perilous Castle. Let me enumerate some of the more obvious cognates. To III are related all the obedience tests, listed by Kittredge, in *Ider*, *Humbaut*, and the *exempla*. To V
the Isle d'Or episode in *Le Bel Inconnu* seems to be related.[88] VII is, of
course, akin to the whole *Lit Périlleux* group. VIII is related to the
Pèlerinage Charlemagne,[89] and more remotely to the Montesclaire adventure in the *Conte del Graal*. The *Mule Sans Frein* lies between VIII and
IX. The Ade episode in *Lanzelet* seems to be a fusion of VIII and XIV.
IX, as I have already pointed out, through its contamination from the
Welsh Bran cycle, is connected with the Bran de Lis combat and the
fights of Gawain and Bohors in Corbenic. X, if we realize that Lyones
and Lynete owe their separate existence to the requirements of the story
and were originally one person, is certainly close kin to the tale in
Crestien's *Charrette* where a damsel first tempts Lancelot to lie with her
and then subjects him to an attack by her servants bearing axes. XI bears
affinity to the whole Beheading Test group. XII has close analogs in

---

[87] *Romanische Forschungen*, XLV (1931), 66–94. *Speculum*, VIII (1933), 415 ff.
[88] Cf. Krappe in *Romania*, LVIII (1932), 426, for other Irish elements.
[89] *Mod. Phil.*, XXV (1928), 335–340.

Peredur and *Diu Krone*. Branches IV and IX of *Perlesvaus* contain recognizable though confused fragments of the Visit to the Perilous Castle. And the list might be greatly extended.

Let me repeat: Can all these stories be satisfactorily derived from Crestien de Troyes or his immediate followers according to the scheme of chronological development adopted by Bruce and Professor Golther?

Scotland and the Arthurian Legend

(Proceedings of the Society of Antiquaries of Scotland Vol. LXXXIX, Session 1955-1956)

SCOTLAND AND THE ARTHURIAN LEGEND.

In approaching the vast body of legends which grew up about the name of a hero called Arthur, one is faced with innumerable questions, but none looms up so promptly and so obviously as the question of historic fact: Did the Arthur of legend live, or was he a mythical figure? Not so long ago there were scholars of eminence who seriously believed that he was in origin a bear-god or an agricultural divinity, arguing from the linguistic roots *art* and *ar*.[1] But now there is an almost unanimous vote of both philologues and historians that he was a man of flesh and blood. Professor Kenneth Jackson, who is unsurpassed in his command of the various kinds of evidence, has expressed himself in a chapter due to be published in 1958 as follows: "Did King Arthur ever really exist? The only honest answer is 'We don't know, but he may very well have existed.' The nature of the evidence is such that proof is impossible."

In spite of this noncommittal answer Jackson does offer a good deal of testimony—some of it set down within a hundred years of the period when the hero of the Britons lived if he lived at all—and I believe that the latest and most authoritative writers on Britain in the Dark Ages—Oman, Collingwood, Hodgkin and Stenton—display no scepticism on the subject.[2] Though conclusive proof is lacking, it is hard to believe that the passionate devotion of the Welsh, Cornish and Bretons to the memory of Arthur was evoked by a med..val and male Mrs Harris. In spite of the silence of Gildas and others writing in the 6th century, it is far more likely than not that a British commander named Arthur flourished about the year 500, perhaps a little earlier or a little later.

The next question which I should like to raise is: Did the historic Arthur have any particular connection with what is now Scotland? Was he a Briton from the north like Cunedda? Or did he conduct campaigns like those of William Wallace (who, to judge by his name, must have been of Welsh ancestry) north of the Tweed and the Solway Firth? Skene first

---

[1] J. Rhys, *Studies in the Arthurian Legend* (Oxford, 1891), pp. 25–40. E. K. Chambers, *Arthur of Britain* (London, 1927), pp. 206–11.

[2] C. Oman, *England before the Norman Conquest*, 8th ed. (London, 1938), pp. 211 f. F. M. Stenton, *Anglo-Saxon England* (Oxford, 1943), pp. 3 f. R. H. Hodgkin, *History of the Anglo-Saxons*, 3rd ed. (Oxford, 1952), pp. 122, 182.

elaborated the thesis that Arthur's military career was confined to the North,[1] and a Fellow of the Society of Antiquaries, John S. Stuart Glennie, published in 1869 an impressive essay, *Arthurian Localities*, supporting Skene.[2] Both relied largely on the identification of the sites of Arthur's battles, as given by Nennius, with places in Scotland. Nennius, be it remembered, was a Welsh priest who, early in the 9th century, collected a miscellaneous body of facts, and what purported to be facts, about British history. In an oft-quoted passage,[3] dealing with the period right after the death of Hengist, Nennius says that Arthur fought against them—apparently the Saxons and the Jutes of Kent—and defeated them in twelve battles. He gives the name of the place where each victory occurred, and, since four battles are listed as occurring in one place, there are nine names in all. It is, of course, easy to sit down with a large-scale map of Northern England and Southern Scotland and match each of the nine names in Nennius with something resembling it on the map. That is what Skene and Glennie did. But Professor Jackson submitted the list to scientific scrutiny,[4] and found that only one site can be placed with any certainty in Scotland, namely, *silva Celidonis* or *Coit Celidon*, which is, of course, the Caledonian Forest. But it is hard to see how a general, operating against the Saxons and Jutes about the year 500, could have encountered them in Strathclyde or the vicinity, where, so far as we know, there were no Germanic invaders then or later. The same objection holds against *Urbs Legionis*, *i.e.*, Chester. Jackson concludes that the one authentic victory listed by Nennius is that of *Mons Badonis*, and that if it was won by Arthur about 500, it must have been fought on the eastern border of the Salisbury Plain, near Swindon or Faringdon. The other battle sites, wherever they actually were, may have witnessed the prowess of Arthur, or they may not. A priest of South Wales, living three hundred years later, is no trustworthy witness on matters of detail.

Glennie found corroboration for his thesis in all manner of local associations.[5] He maintained that "at or in the neighbourhood of every one of these battle-sites thus identified, we find existing, from the time of our oldest charters, and other documents, to this day, places with Arthur's name, or traditions of Arthur's history." There are two weaknesses in this argument. In the first place, associations which go no farther back than the 12th century—and none of them do—carry little weight, for even before 1100 the renown of Arthur was beginning to spread beyond Wales. In the second place, if such evidence is valid, Wales and the Welsh border

[1] J. S. Stuart Glennie, *Arthurian Localities* (Edinburgh, 1869); also published as introduction to Early English Text Soc., No. 36.

[2] W. F. Skene, *Four Ancient Books of Wales* (Edinburgh, 1868), I, 52–58.

[3] Chambers, *op. cit.*, pp. 1–12, 238 f. F. Lot, *Nennius et l'Historia Brittonum* (Paris, 1934), I, 194–6. E. Faral, *Legénde Arthurienne* (Paris, 1929), III, 38 f.

[4] *Modern Philology*, XLIII (1945), 44–57.

[5] Glennie, *op. cit.*, p. 108.

would have a stronger claim, for, in the *Mirabilia* included in Nennius' book, Arthur is connected with a cairn in Brecknockshire and a burial mound in Herefordshire,[1] and that is about four centuries earlier than any similar topographical links with Arthur are recorded for Scotland. As for later times, Welsh toponymy and folk-tradition can match those of Scotland as evidence of interest in Arthur. But in neither country does the existence of an Arthur's Oven or an Arthur's Table mean that the historic hero ever bivouacked there.

Of course, Arthur might have been a Briton of the North, but he could with equal probability have come from Cornwall or Wales. Indeed, he might have been born in eastern England before it was overrun by the Saxons and Angles. That Arthur lived and gave the Saxons a good thrashing in the South of England about the year 500 seems pretty clear, but where he was born, no one knows nor is there the slightest probability that anyone ever will know. Some day a pillar stone marking the true place of his burial (as distinct from the hollow oak found at Glastonbury in 1191) may be dug up, but that his birth certificate or baptismal register will come to light is something that even the most sanguine cannot hope for.

Another ardent believer in Arthur's activities in the North is Professor Nitze.[2] For him Arthur was a Roman, Lucius Artorius Castus, commander of the Sixth Legion, who is on record as fighting in Dalmatia and Armorica, and who may have fought in Britain as well against the Picts and Scots. But he lived in the 2nd century, and I find it hard to understand how this Roman general, even though his middle name was Artorius, was converted into the champion of the Britons against the Saxons in the 5th century or slightly later, and how he came to rouse the ardent loyalty of all the descendants of the Britons—Welsh, Cornish and Bretons—for a thousand years. Lucius Artorius Castus certainly lived and made history in a small way in Britain in Hadrian's time, but he was not our Arthur.

A remarkable early reference, presumably to the Arthur of Nennius, has been brought to the fore in recent years, and it brings us, though not Arthur, back to the North again. There is a Welsh poem called the *Gododdin*, dealing with a defeat inflicted on the Britons of Southern Scotland by the Angles.[3] This poem, in its original form, is now accepted by Welsh scholars as a composition of about the year 600. In it a certain British warrior is said to have "glutted black ravens on the rampart of the city, though he was not Arthur." That is, he slew many Angles, but his prowess was not equal to that of Arthur. What can one infer from this fleeting allusion? Not that Arthur was a North Briton, not that he came from the same region north of the Tweed as did most of the warriors celebrated in the

---

[1] Chambers, *op. cit.*, pp. 239 f. Lot, *op. cit.*, p. 216. Faral, *op. cit.*, III, 61.

[2] *Pub. Mod. Lang. Assoc.*, LXIV (1949), 585–96.

[3] *Gododdin*, ed. I. Williams (Cardiff, 1938). Discussed by Williams, *Lectures on Early Welsh Poetry* (Dublin, 1944), pp. 65–70, and by K. H. Jackson in *Antiquity*, XIII (1939), 25–34.

poem, but simply that his reputation had reached the North and become established there round the year 600. There is nothing in the *Gododdin* to force us to reject the historic probability that Arthur had achieved his pre-eminence by his campaigns against the Saxons in Southern England.

In fact, it seems to me very significant that the other early Welsh poems, which are roughly contemporary with the *Gododdin* and which deal with historic figures of the same general area, King Urien of Rheged and his son Owein, there is no further mention of Arthur.[1] This silence would be unnatural if he had won any great victories in the North two or three generations earlier. This silence would be quite natural if one thinks of Arthur as one who fed the ravens with the carcases of Saxons in the Thames Valley or on the Berkshire Downs, where about 500 the Saxons would be found. It is the reputation of Arthur in the North which is attested by the *Gododdin*, not his activity in any particular part of Britain. Even Nennius' specific reference to the victory of the Wood of Celyddon must be discounted on Nennius' own testimony that Arthur fought against Octha, King of Kent.

There is a long gap between Nennius and the next author to link Arthur with Scotland. A Flemish cleric, Lambert of St Omer, in a work entitled *Liber Floridus* and dated 1120 makes the following remarkable statement:[2] "There is in Britain, in the land of the Picts, a palace of the warrior Arthur, built with marvelous art and variety, in which the history of all his exploits and wars is to be seen in sculpture. He fought twelve battles against the Saxons who had occupied Britain." Lambert then gives a list of the twelve victories of Arthur according to Nennius. What could have suggested this reference to the sculptures in the land of the Picts? We do not know but we can guess. A Corpus Christi Cambridge manuscript, a century or so later in date than Lambert's work, has a gloss on Nennius which states that Carausius, the emperor, built a round house with polished stones (*politis lapidibus*) on the bank of the River Carron.[3] Dr Steer of the Ancient Monuments Commission points out that this gloss refers to the Roman temple which was known as early as 1293 as the Oven of Arthur, for it too was round and made of polished stones and lay near the River Carron.[4] Did Lambert find a similar gloss in his copy of Nennius—a gloss which connected this building with Arthur rather than Carausius? Could he then have converted the polished stones into sculptures and found a subject

---

[1] I. Williams in *Proc. of Brit. Acad.*, XVIII (1932), 270 ff. Morris-Jones in *Y Cymmrodor*, XXVIII (1918), 64–71, 151–99.

[2] Faral, *op. cit.*, I, 256 n. Migne, *Pat. Lat.*, CLXIII, col. 1012. R. S. and L. H. Loomis, *Arthurian Legends in Medieval Art* (New York, 1938), p. 15.

[3] Lot, *op. cit.*, I, 165, n. 8. John Leslie, bishop of Ross, expressed the opinion in *De Origine Moribus et Rebus Gestis Scotorum* (1578) that Arthur was the builder of a stone house formerly existing not far from the River Carron.

[4] Glennie, *op. cit.*, pp. 42 f.

for the sculptures in Nennius' list of Arthur's victories? These questions cannot be answered in the affirmative or the negative; but such efforts to elaborate the scanty materials available were characteristic of other authors than Lambert of St Omer. Geoffrey of Monmouth was writing a few years later, say in the early eleven-thirties, and it is abundantly clear that the *Historia Regum Britanniae* is largely compounded of the rough stones of tradition freely shaped and adorned by Geoffrey's imagination.

In 1125, five years after the composition of the *Liber Floridus*, William of Malmesbury completed the *Gesta Regum Anglorum* and testified[1] that Arthur was the subject of fantastic tales told by the Bretons: "Artur de quo Britonum nugae hodieque delirant"—very significant testimony to the role played by Breton story-tellers in the diffusion of the fascinating but wild and incoherent traditions which had gathered about Arthur. William did not associate Arthur in any way with Scotland, but he did mention Arthur's nephew Gawain under the name Walwen, and said that he had reigned over Walweitha, that is, Galloway.[2] First, it should be observed that the form Walwen is not Welsh; nothing resembling it ever appears in a Welsh text, and it is most probable that the chronicler heard it from Breton lips—a corroboration of his testimony about the circulation of Breton tales about Arthur. All this, of course, is easy to understand when one realizes that many Breton lords fought for William the Conqueror[3] at Hastings and were rewarded with lands, and others followed after. Sir Frank Stenton declared: "There is hardly an English county in which the Breton element is not found, and in some counties its influence was deep and permanent." For example, there was the great Breton earldom of Richmond in Yorkshire.[4] Breton lords would be followed, of course, by Breton entertainers and would welcome professional story-tellers to relieve the tedium of long winter evenings when there was no television and no radio. Bédier was clear on the point: after the battle of Hastings "toute la civilisation normande se trouva brusquement transplantée telle quelle dans les châteaux d'Outre-Manche, et les jongleurs armoricains y suivirent leurs patrons: jongleurs armoricains, mais plus qu'a demi romanisés, mais vivant au service de seigneurs français, et contant pour leur plaire."[5] This is a fact of capital importance. Breton story-tellers and singers would be bilingual and could address Anglo-Norman audiences as well as Breton. Devoted to the memory of their ancestral hero, they drew heavily on the Welsh store-house of romantic fiction about Arthur. They adapted it to

---

[1] Chambers, *op. cit.*, p. 250. William of Malmesbury, *Gesta Regum Anglorum*, ed. W. Stubbs, Rolls Series, I, 11. R. S. Loomis, *Wales and the Arthurian Legend* (Cardiff, 1956), pp. 183–5.

[2] Chambers, *op. cit.*, p. 250. William of Malmesbury, *op. cit.*, II, 342.

[3] F. M. Stenton, *1st Century of English Feudalism* (Oxford, 1932), pp. 24 f., 28.

[4] *Victoria History of the County of York, North Riding*, ed. W. Page (London, 1914), pp. 2 f. *Annales de Bretagne*, XLIII (1935), 265 ff.

[5] Thomas, *Tristan*, ed. J. Bédier (Paris, 1905), II, 126 f.

the taste of Anglo-Normans and Frenchmen and thus spread his fame and that of his Round Table throughout the western world.[1]

The fact, however, that William of Malmesbury made Gawain king of Galloway probably has no significance. In the Middle Ages no principle of historiography was more solidly established than the idea that places took their names from persons. The early history of Rome was sufficient guarantee for it, and so was Vergil's *Aeneid.* William, therfore, had no difficulty in believing that Walweitha, Galloway, took its name from Walwen, Gawain. But there is nothing to support this derivation, and I have elsewhere presented ample evidence to show that the name Walwen or Gawain had an origin which completely eliminates the possibility of a connection with Galloway.[2] Indeed, two scholars of eminence, J. D. Bruce and Edward Brugger,[3] agree that the association is no better than Geoffrey of Monmouth's linking King Leir with Leicester and Coel with Colchester.

As for Geoffrey himself, everyone knows that he was the perpetrator of one of the most successful hoaxes in the world's history, the *Historia Regum Britanniae* (c. 1136). Though born probably at Monmouth, and for a large part of his life a resident of Oxford, he was almost certainly of Breton extraction. Sir John Lloyd, Sir Edmund Chambers and Tatlock all came to this conclusion in view of his marked bias in favour of the Bretons as against the Welsh,[4] and in one manuscript he actually refers to himself as Brito.[5] That in the 12th century did not mean a Welshman, for he says himself that after the time of Cadwallader the Welsh "non vocabantur Britones sed Gualenses." [6] He conceived the bold idea of fabricating a history of Britain from the beginnings, taking advantage of the enormous prestige which the Breton story-tellers had built up around their ancestral hero. In the phrase of William of Newburgh, he even made the little finger of Arthur thicker than the loins of Alexander the Great.[7] But he did his work so cleverly that William was one of the very few who saw through the sham. Almost everyone else accepted the *Historia Regum Britanniae* as a veracious chronicle.

Geoffrey also linked Gawain with Scotland and in a similar, though not the same, way as William of Malmesbury. He decided that Lothian

[1] R. S. Loomis, *Arthurian Tradition and Chrétien de Troyes* (New York, 1949), pp. 15–22, 27–32. *Göttingische Gelehrte Anzeigen*, 1890, pp. 788 ff. *Kultur der Gegenwart*, ed. P. Hinneberg (Berlin, Leipzig, 1909), Teil I, Abt. XI, I, 11–15, 60–65. *Zeits. f. franz. Sprache u. Literatur*, XX[1] (1898), 79–162; XLIV[2] (1922), 78–87.   [2] Loomis, *Arthurian Tradition*, pp. 146–54.

[3] J. D. Bruce, *Evolution of Arthurian Romance* (Baltimore, Halle, 1923), I, 21 n. *Zeits. f. franz. Sprache*, XXXIII[2] (1908), 59 f.

[4] *English Historical Review*, LVII, 466 f. Chambers, *op. cit.*, pp. 23 f., 90. J. S. P. Tatlock, *Legendary History of Britain* (Berkeley, Calif., 1950), 396–402, 439 f., 443.

[5] Faral, *op. cit.*, III, 189, variants.

[6] Loomis, *Wales and the Arthurian Legend*, pp. 181–4. Giraldus Cambrensis says (*Opera*, ed. Dimock, Rolls Series, VI, 179): "Usque in hodiernum, barbara nuncupatione et homines Wallenses et terra Wallia vocitatur."

[7] *Chronicles of the Reigns of Stephen, Henry II and Richard I*, ed. R. Howlett, Rolls Series, I, 11.

got its name from a certain Loth,[1] known in Breton tradition as the father of Gawain.[2] So Gawain became for Geoffrey and his translators heir to the lordship of Lothian. Nothing much came of this, however. A rival tradition was soon in the field, which made Loth king of Orkney, and as a result Gawain and his brothers are much more commonly associated in the romances with the Orkney Isles than with Lothian.[3]

Geoffrey arbitrarily took over Urien, historic king of Rheged in the late 6th century and ancestor of the present Lord Dynevor,[4] made him a contemporary of Arthur, and represented him as restored to his royal throne of Moray by the generous Arthur.[5] Likewise Angusel, king of Albania, that is, Scotland between Lothian and Moray, was restored by Arthur to his kingdom.[6] Geoffrey later makes it quite plain that Urien held Moray and Angusel held Albany as Arthur's vassals; they were invited to the coronation as "reges subditi." [7] There can be no doubt of the implications of this claim, and the history of Scotland might have been somewhat different if it had not been made. For when Edward I in 1301 had his secretaries draw up a statement of his rights to the overlordship of Scotland, they based it largely on Geoffrey's *Historia*.[8] It is not unlikely that the Oxford *magister*, sitting at his desk, had a fatal influence on Scottish-English relations, and it was all done by scribbling a few lines with his quill pen.

But Geoffrey's book had a more immediate and romantic effect in Scotland. Characteristically, he had created from the Welsh name for the city of York, Ebrauc, a king of Britain named Ebraucus,[9] and placed his reign to synchronize with that of King David of Judea. Geoffrey credited Ebraucus with the foundation not only of York but also of three other towns: Alclud, Castellum Puellarum and Mons Dolorosus—four foundations in all.[10] Alclud, defined as lying in the direction of Albany, is easily recognised as Dumbarton on the Clyde, but what did Geoffrey mean when he wrote Castellum Puellarum? He gives it as an alternative name for *Oppidum Montis Agned*, but that does not help us much, for though Nennius placed Arthur's eleventh battle at Mons Agned, Professor Jackson assures us that it is impossible to identify the site[11] and the *Historia* merely implies that it, like Alclud, was "versus Albaniam." However, we do know that in 1141 King David of Scotland came down into England to fight on behalf of his niece, the Empress Matilda, against the supporters of King Stephen.[12] In

[1] Faral, *op. cit.*, III, 225, 237.
[2] Loomis, *Arthurian Tradition*, pp. 148–50.
[3] *Ibid.*, pp. 71 f.
[4] See early editions of Burke's *Peerage* under Dynevor.
[5] Faral, *op. cit.*, III, 237.   [6] *Ibid.*
[7] *Ibid.*, III, 242, ". . . reges etiam et duces sibi subditos ad ipsam festivitatem convocare. . . ."
[8] T. Rymer, *Foedera*, ed. Clerke and Holbrooke (London, 1816), I, 932. *Speculum*, XXVIII (1953), 121 f.
[9] Tatlock, *op. cit.*, p. 12.
[10] Faral, *op. cit.*, III, 97.
[11] *Modern Philology*, XLIII, 52.
[12] *Chronicles of the Reigns of Stephen*, etc. ed. Howlett, III, 75–83.

this enterprise he was allied with his nephew, Robert of Gloucester, and spent several weeks at Oxford. Now Robert was the principal dedicatee of Geoffrey's *Historia*[1] and must have possessed a copy. Geoffrey was living at Oxford.[2] It is hard to believe that Robert did not mention the sensational new history to King David, and call his attention to the many references to Scotland. One can well imagine that he proposed that such a knowledgeable man as the author be summoned to the royal presence and that a dialogue ensued, somewhat like this: "Master Geoffrey, I see that Ebraucus founded three cities in the North. I recognise Alclud, the fortress on the Clyde; but where and what is this Castellum Puellarum?" Geoffrey replied: "Sire, it is your own royal fortress of Edinburgh." This dialogue, of course, is vouched for by no contemporary, but it is certain that in the next year, 1142, King David began using Castellum or Castrum Puellarum as an alternative title for his castle of Edinburgh.[3] The name remained for centuries an official designation in chronicles and documents, and in at least two French texts composed within a decade or two of 1200, *Fergus* and *Doon*, the identification of the Château des Pucelles with Edinburgh is clear.[4]

The title has always been a mystery; why should Auld Reekie be known as the Castle of Maidens?[5] The *Chronicle of Lanercost* offered the explanation that King Edwin, the founder, placed his seven daughters there for safety.[6] In recent times it has been urged that the name was due to a nunnery established by St Monenna.[7] But this is a mere guess, for there is no record of such a house of virgins. Furthermore, why would David suddenly start using Castellum Puellarum in the year 1142, when the saint had been in her grave for over 250 years? It is far more likely that the title was derived from Geoffrey.

It is probable, moreover, that Geoffrey did not invent the title and arbitrarily apply it to Edinburgh. For early in the 13th century the author of the Breton lai of *Doon* not only identified the Château des Pucelles with Daneborc, but he also told a story of a beautiful and proud virgin, mistress of the country, who dwelt there with her maidens.[8] She was won, however, by the hero Doon and gave birth to a son, whose story bears a marked resemblance to that of Gawain:[9] he is born out of wedlock; after he is grown up, his

[1] Chambers, *op. cit.*, pp. 41–44.   [2] *Ibid.*, p. 23.
[3] A. C. Laurie, *Early Scottish Charters Prior to* A.D. *1153* (Glasgow, 1905), pp. 112, 123, 146. G. Chalmers, *Caledonia* (Paisley, 1887–92), IV, 555–9.
[4] *Fergus*, ed. E. Martin (Halle, 1872), p. 106. *Romania*, VIII (1879), 61.
[5] On places called Maiden Castle, see R. E. M. Wheeler, *Maiden Castle, Dorset* (Oxford, 1943), pp. 8–11. J. Rhys, *Celtic Folklore, Welsh and Manx* (Oxford, 1901), I, 156 f.; Camden, *Britannia*, rev. E. Gibson (London, 1753), II, 822; Leland's *Itinerary*, ed. L. Toulmin Smith (London, 1909), IV, 31; V, 147.
[6] *Chronicon de Lanercost*, ed. J. Stevenson (Edinburgh, 1839), p. 179; trans. H. Maxwell (Glasgow, 1913), pp. 144 f.
[7] *Speculum*, XVII (1942), 253. W. J. Watson, *Place Names* (Edinburgh, 1926), p. 156.
[8] *Romania*, VIII, 61–64.
[9] Loomis, *Arthurian Tradition*, pp. 112 f. *Romania*, XXXIX (1910), 19–23. H. O. Sommer, *Vulgate Version of the Arthurian Romances* (Washington, 1909–16), II, 317.

mother sends him away with a ring as a recognition token; he meets his father incognito in combat, overthrows him, and only when his father asks his name, does recognition follow. Now in early French romance Gawain's mother was named Morcades, and Morcades also appears as a queen in a castle of ladies.[1] Most important is the fact that in four romances Morcades is the wife of King Loth of Lothian.[2] Other facts show that Morcades is simply a variation on the name Morgain la Fée.[3]

So we know that the Castle of Maidens was Edinburgh. We know that the mistress of the Castle of Maidens was Morgain la Fée. We know that, though she had various lovers and at least two husbands, one of them was King Loth of Lothian. As Queen of Lothian, Morcades or Morgain could have dwelt in several castles with her attendant maidens, but none would have suited her so well as the great fortress of Edinburgh. Once the tradition was established that Morgain la Fée was wooed and won by Loth, the eponymous king of Lothian, it was a matter of plain logic that Edinburgh was the Castle of Maidens.

What happened then was this, as I see it. In the early years of the 12th century and later, Breton *conteurs* came across the Tweed to find a welcome from the Breton and Norman lords. It is not without significance that the first Scottish ancestor of the Stuart line was a Breton, whom David I appointed his *dapifer* or steward. The Breton entertainers were only too ready to localise their tales wherever they found patrons, and they have left their traces in three Breton lais centered in Scotland—*Doon*, already mentioned, *Desiré* and *Gurun* (preserved only in a Norse translation).[4] They were presumably responsible for linking Morgain la Fée to King Loth, for linking Loth to Lothian, and for thus placing Morgain and her maidens in Edinburgh castle. I have little doubt that Geoffrey, himself a Breton, had picked up this tradition when he boldly placed the Castellum Puellarum among King Ebraucus' foundations in the North. It is proof of his astuteness that he so often appropriated to his uses traditions which already enjoyed a certain currency.

A remarkable confirmation of this inference regarding the connection of Morgain la Fée with Edinburgh comes from the ballad, *The Queen of Scotland*,[5] collected by Peter Buchan, corresponding member of the Society of Antiquaries of Scotland. Scholars recognised over sixty years ago that the latter part of this poem told a story obviously parallel to a story of Caradoc of the Short Arm related in the first continuation of Chrétien de Troyes's

[1] *Romania*, xxxix, 19–23. J. L. Weston, *Legend of Sir Perceval* (1906–9), i, 193.

[2] Loomis, *Arthurian Tradition*, p. 114.

[3] *Ibid.*, pp. 112–6, 302–6, 451–7.

[4] *Ibid.*, pp. 112–6, 269–72, 290 f. *Desiré, Graelent, and Melion*, ed. E. M. Grimes (New York, 1928), pp. 52–75. *Studia Neophilologica*, xiv (1942), 1–24.

[5] F. J. Child, *English and Scottish Popular Ballads*, v, 176 f. P. Buchan, *Ancient Ballads and Songs of the North of Scotland* (Edinburgh, 1828), i, 46–49.

Perceval.[1] The ballad, therefore, contained Arthurian material dating back to the year 1200. What about the first part of the *Queen of Scotland*? Three points are noteworthy: 1. The Queen's abode is "Reekie's towers," *i.e.*, Edinburgh Castle; 2. Her bower has "pictures round it set." 3. She tries to seduce the young hero, in vain. Now we have seen that Morgain was the mistress of the Castle of Maidens; three medieval authors give elaborate descriptions of the mural paintings in her palace;[2] she repeatedly tried to seduce knights of Arthur's court, and was rebuffed. All of these traditions are represented in the French *Mort Artu*, which places Morgain's castle, where she had tried to seduce Lancelot in vain, within two days' ride of Edinburgh (Taneborc), describes its mural paintings, and tells how Arthur was served at table and attended to his bedchamber by damsels only.[3] This French romance and the Scottish ballad, though separated by an interval of more than six centuries, preserve variant versions of the same tradition. The association of Morgain with Edinburgh was, therefore, very old and very persistent, even though her name was early lost and she became the anonymous Queen of Scotland.

One may be struck by the inconsistency of these traditions about the mistress of the Castle of Maidens. Can it be that the betrayed and deserted virgin of the lai of *Doon*, the wife of King Loth of Lothian, mother of Gawain, and the lustful temptress of the Scottish ballad were originally one and the same, were all avatars, as it were, of Morgain la Fée? Anyone who makes the slightest investigation of this fascinating figure in medieval literature will find that she is an extreme example of Vergil's characterisation of her sex: "varium et mutabile."[4] And Mark Twain's Connecticut Yankee, who had made her personal acquaintance, declared: "I have seen a good many kinds of women in my time, but she laid it over them all for variety."

Not only was Geoffrey's Castellum Puellarum taken seriously as a name for the Scottish capital, but the third of King Ebraucus' foundations, Mons Dolorosus, was also identified with what was probably the most imposing Roman ruin in all Scotland, the fort of Trimontium in the parish of Melrose.[5] The author of *Fergus*, Guillaume le Clerc, writing early in the 13th century, shows a detailed and accurate knowledge of Scottish geography from Carlisle and Jedburgh in the south to Dunnottar Castle in the north.[6]

[1] *Modern Language Notes*, XIII (1898), 417 ff. *Romania*, XXVIII (1898), 214–31. *Continuations of the Old French Perceval of Chrétien de Troyes*, ed. W. Roach (Philadelphia, 1949), I, liii, 169–223.

[2] R. S. and L. H. Loomis, *Arthurian Legends*, pp. 16 f., 24 f.

[3] *Mort le Roi Artu*, ed. J. Frappier (Paris, 1936), pp. 44–47.

[4] R. S. Loomis, *Wales and the Arthurian Legend*, pp. 105–30.

[5] J. Curle, *Roman Frontier Post and Its People, the Fort of Newstead in the Parish of Melrose* (Glasgow, 1911).

[6] Brugger in *Miscellany of Studies in Romance Languages and Literatures in Honour of L. E. Kastner* (Cambridge, 1932), pp. 94–107. M. D. Legge, "Some Notes on the *Roman de Fergus*," in *T. Dumf. and Gall. A.S.*, XXVII (1950), 165–7.

He makes it quite plain that he identified Mont Dolerous with a fortress, overhanging a deep ravine, and that an alternative name was Maros (Melrose).[1] When I inquired of Mr Angus Graham, the Secretary of the Ancient Monuments Commission for Scotland, as to what this could mean, he promptly recognised it as a description of Trimontium. Surely anyone seeking to identify the remains of a city or fortress, allegedly founded in remote antiquity, could not have done better than to pitch on the imposing ruins of Trimontium, even though they did not actually go back to the days of Geoffrey's Ebraucus or the biblical David. Not only did the author of *Fergus* know Trimontium as Mont Dolerous, but even earlier, in 1171, the abbot of Melrose was referred to as the abbot of Mons Dolorosus,[2] obviously because the original site of Melrose Abbey lay not more than a mile or two from the great Roman fort on the Tweed.

Whereas the connection of King Loth and his wife Morcades or Morgain with Edinburgh was due to the artificial and comparatively late association of Loth with Lothian, there were earlier and rival traditions, and one of them linked Lothian to the Arthurian hero, Yvain or Ewain. Chrétien de Troyes referred about 1170 to an Yvain de Loenel, and Loenel is easily recognised as a corrupt form of Loeneis, a French name for Lothian.[3] Now, as a matter of historic fact, Owein, the original of Yvain, was the son of Urien, King of Rheged, and fought with his father against the sons of Ida, kings of Bernicia, late in the 6th century.[4] The authorities cannot place Rheged with certainty,[5] but Owein's activities would surely have taken him, if not into Lothian, at least into neighbouring territory. Apparently a tradition connecting Owein the son of Urien with what is now the Scottish Border Country lasted from the 6th to the 12th century. It is found not only in the name, Yvain de Loenel, but also in a *Life of St Kentigern*,[6] written between 1147 and 1164, which records that Ewen, son of King Urien, celebrated by the *histriones*,[7] that is, professional story-tellers, wooed the step-daughter of Leudonus, King of Leudonia (Lothian), surprised her beside a brook, ravished her, and begat on her the future St Kentigern. Leudonus is, of course, a fictitious character, invented to account for the name of his kingdom, Leudonia, just as Brutus of Trojan descent was invented to account for the name Britannia, and as Albanact was invented by Geoffrey of Monmouth to explain the name Albania. So we have the testimony of the *Life of St Kentigern* that in the middle of the 12th century

[1] *Fergus*, ed. E Martin, Halle, (1872), p. 121.

[2] A. O. Anderson, *Early Sources of Scottish History* (Edinburgh, 1922), II, 275.

[3] Chrétien de Troyes, *Erec*, ed. W. Foerster (Halle, 1890), vs. 1707. *Modern Philology*, XXXVIII, 282–6. For various forms of Lothian see *ibid.*, XXII, 186–91.

[4] F. Lot, *Nennius*, I, 73–75, 202, 224. Faral, *op. cit.*, III, 43.

[5] *Proc. of the Brit. Acad.*, XVIII, 292. Watson, *op. cit.*, p. 156. H. M. Chadwick, *Early Scotland* (Cambridge, 1949), pp. 144–60.

[6] *Lives of St Ninian and St Kentigern*, ed. A. P. Forbes (Edinburgh, 1874), 245–7.

[7] "Histrionum" is the correct reading of the manuscript, not "historiarum." *Romania*, XX (1893), 566.

a story was current that Owein or Ewen, son of Urien, was the lover of the step-daughter of the King of Lothian.

Still another and highly elaborated form of this tradition is preserved in Chrétien de Troyes's poem *Yvain*, composed between 1176 and 1181.[1] Chrétien not only refers in *Erec* to Yvain de Loenel, but in the later poem he tells how Yvain, son of Urien, setting out from Carlisle, came to a spring, killed the champion who defended the spring, and married his widow. This widow, we are told, was named Laudine and was the daughter of Duke Laudonez or Laudunet. Is it not obvious that Chrétien has preserved in the name of Yvain's bride, Laudine, and in that of her father, Laudonez, the very same tradition which the *Life of St Kentigern* gives us as to Ewen's amour with the step-daughter of the King of Leudonia? Though the nature of the amour differs widely in the two accounts, there can be little doubt that both have their origin in a legend that Owein was the lover of the King of Lothian's daughter.

We have two other versions in Arthurian romance of what must have been a vigorous tradition about the wooing and winning of the Lady of Lothian. In both the author has substituted his own hero for the traditional lover Owein. The author of *Fergus* relates that his hero, like Yvain, set out from Carlisle, soon after met "la dame de Lodien," and after many adventures wedded her at Jedburgh (Gedeorde).[2] Significantly, two *puceles* from a castle near by were invited to the nuptials, presumably in reference to Edinburgh as the Château des Puceles. Thus the romance of Fergus and the Lady of Lothian gives us a third form of the tradition which appears in the *Life of Kentigern* and in Chrétien's *Yvain*.

A fourth form is to be found in Malory's tale of Gareth of Orkney in the seventh Book of the *Morte d'Arthur*. Gareth takes the place of Yvain as hero, and his adventures at several points resemble those of Fergus, particularly in the great tournament which precedes the wedding.[3] Now Gareth's bride is Dame Lyones, and Lyones is Malory's form of Lothian. Quite clearly, then, a common tradition underlies the love stories of Fergus and "la dame de Lodien" and of Gareth and Dame Lyones.

It is highly probable that Malory's source for his seventh Book was an Anglo-Norman romance at least as old as *Fergus*, even as old as Chrétien's *Yvain*.[4] There existed, then, in the 12th century a flourishing tradition, first attached to the historic Owein, son of Urien, telling how he won the hand of the Lady of Lothian. The author of the *Life of Kentigern* refers explicitly to the tales of the *histriones* about Ewen, and one may safely

---

[1] Loomis, *Arthurian Tradition*, pp. 291, 301–3. Chrétien de Troyes, *Arthurian Romances*, Everyman's Lib., pp. 180–208.

[2] *Fergus*, ed. E. Martin.

[3] *Ibid.*, pp. 177–89. Malory, *Morte d'Arthur*, Bk. VII, ch. 27–31. Loomis, *Arthurian Tradition*, pp. 115 f.

[4] Loomis, *Arthurian Tradition*, pp. 439 f.

infer that this romantic legend, with its variations, was popularised by professional raconteurs, who, like actors, would employ intonation and gesture to give life and fire to their narratives. We can imagine that stories of the Lady of Lothian would be listened to with particular attention in the halls of the Anglo-Norman families who settled in the Lowlands of Scotland in the reign of David I. It is no wild fancy that Walter the Breton, ancestor of the Stuarts, with lands in Renfrewshire, was one of those who extended hospitality to the *histriones*, also of Breton extraction, who could tell him tales of Ewen and the Lady of Lothian or sing a lai of Doon and the mistress of the Castle of Maidens.

Chrétien followed his *Yvain* with his last and incomplete poem, *Perceval* or the *Conte du Graal*, composed about 1182. After about 6500 lines he interrupted the adventures of Perceval to take up those of Gawain and brought him to the borders of Galvoie.[1] Gawain was warned of the danger of crossing the border but insisted on proceeding. He came to a river, was ferried across to a magnificent castle inhabited by ladies, and after some strange adventures in this Castle of Ladies, was ferried back across the river and succeeded in vanquishing the knight who guarded the water-crossing of Galvoie.

Now Galvoie is unquestionably Galloway, and one remembers that William of Malmesbury as early as 1125 represented Gawain as King of Galloway. Moreover, Galloway was bounded by the River Nith. The late Professor Ritchie in his very informative lecture on *Chrétien de Troyes and Scotland*[2] pointed out that Robert Manning of Brunne, writing in 1328, identified the Castle of Maidens, not with Edinburgh, but with Caerlaverock, and Caerlaverock stands at the mouth of the Nith. It looks as if Ritchie had a strong case for identifying Chrétien's Castle of Ladies, situated on the border river of Galloway, with Caerlaverock.

But there is a stronger case, I believe, against it. If Gawain was conceived as King of Galloway, he should have had no difficulty in entering his own kingdom. Wolfram von Eschenbach, who, though dependent largely in his *Parzival* on Chrétien, had other traditional sources, called the river on which the Castle of Ladies stood Sabins,[3] and this has been recognised

---

[1] Chrétien de Troyes, *Percevalroman*, ed. A. Hilka (Halle, 1932), vss. 6600–8648.

[2] R. L. Graeme Ritchie, *Chretien de Troyes and Scotland* (Oxford, 1952), pp. 10, 23. Compare Loomis, *Arthurian Tradition*, p. 502, index sub Scottish Tradition. Though admiring Ritchie's lecture and feeling no prejudice against Scottish influence on Arthurian romance, I believe several of his suggestions erroneous.* His derivation of Esclados from Calathros (the Carse of Falkirk) and his equation of Calathros with Calatir are questionable. See Loomis, *ibid.*, pp. 112, 282. His statement that Chrétien never referred to a real person is mistaken. *Ibid.*, p. 492. There is no evidence that anyone acquainted with British geography of the 12th century called the Britons of Cumbria *Walenses* or *Waleis*. Estregale⁸ is not Strathclyde but South Wales. *Ibid.*, p. 71. The name Erec does not derive from Rhydderch but from Breton Guerec. *Ibid.*, pp. 70–74. There are three Welsh place-names in Chrétien's *Perceval*; Carlion, Gomeret, and Scaudone representing scribal corruptions of Caerleon, Gwynedd and Snowdon. *Ibid.*, pp. 481, 484, 490. The Roche de Sanguin is not likely to be Sanchar. *Ibid.*, p. 490.

[3] Loomis, *Arthurian Tradition*, p. 451.

by Germanists as the Severn, Geoffrey of Monmouth's *Sabrina flumen*. The Severn was well known in the Middle Ages as the old boundary between England and Wales.[1] Moreover, the French romance, *La Queste du Saint Graal*, confirms this identification of the river by telling how Galahad, like Gawain, was warned against crossing the borders, came to the River Severn, where stood the Castle of Maidens, overcame the knights who guarded the boundary, and was welcomed by the maidens.[2] Thus Wolfram and the author of the *Queste*, writing within a generation or so of Chrétien, agree that the boundary was the Severn, and this is corroborated by the Welsh *Peredur*, of about the same date, which makes Kaer Loyw, Gloucester, the abode of nine enchantresses,[3] and, of course, Gloucester is on the Severn. The converging testimony of Wolfram, the *Queste du Saint Graal*, and *Peredur*, pointing toward the Severn, proves that besides the tradition which localised Morgain's Castle of Maidens at Edinburgh, there was another which placed it on the border stream between England and Wales. Chrétien seems to have erred, then, in placing it on the border not of Gales (Wales) but of Galvoie (Galloway).

For this departure from tradition Ritchie provides an adequate and realistic motive.[4] The patron for whom Chrétien undertook the composition of *Perceval* was Philip, Count of Flanders, who supported William the Lion against Henry II and in 1173 sent troops to aid him. But after the King of Scots was captured in 1174, the sons of Fergus of Galloway revolted against his authority, slew all the strangers whom they could lay hands on, and destroyed the royal castles. For several years the Nith was a frontier between Galloway and the rest of Scotland, and a very dangerous one to cross. It is quite understandable, therefore, why Chrétien would have shifted the adventures of Gawain at the Castle of Maidens from the border of Gales to the border of Galvoie, and described the latter as one that no knight could pass and expect to return. To Philip of Flanders in 1182 the border of Galloway meant much more than the border of Wales. If Robert Manning one hundred and fifty years later identified the Castle of Maidens with Caerlaverock, he may well have come to this conclusion on the basis of Chrétien's poem or some derivative from it.

From the 13th-century documents we get new evidence of the tendency to make Arthurian connections with Scotland. A marginal note in a manuscript of Nennius tells how Arthur brought back from the Holy Land an image of the Virgin which he carried on his shoulders at the victory of Castellum Guinion, and how the fragments of this image were held in great veneration at Wedale.[5] A later hand added the information that Wedale

---

[1] *Ibid.*

[2] *Queste del Saint Graal*, ed. A. Pauphilet (Paris), pp. 46–51. Malory, *Morte d'Arthur*, Bk. XIII, ch. 14, 15.

[3] Loomis, *Arthurian Tradition*, p. 455. J. Loth, *Mabinogion*, 2nd ed. (Paris, 1913), II, 75 f.

[4] Ritchie, *op. cit.*, pp. 17 f.   [5] F. Lot, *op. cit.*, I, 195, n. 8.

was a town in Lodonesia (Lothian) six miles from the noble monastery of Melrose.   There is a consensus of opinion that this refers to Stow in the valley of Gala Water, where the church and a spring nearby are dedicated to St Mary.[1]

Stuart Glennie cited a document of the year 1293, referring to a "furnus Arthuri" or oven of Arthur, and he identified it with the building, already mentioned, on the bank of the River Carron, which was known centuries later as Arthur's O'on.[2]   Evidently the notion that any unexplained ancient structure went back to the days of Arthur was as well established in Scotland as it was in Wales or Cornwall.

From 14th-century documents Glennie collected further examples of the same tendency.   In 1339 David de Lindesay made a grant to the monks of Newbattle of certain lands bounded on the west by a line starting at the "fons Arthuri," the spring of Arthur.[3]   From a parliamentary record of 1367 we learn that Dumbarton was called "castrum Arthuri."[4]

One of the most curious and important of all the Arthurian localisations in Scotland is the identification of Sinadon with Stirling, which I have already treated elsewhere.[5]   This alternative name for Stirling is first given by Froissart, who was secretary for Queen Philippa of England between 1361 and 1368.   In 1365 he made an excursion into Scotland, sedulously gathering material, and when he visited Stirling he was gravely informed that this castle was in the old times of King Arthur called Sinaudon, and there on occasion the knights of the Round Table resorted.[6]   Now we have plenty of records about Stirling before 1365, but nowhere can one discover any verification of the claim that Sinaudon was an ancient name for Stirling.[7] It was, in fact, a name which turns up, not infrequently, in Arthurian romance in various but recognisable forms.[8]   In Biket's *Lai du Cor*, an Anglo-Norman poem which goes back to Chrétien's time, a King of Sinadoune was present at one of Arthur's feasts.   In a continuation of Chrétien's *Perceval* the boy hero declares that he was born at Sinadon.   Béroul, the author of a poem about Tristan (*c.* 1200), represented Isolt's squire as departing from Tintagel in Cornwall, coming to Caerleon in South Wales, and arriving at Isneldone, where he found Arthur seated at the Round Table.   *Le Bel Inconnu,* dealing with the career of Guinglain, Gawain's son, describes Sinadon as a ruinous town.[9]   In it the daughter of the King of Wales was imprisoned in the form

---

[1] Glennie, *op. cit.,* pp. 76 f.   F. J. Snell, *King Arthur's Country* (London), p. 213.   Faral, *op. cit.,* I, 148 f.

[2] Glennie, *op. cit.,* pp. 42 f.   Chalmers, *Caledonia,* I, 425.

[3] Glennie, *op. cit.,* pp. 83 f.

[4] *Ibid.,* p. 88.

[5] Loomis, *Wales and the Arthurian Legend,* pp. 1–18.

[6] Froissart, *Oeuvres,* ed. Kervyn de Lettenhove (Brussels, 1867), II, 313.

[7] W. C. Mackenzie, *Scottish Place-names* (London, 1931), p. 81.

[8] Loomis, *Wales and the Arthurian Legend,* p. 11.

   Ibid., pp. 11 f.   Renaut de Beaujeu, *Bel Inconnu,* ed. G. P. Williams (Paris, 1929).

of a dragon. The hero broke the spell by kissing the monster, she was at once transformed into a matchless beauty,[1] and the two were wedded in the city of Sinadon, now restored from its ruinous state. We are told that it was the capital of Wales. If we glance once more at Malory's seventh Book, we discover that Gareth was wedded to Dame Lyones at Kynke Kenadonne, described as a city and a castle "on the sands which marched nigh Wales." [2] It requires no Sherlock Holmes to perceive that Malory created the form Kenadonne by mistaking the *C* of a form Cenadonne for a hard *c* and, as he did elsewhere, substituting *k*.[3]

Such indications as we have, therefore, indicate that Sinadon or Senadon was in Wales, and several great scholars—Sir John Rhys, Gaston Paris, and J. D. Bruce—recognised in the word a form of Snowdon.[4] They were right as far as they went, but they did not go far enough. After all, Snowdon is a mountain, not a town or a castle. The name Snaudon, however, was current in slightly different spellings as an appellation of the whole region about the mountain, as Snowdonia is to-day. What we should look for is a town in that region which was sufficiently imposing as to impress beholders as worthy to be the capital of Wales in Arthur's time. Gaimar, the chronicler, writing about 1150, gives us the clue.[5] He says that there were three renowned cities of Wales, and the first and second named by him are easily identified as Caerleon and Caerwent, the Roman walled towns of South Wales. The third Gaimar called "la cité de Snauedun." This can apply only to the important Roman fortress of Segontium, situated on a hilltop, overlooking the Menai Strait, where at low tide the sandy flats are conspicuous. Even as early as Nennius' day legends had begun to attach themselves to the ruins of Segontium, and the Welsh tale, the *Dream of Maxen*, is partly localised there.[6] Just as Caerleon in South Wales became famous as a resort of Arthur, so apparently did Segontium in North Wales under its Anglo-Norman name of "la cité de Snaudon," and in its forlorn state it offered a perfect setting for the eerie story of the dragon princess of Wales.

But when one visits the site of Segontium to-day, though one may still look down from it on the sands of the Menai Strait, only the foundations remain. Edward I is known to have removed ashlar in 1283 from the Roman ruins and to have used it in the building of the stately castle we see at Caernarvon to-day.[7] The "cité de Sinadon" no longer existed except as

---

[1] For the history of this motif see *Studi Medievali*, XVII (1951), 104–13, and Ulrich von Zatzikhoven, *Lanzelet*, trans. K. G. T. Webster (New York, 1951), pp. 224–6.

[2] Malory, *Morte d'Arthur*, ed. H. O. Sommer (London, 1889), I, 213, 269 f.

[3] Loomis, *Arthurian Tradition*, p. 116, n. 49.

[4] Rhys, *Celtic Folklore*, II, 562. *Histoire Littéraire de la France*, XXX (1888), 174 n. Bruce, *Evolution*, II, 196.

[5] Gaimar, *Estorie des Engles*, ed. Hardy and Martin, Rolls Series (London, 1888), I, 285.

[6] Loomis, *Wales and the Arthurian Legend*, pp. 3–9. *Mabinogion*, trans. G. and T. Jones, Everyman's Lib., pp. 79–85.

[7] *Cymmrodor*, XXXIII (1923), 94.

heaps of rubble and grassy mounds. In a generation or two nobody had any idea where it was, and anyone who wanted to could claim it. The Scots were the first to put in their claim; in fact, they put in two claims. Barbour in his *Bruce*, Book IV, says that Kildrummy Castle, near Aberdeen, was called Snawdoune.[1] That was in 1375. Ten years earlier Froissart heard the other claim at Stirling.

It was this latter claim which has reverberated down the years. William of Worcester in the 15th century asserted: "Rex Arturus custodiebat le round table in Castro de Styrlyng, aliter Snowden West Castell." [2] Sir David Lindsay, in the *Complaint of the Papingo* (after 1530) carried on the pleasant illusion:[3]

> Adew, fair Snawdoun, with thy towris hie,
> Thy Chapell-royall, park, and Tabyll Round.

Sir Walter Scott recalled in the *Lady of the Lake* that "Stirling's tower of yore the name of Snowdoun claims." At this very day, as I have been informed by Mr Angus Graham, the title of Snowdon Herald is customarily bestowed on the Lyon King of Arms on his retirement. The title, mentioned first in 1448, doubtless derives from the romantic name of Stirling Castle, but ultimately it goes back to the Anglo-Norman name for the Roman fort overlooking the Menai Strait, "la cité de Sinadon."

Stuart Glennie mentioned, of course, the most familiar testimonial to the vogue of Arthurian romance, namely, Arthur's Seat, and carried the name back to the end of the 15th century.[4] Kennedy in his flyting with Dunbar refers to "Arthur's Sate or ony Hicher Hill." If there has ever been any legend linked to those magnificent crags, it has not come to my notice. Of one thing we can be sure: the name has no evidential value for Arthur's campaigning against the Angles in the neighbourhood of Edinburgh.

A famous figure associated with Arthur is Merlin, and by 1150, when Geoffrey of Monmouth wrote the *Vita Merlini*, the wizard was already represented as resorting in a fit of madness to the Caledonian Forest, and until very recently his supposed grave was to be seen at Drummelzier.[5] It is possible, moreover, that between 850 and 1150 a Welsh poem was composed, *Afallennau* (*The Appletrees*), in which Myrddin speaks of his miserable state in the Coed Celyddon. But the connections of Merlin with Scotland and the Scottish legend of Lailoken are far too complex to be discussed here, and I must refer the reader to H. M. and N. K. Chadwick, *The Growth of Literature*, I, pp. 105–14, 123–32, 453–57, and to a chapter by Mr Jarman in *A History of Arthurian Literature in the Middle Ages*, to be published in 1958, for the best-informed opinion on the subject.

---

[1] *Bruce*, Bk. IV, vs. 181.
[3] *Ibid.*, p. 58.
[5] *Ibid.*, pp. 72 f.

[2] Glennie, *op. cit.*, p. 57.
[4] *Ibid.*, p. 53.

Though, far into the 15th century, the Scots were eager to share with England in the glories of Arthur, it seems that with the accession of the Tudors Arthur's prestige was so successfully manipulated in the interest of the dynasty that one mode of attack on England was to debase Arthur and to undo the work of Geoffrey of Monmouth. In 1527 Hector Boece, first Principal of the University of Aberdeen, published the *Scotorum*, *Historia*, and proved himself a patriot indeed, but as a historian he stooped to the level of the Oxford *magister*. His method is quite obvious. First, Arthur was a bastard. To quote from the translation by Bellenden,[1] "the treuth is, that Uter gat him on ane othir mannis wife." Loth, on the other hand, is King of the Picts, and, as husband of Uter's legitimate daughter Anna, was "richt commovit that Arthur, gottin in adultrie, suld be preferrit to his childrin, gottin in lauchfull bed, and just heritouris of the crown of Britane."[2] It was Arthur who, it is said, instituted the practice of gormandising for thirteen days after Christmas, and as a consequence his army became so effeminate and soft that for many years they did little "displeasure" to the Saxons. When, at the great battle which Boece does not name but which is easily identifiable as that of Mount Badon, the Saxons under Colgern and Childrik fled or surrendered to Arthur, the credit for the victory is not his but belongs to the Picts under Loth. Doubts, amply justified of course, are cast on Arthur's conquests. When, after Loth's death, the Britons recognised not Modred but Constantine as Arthur's heir, Modred protested, and it was in a lawful quarrel, not in rebellion, that he met Arthur in the fatal battle. The Humber, not the Camblan River, ran red with blood; Arthur, Modred, and Walwan were slain; Guanora, her ladies, and her knights were captured and brought to the castle of Dundee. At Meigle is her sepulchre, held in special reverence of the people, "as the title writtin thairupon schawis: 'All wemen that strampis on this sepulture sall be ay barrant, but ony frute of thair wamb, siclike as Guanora was.'" Apparently, then, a local tradition was already in existence before Boece wrote, and by the time that the poet Gray visited Meigle in 1765 and saw the tomb, the women of the place were prepared to assert that Queen Wanders "was riven to dethe by staned-horses for nae gude that she did."[3] Thus in the interests of Scottish nationalism Arthur and his fair spouse were loaded with ignominy and Modred was whitewashed and exalted, much as Richard III has been in recent times.

Up to this point my paper seems to consist mainly of negatives. Arthur himself, so far as we know, never crossed the Tweed. Gawain never reigned

[1] Boece, trans. J. Bellenden (Edinburgh, 1821), II, 66–86. See R. H. Fletcher, *Arthurian Material in the Chronicles, Studies and Notes in Philology and Literature*, x (1906), 246.

[2] Already Fordun (1384–7) had made this point, but justified the choice of Arthur in preference to Galwanus and Modred as dictated by necessity, since the latter two were mere children when Uther died.

[3] *Correspondence of Thomas Gray*, ed. P. Toynbee and L. Whibley (Oxford, 1935), II, 891.

in Galloway. His father Loth had no connection with Lothian except through the accidental similarity of the two names. The identification of the Castle of Maidens with Edinburgh was nothing but a false inference from the supposition that Morgain la Fée, as King Loth's wife, must have resided in the principal fortress of Lothian. Sinadon was not Stirling, but the city of Snowdonia, the Roman fort of Segontium. Gawain's adventures at the perilous border river of Galloway had, originally, no connection with the Nith but with the Severn. But I have shown that the probabilities are strongly in favour of the activities of the historic Owein, son of Urien, as well as the romantic affairs of Yvain, having extended into regions included in the old Lothian.

After all these denials and doubts, I may conclude on a more positive, more affirmative note. Tristan or Tristram was a historic personage, a King of the Picts, and that means, of course, that Scotland can claim him as one of its most famous sons. Probably no statement about him in the great romance of the Middle Ages is true; he did not live in or near Arthur's time; even his tragic love for Isolt is the invention of a later age. But that Drust, son of Talorc, was a Pictish king of the Dark Ages and that he was the original of the Tristan of romance is not a private opinion of mine, but is now the widely accepted view of Arthurian specialists. First broached by Heinrich Zimmer, the theory has been adopted by Ferdinand Lot, Joseph Loth, Deutschbein, Brugger, Bruce, Bédier, and Mrs Bromwich.[1] I do not know of any scholar who is familiar with the texts and the evidence who rejects it.

In the *Chronicle of the Picts* a Drust, son of Talorcan, is recorded as reigning about the year 780.[2] Apparently his reign was uneventful and short. But it is demonstrable that a romantic story of the Perseus and Andromeda type grew up about him which is reflected, not only in the Irish saga of *The Wooing of Emer*, but also in the French romance of Tristram.[3] As Bédier long since worked out the itinerary,[4] the tradition passed from Scotland through Wales, Cornwall and Brittany into France and England. Drust, son of Talorcan, appears in Welsh as Drystan, son of Tallwch. He becomes the lover of Esyllt, wife of March, and eventually a contemporary of Arthur's. Miss Schoepperle proved that the tragic tale of adultery was elaborated under the influence of the Irish saga of Diarmaid and Grainne.[5] From Wales the legend passed on to the SW., King Mark became King of

---

[1] *Zeits. f. franz. Sprache u. Literatur*, XIII [1] (1891), 58 ff. *Romania*, XXV (1896), 15. *Comptes Rendus de l'Académie des Inscriptions*, 1924, p. 128. *Beiblatt zur Anglia*, XV (1904), 16–21. *Modern Philology*, XXXIII, 231. J. D. Bruce, *Evolution*, I, 178 f. Thomas, *Tristan*, ed. Bédier (Paris, 1905), II, 105–8. R. Bromwich in Trans. Hon. Soc. of Cymmrodorion, 1953, pp 38 f.

[2] A. O. Anderson, *Early Sources of Scottish History* (Edinburgh, 1922), I, cxiii, cxxvii, n. 2.

[3] *Beiblatt zur Anglia*, XV, 16–21. Thomas of Britain, *Romance of Tristram and Ysolt*, trans. R. S. Loomis (New York, 1951), p. XX.

[4] Thomas, *Tristan*, ed. Bédier, II,

[5] G. Schoepperle, *Tristan and Isolt*, II, 395 ff. J. F. Campbell had already noticed the relationship in his *Popular Tales of the West Highlands* (London, 1890–3), IV, 240. See also *Romania*, LIII (1927), 92–95.

Cornwall, and his castle was identified with Tintagel, where the shattered walls, the cliffs, and the little cove are forever associated with the star-crossed lovers. Thence to Brittany, where we find a Tristan, lord of Vitré, in the first half of the 11th century.[1] There the story of the Second Isolt, Isolt of Brittany, was added, and the death of Tristram was localised;[2] there, as late as the 19th century, vestiges of the tradition survived in the form of folk-tales.[3] In the course of the 12th century the long romance of Tristram and Isolt was fully formed, was popularised by Breton *conteurs*, and taken up by poets of remarkable power. By the 13th century there was no branch of the Arthurian cycle more familiar throughout Europe, and Tristram and Isolt had become proverbial as ideal lovers.[4]

In spite of the migration of the legend through Wales, Cornwall and Brittany, two place-names embedded in the French romances still remained to suggest its Scottish origin. From these French texts through Malory comes the familiar association of Tristram with Lyonesse, the land of his birth. Most of us have been brought up to believe that Lyonesse was a region lying W. of Land's End and long since sunk beneath the Atlantic waves. Mr Bivar, however, in his penetrating article, "Lyonesse: the Evolution of a Fable,"[5] has demonstrated that this notion arose in the 17th century as the result of curious confusions, and Arthurian students have been aware for more than fifty years that Lyonesse was one of Malory's spellings of Leonois, and that Leonois or Loonois was a common French name for Lothian. Though, of course, Drust, the Pictish king of the 8th century, could not have known Lothian except as a troublesome neighbour, then settled by the Angles, it is probable that the association of Tristram with that region means that the derivation of the romance from Scotland was not completely forgotten.[6] This probability is strengthened by the fact that the poems of Eilhart von Oberg and Béroul state that when Tristram and Isolt were banished from King Mark's court, they fled to the forest of Morrois, and the only likely identification of Morrois is Moray— a very natural retreat for an exiled Pictish hero. I believe that the great majority of Arthurian scholars would agree with Bédier that Scotland was not only the birthplace of the historic Drust, but also of his legend.

By the early 13th century the romances of the Round Table, in oral and written form, had spread throughout Latin Christendom from Iceland to the Holy Land. Now they form an integral part of Western culture. But they are peculiarly the heritage of the English-speaking peoples, and this heirloom has deeply impressed upon it the mark of Scotland. Unless

---

[1] *Revue de Bretagne*, XVIII, 435–9.
[2] Thomas of Britain, *Romance of Tristram*, trans. Loomis, pp. XXVII f.
[3] *Annales de Bretagne*, LVI (1949), 203–10.
[4] For popularity of Tristan romance in medieval art see R. S. and L. H. Loomis, *Arthurian Legends*.
[5] *Modern Philology*, L (1950), 162–70.
[6] *Romania*, XXV (1896), 16 ff. J. D. Bruce, *Evolution*, I, 179, 180, n. 42.

the late Professor Ritchie and I are completely mistaken, this Scottish impress on Arthurian literature is mainly due to professional reciters and singers of the 12th century who found a welcome in Scotland and who gave their tales and their lais a setting that would appeal to their auditors. Even when they returned to England or to France, they retained the Scottish localisation.

May I be so bold as to suggest that a translation into English of the unfamiliar and almost inaccessible (except in large libraries) Breton lais— *Desiré, Doon* and *Gurun* (Norse)—and of the romance of *Fergus*, accompanied by an introduction and commentary, would be a service to Scotland, even perhaps a profitable publishing venture?

More Celtic Elements
in
Gawain and the Green Knight

(The Journal of English and German Philology Vol. XLII, No. 2, pp. 149-84.)

MORE CELTIC ELEMENTS IN *GAWAIN*
AND THE GREEN KNIGHT

Since 1888, when Gaston Paris revealed the derivation of the Beheading Test in *Gawain and the Green Knight* from *Bricriu's Feast*, the evidence for Irish influence on the Middle English masterpiece has steadily accumulated. A number of striking elements, however, seemed to have no Irish or Celtic ancestry, but to represent the felicitous fancies of anonymous French adapters or of the English poet himself. To this view I was myself inclined until within the last year I was forced to examine the poem from several new angles. The results of this inquiry form the subject of the following pages.

I. BERCILAK'S GIRDLE. Every reader of *Gawain and the Green Knight* remembers the green silk girdle, or belt, or *lace* (the three words are used synonymously) which Sir Bercilak's wife persuaded Gawain to accept before his testing at the Green Chapel. She recommended it because of its magic virtue (vss. 1851 ff.).

> "For quat gome so is gorde with þis grene lace,
> While he hit hade hemely halched aboute,
> Þer is no haþel vnder heuen tohewe hym þat myȝt,
> For he myȝt not be slayn for slyȝt vpon erþe."

Later Bercilak informed Gawain that it was his own girdle which his wife, at his instigation, had urged upon the hero (vss. 2358 ff.).

> "For hit is my wede þat þou wereȝ, þat ilke wouen girdel,
> Myn owen wyf hit þe weued, I wot wel for soþe.
> Now know I wel þy cosses, and þy costes als;
> And þe wowyng of my wyf: I wroȝt hit myseluen.
> I sende hir to asay þe. . . "

Presumably Bercilak was wearing it when he appeared as the Green Knight at Arthur's Court, for some magic influence enabled him to come through the beheading alive—"he myȝt not be slayn for slyȝt vpon erþe"—and he was wearing a green belt at the time, as the following lines prove (vss. 161 ff.):

> And alle his vesture uerayly watȝ clene verdure,
> Boþe þe barres of his belt and oþer blyþe stones,
> Þat were richely rayled in his aray clene
> Aboutte hymself and his sadel, vpon silk werkeȝ.

157

Twice there is reference to the pendants attached to the girdle (vss. 2038, 2431). Finally we read that on his return to Arthur's court Gawain wore the belt "abelef as a bauderyk bounden bi his syde, loken vnder his lyfte arme," and that, following suit, all the knights and ladies of the Round Table agreed to wear a similar baldric of bright green (vss. 2485–88, 2515–18).

All that is said of Bercilak's girdle would seem natural to readers of the poem. Cinctures possessing various magical virtues were not uncommon in traditional literature;[1] real belts of lion's skin belonged to Piers Gaveston (d. 1312) and Charles V of France, and evidently were credited with supernatural powers;[2] others were adorned with talismanic devices or formulas.[3] Light silk girdles, decked with gold "bars" and jewels, were worn indifferently by men and women,[4] so that there was nothing surprising in the fact that Bercilak's girdle was worn not only by himself and Gawain but also by his wife. Pendants like those

[1] G. L. Kittredge, *Study of Gawain and the Green Knight* (Cambridge, Mass., 1916), pp. 139 f. Stith Thompson, *Motif Index of Folk-Literature*, II (Bloomington, Indiana, 1933), 109, 165, 170. K. Meyer, A. Nutt, *Voyage of Bran* (London, 1895–1897), I, 83. J. Bédier, *Légendes épiques*, ed. 3 (1929), IV, 159. *Sowdone of Babylon*, ed. E. Hausknecht, *EETSES* (London, 1881), pp. 66–68. A. Hertel, *Verzauberte Oertlichkeiten u. Gegenstände in der altfranzösischen erzählenden Dichtung* (Hannover, 1908), pp. 67 f. *English and Scottish Popular Ballads*, ed. H. C. Sargent, G. L. Kittredge (Boston, 1904), p. 60. *Roman de la Rose*, ed. E. Langlois, *SATF*, II (Paris, 1920), vss. 1067 ff. Chaucer, *Complete Works*, ed. F. N. Robinson (Boston, 1933), pp. 674 f. T. P. Cross, C. H. Slover, *Ancient Irish Tales* (New York, 1936), p. 483. J. A. MacCulloch, *Medieval Faith and Fable* (London, 1932) p. 40. Snorri Sturluson, *Prose Edda*, trans. A. G. Brodeur (New York, 1929), pp. 121 f. Bede, *Life of Cuthbert*, ch. 23.

[2] Joan Evans, *Magical Jewels of the Middle Ages and the Renaissance, Particularly in England* (Oxford, 1922), p. 119. On page 136 she notes that a woman's girdle (A.D. 1451) was ornamented with figures of the Three Kings, which were regarded as a talisman.

[3] C. Enlart, *Manuel d'archéologie française*, III (Paris, 1916), 279 f. Unfortunately Enlart supplied no specific reference.

[4] *Ibid.*, p. 275. "Sous le règne de Philippe Auguste, c'est le type masculin de la ceinture qui s'étend au costume féminin: la ceinture uniforme pour les deux sexes . . . " Chaucer, ed. Robinson, pp. 22, 674 f. F. H. Crossley, *English Church Monuments* (London, 1921), pp. 16, 159, 232. Prior and Gardner, *Mediaeval Figure Sculpture in England* (Cambridge, 1912), fig. 777. E. G. Millar, *English Illuminated MSS. of the XIV and XV Centuries* (Paris, 1928), pl. 68, 70. In the two early 13th century German romances to be discussed below the magic girdles were worn both by men and women.

mentioned have survived.[5] Wearing a belt as a baldric over one shoulder was known in the fourteenth century, though common only in hunting costume as a means of suspending the horn.[6] The employment of girdles as gifts or love-tokens was familiar both in romance and in reality.[7]

Doubtless the fact that the magic girdle was a commonplace of fiction, was described in *GGK* in accordance with conventions of the time, and did not occur in any version of the Beheading Test or the Temptation, regarded by Kittredge as the chief traditional elements in the poem, led that great scholar to reject the girdle as a survival from Celtic story.[8] Similar considerations and the plausible hypothesis that the green *lace*, worn baldric-wise by the members of Arthur's court, was introduced to connect the poem with some chivalric order brought Professor Hulbert to the conclusion that it was merely an adaptation of "a customary feature of fairy stories."[9] Both failed to follow up the suggestion of Miss Weston, in the slimmest but perhaps the soundest of her Arthurian books,[10] that the appearance of a similar girdle in the possession of Gawain in two German romances and in the possession of Gawain's counterpart, Cúchulainn, in a very early Irish saga demanded closer examination of this feature. The evidence since accumulated shows that the plot of *GGK* is much more deeply indebted to Irish tradition than Kittredge dreamed. Professor Hulbert emphasized the debt to the love story of Cúchulainn and Bláthnat, and Professor Nitze empha-

---

[5] Enlart, *op. cit.*, III, fig. 310.

[6] *Ibid.*, fig. 368. M. Bernath, *Malerei des Mittelalters* (Leipzig, 1916), fig. 296. *Victoria and Albert Museum, List of Rubbings of Brasses* (London, 1915), pl. 35. J. R. Planché, *Cyclopaedia of Costume* (London, 1876), pp. 30 f.

[7] Enlart, *op. cit.*, III, 278, n. 2. Marie de France, *Lais*, ed. K. Warnke, ed. 3 (Halle, 1925), *Guigemar*, vss. 568–72. H. J. Chaytor, *Troubadours in England* (Cambridge, 1923), p. 10. H. O. Sommer, *Vulgate Version of the Arthurian Romances*, III, 395; V, 84. Andreas Capellanus, *Art of Courtly Love*, trans. J. J. Parry (New York, 1941), Bk. II, ch. 7, sec. 21. Note that in *GGK*, vss. 1874, 2033, the girdle is called a *luflace* and a *drurye*.

[8] Kittredge, *op. cit.*, pp. 139 f. On realism of Middle English romances cf. D. Everett, *Essays and Studies of the English Association*, XV (1929), 103 ff.

[9] *MP*, XIII (1916), 707–18.

[10] J. L. Weston, *Legend of Sir Gawain* (London, 1897), pp. 100–2. In her later books Miss Weston unfortunately abandoned the promising start she had made in the study of Celtic origins.

sized the analogs in seasonal ritual.[11] Miss Buchanan was able to list thirty-one features derived from the complex of stories about Cúchulainn, Cúroi, and Bláthnat.[12] I propose to show that the belt of *GGK* is derived from this group of Irish stories by the following points:

1. The appearance of a magic protective girdle in *GGK* and the two other Arthurian romances, *Wigalois* and *Diu Krone*, is due not to coincidence, but to a common tradition as old as the twelfth century. 2. The origin of this tradition in the Cúchulainn-Cúroi-Bláthnat complex of stories is rendered plausible by the profound influence of this complex on early Welsh literature and numerous Arthurian romances, especially on *GGK*. 3. In one of the stories in this complex, *The Violent Death of Cúroi*, a girdle appears in association with the prototypes of the Green Knight, his wife, and Gawain,—namely, Cúroi, Bláthnat, and Cúchulainn. 4. The story of this girdle corresponds in ten points to the story of the cincture in the Gasozein episode in *Diu Krone*. 5. The story of the girdle in *Wigalois* must be an offshoot from the same stock of tradition since it offers analogies to the girdle stories in *Diu Krone* and *GGK* and a close parallel to the Irish story of Cúchulainn and his son Connla. 6. Cúchulainn in *The Cattle-Raid of Cooley* wears a battle-belt which, whether it was identical with the one in *The Violent Death of Cúroi* or not, probably indicated its nature. Arrows and spears would bound back from Cúchulainn's belt as if from stone or horn. 7. In any case, since *The Violent Death of Cúroi* influenced the plot of *GGK* and supplied ten points in the Gasozein episode in *Diu Krone*, it is fair to conclude that the precious girdle which Cúroi possesses in the Irish saga must be the original of the magic girdle which Cúroi's counterparts, Bercilak and Gasozein, possess in the romances.

[11] *MP*, xiii, 434–58.

[12] *PMLA*, xlvii (1932), 315–38. From her list I would subtract no. 5, since the Irish, "dos bili mor fair," does not mean "upon him the bushiness of a great tree," but "on him a bush of a large sacred tree." Since it was large enough to shelter 30 bullocks, the bush could hardly have been Cúroi's hair, as Zimmer and Thurneysen surmised. A possible parallel is to be found in Manannán's appearance at Tara with a silver branch on his shoulder; "craebh airgid co tri hublaib oir fria ais." (Stokes, Windisch, *Irische Texte*, ser. 3, vol. i, p. 193). I would add to Miss Buchanan's list of parallels the protests of Cúchulainn and Gawain against the delays of Cúroi and Bercilak. Cf. Kittredge, p. 38.

1. The three magic girdles of Arthurian romance possess much the same advantageous properties in combat and occur in inter-related plots. Compare with the assurance given to Gawain in *GGK* concerning the *lace*, the following assurance given to Gawein in *Wigalois* (c. 1207) concerning the girdle.[13]

> "Behalt in unz an iuwern tôt
> und sît sicher vor aller nôt:
> wan daz ir siglôs sît ersehen
> daz ist von sîner kraft geschehen. . .
> iun mac nû nimmer missegên;
> ân angest müget ir bestên
> swaz vreise ir in der welte welt."

Much the same general nature belongs to the talisman in Heinrich von dem Türlin's *Krone* (c. 1220).[14]

> "Der gürtel hât sô grôz kraft,
> Swer in treit ist sô werhaft,
> Daz in niemen kan gewinnen. . .
> Sîn tugent unde sîn lîp
> Wirt dâ von gerîchet."

What of the narrative settings in which the three cinctures are found? In all three poems a stranger knight from a far-off land arrives at Arthur's court wearing or bringing the girdle; in all three Gawain encounters him in the ax test or in combat; in all three the outcome is dependent on the talisman; in all three Gawain is entertained by the stranger knight and his wife in his castle.[15] In the two German poems the stranger knight offers the

---

[13] Wirnt von Gravenberc, *Wigalois*, ed. J. M. N. Kapteyn, *Rheinische Beiträge u. Hilfsbücher zur Germ. Philologie u. Volkskunde*, IX (Bonn, 1926), vss. 611 ff. Trans.: "Keep it to the time of your death and be secure against all danger. For that you have appeared unvictorious has happened through its power. . . . Never may things go amiss with you now. Without fear you can face whatever terror you may choose in the world." A full summary is given in P. Piper, *Höfische Epik* (Stuttgart), II, 209–13.

[14] Heinrich von dem Türlin, *Diu Krone*, ed. G. H. F. Scholl, *Bibliothek des Literarischen Vereins in Stuttgart*, XXVII (Stuttgart, 1852), vss. 4870 ff. Trans.: "The girdle has such great potency that whoever wears it is so protected that no one can vanquish him. . . . His valor and his body is strengthened by it." A full summary is given in Piper, *op. cit.*, II, 264–66, 273–75, 290.

[15] *Wigalois*, pp. 13–33; *Krone*, pp. 183 f., 287 f., 342 f. It is noteworthy that in the German poems the knights Fimbeus and Joram are both kings, and that their counterpart in *GGK*, Bercilak, is according to the ms. (vs. 992) also a king, and his wife (vs. 1770) is called a "pryncece."

girdle to Queen Ginover as a gift; it confers on her great beauty or wisdom; she rejects it; Gawein fights for it.[16] In *GGK* and *Wigalois* the stranger knight who brings the girdle to Arthur's court challenges the knights of the Round Table; he later becomes Gawain's hospitable host in his castle, introduces him to the ladies of his household,—an older woman and a younger woman of superlative beauty,—and openly encourages or secretly connives at the love of Gawain for the latter.[17] In *Diu Krone* the girdle functions in two interlocking episodes, both of which have their analogies with *GGK*. In the Fimbeus episode[18] we have a figure corresponding to "Morgne the goddes" in *GGK;* in the household of the stranger knight who comes with the girdle to Arthur's court there is a fay who cherishes a grudge against the fellowship of the Round Table and sends her emissaries to Arthur's court to humiliate them. Later in the same episode, when Gawain visits the stranger knight's castle, he is the object of a plot between the host and his wife, just as in *GGK*. Even more marked and detailed is the parallelism between the Gasozein episode in *Diu Krone*[19] and the latter part of *GGK*. Both poems relate the close of a Christmas festival and the departure of the guests on December 28 or 29. The hosts, Bercilak and Arthur respectively, spend the 29th in the chase. Their wives, at this or some previous time, bestow girdles as love-tokens on Gawain and Gasozein,—girdles which protect the wearer in combat. Gawain behaves with strict chastity toward Bercilak's wife; Gasozein later promises to preserve the honor of Arthur's wife. Gawain comes to his rendezvous with Bercilak on January 1 beside a brawling stream; Gasozein comes on the night of December 29 to a ford, and meets Arthur. The encounters end hap-

---

[16] *Wigalois*, pp. 13–25; *Krone*, pp. 287–89.   [17] *Wigalois*, pp. 21–46.

[18] *GGK*, vss. 1830–75, 2361 f., 2446–62. *Krone*, pp. 60, 183, 285 ff., 305 ff., 342 f.

[19] Vss. 3356–5080, 10458–12468. An excellent summary is given by Professor Webster in *Englische Studien*, XXXVI, 341–46. On the Arthurian relationships of this episode cf. *ibid.*, pp. 337–60; *Historia Meriadoci and De Ortu Walwanii*, ed. J. D. Bruce (Baltimore, 1913), pp. lvii f. Gasozein de Dragoz appears, as Webster notes, as Gasoain d'Estrangot in the *Vulgate Lancelot* (H. O. Sommer, *Vulgate Version*, LI, 119), and there is reference to a combat between him and Gauvain before the King. He is probably identical also with a certain Gosangos who in the *Livre d'Artus* (Sommer, *Vulgate Version*, VII, 29, 36 f., 132) displays his valor, loves the Queen, is beloved by her, and between whom and Gauvain there was a great battle.

pily. Bercilak and Arthur reveal their identity to Gawain and Gasozein. Gasozein proposes another encounter with Arthur at the end of a year whereas Gawain has met Bercilak as the consequence of such a proposal.

Despite the many differences, there are certain features common to all three romances and even more elaborate correspondences between the three pairs. Since the German poems cannot be the source of *GGK* and must themselves rest on antecedent French originals, the only explanation for the triangular relationship between *GGK*, *Wigalois*, and *Diu Krone* is a common fund of French tradition dating back to the twelfth century. The talismanic belt, therefore, is no addition of the English poet or of his immediate French source, as Kittredge suggested, but an integral part of the *Matière de Bretagne*.

This conclusion is not to be wondered at but was rather to be anticipated since similar complex relationships have already been demonstrated between each of these three poems and other Arthurian romances. Kittredge, Professor Hulbert, Miss Buchanan, and I have done this for *GGK*;[20] Saran, Schofield, and Heuckenkamp for *Wigalois*;[21] Miss Weston, Bruce, Orlowski, Warnatsch, Webster, Dr. Boll, and Professor Cross for *Diu Krone*.[22] The three poems in which the talisman appears are organic outgrowths from the mass of Round Table fiction circulating in the twelfth century.

2. The organic connection of the three poems with early Arthurian tradition takes on added significance when we realize that one of them, *GGK*, has been shown to derive its plot in large measure from a group of famous Irish stories,[23] some of them authoritatively dated in the eighth century,[24] which exerted a

[20] Kittredge, *op. cit.; MP*, XIII, 55–67; *PMLA*, XLVII, 331 ff., XLVIII, 1000 ff.

[21] F. Saran, *Ueber Wirnt von Grafenberg u. den Wigalois, Beiträge zur Geschichte der Deutschen Sprache*, XXI (1896); W. H. Schofield, *Studies in Libeaus Desconus, Studies and Notes in Philology and Literature*, IV (Boston, 1895); F. Heuckenkamp, *Chevalier du Papegau* (Halle, 1896), pp. viii ff.

[22] Weston, *op. cit.*, cf. Index sub *Diu Krone;* Weston, *Gawain at the Grail Castle* (London, 1903), pp. viii ff.; *Historia Meriadoci*, ed. J. D. Bruce, pp. lvii f.; *Damoisele à la Mule*, ed. B. Orlowski (Paris, 1911), pp. 41–64; O. Warnatsch, *Der Mantel, Germanistische Abhandlungen*, II (Breslau, 1883), 111 ff.; L. L. Boll, *Relation of Diu Krone of Heinrich v. d. Türlin to La Mule sans Frein* (Washington, 1929); *Englische Studien*, XXXVI (1906), 340–51; T. P. Cross, W. A. Nitze, *Lancelot and Guenevere* (Chicago, 1930), pp. 27 f.   [23] *PMLA*, XLVII, 315 ff.

[24] R. Thurneysen, *Irische Helden- und Königsage* (Halle, 1921), p. 431.

great influence on early Welsh literature and also on a number of the stock themes of Arthurian romance. Indeed it is possible to assert that no other Irish sagas have impressed themselves so clearly and so frequently on the plots of the Arthurian cycle as has the group of tales centering round the figures of Cúroi, Cúchulainn, and Bláthnat. As we should expect, these stories passed through Wales. Professor Gruffydd, who made a profound study of their influence on Blodeuwedd's betrayal of Llew in *Math Vab Mathonwy*, asserted:[25] "The story of Cúroi's death was well known in Wales." Professor Cross concurs:[26] "It is important to observe that the Cu Roi story was known in early Welsh literature." He also summarizes *The Violent Death of Cúroi* as one of the Celtic abduction tales which set the pattern for the abduction of Guinevere in its many forms.[27] Kittredge adduced, besides *GGK*, four French romances in which the testing of Cúchulainn by Cúroi reappears in the form of Beheading Games.[28] I have shown that this same complex of Irish stories has influenced many other familiar situations and motifs in Arthurian romance, including the Turning Castle and the Perilous Bed.[29]

Particular emphasis should be laid on *The Violent Death of Cúroi* as a source of Arthurian matter. To it, as Miss Buchanan showed, *GGK* owes three features—the color of the Green Knight's vesture, Gawain's delay of a year, his search for the Green Chapel. Miss Schoepperle, followed by Professor Cross, pointed out its general kinship with the various versions of the abduction of Guinevere,[30] and it is manifestly the main source of two other abduction stories in the Arthurian cycle. Briefly the Irish saga of the eighth or ninth century may be summarized thus:[31]

The gigantic Cúroi carried off Bláthnat (Little Flower) from her lover[32] Cúchulainn to his fortress. Cúchulainn obtained secret access to her there and arranged

---

[25] W. J. Gruffydd, *Math Vab Mathonwy* (Cardiff, 1928), p. 266.

[26] Cross, Nitze, *op. cit.*, p. 41, n. 2.   [27] *Ibid.*, pp. 39–41.

[28] Kittredge, *op. cit.*, pp. 26–66.   [29] *PMLA*, XLVIII, 1000 ff.

[30] G. Schoepperle, *Tristan and Isolt* (Frankfort, New York, 1913), II, 427–29, 528–37; Cross, Nitze, *op. cit.*, pp. 38–41, 47 ff. I hope to show further influences on Arthurian romance in a study of Chrétien's sources.

[31] Thurneysen, *op. cit.*, pp. 432–35, 441–44.

[32] Cross, *op. cit.*, p. 52, n. 1, aptly remarks: "Blathine's complicated love story makes it difficult to say whether she was the wife of Cu Cuchulinn or of

to bring an army to attack the fortress. During the conflict, Bláthnat betrayed Cúroi, by giving the sword with which alone he could be slain to Cúchulainn. Foreseeing his doom, Cúroi cried, "No secret to women!" and was promptly beheaded.

Compare this with an episode in the *Vulgate Lancelot:*[33]

The gigantic Carado carried off a damsel, whose name we can infer was Floree,[34] from her lover to his castle. Lancelot, accompanied by a large army, attacked the fortress. During the conflict, the damsel betrayed Carado by giving the sword with which alone he could be slain to Lancelot. Foreseeing his doom, Carado cried, "Alas, that which I loved best in the world has slain me!" Carado was presently beheaded.

Compare also this episode in *De Ortu Walwanii.*[35]

Milocrates carried off a damsel to his palace. Walwanius (Gawain), learning that she was in love with him, obtained secret access to her there, and arranged to bring an army to attack the palace. She gave him the sword of Milocrates,

---

Cu Roi or of either." Likewise Gruffydd says (*op. cit.*, p. 128) that the Balor story "belongs to the tradition of the earlier Cuchulain saga, where marriage, as we know it, did not count. Indeed, in the *Mabinogion*, the institution of marriage is not recognized, and the usual phrase for a man and a woman beginning to cohabit, whether legitimately or otherwise, is 'he slept with her.' " The uncertainty as to Bláthnat's status made it almost inevitable that the relationship of her Arthurian descendants to the Arthurian descendants of Cúchulainn and Cúroi shows every variety conceivable.

[33] Sommer, *Vulgate Version*, IV, 114, 135–37. Cf. *Studi Medievali*, Nouva Serie, III (1930), 295 f.

[34] This damsel was married to Melyant le Gay (Sommer, IV, 139), whereas we learn from the *Livre d'Artus* (*ibid.*, VII, 115) that Meliant de Lis was married to a certain Floree, whose love affair with Gauvain in her father's castle shows marked resemblances to that of Bercilak's wife with Gawain. Cf. *infra*, p. 164. Florie was evidently a traditional name for Gawain's mistress or wife. Cf. *PMLA*, XLVIII, 1014, 1021; R. S. Loomis, *Celtic Myth and Arthurian Romance* (New York, 1927), pp. 22, 228. Both the Meliants mentioned above, like Chrétien's Meleagant, are descended, I believe, from Welsh Melvas, who was apparently a notorious abductor. Cf. Cross, Nitze, *Lancelot and Guenevere*, pp. 21, 26, and n. 1, 29, 47, n. 2. It is at least a remarkable coincidence with the betrayal of Carado by the damsel that in the earliest version of *Amicus and Amelius*, that of Radulphus Tortarius (ca. 1090), Amicus in the course of a combat with the redoubtable Adradus broke his sword and was in dire straits until a damsel sent him the mighty sword of her father with which he slew Adradus, whereas in the next oldest version of the Amicus story, the Anglo-Norman romance (12th century), the damsel is called Florie. Cf. *Amis and Amiloun*, ed. MacE. Leach, *EETS* (1937), p. 103; *Amis and Amiloun*, ed. E. Kölbing (Heilbronn, 1884), pp. 127 ff.

[35] *Historia Meriadoci*, ed. Bruce, pp. 62–72.

which was destined to be the latter's doom. During the conflict which followed, Walwanius beheaded Milocrates with his own sword.

To repeat, the group of stories concerned with Cúroi, Cúchulainn, and Bláthnat have left more traces on Arthurian romance than has any other body of Irish fiction.

3. The bearing of this fact on the problem of Bercilak's girdle becomes apparent when we observe that one version of *The Violent Death of Cúroi* mentions among several treasures a precious girdle, that these treasures came into the possession of Cúroi, the recognized original of Bercilak, and that another version represents Cúroi as wearing a girdle when he came to the court of Ulster and carried off Bláthnat, or Bláthine, the original of Bercilak's wife. Evidently *The Violent Death of Cúroi* deserves further scrutiny since its influence on Arthurian romance is certain and since it contains a girdle associated with the prototype: of the very persons who wear the magic cincture in *GGK*. A fuller résumé of the saga follows.[36]

In a raid on the home of Echde Echbel in Cantire (Scotland) Cúchulainn and a young man (Cúroi in disguise) brought away the captive maiden Bláthine, who loved Cúroi, and also certain valuable possessions, among which is listed the girdle of Uar Galmar (Uar the Brave). In dividing the spoils the treasures were given to Cúroi, but in violation of his promise Cúchulainn kept the captive Bláthine for a year. At the end of that year and again at the end of the next Cúroi returned to the court of Ulster to claim Bláthine, but was refused. When he was refused a third time, Cúroi seized the woman and other booty, and according to another version he placed some of it in his girdle.[37] As he made off,

---

[36] Thurneysen, *op. cit.*, pp. 432–45. For reconstructed Irish text and translation into German cf. *Zeits. f. celt. Philologie*, IX (1913), 190–96. In the ms. the girdle is referred to as "criss uairgal mair," and the translation "of Uar Galmar" is doubtful. According to the 12th century version of *The Fate of the Children of Turenn* Uar was one of the three gods of Dana (*Zeits. f. celt. Phil.*, XII, 1918, p. 241): "Tri De Donand. i. tri meic Bresa meic Elathan, batar he a n-anmand .i. Brian ocus Huar acus Hiuchor." Peter O'Connell says Uar was one of the sons of Turenn (Joyce, *Old Celtic Romances*, Dublin, 1920, p. 11). In *The Cattle-Raid of Regamon* from the Yellow Book of Lecan the Morrígan gives Dáire mac Fiachna a long name beginning with Uar (A. H. Leahy, *Heroic Romances of Ireland*, London, 1906, II, p. 132).

[37] According to the second version of *The Violent Death of Cúroi* (Thurneysen, p. 441; *Eriu*, II [1905], 21) Cúroi collected the birds in his girdle, "cordait na heonu ina chris," and these birds are called in an earlier passage "na tri fira Ochaine," and are said to have perched on the ears of Iuchna's (that is, Echde's) cows, and the caldron was filled with milk while the birds sang. Best translated "tri fira Ochaine" as "the three men of Ochain," and Thurneysen in *ZCP*, IX,

Cúchulainn overtook him and a fierce combat ensued in which Cúchulainn was hurled thrice to the earth. Cúroi abducted the woman to his fortress, and there followed in time the clandestine visit of Cúchulainn and the betrayal of Cúroi by Bláthine already summarized above.

Unfortunately this earliest version of the abduction of "Little Flower," though it preserves the tradition of a precious girdle, tells us nothing of its properties and leaves us to infer that it was granted to Cúroi as part of the treasure of Echde, and in none of the later versions is it even mentioned except that it is probably the girdle which Cúroi is wearing in the twelfth-century version when he appears for the third time to claim Bláthnat. But in view of the summary nature of these versions, it is reasonable to suppose that the girdle was once an important feature in the famous abduction story. To judge by the analogy of *GGK* and the Gasozein episode, Bláthnat must have given Cúroi's belt to Cúchulainn before the final battle. The act would accord with her notorious treachery on this occasion, and the transfer of the talisman would serve to explain why Cúroi, who had triumphed so completely over Cúchulainn in their first struggle when he wore the girdle, was himself slain in the second.

4. This surmise receives a neat confirmation from the fact that this abduction story is paralleled in ten points by the Gasozein episode in *Diu Krone*, in which the magic girdle appears.[38]

Queen Ginover gave the protective girdle as a love-talisman to Gasozein, a knight whom she evidently favored. Near a ford in the neighborhood of Arthur's court, Gasozein overthrew three knights of the Round Table, but was less successful against Arthur. On learning the King's identity, Gasozein declared that Ginover had loved him and had been his captive, but that Arthur had taken her

---

214 was moved to wonder why the birds should be men from a place in County Louth. "Was haben aber Vögel aus dieser irischen Gegend mit den Überseeischen Wunderkühen zu schaffen?" Prof. Vernam Hull, whom I have always consulted in Irish textual matters with profit, generously informs me that he believes, *fira* in the passage above is the regular acc. pl. of *fir*, which as a noun meant "truth," then "proof," then *"Wahrheitsbeweis."* Further light is shed on the matter by a gloss in the eighth-century *Lament for Cúroi* (*Eriu*, II, 5 f.), where "Firu Ochaine huargus" is glossed by "laimdei beca tuctha anall imaille frisin n-ingin," that is, "little hand-gods [images] which were brought from yonder with the damsel." Prof. Hull writes: "If I am correct, images were made of the birds, which were used apparently to swear by or as testimonials for the veracity of a statement." It was probably, then, talismanic images, not living birds, which Cúroi put in his belt when he carried off Bláthnat from Cúchulainn.

[38] Cf. *supra*, n. 19.

away from him against his will. He displayed the girdle as a token of her love, and proposed to fight Arthur for her possession that day, and with any of his knights at the end of a year. When Gasozein later presented himself to win the queen from Arthur, it was decided to let her choose between them, and when she denied his claim, he departed crestfallen. But when she fell into the hands of a certain Gotegrin, Gasozein appeared on the scene and forced her to ride away with him. As he was about to ravish her, Gawein providentially came to the rescue and a terrific combat ensued. Gawein had the best of it, and brought the queen back to Arthur's court. (It is perhaps not irrelevant to note that this episode is followed by another in which the Beheading Test occurs, and Cúroi is clearly recognizable as the ugly, ax-bearing lord of a revolving castle, as he is in *The Feast of Bricriu*.[39])

Compare this tale with the abduction of Bláthine summarized above. Despite contaminations, interpolations, and the fairly obvious doubling of the abduction of the unfortunate Ginover, it betrays ten correspondences to *The Violent Death of Cúroi*.

Diu Krone	*The Death of Cúroi*
1. Ginover had loved Gasozein.	1. Bláthine had loved Cúroi.
2. Ginover had been the captive of Gasozein.	2. Bláthine had been carried off captive by Cúroi.
3. Ginover had been taken from Gasozein against his will by Arthur.	3. Bláthine was held by Cúchulainn against Cúroi's will.
4. Gasozein claimed Ginover from Arthur as his right.	4. Cúroi claimed Bláthine from Cúchulainn as his right.
5. Gasozein had a girdle given him by Ginover.	5. Cúroi had a girdle which he had captured with Bláthine.
6. Gasozein brought this girdle when he claimed Ginover.	6. Cúroi was wearing a girdle when he claimed Bláthine.
7. Gasozein proposed to fight for Ginover again at the end of a year.	7. Cúroi fought for Bláthine after the lapse of a year.
8. Gasozein's claim to Ginover was rejected.	8. Cúroi's claim to Bláthine was rejected.
9. Gasozein carried off Ginover from Gotegrin by force.	9. Cúroi carried off Bláthine by force.
10. Gawein rescued Ginover in a terrific combat with Gasozein.	10. Cúchulainn rescued Bláthine in a terrific combat with Cúroi.

Given the certainty that *The Death of Cúroi* was well known in Wales and penetrated in various forms into Arthurian romance, particularly into the two abduction stories cited above from the *Vulgate Lancelot* and *De Ortu Walwanii*, who can doubt

---

[39] R. S. Loomis, *op. cit.*, pp. 49, 112–14. On the revolving castle cf. *ibid.* pp. 166–75, and *PMLA*, xlviii, 1005, 1010, 1016, 1019–21.

that we have in the Gasozein episode another instance of that penetration? And since we have already identified Gasozein's girdle with the Green Knight's *lace*, and have seen that Gasozein plays the role of Cúroi in the abduction story, just as the Green Knight plays the role of Cúroi in the Beheading Test, who can doubt that both these girdles of Arthurian romance are derived from Cúroi's girdle?

5. Whereas the Gasozein episode in *Diu Krone* offers the strongest proof of the Irish origin of the magic girdle, further confirmation may be found in the early history of the girdle in *Diu Krone* and in *Wigalois*. Heinrich von dem Türlin tells us:[40]

The girdle given to Gasozein by Ginover had originally been worked by the fay Giramphiel for her husband, King Fimbeus. Fimbeus appeared at Arthur's court and offered it to Ginover as a gift. Though she refused it, he left it with her. It conferred great beauty upon her, and she persuaded Gawein to fight Fimbeus for it. During the conflict, though Fimbeus wore the girdle, the gem in which its potency lay[41] fell out, and Gawein, picking it up, won both the combat and the girdle for Ginover.

Wigalois begins with a similar story:[42]

A certain King Joram from a far country appeared before the wall of Arthur's castle, and presented to Ginover a girdle, which she might keep or return to him the next morning.[43] Testing its powers, she found it conferred on her great knowledge. By Gawein's advice she returned it to Joram. He challenged the knights of the Round Table to fight him for it, and unhorsed them easily without use of the girdle. When Gawein sallied forth, Joram wore the talisman and so vanquished him also.

It hardly needs demonstration that though the outcome of the stranger knight's combat with Gawein differs in the two romances, the basic tradition is the same. Considering, moreover, that we have here again a stranger knight wearing a magic girdle, appearing at Arthur's castle, displaying a marked interest in his Queen, challenging and vanquishing his knights, and finally meeting in combat the Queen's champion, Gawein, it seems

[40] Pp. 183 f., 287 f.

[41] For the gem as source of the girdle's potency cf. Joan Evans, *Magical Jewels of the Middle Ages*, p. 119; Chaucer, ed. Robinson, p. 674 f., vss. 1085–1102; *Roman de la Rose*, ed. E. Langlois, II, vss. 1067–82.

[42] Pp. 13–27.

[43] The girdle is depicted twice in the Wigalois murals at Runkelstein. Cf. R. S. and L. H. Loomis, *Arthurian Legends in Medieval Art* (New York, 1938), figs. 171, 183.

probable that these two stories embody the same basic tradition as that already found in the Gasozein episode. If this conclusion be accepted, then the magic girdle is three times involved in a sequence of events which ultimately derived from *The Violent Death of Cúroi*, and dimly reflects Cúroi's coming to the court of Ulster, wearing a girdle, his claiming Bláthine, the refusal of his claim, and his combat with Cúchulainn. *Wigalois*, which represents Gawein as vanquished by the stranger knight, seems to reproduce the humiliating outcome of Cúchulainn's first struggle with Cúroi, whereas the Fimbeus adventure in *Diu Krone*, which ends with Gawein's victory, may have been influenced by the outcome of Cúchulainn's final battle with Cúroi. Basically the two episodes in *Diu Krone* and the one episode in *Wigalois* were the same.

It is important at this point to recall that when the authors of *Diu Krone* and *Wigalois* continue the stories of King Fimbeus and King Joram respectively, they follow traditions which are found in *GGK*, thus proving once more that all three romances drew for these adventures on a common ultimate source. Giramphiel, the wife of Fimbeus and a "fei," nurses a grudge against the knights of the Round Table, particularly Gawein; she sends emissaries to the court to humiliate them by means of the glove test; she and her husband later entertain Gawein in their castle; there is a second encounter between her husband and Gawein outside the castle, and the latter again emerges victorious.[44] The parallelism with the English poem needs no elaboration. In *Wigalois* there is a continuation of the Joram adventure which likewise has a parallel with *GGK*. As already noted, Joram, the stranger knight from afar, after his combat with Gawein at Arthur's court, becomes Gawein's hospitable host in his castle, introduces him to the ladies of his household, an older woman and a younger woman of ravishing beauty, and encourages Gawein's love for the latter. The resemblance to the latter part of *GGK* is too marked to be due to coincidence.

As Miss Buchanan and I have made clear,[45] this part of *GGK* is based largely on Cúchulainn's visit to Cúroi's Fortress, as found in *Bricriu's Feast*,[46] and nothing could confirm more neatly

---

[44] Cf. *supra*, n. 18.   [45] Cf. *PMLA*, xlvii, 325–27; xlviii, 1005–24.
[46] *Feast of Bricriu*, ed. G. Henderson (London, 1889), pp. 101–15.

my thesis that the ambiguity of Cúroi's attitude toward Cúchulainn in that tale was responsible for the strange and multifarious developments of the tale in Arthurian romance[47] than the variant attitudes of the counterparts of Cúroi and Bláthnat toward Gawain in *GGK* and the German romances. Let us remember that in the Visit to Cúroi's Fortress Cúroi is represented as arranging for Cúchulainn's hospitable reception and as awarding to him the sovranty of Ireland's heroes—acts which seem to indicate a friendly disposition; on the other hand, Cúroi is evidently responsible for the attacks on his guest and in fact is his most formidable antagonist, the *Scáth.*[48] Bláthnat's attitude likewise is somewhat ambiguous; in entertaining Cúchulainn and in knowing full well of Cúchulainn's evil plight, is she an accessory to Cúroi's designs on her guest's life, or, as there is much evidence to show,[49] is she even here the loyal mistress of Cúchulainn? This Irish tale certainly does not make it clear whether Cúroi and Bláthnat were the friends or the foes of Cúchulainn. One interpretation has been adopted in *Diu Krone:* Fimbeus and his wife are consistently hostile to their guest Gawein. The opposite interpretation has been adopted in *Wigalois:* Joram and his wife are consistently friendly. In *GGK* Bercilak is an odd, though comprehensible, mixture of hostility and friendliness; and his wife, though her motives appear to be inimical, makes love to her guest and actually gives him her husband's girdle which has the power to protect him from her husband's blow. These variations in the three cognate girdle stories are partly explained by the dubious roles of Cúroi and Bláthnat in the Visit to Cúroi's Fortress.

We have seen that the girdle story in *Wigalois* parallels that in *GGK* to the extent that Gawein goes to the castle of the wearer of the girdle, is there hospitably entertained by the ladies

[47] *PMLA*, xlviii, 1006 ff.

[48] *Ibid.*, p. 1006. Note, moreover, that in the *Feast of Bricriu*, p. 108, l. 11, Cúchulainn addresses the *Scáth* as "bachlaig," and that Cúroi on pp. 116 ff. is regularly referred to by the same noun meaning "herdsman."

[49] *Feast of Bricriu*, ed. Henderson, p. 113. "Blathnat, wife of Curoi, made speech: 'Truly, not the sigh of one dishonored but a victor's sigh of triumph'. " This is apparently an exclamation of sympathy and joy. Full confirmation is found in the numerous derivates from the Visit to Cúroi's Castle in Arthurian romance, in which the hostess is clearly enamored of the hero. Cf. *PMLA*, xlviii, 1012–16, 1022–31, and *infra*, n. 50.

of the household, an older dame and a very beautiful young woman, and enters into an amorous relationship with the latter, which is encouraged by his host. But it is somewhat disconcerting to find that instead of the surreptitious and vain advances of the lady to Gawain during the absence of the host, *Wigalois* tells of an honorable marriage between the hero and the host's niece, and of the birth of a son destined to great renown; and the girdle, instead of being given by the lady to Gawein, is entrusted by Gawein to the lady as a gift for their son. Does the parallel break down? Are the earlier analogies merely fortuitous? The name of Gawein's bride, Florie, reassures us, for it suggests derivation from Bláthnat, "Little Flower," and actually directs us to a story which forms a perfect link between *Wigalois* and *GGK*. In the *Livre d'Artus*[50] Gauvain comes to the castle of King Alain, is most hospitably received by him, his wife, and his daughter Floree. During the night Floree comes to her guest's bed secretly, finds him half asleep, and her amorous behavior results in his begetting on her "un fil qui molt fu puis de grant proesce." Gauvain learns that dangers await him in the neighborhood, and when he departs, his host gives him an attendant to act as guide.

It is not hard to discern here a story which parallels in part the visit of Gawain to the Green Knight's castle, and in part the visit of Gawein to Joram's castle. The latter evidently furnishes a traditional continuation of Gauvain's liaison with Floree, linking it to the story of the birth and youthful exploits of Gauvain's famous son, Guiglain or, as he is called in the German romance, Wigalois.[51] And it is perfectly clear why the author of *Wigalois* has suppressed the liaison with the host's daughter, which we find in the *Livre d'Artus*. Either the German poet or the composer of his French source wished to remove the blot on

---

[50] H. O. Sommer, *Vulgate Version*, VII, 108–12. The connection between the two Flories has been noted already by Sommer, *ibid.*, 110, n. 1; Freymond, *Zeits. f. Franz. Sprache u. Lit.*, XVIII (1895), 50, n. 2; Schofield, *Studies in Libeaus Desconus*, p. 236, n. 1.

[51] On the name cf. R. S. and L. H. Loomis, *Arthurian Legends in Medieval Art*, p. 79. Besides the influence of the saint's name Guingalois, the French form of Winwaloe (U. Chevalier, *Répertoire des sources historiques du Moyen Age* [Paris, 1903–1904], I, 1990), the name has been etymologized as Gwi von Galois (vs. 1574) by Wirnt, who has mistakenly treated the adjective *galois* (Welsh) as if it were the noun *Gales* (Wales).

the scutcheon of his young hero, Wigalois, and so erased the scenes of temptation and clandestine union and made Wigalois' mother, Florie, the honorable bride of Gawein.

The remainder of the story of Gawein and Florie in *Wigalois*[52] offers strong support for this thesis, for, though it no longer follows the story of Cúchulainn and Bláthnat, it does follow distinctly the pattern of another famous liaison of Cúchulainn's, more suitable to the author's purpose, leading on, as it does, to the birth of a son Connla.

According to the German romance, Gawein, after six months of wedded life, leaves Florie pregnant and returns to his own land, entrusting to her the magic girdle and directing that it should be given to his expected son. Wigalois is born, and after twenty years of expert training in arms and accomplishments under the tutelage of a certain queen (note the strangeness of this education by *ein rîchiu künigin*, hitherto unmentioned), he sets out to find his father. A youth of Arthur's court meets him, praises the prowess of the knights of the Round Table, and urges him to join them. When Wigalois comes to court, he provokes the wonder of all by sitting on a perilous seat. He refuses to tell his father's name, and wears the magic girdle concealed so that no one, not even his father, knows who he is.

Anyone familiar with Irish saga will recognize here the outline of the story of Cúchulainn's son Connla as found in *The Wooing of Emer* and *The Tragic Death of Aife's Only Son*, which are as old as the ninth century.[53]

Cúchulainn, during his stay on the Continent, lies with the Princess Aife, sister of the woman-warrior Scáthach, and herself "the hardest woman-warrior in the world." Before returning to Ireland, he leaves with the pregnant Aife a ring for his son. When it fits the boy, he is to seek his father, but he is under a spell not to reveal his identity to any man. After seven years, during which the precocious Connla has been given expert training in arms by Scáthach, he sets out for the court of Ulster. As he approaches, he provokes the wonder of King Conchobar and his warriors by his feats. One of them goes to meet him, extols the glory of the court and urges him to come to the king. But Connla refuses to reveal his name and meets his death in combat with his father.

Particular strength is lent to this analog with the story of Wigalois by the fact that the German romance retains the marked feature of the boy's training by a woman. The discrepancies between the Irish and German versions are not hard to ac-

[52] *Wigalois*, pp. 47–68.
[53] Thurneysen, *Irische Helden- und Königsage*, pp. 391, 404–6. Cross, Slover, *Ancient Irish Tales*, pp. 166 f., 172–74.

count for. The originator of the latter version naturally could not afford to let his youthful hero be slain at the outset of his career, for then there would be no romance of Wigalois; and accordingly he excised the fatal combat of father and son. The substitution of the girdle for the ring as the gift of the father to his future son is quite understandable, since the originator of the Wigalois story, having found no use for the cincture in his modification of the Gawain-Florie amour, simply carried it over into the sequel as a more fitting gift than a ring from a warlike father to a warlike son.[54]

The romance of *Wigalois*, then, by its analogies with *GGK* and *Diu Krone* demonstrates its derivation from the same basic stock of Irish story, and by its continuation with the *enfances* of Gawein's son displays its affinity with another famous Irish saga.

6. We may now, I trust, feel secure in the conclusion that Bercilak's belt was an integral part of the tradition developed from ancient Irish tales of Cúroi, Cúchulainn, and Bláthnat. Of Cúroi's girdle, the probable original, no Irish text discloses the properties. But the unanimity of *GGK*, *Diu Krone*, and *Wigalois* in ascribing to the traditional belt the power of preserving the hero from bodily harm in combat is good reason for supposing that its archetype possessed the same power. Thus we are led to reconsider Miss Weston's suggestion that Cúchulainn's belt, described in the eighth-century saga of *The Cattle-Raid of Cooley*,[55] may be related to Gawain's *lace*.

Over him [Cúchulainn] he put on the outside his battle-girdle (*cath-chriss*) of a champion, of rough, tanned, stout leather cut from the forequarters of seven ox-hides of yearlings, so that it reached from the slender parts of his waist to the stout parts under his arm-pits. He was used to wear it to keep off spears and points and irons and lances and arrows. For in like manner they would bound back from it as if from stone or rock or horn they rebounded.

It is, of course, impossible to assert that this is the selfsame girdle which Cúroi wore when he came to the court of Ulster,

---

[54] The originator of the story has also found a new use for the girdle as an explanation of Gawein's failure to return to his beloved Florie; without this talisman, which Gawein had left with her, he was unable to find his way back.

[55] J. Dunn, *Ancient Irish Epic Tale, Tain Bo Cualnge* (London, 1914), p. 188. For Irish text cf. *Die altirische Heldensage Tain Bo Cualnge*, ed. E. Windisch (Leipzig, 1905), p. 361; *Lebor na Huidre*, ed. R. I. Best, O. Bergin (Dublin, 1929), p. 198, ll. 6415–20.

carried off Bláthnat, and fought with Cúchulainn, or that it is the girdle of Uar Galmar which presumably was included in the booty carried off by Cúroi and Cúchulainn from Echde. No Irish text justifies the identification of the two girdles. It is possible to say, however, that Arthurian traditions demonstrably based on *The Violent Death of Cúroi* seem to show a persistent tendency to pass the girdle about between the counterparts of Cúroi and Cúchulainn. What can this mean except that at a fairly early stage in the growth of the tradition Cúchulainn was credited with the possession of a belt similar to Cúroi's, if not identical with it? Miss Weston's suggestion that Cúchulainn's battle-belt was the original of Bercilak's and Gawain's *lace* deserves, therefore, every respect.

7. Though no decisive evidence exists on this point, the evidence presented above for the dependence of *GGK* and many of the episodes in *Diu Krone* and *Wigalois* on the complex of stories about Cúroi, Cúchulainn, and Bláthnat, particularly on *The Violent Death of Cúroi*, seems more than adequate to demonstrate the derivation of these girdles in Arthurian story from the girdle in that Irish saga. And we may safely add the green *lace* to Miss Buchanan's list.

II. THE PENTANGLE. This conclusion as to the girdle which is so conspicuous a feature in Gawain's adventures with the Green Knight and his lady prompts me to hazard a suggestion as to the device which, according to *GGK*, vss. 619–65, the hero bore on his shield and for which thus far no parallel in Arthurian heraldry and no explanation in history has been found.

> Then þay schewed hym þe schelde, þat was of schyr gouleʒ
> Wyth þe pentangel depaynt of pure golde heweʒ.

As is explained, this five-pointed star is called the endless knot "because its interlacing lines are joined so as to be continuous, and if followed out they bring the tracer back always to the same point."[56] It is also explained that Gawain is virtuous in five ways and in respect to five things: the five senses, the five fingers, the five wounds of Christ, the five joys of Heaven's Queen, and the five virtues. It is obvious that this symbolical interpretation of

[56] *Sir Gawain and the Green Knight*, ed. J. R. Tolkien, E. V. Gordon (Oxford, 1925), p. 92. On number 5 cf. V. F. Hopper, *Medieval Number Symbolism* (New York, 1938), index.

the pentangle is due to the common association of the number five with these things. For example, John of Gaunt prescribed in his will that five candles be placed round his bier "en l'onur des cink plaies principalx nostre seigneur Jesu, et pur mes cynk scens lesquelx j'ay multz negligentment despendie."[57] Professor Hulbert remarks that in the fifteenth century the pentangle "was certainly Christian, because it was then used on the seal of the Carmelite Priory of Aberdeen."[58] I have noted it also on an eleventh or twelfth century capital from a church at Frías, near Burgos, now in the Cloisters Museum, New York City; on a tomb in the monastery of Montmajour; and in the illumination (fol. 141 v) of the Tiptoft Missal, done in England, ca. 1325, and now in the Morgan Library, New York City.

The attribution to Gawain of the symbolic pentangle, gold on a red field, as his armorial charge is unique, and may, of course, be a pure invention of the English poet. On the other hand, it may be founded on a tradition. *Wigalois* is unique in assigning to Gawain's son a golden wheel on a black ground as his device,[59] and here the odds in favor of traditional origin are strong. For not only does the name of the hero go back through the French form Guiglain to Irish Cúchulainn,[60] but the association of Cúchulainn with a wheel is noteworthy. Three times does it appear. In *The Wooing of Emer* Cúchulainn is given a wheel which he is to follow as it rolls swiftly across half the Plain of Ill Luck.[61] In *The Feast of Bricriu* he hurls a wheel higher than either of his two rivals; this is called the wheel-feat (*rothcless*).[62] In the earliest ms. of *The Cattle-Raid of Cooley* (ca. 1100) we read that his shield was "dark red, dark crimson with five wheels of gold."[63] These repeated associations of Cúchulainn with wheels are hardly fortuitous, since the wheel was a familiar solar symbol[64]

---

[57] S. Armitage-Smith, *John of Gaunt* (1904), p. 421.

[58] *MP*, XIII, 724. It may be significant that the pentangle remained a talismanic symbol in Wales even in the 19th century. Cf. M. Trevelyan, *Folklore and Folk-stories of Wales* (London, 1909), pp. 234 f.

[59] Ed. Kapteyn, vss. 1826–31.   [60] Cf. *supra*, n. 51.

[61] Thurneysen, *op. cit.*, p. 389. Cross, Slover, *op. cit.*, p. 164.

[62] Ed. G. Henderson, pp. 80–83.

[63] J. Dunn, *op. cit.*, p. 196. *Tain Bo Cualnge*, ed. Windisch, p. 393, n. 3. *Lebor na Huidre*, ed. Best, Bergin, p. 202, ll. 6559 f.

[64] R. S. Loomis, *Celtic Myth and Arthurian Romance*, p. 318. *Etudes celtiques*, III (1938), 58. *Mannus*, I (1909), 53 ff., 169 ff. P. W. Joyce, *Social History of Ancient Ireland*, I, 59. *Proceedings of Royal Irish Acad.*, XXXIV, C, 366 f.

and Cúchulainn has long been recognized as possessing solar traits.[65] Hardly fortuitous is the reappearance of a golden wheel on the shield of Wigalois, who derives his name ultimately from Cúchulainn's, and whose love for Larie and whose adventure in the castle of Roaz I have shown elsewhere[66] are derived from Cúchulainn's love for Bláthnat and his adventures in Cúroi's fortress.

If, then, the golden wheel on Wigalois' shield can be traced with great probability back to the five golden wheels on Cúchulainn's shield, it is surely not improbable that the five-pointed device on Gawain's shield may have the same origin. For, as we have seen, *GGK* is saturated with Irish tradition; Gawain is here the counterpart of Cúchulainn; the tinctures, gold on red, are common to the shields of both, and so is the number five. The substitution of the pentangle for the five wheels would be perfectly natural, since like a multitude of other details in Arthurian romance it exemplifies the effort to give meaning to the meaningless. In one of the most pregnant passages of Arthurian criticism M. Pauphilet says of the Grail legend:[67]

Tout y est imprégné de la troublante poésie du hasard, de l'illogisme et du rêve. ... L'imagination est ravie, mais l'intelligence déconcertée: elle aspire à ordonner ce chaos charmant. L'auteur de la *Queste* était loin de se douter que tout cela n'avait pas été une vaine fantasmagorie, et que ces contes étranges n'étaient pour la plupart que l'expression déformée d'antiques croyances paiennes. Mais il eut la clairvoyance rare de comprendre qu'en l'état où les Français de son temps le trouvaient, le merveilleux celtique, malgré son charme incomparable, n'était plus qu'une forme vide. Ce qu'il y introduisit, ce fut naturellement sa conception chrétienne de l'univers et de l'homme.

This process of modification and reinterpretation which Pauphilet divined so clearly in the *Queste del S. Graal* is clearly visible throughout *GGK*. We have passed from a world of myth to one of Christian ethics and symbolism. And though the pentangle may not be equated by rigid laws of geometry with the five wheels of Cúchulainn's shield, yet the presuppositions are in favor of just such an evolution. Not only the green girdle but also the golden device may be survivals from Irish tales of the Cúchulainn cycle. They may bring up to thirty-three the number of traditional Irish features in *GGK*.

[65] R. S. Loomis, *Celtic Myth*, p. 47. *Studi medievali*, N. S., III (1930), 291.
[66] *PMLA*, XLVIII (1933), 1000–21.
[67] A. Pauphilet, *Etudes sur la Queste del S. Graal* (Paris, 1921), pp. 192 f.

III. WELSH ELEMENTS. There are four features of the English romance for which no Irish source has been or can be, I believe, found: Gawain's host is emphatically a huntsman; during his absence Gawain, left alone with his wife, maintains an honorable chastity; it is by a covenant that a year elapses between the first and second encounters of Gawain with the Green Knight; the second encounter takes place, not in the royal palace or beside a loch as in the two Irish versions of the Beheading Test, but by a brawling brook.

Three, at least, of these features do not seem to have been conceived in the brain of the English poet, for they appear in cognate Arthurian tales and were therefore deeply imbedded in the tradition. These three and perhaps the fourth are recognizable in the very Gasozein episode in *Diu Krone*,[68] which shows such marked resemblance to *GGK*. Arthur, like Bercilak, spends in hunting the late December day before his meeting with the wearer of his wife's protective girdle; the meeting takes place near a ford; Gasozein proposes another encounter a year later; he promises that if in the meantime he gains possession of Ginover, he will respect her chastity. The Guingambresil episode in Chrétien's *Conte del Graal* presents another marked parallel to *GGK*,[69] and here we can discern two of the non-Irish elements. In response to the challenge of Guingambresil, the stranger knight, at Arthur's court, Gauvain sets out and is entertained hospitably in the castle of a noble huntsman; during his host's absence in the chase, Gauvain engages in a compromising affair with the lady of the castle; he agrees to meet Guingambresil, his challenger at Arthur's court, at the end of a year. Here the huntsman host and the pledge to an anniversary encounter are non-Irish features which we have already noted in *GGK*. They and the encounter at the riverside and, perhaps, the chastity motif in connection with the huntsman's wife are a part of the basic tradition. If these four elements did not spring from Irish saga, where did they have their origin?

I was myself astonished when I realized that all four were present in the first episode of the eleventh-century mabinogi of

[68] Cf. *supra*, n. 19.
[69] *PMLA*, xlviii, 1023–27. Chrétien, *Conte del Graal*, ed. Hilka (Halle, 1932), vss. 4747–4813, 5703–6215.

Pwyll.[70] I was even more astonished to realize that the very same Welsh episode accounted for most of the outstanding features in the Gasozein story which were not derived from the *Violent Death of Cúroi*. Could it be a coincidence that *GGK* on the one hand shared with the Gasozein episode the parallels of the break-up of the Christmas party, the host's hunting throughout December 29, his wife's giving the protective girdle as a *drurye* to his opponent, the encounter near a stream; and that, on the other, *GGK* and the Gasozein episode should find an explanation of their non-Irish features in the same Welsh source? Let me sur-marize that source.[71]

Pwyll, Prince of Dyfed (Southwestern Wales), met in a forest glade a huntsman, clad in gray wool, on an iron-gray horse. He revealed himself as Arawn, King of Annwn (the Other-World or Faerye), and admitted that he had suffered defeat at the hands of Hafgan (Summer White),[72] a king from Annwn. When Pwyll agreed to fight Hafgan in Arawn's stead at the end of a year at a ford, Arawn sent Pwyll to his faery palace in his own form. There Pwyll dwelt for a year, sharing the same bed with Arawn's most beautiful wife, yet turning his face resolutely to the wall. At the year's end, Arawn fulfilled his bargain, met "Summer White" at the ford by night in the presence of all their nobles. It was proclaimed that none should intervene between the two combatants. Pwyll dealt "Summer White" one fatal blow, and then departed to his own dominion.

Here, then, are the four non-Irish features noted in *GGK:* the noble huntsman who introduces the hero as a guest into his household; the huntsman's wife, whose embraces the hero spurns; the anniversary combat; its localization at a river-crossing. Moreover, there are additional parallels in the Gasozein episode. There Arthur, the huntsman, engages by night in an indecisive combat near a ford with a knight in strangely summery costume, clad in a white shirt, with white shield and spear, and riding a white horse. Both reveal their names. Gasozein proposes another combat at the end of the year, during which he will will not touch the queen. A second encounter takes place in the presence of all Arthur's nobles. It is proclaimed that none should

[70] On probable date cf. *Pedeir Keinc y Mabinogi*, ed. Ifor Williams (Cardiff, 1930), pp. xxxvi–xli; *Transactions of Honourable Soc. of Cymmrodorion*, 1912–1913, p. 64.

[71] For Welsh text cf. *Pedeir Keinc*, ed. Williams, pp. 1–6. For French translation cf. J. Loth, *Mabinogion* (Paris, 1913), I, pp. 81–90. For English translation, cf. *Mabinogion*, ed. A. Nutt (London, 1904), pp. 3–8.

[72] J. Rhys, *Studies in the Arthurian Legend* (Oxford, 1891), p. 281.

intervene. In the first onset, Gasozein evades Arthur's thrust, and the battle ends.

Are all these parallels, between *GGK* and *Diu Krone*, between *GGK* and *Pwyll*, between *Diu Krone* and *Pwyll*, meaningless coincidences?

Differences between the members of this story-group are, of course, inevitable, since each member contains not only the common element but certain manifestly extraneous elements. *GGK* is dominated mainly by the two Irish versions of the Beheading Test. The Gasozein episode in *Diu Krone* has absorbed the Irish themes of *The Violent Death of Cûroi*, as we have observed, and of the boastful king, found in *The Violent Death of Fergus Mac Léite*.[73] The Pwyll episode, as Nutt and Professor Gruffydd have shown,[74] has been subjected to another Irish influence, *The Birth of Mongan*, which surely supplied the compact between mortal and god, the visit of one in the other's shape to the latter's home and bedchamber, and the intervention of one in the other's battle.

The significant point is that these various Irish influences on *GGK*, the Gasozein episode, and the Pwyll episode account for most of the differences. If we subtract the Irish elements from these three stories, we have left a basic plot, which we may thus reconstruct.

There was a supernatural king (*GGK*, P), who was clad in gray (P, changed to green in *GGK*) and rode a gray (P, changed to green in *GGK*) horse. He hunted with a pack of hounds (*GGK*, P, K) between Christmas and Twelfth Night (*GGK*, K, Welsh folklore). During his absence but with his connivance a guest was entertained in his magnificent home by his most beautiful wife, but maintained strict chastity in spite of temptation (*GGK*, P). The guest went to a rendezvous for an anniversary encounter (*GGK*, P). It took place at night (P, K) at a river crossing (*GGK*, P, K). One of the participants was a horseman called "Summer White" (P), or was lightly clad in white both summer and winter (K).

---

[73] Thurneysen, *Irische Helden- u. Königsage*, p. 542. This seems to be the closest Celtic parallel to the many occurrences of this theme in Arthurian fiction. Cf. *Historia Meriadoci and De Ortu Walwanii*, ed. J. D. Bruce, pp. lvii, 85 f.; *Merveilles de Rigomer*, ed. W. Foerster (Dresden, 1908), I, 470–82; *Hunbaut*, ed. Stürzinger and Breuer (Dresden, 1914), pp. 2–4; *L'Atre Périlleux*, ed. B. Woledge (Paris, 1936), p. 216 f.; F. J. Child, *English and Scottish Popular Ballads* (Boston, 1882–1898), I, 274 f. Cf. also W. Map, *De Nugis Curialium*, trans. Tupper and Ogle (London, 1924), p. 92.

[74] K. Meyer, A. Nutt, *Voyage of Bran*, II, 16. *Trans Hon. Soc. Cymmrodorion*, 1912–1913, pp. 72–80.

This encounter, or a later, was held in the presence of nobles (P, K); a warning against interference was proclaimed (P, K); and after a single blow the combat ended (P, K).

It cannot be a freak of chance that traces of this story are sharply imprinted, though in different ways, on two narratives so interlocked as *GGK* and the Gasozein episode.

What more can one discover about this Welsh tradition? Hafgan, "Summer White," evidently furnished Gasozein with his white shirt, worn both winter and summer, his white horse, shield, and banner, and determined his habit of fighting by night at a ford. The fourteenth-century poet, Dafydd ap Gwilym, casts more light on the subject, for he represents Haf, "Summer," as a person.[75] Summer is a prince (*Tywysawg*). He departs to his own land of Annwn to escape the gales of winter. His favored month of May is personified as a horseman (*marchog*), and is contrasted with the rigors of January. Professor T. Gwynn Jones remarks with penetration:[76] "The poems attributed to Dafydd, and many others, derive much of their 'natural magic' from legends, and what often passes for imagination on the part of the bards is basically the symbol of a nature cult." We need not hesitate to identify Dafydd's Haf, the personification of Summer, with the Hafgan of Pwyll. This being so, what of his victory over Arawn, the gray huntsman with his pack of hounds?

Modern Welsh folk-custom and folklore give an answer. As late as the nineteenth century in South Wales a ritual conflict between Summer and Winter was enacted yearly.[77] Two companies of young men were formed. The captain of the summer

---

[75] For Welsh text and free English trans. cf. Dafydd ap Gwilym, *Fifty Poems*, trans. H. I. and D. Bell (London, 1942), pp. 252–59. T. Gwynn Jones, *Welsh Folklore and Folk-Custom* (London, 1930), p. 154.

[76] *Op. cit.*, p. 154.

[77] M. Trevelyan, *Folklore and Folk-stories of Wales*, p. 53. Similar customs are found in Scandinavian and Germanic lands. Cf. J. G. Frazer, *Golden Bough*, ed. 3, IV, 254 ff.; J. Grimm, *Teutonic Mythology*, trans. Stallybrass (London, 1883), II, 758–69; W. Hone, *Every-day Book* (London, 1838), I, 358 f. It is remarkable that near Breitenbrunn in Oberpfalz "Sommer" speaks of his "weissen G'wand," and speaks twice of his country as "das Sommerland," which seems to be the equivalent of the "aestiva regio" to which Melvas carries off Guinevere, discussed below. Cf. *Bavaria, Landes und Volkskunde des Königreichs Bayern* (Munich, 1863), II, 260. In Lower Austria and Moravia also "Sommer" is clad in white. Cf. Frazer, *op. cit.*, IV, 257. In Switzerland he wears only a shirt. Cf. Grimm, *op. cit.*, II, 769. In most of these instances he carries a green bough.

forces rode horseback, wore a white smock, and was crowned with flowers. The captain of the winter's forces was mounted, was dressed in furs, and carried a blackthorn stick. A sham battle took place in some common or wasteland, and the softer season gained the victory. This would be the natural outcome of a symbolic struggle fixed, as this was, on the first of May, *Calan Haf*, the great Celtic festival of the beginning of summer. In the impersonator of Summer we recognize a counterpart to Dafydd's rider, Haf, from Annwn; to Hafgan, "Summer White," a king from Annwn; and to Gasozein, clad only in a white shirt both summer and winter, and riding a white horse.

If Hafgan is Summer, Arawn his antagonist, clad in gray wool, should be Winter. In the same collection of Welsh folklore which describes the annual combat we read:[78] "In some part of Wales it was stated that Arawn and his *Cwn Annwn* [Hounds of the Other World] hunted only from Christmas to Twelfth Night, and was always accompanied by a howling wind." "In Glamorgan, Brecon, and Radnor Arawn, the master of these hounds, rides a gray horse and is robed in gray." "Stories about the Brenin Llwyd, the Grey King, or Monarch of the Mist, were told in most of the mountainous districts. . . . He was represented as sitting among the mountains, robed in grey clouds and mist." The hounds of Annwn are sometimes called *Cwn Wybir*, and *wybir*, according to Rhys, derives from Latin *vapor*, and means a condensed floating white cloud.[79] Arawn's gray woolen coat, his association with gray mists and howling winds, his predilection for the midwinter season, mark him out as the perfect antagonist of Hafgan in an annual struggle for mastery. He is the lord of winter and its storms. His baying hounds are the roaring blasts.

Students of folklore will perceive in Arawn a familiar figure; this wintry huntsman haunts not only the lonely mountains and valleys of Wales, but has been seen and heard by the peasantry

[78] Trevelyan, pp. 53, 48, 69.

[79] T. Gwynn Jones, *Welsh Folklore and Folk-Custom*, p. 203. *Black Book of Carmarthen*, ed. J. Gwenogvryn Evans (Pwllheli, 1906), p. xiv, n. 17. Rhys, *Studies in Arthurian Legend*, p. 156, n. 1. For further information on the *Cwn Annwn*, cf. Trevelyan, pp. 47–53; J. Rhys, *Celtic Folklore, Welsh and Manx* (Oxford, 1901), I, 214–17.

throughout most of Europe.[80] His company is known by many names: *La Chasse Furieuse, Die Wilde Jagd, Nachtjaeger, Odinsjaeger, La Mesnie Hellequin, Familia Arturi*, etc.[81] It is of very great significance that from the Shetlands to the Pyrenees, as Professor Archer Taylor has shown, folk tradition identified Arthur with the leader of the phantom chase.[82] Arthur's playing the part of Arawn in the Gasozein episode is therefore no isolated instance of this identification. Many are the interpretations given to the Wild Hunt by popular fancy or by scholarly mythologists. But Grimm and Mogk recognized that the most persistent features of this phenomenon in German folklore indicate that it is a myth of wind and storm, and Sébillot on the basis of the French evidence came to the same conclusion.[83] Despite the multitudinous variations in the European traditions of the wild hunt, it is surprising to discover even in German territory many parallels to the Welsh legends of Arawn. In German folklore, too, we find the huntsman riding only in the twelve days between Christmas and Twelfth Night, or whenever the storm-wind howls.[84] He wears a long gray coat, and his horse is gray.[85] He is met in a forest glade or by a stream.[86] He is attended by a pack of baying hounds.[87] He re-appears at the same place at the end of a year.[88] Though, both in Welsh and Continental folklore, this

[80] H. Plischke, *Sage vom wilden Heere im deutschen Volke* (Eilenburg, 1914)' p. 27. "Bei allen Völkern Europas lässt sich die Erscheinung, die man in Deutschland das wilde Heer nennt, nachweisen, in den Hauptzügen, ja sogar in der Benennung, zumeist übereinstimmend. . . . Es zeigt sich, wenn der Sturm besonders brausend durch das Land fährt und die Nächte am dunkelsten und unheimlichsten sind."

[81] For bibliography cf. S. Thompson, *Motif-Index of Folk-Literature*, II, 388–401; Plischke, *op. cit.*, pp. vii–xii; P. Sébillot, *Folklore de France* (Paris, 1904), I, 165–78; *MP*, XXXVIII (1941), 289, n. 2; M. Latham, *Elizabethan Fairies* (New York, 1930), pp. 97 f. Prof. Archer Taylor has generously added the following: M. Murguia, *Gallica*, p. 382, n. 2; E. L. Urlin, *Festivals, Holy Days, and Saints' Days* (London, 1915), pp. 148 f.; A. Dagnet, *Au pays fougerais* (1899).

[82] *Romanic Review*, XII (1921), 286–88.

[83] Grimm, *Teutonic Mythology*, trans. Stallybrass, III, 918–48. H. Paul, *Grundriss der Germ. Philol.*, ed. 2, III (Strassburg, 1900), pp. 333–37. Sébillot, *op. cit.*, I, 165 ff.

[84] Grimm, III, 921. Plischke, pp. 53 f.   [85] Grimm, III, 931.

[86] V. Schweda, *Sagen vom wilden Jäger . . . in der Provinz Posen* (Gnesen, 1915), pp. 11–14.   [87] Plischke, pp. 32 f.

[88] Grimm, III, 921. Plischke, pp. 73 f.

phantom hunter has been identified with the Devil or with some wicked mortal, and his tumultuous rout has been interpreted as a troop of lost souls, yet these are obviously the Christian interpretations of a widespread pagan myth. The Gray Huntsman was first created by the imagination of our European ancestors as an embodiment of Storm and Winter. The Welsh alone, it would seem, introduced him into the independent tradition of the mythical conflict.

The same antagonism between Winter and Summer which reflected itself in the nature lyrics of Dafydd ap Gwilym and was dramatized in the ritual combats of the Welsh folk, evidently lay behind the yearly conflict at the ford between the kings of Annwn, gray Arawn (or his substitute) and "Summer White."[89]

We possess what appear to be two other Welsh versions of the annual combat, and in them, significantly enough, it is represented as a struggle for the love of a lady. In *Kulhwch and Olwen* Gwynn ab Nudd, who was, like Arawn, king of Annwn and a huntsman, carried off the virgin Creiddylad to his home, which a later Welsh tradition localized at Glastonbury.[90] Her husband, Gwythyr ab Greidyawl, "Victor son of Scorching," gathered an army and went in pursuit. Arthur intervened and decreed that Creiddylad should remain inviolate, and that the two rivals should fight for her every *kalan Mei*, first of May, till the Day of Doom. What is evidently a variant of the same tradition occurs in the *Vita Gildae* of Caradoc of Lancarvan.[91] Melvas, king of the *aestiva regio*, "Summer Land,"[92] carried off Guinevere to his

---

[89] In Glamorganshire there was a folk tradition of a battle between fairies mounted on white steeds and others mounted on black steeds. The army on white horses won, and the whole scene dissolved in mist. This is probably another reflection of the mythical combat between summer and winter. Cf. W. Sikes, *British Goblins* (London, 1880), p. 107.

[90] Loth, *Mabinogion*, I, 331 f., 314, n. 1. Baring-Gould and Fisher, *Lives of the British Saints* (London, 1913), IV, 377. J. Rhys, *Celtic Folklore, Welsh and Manx* (Oxford, 1901), I, 203, 216.

[91] *Cymmrodorion Record Series*, II (London, 1901), p. 410. E. K., Chambers, *Arthur of Britain*, pp. 263 f. On date cf. Tatlock in *Speculum*, XIII (1938), 139–52.

[92] Already in Caradoc's book a false etymology has led to the identification of this summer land with Somerset (just as a similar false etymology led to the identification of Maheloas' "isle de voirre" with Glastonbury). Today Gwlad yr Hav, "Land of Summer," is Welsh for Somersetshire, but some recollection of the fabulous country remains. J. Rhys, *Studies in Arthurian Legend*, pp. 241, 346, n. 1.

fortress at Glastonbury, interpreted as *insula vitrea*, and after a year's interval Arthur gathered an army to win back his queen. Gildas intervened and Guinevere was restored.

In the poems of Chrétien de Troyes the same basic myth can be detected. In *Erec* there is mention of Maheloas, lord of the "isle de voirre," where there is never storm or thunder or winter.[93] All scholars agree that this lord of a summer country is identical with the Melvas of Caradoc and with Chrétien's Meleagant, who is prince of the water-girdled land of Goirre, in which name for excellent reasons we may detect a corruption of *isle de voirre* and the equivalent of *insula vitrea*.[94] Meleagant, like Melvas, abducted Arthur's queen. She remained inviolate through the intervention of King Baudemaguz.[95] When her lover Lancelot came to her rescue, he fought one indecisive combat with Meleagant.[96] Meleagant appeared at Arthur's court and demanded another duel after the lapse of a year.[97] It took place in a meadow, green and fresh at all seasons, and beside a stream.[98] The kinship of this narrative, despite all accretions, to the Melvas and Gwynn stories is fairly clear. It is possible to discern also traces of the *Pwyll* version. Gauvain offered to take Lancelot's place in his final combat with Meleagant; being refused, he removed his arms, and Lancelot put them on.[99] This seems to be a reminiscence of Pwyll's taking Arawn's place and shape. Moreover, this combat in both the *Charrette* and *Pwyll* takes place before an assembly of nobles.

Noteworthy is the fact that not only in the stories of Gwynn and Meleagant was the lady emphatically not violated by her abductor, but the same point is emphasized in *L'Atre Périlleux*.[100] Escanor was not permitted to lie with the damsel he carried off.

[93] Ed. Foerster, ed. 3 (Halle, 1934), vss. 1946 ff. On the isle of glass cf. *PMLA*, LVI (1941), 925 f., 928, 933–35. On Melvas and Meleagant cf. T. P. Cross, W. A. Nitze, *Lancelot and Guenevere*, p. 21, n. 4; p. 47, no. 2.

[94] For proof of this cf. *PMLA*, LVI, 926.

[95] Chrétien de Troyes, *Karrenritter*, ed. W. Foerster (Halle, 1899), vss. 3378–80, 4068–75. Cf. Cross and Nitze, *op. cit.*, p. 51.

[96] Vss. 3600 ff.   [97] Vss. 6167 ff.   [98] Vss. 7008–19.

[99] Vss. 6221 ff., 6768 ff. Note that in vss. 6931 f. Gauvain 'tost se desarme" and "Lanceloz de ses armes s'arme," Since Lancelot has arrived unarmed, it is clear that he takes Gauvain's war-gear.

[100] Ed. B. Woledge, pp. 32 ff., 55 ff. Brun de Morois, the abductor of Guinevere in *Durmart* (ed. E. Stengel, Stuttgart, 1873, vss. 4220 ff.), declares that he will not ravish her before sunset.

It is hardly a coincidence, therefore, that Gasozein promised that even if he won Ginover by arms from her husband, he would not lie with her for a year. There must have been a very strong Welsh conviction that the lady involved in the annual combat main-tained her chastity, thus long. But though the tradition was uni-form, the explanations varied. Gwynn, Meleagant, and Escanor could not ravish the ladies whom they abducted by reason of outside intervention. But with Gasozein the promise to refrain was voluntary.

In *Pwyll* and *GGK*, though there is no abduction, and no love-rivalry is involved in the annual encounter, yet there can be little doubt that the chaste conduct of the hero, when left alone with the wife of his huntsman host, reflects the same tradi-tion as the inviolate chastity of other ladies involved in the com-bats of summer kings and their opponents. The inventor of the plot of *Pwyll* adopted friendship as a motive for his hero's noble conduct, and cleverly combined it with his traditional matter. The inventor of the plot of *GGK* naturally motivated Gawain's conduct by presenting him as a paragon of Christian knighthood, much as the pentangle, symbolic of Christian virtues, seems to have taken the place of solar symbols.

The more one scrutinizes the formation of *GGK*, the more one sees that there was reason in it. What reason, then, was there for superimposing the Welsh traditions of the combat at the ford on the Irish sagas of the several encounters of Cúroi and Cúchulainn? Why does this same combination occur in the Gasozein and Guingambresil stories and in the Scottish romance of *Egar and Grime?*[101] The reason may well be that, whereas modern scholars are in most instances averse to recognizing mythical meanings,—and considering some of the specimens of mythologizing which one sees in learned journals even today,[102]

[101] *Eger and Grime*, ed. J. R. Caldwell (Cambridge, 1933). The friendship motif; the defeat of one friend by a supernatural champion at a ford; the victory of the other friend, impersonating him; the hospitable lady,—all these features (and more) derive from the Welsh ford complex. The solar features of the super-natural champion; the lady who hates him and reveals to her lover the secret of his strength; the magic sword required to slay him,—these seem to reflect Cúroi and Bláthnat.

[102] With all due deference to the prodigious learning of Dr. Krappe, his articles in *Speculum*, XIII (1938), 206, and in *Etudes celtiques*, III (1938), 27, seem to me to furnish excellent illustrations.

they may be pardoned a certain prejudice,—yet the Welsh and Breton conteurs had no such antipathies. Even their French and German successors had some realization of the mythical nature of their legends, and the Middle English *Sir Orfeo* is a most skillful effort in blending classic and Celtic myths.[103]

The Welsh doubtless perceived a certain basic resemblance in the meanings of the combat at the ford and of the encounters between Cúroi and Cúchulainn. To be sure, as I have maintained and as Professor Nitze, on the basis of the Beheading Test in *Perlesvaus*, has strongly urged, the basic Irish pattern seems to consist of the annual slaying of a solar divinity (or a human representative) and his replacement by another. This is a somewhat different seasonal concept from the Welsh combat of summer sun and winter storm. And yet it was possible to detect analogies. Cúroi was preceded by a heavy dark cloud; he was clad in a dark gray mantle; his ax descended with the noise of a wood tempest-tossed in a night of storm.[104] He was evidently the counterpart of Arawn. Cúchulainn could withdraw his golden hairs into his head, which then became red with blood; he radiated intense heat and melted snow; he was son of the sungod Lug.[105] Evidently, he embodied solar forces, was a natural antagonist to Cúroi (even though Cúroi, too, had his solar phases) and was therefore the counterpart of Hafgan. Three times Cúroi came to demand Bláthnat, "Little Flower," from Cúchulainn, each time at the end of a year. He defeated Cúchulainn and brought away Bláthnat, but at the end of a year Cúchulainn sought him out, slew him, and brought away the flower lady. The battle for her lasted from November 1, the beginning of winter (as Mayday was the beginning of summer), till the middle of spring. Here, obviously, was a seasonal myth, which had its analogs in the Welsh tales of abduction and annual combats. What more natural than that there should be many efforts at fusion? And it is a happy confirmation of this theory that still in *GGK* Bercilak had a glance like lightning and his appearance at the rendezvous was heralded by a harsh roar as if he had been whetting his ax;[106] that Gawain's solar sympathies became one

---

[103] Loomis, *Celtic Myth*, pp. 303–8. On *Orfeo* cf. *MLN*, LI (1936), 28–30.

[104] Loomis, *Celtic Myth*, p. 50.

[105] *Ibid.*, p. 47. *Feast of Bricriu*, ed. G. Henderson, p. 33.

[106] Vss. 199, 2199–2204. Cf. the noise which precedes the approach of Esclados to the perilous fountain in *Ivain*, vss. 481, 813; and the thunder in *Owain*, trans. Loth, *Mabinogion*, II, 12 f., 17, 29.

of the commonplaces of Arthurian romance; that Gasozein, as
the defender of the ford, retained the summery whiteness of
Hafgan.

That there were also genetic relations between *GGK* and folk
ritual has already been suggested by Sir E. K. Chambers and
Professor Nitze.[107] Chambers was naturally misled by the greenness of Bercilak into taking him for a "green man," a vegetation
spirit of the Mannhardt school. But since we have deduced his
ancestry from Cúroi and Arawn, neither of whom has any vegetable traits or green garments, and both of whom are clad in gray,
we must abandon this view. As I pointed out long since,[108]
Bercilak's verdant hue is due not to summer verdure, but to the
ambiguity of the Welsh word *glas*, which may mean either gray
or green. Probably A. B. Cook and Professor Nitze were right,
however, in attaching significance to the cluster of holly borne
by the Green Knight.[109] Captain Winter in the Welsh ritual con-
bat carried a blackthorn stick, and the blackthorn still blossoms
about Christmas time in the British Isles.[110] In Hampshire, according to Gilbert White, the season when the cold north east
winds blow and the blackthorn flowers was called "blackthorn
winter."[111] In one South Welsh district the king of Winter was
crowned with holly for obvious reasons.[112] It was of course
equally fitting for Bercilak as the personification of the same
season to carry the appropriate holly. These glossy leaves and
coral berries may well be a contribution of folk-custom, rather
than myth, to Romance. There may be other details, such as
Gasozein's white shirt[113] and the songs which he sings,[114] which
derive from ritual. But in the main, I believe, the case is clear:
Cúroi, Cúchulainn, Bláthnat, Arawn, king of Annwn, his wife,
and Hafgan were not human representatives of the powers of
nature, but the divine embodiments of them. The stories which

[107] E. K. Chambers, *Medieval Stage* (Oxford, 1903), I, 185 f. *MP*, XXXIII
(1936), 361 f.

[108] Loomis, *Celtic Myth*, p. 59. *PMLA*, XLVIII, 1004, 1008, 1029 f. Cf.
Kittredge, *op. cit.*, 197.   [109] *Folklore*, XVII (1906), 339. *MP*, XXXIII, 357 f.

[110] Chambers, *Medieval Stage*, I, 252, n. 3.

[111] Cf. *NED*, sub blackthorn.

[112] T. Gwynn Jones, *Welsh Folklore and Folk-Custom*, p. 153. Cf. Chambers,
Medieval Stage, I, 251, 253.   [113] Cf. *supra*, n. 77.

[114] Gwynn Jones, *op. cit.*, p. 154. "Songs called *Carolau Haf*, 'Summer
Carols,' were sung" by Welsh peasants celebrating Mayday.

went into the making of *GGK* were myths. Let me quote the great scholar, W. P. Ker.[115]

Whether in the Teutonic countries, which in one of their corners preserved a record of old mythology, or in the Celtic, which allowed mythology, though never forgotten, to fall into a kind of neglect and to lose its original meaning, the value of mythology is equally recognizable, and it is equally clear that mythology is nothing more nor less than Romance.

IV. "MORGNE THE GODDES." It is not hard to understand the role of Bercilak's wife, once it is realized that she is a blend of Bláthnat and Arawn's wife. But what of the old dame, "Morgne the goddes," who sent Bercilak as her emissary to Arthur's court to reave the wits of his knights and to frighten Gaynour? Is she an arbitrary addition, as Kittredge[116] believed? We have already observed in *Wigalois* a somewhat analogous figure in the older woman in Joram's castle. In *Diu Krone* there are confused indications that Fimbeus, the Green Knight's counterpart, had not only a wife who conspired with him against Gawain, but also an *amie*, a "gotinne," his wife's sister, who sent her emissaries to Arthur's court with malignant intent,—[117] all of which reminds us of Morgne and her role. What further evidence is there that the "goddes" of the Green Knight's household was traditional?

Let us remember that Bercilak's wife fills in part the role of the wife of the wild huntsman, Arawn. In Continental legends the phantom rider was often provided with a female substitute or counterpart, and medieval clerics repeatedly identified her with Diana, "paganorum dea."[118] There is at least one witness that in Arthurian tradition the mistress of the huntsman was Morgue or Morgain la Fée. In 1276 Adam de la Halle, who shows considerable familiarity with folk and faery lore, represented her as resolving to take as her lover for all her days Hellekin, the famous chief of the "chasse furieuse," and "le gringneur prinche qui soit en faerie."[119] Here, then, is a possible explanation for

[115] W. P. Ker, *The Dark Ages* (New York, 1904), p. 47.

[116] Kittredge, *op. cit.*, pp. 131–33.

[117] *Diu Krone*, vss. 4885–88, 23058–93, 23223–69, 24904–6.

[118] Plischke, *Sage vom Wilden Heere*, pp. 47 ff.

[119] A. Rambeau, *Die dem Trouvere Adam de la Hale Zugeschriebene Dramen* (*Ausgaben u. Abhandlungen aus dem Gebiete der Romanischen Philologie*, LVIII, 1886), p. 91, vss. 758 f.; p. 92, vss. 827–30. On Hellekin cf. O. Driesen, *Ursprung des Harlekin* (*Forschungen zur Neueren Literaturgeschichte*, XXV, 1904), pp. 25–

Morgne's presence in Bercilak's castle; she was a traditional mistress of the leader of the Wild Hunt, a counterpart of Arawn's wife.

A much more cogent argument for Morgne's original identity with Arawn's wife lies in the episode of the Perilous Ford in the *Didot Perceval*.[120] Here we have a beautiful fay, who, since she and her sisters could transform themselves into birds and had a home in Avalon, can be unhesitatingly identified with Morgain la Fée, who with her sisters could change her form and fly through the air on wings,[121] and who had her home, of course, in Avalon. This same fay dwelt in an enchanted palace, and was the *amie* of a knight who guarded the ford, evidently on a year-long basis, and who, when defeated by Perceval, told him to guard the ford for a year in his place. A study which I have been making of the Perilous Ford motif shows that the version in the *Didot Perceval* is shot through and through with genuine Welsh tradition. Here then is a situation which gives every sign of being derived from the episode of Arawn, his wife, and the annual combat at the ford; and the role of Arawn's wife is assigned to Morgain.[122] Here also is a sufficient explanation of Morgne's appearance in Bercilak's castle; she was a traditional *amie* of the Wild Huntsman and was deeply involved in the annual combats at the ford. As a doublet of Bercilak's wife, she doubtless was taken into the plot of *GGK* at some earlier stage as a result of conflating two variant developments of the Arawn story.

Morgne came legitimately by her title "goddes." Elsewhere she is called *gotinne, dea, déesse,* and *dwywes*.[123] As the daughter of

---

62. Prof. A. Taylor informs me that he believes the name derived from German *Höllchen*.

[120] *Didot Perceval*, ed. W. Roach (Philadelphia, 1941), pp. 70–73, 195–202.

[121] Geoffrey of Monmouth, *Vita Merlini*, ed. J. J. Parry, Urbana, 1925), vss. 922 f. Hartmann v. Aue, *Erek*,[2] ed. M. Haupt (Leipzig, 1871), vss. 5177–79.

[122] It may also be significant that in the *Vulgate Lancelot* Morgain is twice spurned as a mistress by Lancelot, and in the *Roman de Troie*, by Hector (L. A. Paton, *Fairy Mythology of Arthurian Romance*, Boston, 1903, pp. 51 f., 54, 21); and again in the *Vulgate Lancelot*, her damsel, according to her instructions, tries to seduce Lancelot but in vain (Sommer, *Vulgate Version*, IV, 127). Though there is no clear evidence, these episodes seem to be offshoots of a tradition that Morgain was often rebuffed in her amorous advances, and may be derived from the role of Pwyll's wife. Cf. my forthcoming article in *Speculum*, "Morgain la Fée and the Celtic Goddesses."

[123] Loomis, *Celtic Myth*, p. 192. *PMLA*, LVI (1941), 907. Hartmann von Aue, *Erek*, vs. 5161.

Avaloc, and the mother of Ivain by Urien, she is identical with Welsh Modron, daughter of Avallach and mother of Owain by Urien.[124] In a Welsh tale the mother of Owain by Urien declares herself the daughter of the King of Annwn, and haunts a ford where dogs are wont to bark—perhaps the hounds of Annwn.[125] All Celtic mythologists recognize the descent of Modron from Matrona, a Celtic goddess who gave her name to the River Marne.[126] It was a long and a strong tradition which brought Morgne into *GGK*.

Whoever the genius was who worked out the plot of *GGK*, he performed a miracle, for I doubt whether in the whole history of fiction so perfect a narrative structure has been built almost exclusively from such inharmonious and recalcitrant materials. Well might Mr. C. S. Lewis remark apropos of the poem (as well as of Salisbury Cathedral and the *Divine Comedy*) that in these works "medieval art attains a unity of the highest order, because it embraces the greatest diversity of subordinated detail."[127] How diverse and divergent were the traditions which went into the making of *GGK* Mr. Lewis probably did not realize; only a comparative study of the themes of Beheading Test, Temptation, Perilous Castle, Magic Girdle, Gawain's Loves, the Ford Perilous, the Huntsman Host, and the Annual Combat can give one any impression of the complexity and contradictoriness of the matter employed to make this singularly harmonious, neatly dovetailed narrative. Here is an instance where source study, far from detracting from the greatness of a masterpiece, is essential to a full understanding of its greatness. Working with much the same materials, the originators of the plots of *Wigalois* and *Diu Krone* show some ingenuity, but much of the motivation remains unnatural or obscure, connections are often loose, and discrepancies occur. What were the motives of Joram and Fimbeus in coming to Arthur's court and urging Ginover to accept the girdles? Was Gasozein's claim to Ginover true or false? In *GGK* thirty-five or more traditional features have been shaped into an almost flawless plot. And nothing could be neater than the employment of the one non-Celtic element discovered by

[124] *Romanic Review*, xxix (1938), 176 f.

[125] *Aberystwyth Studies*, iv (1922), 105.

[126] J. Rhys, *Hibbert Lectures*[2] (London, 1892), pp. 28 f. T. Gwynn Jones, *Welsh Folklore*, p. 17. *Cymmrodor*, xlii (1930), 140. Hastings, *Encyclopedia of Religion*, iii, 292.   [127] *Allegory of Love* (Oxford, 1936), p. 142.

Professor Hulbert.[128] It would seem a hopeless task to find any causal connection between the Welsh tradition of the hero's chaste behavior toward the huntsman's wife, the Irish tradition of the treacherous wife who bestows her husband's protective girdle on her lover, and the Irish tradition of the Beheading Test. Yet the creator of the plot of *GGK* found in the extraneous motif—the exchange of winnings—a perfect solution. It was a stroke of genius.

For this triumph in narrative architecture we cannot give the credit to the English poet. At least, nothing in his other works suggests any such power. Besides, no one in the fourteenth century had access to the many lost *contes* which the creator of the plot must have used if he were to include the 37 or 38 features derived from Celtic tradition. Most of these *contes* must have been lost in that century, since even a royal collector, Charles V, possessed little or nothing that is not extant today. That the *Gawain* poet had eight or ten French tales representing the various forms of the Cúchulainn-Cúroi-Bláthnat complex and the Hafgan-Arawn encounter, is incredible. His contribution lay rather in the brilliance of the descriptions, in the subtlety and naturalness of the characterization, particularly of Gawain, and in the pulsating vitality of the action. These qualities we find in the other poems of the Cotton ms. and in some of the works of the alliterative school. The author of the English poem deserves and has received his meed of glory. But the credit for the narrative framework must go elsewhere. Not altogether to one man, for in the Guingambresil and the Gasozein episodes, in the *Carl of Carlisle* and the *Chevalier à l'Espée*, we can perceive fumbling efforts towards the shaping of our plot. Still, most of the glory for this structural miracle must go to some great unknown. He was in all probability a Frenchman, perhaps a contemporary of the architects of Amiens and Rheims cathedrals. At any rate, he shared with them the power of building diverse materials, adjusting diverse claims, shaping diverse traditions into a superb unity.[129]

---

[128] *MP*, xiii (1916), 699–701.

[129] I am greatly indebted to Prof. Archer Taylor and Prof. Henry Savage for their comments on this article at various stages in its development. I also owe my thanks to Prof. Vernam Hull and Prof. Arthur Remy for their kind assistance.

Vandeberes, Wandlebury, and the "Lai de l'Espine"

(Romance Philology Vol. IX, No. 2, pp. 162-167)

Ferdinand Lot, in his *Étude sur le Lancelot en Prose* (p. 143), hardly exaggerated when he observed that, apart from certain easily recognizable names, the author of that cyclic work "construit pour la Grande Bretagne une géographie entièrement fantaisiste." If we turn our attention to the *Vulgate Merlin* continuation, presumably by another author, we find that here too most of the place-names, such as *Carmelide, Estrangore, Arestuel, Listenois, Clarence*, cannot be identified with any region or site. In some instances we are able to detect the origin of the name; for example, *Belande*, the city of King Clarion of Northumberlande, was obviously manufactured by cutting off the first two syllables of *Northumberlande*. *Benoyc*, the realm of King Ban, has been recognized as due to manuscript corruption and misunderstanding of Bran le Benoit,[1] a name which correctly translates the Welsh *Bendigeid Vran* 'Blessed Bran.' Similarly the city of *Cambenic* is doubtless, like *Corbenic*, due to a misreading of *Cor-beneit* 'Blessed Horn,' referring to the horn of plenty of Blessed Bran.[2] *Gorre*, too, taken over from Chrétien's *Lancelot*, goes back to a corrupt reading of *Isle de Voirre* 'Isle of Glass.'[3]

On the other hand, the author does reveal a minimum of knowledge about certain geographical names. He does know that the Saverne, the Hombre, and the Tamise are rivers, that *Dovre* is a port, that *Leycestre* is a town, that *Arondel* and *Windesores* are castles.[4] But he seems utterly ignorant of their situation, placing *Arondel*, for example, in "la marche de Cambenic,"[5] and *Windesores* in Brocheliande![6]

Another identifiable name occurring in the *Merlin* continuation is the castle or city of *Vandeberes* or *Wandeberes*.[7] It is described at some length as situated in a plain with no hill nearer than two leagues.[8] It was protected by ditches, a marsh, and battlemented walls. There were only two gates, each with two locks and two portcullises. As to the geographical location of *Vandeberes* there is more than the usual muddlement. On p. 113 under the form of *Vandaliors* or *Vandelers* it is described as a castle in Cornuaille, besieged by the Saxons. On p. 124 messengers from Cornuaille and Orcanie bring the news that the Saxons are ravaging these lands and are besieging the castle of *Vanbieres*. On p. 132 we read that the city of Corente in Escoce was only twenty Scotch leagues from *Vambieres*, besieged by the Saxons. On p. 164 *Vanbieres* is apparently in the territory of Aguiscant, king of Scotland. Finally on p. 383 we learn that the Saxons abandoned the siege in order to concentrate their forces before Clarence.

The geography of the wars described in the *Merlin* is quite mad, but it is clear that the author had a fixed idea that the Saxons were engaged in a long siege of *Vandeberes* or *Wandeberes*, and that they devastated the country round about. In the Middle English *Arthour and Merlin*,[9] written about 1300, there is the same story, and though the besiegers are consistently referred to as Saracens and though the name of the castle is given in vss. 4245 and 4512 as *Nambire(s)* owing to the misreading of initial *u*, yet in vss. 6930 and 8217 it appears as *Wandlesbiri*. Malory, following (as Professor Vinaver has shown[10]) a greatly abridged version of the *Vulgate Merlin* for a part of Book I, also converted the Saxons into Saracens and mentioned in Chaps. xvii and xviii their burning and slaying the people and their beleaguering the "castell *Wandesborow*."[11]

It can hardly be a coincidence that Gervase of Tilbury in his *Otia Imperialia* (ca. 1211) describes a place called *Wandlebiria*, so called because the Wandali (Vandals) had camped there when they devastated Britain and slaughtered the Christians. Let me quote:

De Wandlebiria. In Anglia ad terminos episcopatus Eliensis est castrum, Cantabrica nomine, infra cujus limites e vicino locus est, quem Wandlebiriam dicunt, eo quod illic Wandali, partes Britanniae saeva Christianorum peremptione vastantes, castra metati sunt. Ubi vero ad monticuli apicem fixere tentoria, planities in rotundum vallatis circumcluditur, unico adinstar portalis aditu patens ad ingressum.[12]

Wandlebiria has been identified with an Iron Age camp, still called Wandlebury, three and a half miles southeast of Cambridge.[13] Now obscured by a surrounding wood, it must once have been a conspicuous feature of the landscape since it lies 240 feet above sea level on the highest point of the Gog-Magog Hills. It is 950 feet in diameter and was surrounded by a triple ditch and vallum, and in the *Victoria County History of Cambridge* we read that "its position, strength, and size make it not improbably the chief stronghold of the region in Early Iron Age times."[14]

Though the author of the *Vulgate Merlin* has converted the Vandals into Saxons, has situated the camp in a plain, and has visualized it as a medieval castle, who can doubt that he had heard of *Wandeberes* just as he had heard of *Arondel* and *Windesores*? Or that the author of *Arthour and Merlin*, though at first he misread the name as *Nambire*, came to recognize it quite rightly as that of the famous hill-fort *Wandlesbiri*? Malory's *Wandesborow*, too, seems to reveal some familiarity with the place.

We can be fairly certain that it was not Gervase's tale, even though it was well known, which provided the little information about Wandlebury embedded in the *Vulgate Merlin*, and there is even less reason to suppose that Gervase was the source of the English romances. Apart from the discrepancies between the *Otia Imperialia* and the *Vulgate Merlin*, there is the fact that any romancer, reading the former text, would surely have made use of the story which follows the description of *Wandlebiria*, a story so arresting that it was taken over into some manuscripts of the *Gesta Romanorum*[15] and was worked by Walter Scott into the fabric of *Marmion*.[16] He summarized it as follows in *Minstrelsy of the Scottish Border*:

Osbert, a bold and powerful baron, visited a noble family in the vicinity of Wandlebury, in the bishopric of Ely. Among other stories related in the social circle of his friends, ... he was informed that, if any knight, unattended, entered an adjacent plain by moonlight and challenged an adversary to appear, he would be immediately encountered by a spirit in the form of a knight. Osbert resolved to make the experiment, and set out, attended by a single squire, whom he ordered to remain without the limits of the plain, which was surrounded by an ancient entrenchment. On repeating the challenge, he was instantly assailed by an adversary, whom he quickly unhorsed, and seized the reins of his steed. ... Osbert returned in triumph with the horse which he committed to the care of his servants. The horse was of a sable colour, as well as his whole accoutrements, and apparently of great beauty and vigour. He remained with his keeper till cock-crowing, when, with eyes flashing fire, he reared, spurned the ground, and vanished. ...[17]

It is most unlikely that, if the author of the *Vulgate Merlin* had read this legend of *Wandlebiria* in Gervase's book, he would have failed to attach it somehow to *Wandeberes*. The odds are that his knowledge of the place came through his ears and did not include the tale of the phantom warrior and his horse.

The Wandlebury legend has been discussed by Arthur Gray in *Proceedings of the Cambridge Antiquarian Society*, XV (1910–11), 53–62, and he declared that it had a "clear relation to the immemorial traditions of Wales and Armorica." Though he adduced no conclusive evidence, he was right, for there is a strong likeness to the *Lai de l'Espine*, a Breton lai assigned by Zenker, the editor, to the second half of the twelfth century.[18] In the lai the plot is complicated by a love affair, and the scene of the nocturnal adventure is not a hill-fort but a ford; otherwise, however, there is a marked parallel to the story of Osbert.[19]

The hero, a young prince, was listening after supper, like Osbert, to tales of bygone days and learned of a place where no coward would dare to watch on St. John's night. Like Osbert, he undertook the adventure and arrived armed on the spot. Like Osbert, he unhorsed his unearthly adversary, seized the latter's steed by the reins, and turned it over to an attendant. Osbert returned with the high-mettled animal, but at cock-crow it broke its bridle and disappeared. Somewhat similarly, the prince returned with the captured horse, but when his wife removed the bridle, the animal was lost (*perdu*).

Though one may place little faith in the author's statement that he found the substance of his lai in the church of St. Aaron at Caerleon,[20] I have shown elsewhere that he employed several unmistakable Celtic motifs.[21] The central motif, the combat at the ford, was recognized as of Celtic origin by Thurneysen as early as 1884, and since then by Jessie Weston and the late Tom Peete Cross.[22] We need have little hesitation, therefore, in regarding the *Lai de l'Espine* as embodying genuine Breton tradition, and in accepting the similar tale of Osbert at Wandlebury as a Breton *conte* which somehow came to be localized at the haunted hill-fort on the Gog-Magog Hills.

If this were a unique example of the attachment of a Celtic tale to a specific site in Britain, its importance would not be great; it might be merely an odd accident. But such medieval localizations of what were very old traditional stories were by no means rare. The abduction of Guenevere by Melvas was an ancient myth, as Cross and Professor Nitze recognized,[23] but the localization at Glastonbury was a tardy development due to a mistaken equation of Glastonbury with the "Isle of Glass."[24] Likewise the well-established tradition of a Castle of Maidens was linked to Edinburgh and to Gloucester as the result of curious reasoning processes.[25] The *Fier Baiser* adventure, which had its roots in the Irish legend of the transformation of the Sovranty of Erin,[26] came to be localized, according to *Le Bel Inconnu*, among the ruins of Sinadon, the old Roman fort of Segontium.[27] Some of these connections were made by the Welsh, for it was Caradoc of Llancarvan who identified Melvas' "Urbs Vitrea" with Glastonbury, and only the ambiguity of *Caer Loyw*, meaning both 'Transparent Fortress' and 'Gloucester,' would account for Chrétien's placing the many-windowed Castle of Ladies on the boundary river, the Severn, and for the placing of the court of the nine sorceresses at Gloucester, according to *Peredur*.[28] Whether the Welsh also set the story of the *Fier Baiser* at Segontium, no one can tell. But to the extent that these localizations appear in French romances, they must have been transmitted by the bilingual Bretons.[29] It is therefore not surprising that it was a Breton legend of a nocturnal encounter and a supernatural horse which Gervase of Tilbury found localized at Wandlebury.

---

[1] R. S. Loomis, *Celtic Myth and Arthurian Romance* (New York, 1927), pp. 145 f. H. Newstead, *Bran the Blessed in Arthurian Romance* (New York, 1939), pp. 157–163.

[2] *Ibid.*, pp. 89–95. Cf. the form *Cambenoyt* in the *Dutch Lancelot*: J. L. Weston, *Legend of Sir Lancelot du Lac* (London, 1901), p. 159.

[3] R. S. Loomis, *Arthurian Tradition and Chrétien de Troyes* (New York, 1949), pp. 218–220. For place-names in Chrétien's *Erec* due to misunderstanding cf. *ibid.*, pp. 107 f., 163–165.

[4] Cf. Index volume of H. O. Sommer's *Vulgate Version of the Arthurian Romances* (Washington, D.C., 1916).

[5] Sommer, *op. cit.*, II, 133, n. 1.

[6] *Ibid.*, II, 163. Sommer's MS here gives the corrupt form *Lindesores*.

[7] Though the MS followed by Sommer, Brit. Mus. Add. 10292, gives the forms *uandaliors*, *uanbieres*, and *uambieres*, the original form is furnished by the coincidence of the Middle English translation, which gives *Vandeberes* (*Merlin*, ed. H. B. Wheatley, EETS, Part I, 1865, p. 172), with the French continuation in Bibl. Nat. fr. 337, which gives *Vandeberes* and *Wandeberes* (Sommer, *op. cit.*, VII, 20, 21). For variant forms of the name in the Middle English romances (Malory, *Arthour and Merlin*, and the *Prose Merlin*) see R. W. Ackerman, *Index of the Arthurian Names in Middle English* (Stanford and London, 1952), p. 238, s. *Vandaler* and *Vandebere*. For forms in *Vulgate Merlin* and *Livre d'Artus* see Sommer, *op. cit.*, Index volume, p. 83, s. *Vandaliors* and *Vandeberes*.

[8] Sommer; *op. cit.*, II, 176.

[9] *Arthour and Merlin*, ed. E. Kölbing, Altenglische Bibliothek, IV (Leipzig, 1890).

[10] *Works of Sir Thomas Malory*, ed. E. Vinaver (Oxford, 1947), III, 1292.

[11] *Ibid.*, I, 37, 40.

[12] Gervasius von Tilbury, *Otia Imperialia*, ed. F. Liebrecht (Hanover, 1856), pp. 26–28. Liebrecht has a long note on the story on pp. 126–128. G. G. Coulton, in *Social Life*

in Britain from the Conquest to the Reformation (Cambridge, 1918), pp. 532–534, gives a translation of the story. Sir Walter Scott in *Minstrelsy of the Scottish Border* adds a footnote to the introduction to the Tale of Tamlane in which he observes the correspondence between Gervase and *Arthour and Merlin*. "In the metrical romance of *Arthour and Merlin* we have also an account of Wandlesbury being occupied by the Sarasins, *i.e.*, the Saxons, for all Pagans were Saracens with the romancers."

[13] Scott, in the footnote just cited, presumed that *Wandlesbury* was *Wodnesbury* in Wiltshire, but Arthur Gray in *Proceedings of the Cambridge Antiquarian Society*, XV (1910–11), 53–62, correctly identified it with the camp near Cambridge.

[14] For description of the camp see *Victoria History of the County of Cambridge*, ed. L. F. Salzman, II (London, 1948), 39–41. The earliest recorded form of the name is *Wendlesbiri* from the tenth century. P. H. Reaney, *Place-names of Cambridgeshire* (Cambridge, 1943), p. 88.

[15] *Gesta Romanorum*, ed. H. Oesterley (Berlin, 1872), p. 253. For English translation see *Gesta Romanorum*, tr. C. Swan, rev. W. Hooper (London, 1905), pp. 300–302.

[16] Marmion, Canto iii, vss. 421–614; Canto iv, vss. 388–454.

[17] W. Scott, *Minstrelsy of the Scottish Border*, Introduction to the Tale of Tamlane.

[18] *ZRPh.*, XVII (1893), 238.

[19] The portion of the lai summarized may be found *ibid.*, pp. 245–255, vss. 165–504.

[20] *Ibid.*, p. 240.

[21] R. S. Loomis, *Arthurian Tradition and Chrétien de Troyes*, pp. 90, 92–94, 130 f., 156, 276 f.

[22] The Celtic nature and origin of the combat at the ford in Arthurian romance has been recognized by R. Thurneysen in *Keltoromanisches* (Halle, 1884), p. 20; J. L. Weston, in *Legend of Sir Perceval* (London, 1906–09), II, 207 f.; T. P. Cross, in *MPh.*, XII (1915), 604, n. 1; R. S. Loomis, *ibid.*, XLIII (1945), 63–71.

[23] T. P. Cross and W. A. Nitze, *Lancelot and Guenevere* (Chicago, 1930), pp. 31 f., 58.

[24] *Perlesvaus*, ed. W. A. Nitze and others (Chicago, 1932–37), II, 58.

[25] Loomis, *Arthurian Tradition*, pp. 111–114, 452–457.

[26] *St. Med.*, XVII (1951), 104–113. Ulrich von Zatzikhoven, *Lanzelet*, tr. by K. G. T. Webster (New York, 1951), pp. 224–226.

[27] *Spec.*, XXII (1947), 527–530.

[28] Loomis, *Arthurian Tradition*, pp. 455–457.

[29] *Ibid.*, pp. 15–21, 27–32.

By What Route did the Romantic Tradition of Arthur Reach the French?

(Modern Philology Vol. XXXIII, No. 3, pp. 225-38)

BY WHAT ROUTE DID THE ROMANTIC TRADITION
OF ARTHUR REACH THE FRENCH?

IN *Celtic myth and Arthurian romance* (New York, 1927) I set forth a hypothesis of the origins and transmission of the Round Table cycle which succeeding years of investigation have convinced me was, in the main, sound, and these pages constitute an attempt to clarify and amplify the matter. In order that I may come to the point without undue delay, let me assume that the cradle of that great romantic tradition does not lie among the ruins of the temple of Zeus at Dodona or in the palace of Agamemnon at Mycenae or on some mountain peak in Persia.[1] After all, we are not on the road to Xanadu, but to Caerleon on Usk. Let me also assume that neither Geoffrey of Monmouth nor Chrétien de Troyes was the "father of Arthurian romance" in the sense that he first created or popularized the fantastic story-patterns characteristic of that cycle.[2] The number of Celtic parallels pointed out in the course of the last fifty years justifies our starting with the further premise that not only was Arthur himself an acknowledged hero of the Celts but also a considerable and fundamental part of his legend was Celtic. These issues, alas, are still under debate, but it is not out of dogmatism that I here exclude them from discussion. One cannot cover all phases of the Arthurian problem in one article, and the assumptions with which I start are, I believe, the conclusions of a majority of those who have made a close study of the

[1] Cf. C. B. Lewis, *Classical mythology and Arthurian romance* (London, 1932); F. von Suhtscheck, *Forschungen und Fortschritte*, VII (1931), 134; *Klio*, XXV (1931), 50.

[2] *Speculum*, III (1928), 16.

subject, surely a majority of those scholars who combine a knowledge of Arthurian romance with some knowledge of Celtic literature. So, postulating that the original part of the narrative elements in legends of the Round Table is Celtic, let me address myself to the question: how did they reach the French?

One outstanding fact established by the researches of the last fifty years is that the greatest number of striking analogs to Arthurian romance is to be found in Irish literature, many of them in Irish texts which have been dated on linguistic grounds before the twelfth century.[3] Of course, Arthurian scholars differ among themselves as to the validity of Irish analogs discovered by other Arthurian scholars. The late Joseph Loth was skeptical of the Tristram parallels discovered by Miss Schoepperle in *Diarmaid and Grainne;*[4] Professor F. N. Robinson expresses himself with extreme caution as to the parallels pointed out by Professor Maynadier between the *Wife of Bath's tale* and the Irish stories of the Sovranty;[5] yet to me a genetic relationship seems to have been demonstrated in both instances. Though upholders of the hypothesis of Celtic origins do not agree on any list of established parallels between Irish and Arthurian tradition, most will agree that there are a considerable number of striking resemblances. To my mind they present a formidable array.

How did these Irish elements reach the French and become imbedded in stories of Arthur and his knights? Were they carried directly from Ireland to France? Were they imported by the Christian missionaries who poured into Frankish territory and founded Luxeuil, Jouarre, Faremoutiers, and Rebais in the seventh century? Or by

[3] The most remarkable analogs are, I believe, to be found in G. H. Maynadier, *The Wife of Bath's tale* (London, 1901); G. L. Kittredge, *A study of Gawain and the Green Knight* (Cambridge, Mass., 1916); G. Schoepperle, *Tristan and Isolt* (New York and Frankfort, 1913); T. P. Cross and W. A. Nitze, *Lancelot and Guenevere* (Chicago, 1930); Nitze, in *Studies in honor of A. M. Elliott* (Baltimore, 1911), I, 19; A. C. L. Brown, in *Mod. phil.*, XVIII (1920), 211–18; A. Taylor, in *Romanic rev.*, IX (1918), 21; A. H. Krappe, in *Zeits. f. franz. Sprache u. Lit.*, LVII (1933), 156; in *Romania*, LVIII (1932), 426; in *Romanische Forsch.*, XLV (1931), 95; L. H. Loomis, in *Mod. lang. rev.*, XXVI (1931), 408; R. S. Loomis, in *Speculum*, VIII (1933), 415; in *PMLA*, XLVIII (1933), 1000; in *Romania*, LIX (1933), 557; T. P. Cross, in *Manly anniversary studies* (1923), p. 284; G. S. Loomis, in *Vassar mediaeval studies* (1923), p. 3; F. Lot, in *Romania*, XXI (1892), 67; A. H. Krappe, *Balor of the Evil Eye* (New York, 1927), p. 132; A. C. L. Brown, *Iwain* (Boston, 1903), p. 80, n. 1; L. A. Hibbard, in *Romanic rev.*, IV (1913), 166; Zenker, in *Romanische Forsch.*, XXIX (1911), 331 ff.

[4] *Rev. celt.*, XXXV (1918), 380.

[5] Chaucer, *Works*, ed. F. N. Robinson (Boston, 1933), pp. 8, 807.

great scholars like Eriugena and Sedulius in the ninth century? Or by later scholars attracted to the monastic and cathedral schools of northern France? It is well to consider the possibility, even though it has not been proposed in print, and must be dismissed at once. The early Irish scholars have left in the libraries of Europe a good many traces of their activity in the form of glosses and poems, but not a trace of heroic and mythical legend.[6] We know much of the interests of Eriugena and Sedulius, but nothing leads us to suppose that native profane sagas were included among them. And though it may well be that later Irish clerics played some part in bringing the legend of Brendan, St. Patrick's Purgatory, and St. Modwenna to the Anglo-Normans,[7] the difference between these strongly ecclesiastical traditions, clearly attached to Ireland by name and localization, and the fictions of Lancelot, Gawain, and Morgan la Fée is enough to demonstrate that the latter could not have been introduced by the same agency. It is obvious that the Irish clergy who visited France did not belong to that class of *filid*[8] who preserved and retold the traditions of Manannán, Lug, Cúroi, Cúchulainn, Midir, and Étáin, but they were interested in Christian learning. Moreover, if these Irish scholars had transplanted into Gaul their native legends of heroes and gods, and if these had taken root there, the later fruitage would have been found scattered throughout the vast orchard of medieval French narrative; they would have cropped out in Carolingian epics and in classical and oriental romance; they would have been common in saintly and religious contexts; they would have formed independent stories betraying by their nomenclature clear signs of Irish origin. But the fact is, these Irish motifs are found, with the exception of the *Pèlerinage de Charlemagne*,[9] only in Breton lais and Arthurian romances. By and large, we may say that it is only in Breton, Welsh, and Cornish localizations, and pre-eminently in association with Arthur,

---

[6] D'Arbois de Jubainville, *Essai d'un catalogue de la littérature épique de l'Irlande* (Paris, 1883), p. cxxxiv: "Nous placerons dans une section à part les manuscrits latins ou grecs qui ne contiennent en fait d'irlandais que des gloses, ou quelques poèmes ou notes formant comme étendue une partie simplement accessoire dans le volume dont il s'agit. C'est le cas de tous les manuscrits continentaux antérieurs au douzième siècle."

[7] J. F. Kenney, *Sources for the early history of Ireland* (New York, 1929), I, 355 f., 369, 412.

[8] R. Thurneysen, *Die irische Helden- und Königsage* (Halle, 1921), pp. 66 ff.; *Mod. phil.*, IX (1911), 121 f.

[9] L. H. Loomis and T. P. Cross, in *Mod. phil.*, XXV (1928), 331.

that we find these Celtic motifs. It is certain that Irish missionaries did not make these associations with Arthur, localize their stories in British territory, and deliberately suppress their Irish names. Neither would the French of their own initiative have been so curiously and consistently intent on canceling all signs of Irish origin and so eager to exalt the renown of a group of British heroes. Direct transmission from Ireland to France is a hypothesis which receives no corroboration from the facts.[10]

If we consider, however, the possibility that the Welsh were transmitters of Irish material, as well as contributors of native stories, we receive at once confirmatory evidence. Miss O'Rahilly[11] and Professor Slover[12] have assembled a mass of facts demonstrating political and literary contacts between Ireland and Wales. Professor Gruffydd has shown how profoundly one of the *Four Branches of the Mabinogi* is saturated with Irish traditions of Lug and Balor.[13] Professor Hyde has pointed out Irish parallels to *Kilhwch and Olwen*.[14] Irish influence on the very Welsh literature which developed into Arthurian romance is a plain fact. Brythonic stories of Bran, Pryderi, Rhiannon, and Llew[15] are, on the one hand, mingled with Irish tales in the *Four Branches of the Mabinogi*, and, on the other hand, are to be definitely detected in Arthurian romance. Here, then, in Wales was not only the logical place for Irish saga to mingle with British myth and hero-legends of Arthur, but also the actual place where historical conditions favored their mingling and where we can observe currents flowing in from Ireland and flowing out to meet us again in French literature. The remains of the Welsh stage in this process of development are so scanty that it is not possible to point to a single story of which we possess the precise intermediate form between the Irish original and

[10] Though in the *Lai de l'Espine* (ed. Zenker, in *Zeits. f. rom. Phil.*, XVII, 233) we read of an Irish harper who sang a "lai d'Orphey," the surviving English lai of *Sir Orfeo* is a blend not only of classical and Irish elements but also of Breton. Cf. *Mod. lang. notes*, LI (1936), 28. We must adopt the alternative suggested by L. A. Hibbard, *Mediaeval romance in England* (New York, 1924), p. 199, that "the bilingual Breton minstrels may have turned the Orpheus story into the form of a lay which the Irish minstrel learned and sang."

[11] C. O'Rahilly, *Ireland and Wales* (London, 1924).

[12] *University of Texas studies in English*, VI (1926), 5; VII (1927), 5.

[13] W. J. Gruffydd, *Math Vab Mathonwy* (Cardiff, 1928).

[14] *Transactions of the fourth Celtic Congress* (Swansea, 1923), p. 39.

[15] *Mod. lang. rev.*, XXIV (1929), 418, 427; *Revue celt.*, XLVII (1930), 39; *Speculum*, VIII (1933), 426–30; *PMLA*, XLV (1930), 432–41.

the French romance. We can, however, say that the famous Irish story of the betrayal of Cúroi by Bláthnat (Little Flower) descends into Welsh as the betrayal of Llew by Blodeuwedd (Flower Face)[16] and into Arthurian romance as the betrayal of Caradoc of the Dolorous Tower by a woman, presumably named Floree, and as the betrayal of Milocrates by his wife in the *De Ortu Walwanii*.[17] Thus we have several Irish, one Welsh, and two Arthurian versions of the same story, though it must be conceded that the Welsh tale does not stand in the direct line of descent.

To the fact that the *Four Branches* and *Kilhwch* afford us a transitional stage between Irish and Arthurian legend we may add that not only was Arthur himself a British hero but also a large number of French Arthurian names can be derived from the Welsh with more or less certainty. Certain names of undoubted Welsh origin are to be found not only in the French romances but in Wace as well: Beduier, Calibore, Gawain, Genievre, Keus, Lot, Merlin, Mordret, Uter Pendragon, and Yder son of Nut. Wace, of course, got these names from Geoffrey of Monmouth, and it may be asked: Is Geoffrey the source of the Arthurian onomasticon? There is one decisive test. Geoffrey provides a list of the notables who attended Arthur's coronation, and Fletcher and M. Faral have shown that the list is largely fabricated from Welsh genealogies.[18] It is of no small significance that not one of these Welsh names, thus unscrupulously borrowed by Geoffrey and repeated by Wace, appears in Chrétien de Troyes or the Vulgate cycle. The same holds true of the non-Celtic names which Geoffrey included among Arthur's chief warriors: Guitart of Poitiers, Gerin of Chartres, Holdin of Flanders, and Borel of Le Mans, except that the last is mentioned once in the *Vulgate Merlin*. Not one of these manifestly spurious names found favor with the French romancers. Why? Because they possessed the critical instinct and the apparatus of a modern scholar, and saw through Geoffrey's little game? Nonsense! The only sane explanation is that the romancers derived their Welsh names, not from Wace, but, however indirectly, from Welsh tradition.

[16] Gruffydd, pp. 260–70.

[17] R. S. Loomis, *Celtic myth and Arthurian romance*, pp. 7, 11–15, 22, n. 36.

[18] R. H. Fletcher, *Arthurian materials in the chronicles* (Boston, 1906), pp. 76 f.; E. Faral, *La légende arthurienne: première partie*, II (Paris, 1929), 276.

This view is substantiated by the fact that the French romancers knew many Welsh names which do not appear in Wace at all. There will be no question that the boar Tortain is derived from the boar Twrch Trwyth, the cat Chapalu from the cat Cath Paluc, Brangien from Branwen, Yseult from Esyllt, Mabon from Mabon, Giflet fils Do from Gilfaethwy son of Don, Maheloas and Meleagant from Maelwas.[19] There are also solid grounds for supposing that Bran de Lis, Brangor, Bron, Brandus des Iles, Morgain la Fée, Niniane, Pelles, Pellinore, Perceval, Pierre, Lancelot, Guahries, and Guirres derived their names from important figures in Welsh, and that Lac and Lion are simply French translations of Llwch and Llew.[20] Arthurian topography, too, has a considerable Welsh element: Caerleon, Cardiff, Glamorgan, Sugales, Destregalles, Norgales, the Chastel de la Marche, which I have identified with Dinas Bran near Llangollen,[21] and Dinasdaron, which is probably a corruption of the same name.[22] What more could one ask as proof of a Welsh contribution to French romance?

At this point one must determine whether or not there was an important tributary flowing into Wales from Southern Scotland, where the Brythonic population of Strathclyde maintained itself for centuries as distinct from the neighboring Picts of Galloway and the Angles of Bernicia. Welsh literature, as Morris-Jones, Anwyl, and Professor Ifor Williams have shown,[23] contains many allusions to this region and its kings and heroes. Dr. Brugger has written voluminously, but less successfully, to prove that the topography of the district is reflected in French Arthurian romance. It is at least certain that Galvoie and Cardoil are Galloway and Carlisle, and fairly probable that Escalot represents Alclut (Dumbarton).[24] Ivain, son of Urien,

[19] J. D. Bruce, *Evolution of Arthurian romance* (Baltimore, Göttingen, 1923), I, 41 (n. 9), 51, 183; J. Loth, *Contributions à l'étude* ... (Paris, 1912), p. 103; *Zeits. f. franz. Sprache u. Lit.*, XLVI (1923), 265–73; J. Rhys, *Studies in the Arthurian legend* (Oxford, 1891), p. 51.

[20] Cf. my *Celtic myth and Arthurian romance*, index, and *Revue celt.*, XLVII (1930), 39 ff.; *Mod. lang. rev.*, XXIV (1929), 418, 427; *PMLA*, XLV (1930), 432–41.

[21] *Miscellany of studies in honour of L. E. Kastner* (Cambridge, 1932), p. 342.

[22] There are three romances which owe their detailed localizations in Celtic territory to late efforts: *Fergus* (cf. *PMLA*, XLIV [1929], 360; *Kastner miscellany*, p. 94); *Rigomer* (cf. Bruce, *Evolution*, II, 246); *Historia Meriadoci*, ed. J. D. Bruce (Baltimore and Göttingen, 1913), p. xxv.

[23] *Cymmrodor*, XXVIII (1918), 187 ff.; *Celtic rev.*, IV (1907–8), 125, 249; *Proceedings of the British Academy*, XVIII (1932), 270.

[24] *Mort Artu*, ed. J. D. Bruce (Halle, 1910), pp. 269 f.

moreover, is without doubt Owain, son of Urien, a prince of the northern Britons in the second half of the sixth century. But the only evidence that story material as well as names from Scotland reached the French is found in the legend of Tristram. Zimmer first pointed out that the Welsh form of the hero's name, Drystan, son of Tallwch, belonged originally to Drust, son of Talorc, a Pictish king of about the year 780.[25] Brugger has demonstrated that Tristram's kingdom of Loenois was Lothian, which, though it may not have been the kingdom of Drust, did include some Pictish territory.[26] Deutschbein in a strangely neglected article clinched the matter by showing that part of the saga of Drust has been preserved in the Irish *Wooing of Emer*, a section of which corresponds strikingly to the romance of Tristram.[27] In this very section a Drust is mentioned as one of the heroes subordinate to Cúchulainn, and in this section alone; the localization is in the Hebrides, not far from Pictish territory. It seems perfectly clear that certain youthful adventures of Tristram, including the human tribute demanded from Ireland, his asking and learning the cause of the mourning, his fight, his wounding, the false claimant, the recognition of the hero in the bath, his rejection of a royal bride, are a part of a saga originally attached to Drust, the Pictish king. This narrative tributary certainly flowed into Wales, and was duly elaborated, as we know, under the influence of the Irish tales of Diarmaid and Grainne.

Cornwall made its contribution also to this and other Arthurian legends. Not only does Tintagel serve as a background to some of the most memorable incidents, not only does King Mark seem to owe his name to a Cornish king of the sixth century, but also the name forms of Gorlois and Modred are not Welsh but Cornish,[28] and it must have been from the southwest that Geoffrey of Monmouth got the traditions of Arthur's birth and his last battle.

[25] *Zeits. f. franz. Sprache u. Lit.*, XIII[1] (1891), 69.

[26] *Mod. phil.*, XXII (1924), 159; *Miscellany of studies* . . . . L. E. Kastner (Cambridge, 1932), pp. 97 ff. On Celtic Tristram legend cf. J. van Dam, in *Neophilologus*, XV (1929), 19 ff.; J. Kelemina, *Geschichte der Tristansage* (Vienna, 1923), pp. 201 ff.

[27] *Beiblatt zur Anglia*, XV (1904), 16. On the transmission of the Tristram legend cf. Thomas, *Tristan*, ed. Bédier, II (Paris, 1905), 103–24; Bruce, *Evolution*, I, 177–86; R. S. Loomis, in *Romania*, LIII (1927), 82 ff.

[28] *Romania*, XXX (1901), 11. The statement that the name Tristram in the form Drustagni is found in Cornwall has been disputed, and Macalister reads it as Cirusinius (*Archaeologia Cambrensis*, LXXXIV [1929], 181).

We now come to the final question: How did this mass of Celtic tradition pass from the Celtic peoples to the French—through the Anglo-Normans, or through the Bretons, or through both? Everything points to the Bretons; nothing, so far as I know, to the Anglo-Normans. Gaston Paris' theory of Anglo-Norman transmission rested on little except a passage in *Waldef* and the presence of a few English words in Marie de France's lais.[29] The passage in *Waldef* asserts that the French translated *Tristan* from an English original; but the internal evidence of Béroul, Eilhart, and Thomas contradicts this statement so flatly that no one today accepts it. If Thomas placed Mark's court at London, it is obviously because he was himself attached to the Angevin court; if Béroul introduced the one word *lovendrinc*, it does not imply an English source for the poem any more than a few French words in an English novel involve a similar conclusion. Though Marie twice gives her lais English titles as well as French, she explicitly says that Bretons composed *Laustic*, and there is nothing English or Anglo-Norman about the names or the setting of *Chievrefoil*. All we know is that Thomas, Marie, and perhaps Béroul wrote for Anglo-Norman readers, but there is no reason to suppose that they took any of their materials directly from Welsh sources.

There are, moreover, two poems, one Anglo-Norman, one English, of which the internal evidence answers clearly the question whether the Welsh transmitted Arthurian stories to their neighbors across the border. The first is the *Lai du Cor*, composed by the Anglo-Norman, Robert Biquet, about 1150. The author knows or has invented a tradition that the magic horn was preserved at Cirencester, not fifty miles from Offa's Dike, and here, if anywhere, in the earliest bit of Arthurian romance in Anglo-Norman, we should expect to find signs of direct importation from Wales. Yet when we look at the name forms which might be expected to resemble the Welsh forms, we find on the contrary names that are even more remote from the Welsh than any similar list in Continental romances. The Bodleian MS furnishes the following forms: Gauuein, Giflet, Iuuein, Mangounz de Moraine, Gauwain, Iuwain, Arzur, Keerz, Kadoin, Goher, Muz, Aguisiaus, Glouien, Kadoiners, Lot, Caratoun, Garadue, Galahal.[30]

[29] *Romania*, XV (1886), 597; XVIII (1889), 510. For criticism of Paris cf. Thomas, *Tristan*, ed. Bédier, II, 315 f.; *Zeits. f. franz. Sprache u. Lit.*, XXXII², 138; *Bonner Studien z. englische Phil.*, IV, xxiii; Bruce, *Evolution*, I, 61 f., 154 n.

[30] Cf. ed. F. Wulff (Lund, 1888).

In this earliest of poems about Arthur written in England and preserved to our time there is not one name which suggests immediate
borrowing from the Welsh.

We turn to Layamon's *Brut*, composed late in the twelfth or early
in the thirteenth century at Arley Regis, not more than thirty-five
miles from Offa's Dike. Bruce demonstrated that two of the most
significant proper names which Layamon added to Wace—Argante
and Melian—find their close counterparts not in Welsh nomenclature
but in French romances.[31] Since Layamon did not inspire the Vulgate
Mort Artu or the *Didot Perceval*, there must have been a common
source. Celtic elements there certainly are in Layamon, but he seems
to have got them through a French medium. One may assert with
some confidence that, whatever the reason, Arthurian material did
not pass from Wales to France across England.

There remain the Bretons. Foerster's claim that they were the
inventors of the romantic tradition of Arthur and that they drew
nothing from Wales and Ireland has been thoroughly shot to pieces.
But his claim that the Breton *conteurs* were an important agency in
the promulgation of the *matière de Bretagne* is supported by an impressive body of facts.[32] It will be unnecessary to do more than recall the
importance of Nantes and the Forest of Broceliande in Chrétien, and
the derivation of the name Erec from the historic Guerec, a count of
Nantes, who died about 980.[33] Add to this the Breton names which
Bédier found in the Tristram legend,[34] and the localization of the
hero's birth and death in Brittany. Add the fact that the names of
Lancelot and Morgain la Fée are best explained as transformations of
Welsh Llenlleawc and Modron under the influence of names recorded
in Breton documents—Lancelin and Morcant.[35] Add, moreover,
names found in Breton documents: Ivanus, recorded in 1083[36] and
representing the transitional form between Welsh Owain and French

---

[31] *Mod. lang. notes*, XXVI (1911), 65; cf. *Rev. of Engl. stud.*, X (1934), 80 f.

[32] Christian von Troyes, *Erec und Enide*, ed. W. Foerster (Halle, 1890), pp. xxxviii f.;
Karrenritter, ed. Foerster (Halle, 1899), pp. cxi–cxxvii.

[33] Lot, in *Romania*, XXV, 588; cf. R. S. Loomis, *Celtic myth*, p. 94.

[34] Thomas, *Tristan*, ed. Bédier, II, 122 f.

[35] R. S. Loomis, pp. 92, 192; *Romania*, LIV (1928), 517; for Lancelin (not, however,
a Breton name) cf. H. Morice, *Mémoires pour servir de preuves*, Vol. I, col. 432.

[36] *Mémoires*, cols. 457, 469. Geoffrey's Eventus, son of Urien, and Evein or Evain, found
in *Tyolet* (vs. 630) and the *Didot Perceval* (J. L. Weston, *Legend of Sir Perceval*, II, 19 n.),
are probably derived from Breton Even, cited frequently after 833.

Ivain; Moraldus, recorded somewhat earlier,[37] palpably the immediate source (whatever may be the ultimate origin) of the name of Tristram's redoubtable opponent, Morhaut. Add the presence on the Modena sculpture, dated 1099–1106, of a name like Winlogee, which is clearly an intermediate form between Breton Winlowen and French Guinloie.[38] Wherever we turn in the French romances we are greeted by names which are obviously Breton or have undergone assimilation to names recorded in Brittany. The onomastic evidence, which is decidedly negative in regard to Anglo-Norman transmission, is decidedly positive in favor of Breton transmission.

Apart from the internal evidence of the romances there is the external evidence assembled by Brugger.[39] It may be summed up in the statement that when William of Malmesbury, Giraldus Cambrensis, and Wace refer to the promulgators of Arthurian story as a class, they speak uniformly of *Britones* or *Bretons*, never of *Wallenses*, *Cambrenses*, or *Gallois*.[40] If it be suspected that William and Giraldus must be referring to Welshmen in spite of the fact that they use a term no longer applied to contemporary Welshmen, note that William speaks elsewhere of Gawain as Walwen,[41] a form unrecorded in Welsh literature, equally remote from Gwalchmei, which the Welsh substituted for French Galvain, and from Gwallt-Avwyn, which, in my judgment, is the Welsh original of Galvain.[42] Note, too, that in the two passages in which Giraldus speaks of a *historico cantore Britone*[43] and of the *fabulosi Britones et eorum cantores* he also speaks of Morganis as carrying Arthur to Avalon to be healed of his wounds. Now both Morgan and Avalon are unknown to the Welsh under these forms; they know only Modron and Avallach.[44] Geoffrey of Monmouth himself cites as his authority for the *Historia regum Britanniae* a book which Walter the archdeacon had brought *ex Britannia;* and

[37] *Mémoires*, col. 436.

[38] *Medieval studies in memory of G. Schoepperle Loomis* (Paris and New York, 1927), p. 222.

[39] *Zeits. f. franz. Sprache u. Lit.*, XX¹ (1898), 79 ff.; XLIV² (1922), 78 ff.

[40] E. K. Chambers, *Arthur of Britain* (London, 1927), pp. 250, 272.

[41] *Ibid.*, p. 250.

[42] *PMLA*, XLIII (1928), 384 ff.

[43] Cf. Nitze, in *Speculum*, IX (1934), 358.

[44] R. S. Loomis, *Celtic myth and Arthurian romance*, pp. 192, 344 f.; J. Loth, *Mabinogion* (Paris, 1913), II, 237, 288; Geoffrey of Monmouth, *Historia*, ed. San Marte (Halle, 1854), p. 374; *Cymmrodor*, VIII (1887), 85.

this must be Brittany, for otherwise an Anglo-Norman could not have brought the book out of "Britain" into England, and Geoffrey himself expressly writes: "Armoricum regnum, quod nunc Britannia dicitur."[45] Even though we dismiss the Breton book as a figment of Geoffrey's imagination, it is significant that he did not cite a Welsh book as his authority; and though he certainly used, as we have seen, Welsh genealogies to concoct a spurious roster of Arthur's knights, the traditional Arthurian names which he did mention—particularly Hider and Galwainus—are obviously closer in form to French Ider and Gauvain than to Welsh Edern and Gwallt-Avwyn.[46] Internal and external evidence makes it plain that even Welshmen of the twelfth century knew and turned to Breton versions of Arthurian story in preference to their own native traditions.[47]

Foerster, though he grossly underestimated the talent and the influence of the Breton *conteurs*, rightly ascribed to them the introduction of the Round Table cycle among the French. To do so they must have spoken French. The *cantores* mentioned by Giraldus must be the professional singers of Breton lais, but their repertoire, though occasionally it touched Arthurian themes, was in the main distinct. The reciters of Arthurian tales must have used prose. Chrétien de Troyes in his *Conte del graal* declares his purpose as "rimoiier le meillor conte ... qui soit contez an cort real,"[48] that is, "to turn into rime the best tale that may be told at a royal court." The continuator, Wauchier, in a passage seldom cited but significant, writes in these terms:

> Mais il sont ore maint vassal
> Qui fabloiant vont par les cours
> Qui les contes font à rebours,

[45] Book V, chap. xii.

[46] Loomis, pp. 345 f.; cf. Zimmer, in *Zeits. f. franz. Sprache u. Lit.*, XII[1], 231.

[47] It might be well to reconsider the oft-cited passage about the return of Rhys ap Tewdwr from Brittany in 1077, bringing with him the system of the Round Table to South Wales, where it had been forgotten, and restoring it in regard to minstrels and bards (cf. *Göttingische gelehrte Anzeigen*, 1890, p. 796). Of late this statement has been rejected because it occurs in the MSS of Iolo Morganwg, who early in the nineteenth century introduced as much confusion into Welsh studies as Macpherson and Villemarqué have done in Gaelic and Breton. Nevertheless Professor Gruffydd says of these MSS in his *Math Vab Mathonwy* (Cardiff, 1928), p. 203 n.: "I refer to this much suspected source with all due reserve, but it may be safely stated that a large portion of the information given in the Iolo MSS. goes back directly or indirectly to genuinely ancient sources." Is it likely that the patriotic Iolo would have concocted a story to the discredit of Wales, and could have by accident fancied a situation so harmonious with evidence of which he knew nothing? Cf. Watkin, in *Transactions of the Honourable Society of Cymmrodorion*, 1919–20, p. 5.

[48] Vss. 63, 65.

> Et des estores les eslongent
> Et les mençognes i ajoingnent,
> Et cil ki l'oent et escoutent
> Ne sèvent que bon conte montent,
> Ains dient ke cil ménestrel
> Qui gisent la nuit en l'ostel,
> Quant on leur fait .i. poi conter
> D'une aventure *sans rimer*,
> Qu'il ont toute l'estore oïe,
> Qu'il jà n'aront jor de lor vie,
> Si lor font tout mençogne acroire
> Et il le sèvent bien aoire
> Et bien acroistre et metre avant.[49]

This passage should be compared with Chrétien's statement that the story of *Erec* was one which "devant rois et devant contes Depecier et corronpre suelent Cil qui de conter vivre vuelent."[50] Wace, however, referring to the same *conteurs* in 1155, is more complimentary to their art if not to their veracity:

> Tant ont li contéor conté
> Et li fabléor tant fablé
> Por lor contes ambeleter,
> Que tout ont feit fables sanbler.[51]

And Peter of Blois about 1190 witnesses that the tragic stories of Arthur, Gawain, and Tristram had the power of moving the listeners to tears.[52] That these *conteurs* were Bretons is shown by the well-known references of Wace:

> Fist Artus la Roonde Table
> Dont Breton dient mainte fable.
>
> E cil deuers Brecheliant,
> Donc Breton uont souent fablant.[53]

Both external testimony and internal evidence confirm the view that the early popularization on the Continent was the work of these anonymous Breton *conteurs*.

Zimmer and M. Bédier have emphasized the close association of Bretons with Normans and Anglo-Normans as a possible explanation

---

[49] C. Potvin, *Perceval le Gallois* (Mons, 1866–71), Vol. IV, vss. 28376 ff.
[50] Vss. 20–22.
[51] Wace, *Brut*, ed. Leroux de Lincy (Rouen, 1838), Vol. II, vss. 10040 ff.
[52] Chambers, p. 267.
[53] Wace, *Brut*, vss. 9998 ff.; *Roman de Rou*, vss. 6395 f.

of the diffusion of Arthurian narrative in France and England.[54] It seems fairly certain that after the Norman Conquest, in which the Bretons had a notable share, Breton minstrels and *conteurs* swarmed into England. The allusions of William of Malmesbury and Giraldus Cambrensis, already cited, and the evidence of Marie de France seem otherwise incomprehensible. It is also highly probable that the Breton *conteurs* found patronage in the Norman kingdoms of Apulia and Sicily, for the cathedral pavement at Otranto, made between 1163 and 1166, displays Arthur riding on a goat,[55] and in the early thirteenth century a tradition that the wounded Arthur still lived on in a palace on Mount Etna is found firmly established.[56] Nevertheless, Breton association with the Normans should not be overrated as a factor in the spread of the *matière de Bretagne*. Professor Levi's thesis and mine that the court of Poitou and Eleanor of Aquitaine herself did much for the vogue of the Tristram romance has commended itself to several scholars.[57] Chrétien might have composed his Arthurian poems even if there had been no contact of Bretons and Normans. Once the *conteurs* of Haute Bretagne had learned to speak French, they were free of the courts of all North France. Their patrons, the kings and counts of whom Chrétien speaks, were not exclusively their neighbors of Normandy or d'Outre-Manche.

Moreover, though these *conteurs* of the twelfth century must have been in the main of Breton extraction, we may concede the possibility of exceptions. It would be strange if by the end of the century there were not some Frenchmen in the profession, retelling and embellishing the tales of their Breton predecessors. The greatest exception to my generalization is the Welshman Bleheris or Bleddri, who alone of all the *conteurs* has left us his name and a reputation.[58] But if we are to judge by the content of the romances which claim him as authority, his repertoire was in no way distinct from the rest of the French cycle;

[54] Thomas, *Tristan*, ed. Bédier, II (Paris, 1905), 126 ff.

[55] *Studi medievali*, II (1906–7), 512, pl. XI; Bertaux, *L'art dans l'Italie méridionale* (Paris, 1904), I, 490.

[56] A. Graf, *Miti, leggende, e superstizioni del Medio Evo* (Turin, 1893), II, 303 ff.; P. S. Barto, *Tannhäuser and the Mountain of Venus* (New York, 1916), pp. 11–16; E. G. Gardner, *Arthurian legend in Italian literature* (London, 1930), pp. 12–15.

[57] *Studi romanzi*, XIV (1917), 177 f.; *Mod. lang. notes*, XXXIX, 322–25; *Romania*, LIII (1927), 89. Cf. *Neophilologus*, XV (1929), 31 f.; *Literaturblatt f. germ. u. rom. Phil.*, XLIX, 170; E. S. Murrell, *Girart de Roussillon and the Tristan poems* (Chesterfield, 1926), pp. 72 ff.

[58] For bibliography of Bleheris cf. *Mod. phil.* XXII, 123 n. Cf. esp. *Mod. lang. notes*, XXXIX, 319; *Romania*, LIII (1927), 82; *Neophilologus*, XV, 30–34.

there is no more knowledge of the topography of Wales; no closer approximation to Welsh name forms; on the contrary, there is the usual sprinkling of Breton names. I take the existence and the influence of Bleheris very seriously, but I am obliged to conclude that he spoke French, made up his repertoire from Breton or French sources, and owed his fame to the fact that he excelled all his confrères in the verve and passion of his recital. But his narrative material, if basically Welsh, had been already acclimated on the Continent.

This paper is largely founded on the researches of Zimmer, Foerster, Dr. Brugger, M. Bédier, and those Celtists who have studied the literary relations between Ireland and Wales. My own contribution, apart from certain details, consists in the attempt to show how the evidence on the origin of the Arthurian legend and its transmission from the Celts to the French can be wrought into a harmonious pattern. Unless I am much mistaken, that evidence is not confused and conflicting, but presents a clear and definite plan. We see Wales as the natural meeting place for Irish and Brythonic myth and saga; we see North Britain and Cornwall making their natural contributions; we see the Bretons of the Continent as the natural links between their cousins the Welsh and their neighbors the French. It is a conception which, to my thinking, is the key to many locks. Problems of nomenclature find an answer; the presence of Irish motifs in every stage of rationalization and decomposition is comprehensible; the sudden interest of the French in an obscure British war-chief is accounted for on the theory of infection by the Bretons; the difference between *Kilhwch and Olwen* and Chrétien de Troyes's romances is comprehensible when we realize that perhaps two centuries of divergent development lie between, leaving only four clear parallels: the ride of the youthful hero to Arthur's court, his demanding a boon, Kai's churlish reception, and the giant herdsman.[59] To understand the characteristic failings of oral tradition and to understand the constant effort, first of the Bretons, later of the French, to bring order and reason and chivalric manners into a beautiful but bewildering mass of story, is, I believe, to understand in large measure the legend of Arthur and his Table Round.

[59] Note the less obvious parallels between *Kilhwch* and Arthurian romance mentioned in Loomis, *Celtic myth*, pp. 73, 100.

Objections to the Celtic Origin
of the
"Matière de Bretagne"

(Romania LXXIX, pp. 47-77)

OBJECTIONS TO THE CELTIC ORIGIN OF THE « MATIÈRE DE BRETAGNE »

In the following article I place myself in a very embarrassing position, since, in dealing with the problem of the origins of Arthurian romance and the extent of its debt to the literature of the Celtic peoples, I shall have some severe criticims to make of both the defenders and the opponents of the Celtic hypothesis, and yet I have had and still have friends on both sides. It is embarrassing to call attention to defects in the work of Sir John Rhys, who showed me when I was a student at Oxford more than forty-five years ago nothing but kindness, and from whose *Hibbert Lectures* and *Studies in the Arthurian Legend* I have derived much information and stimulus. It is equally embarrassing, when I speak of the work of A. C. L. Brown, to be obliged to ignore the maxim " De mortuis nil nisi bonum ", for, though we were friends for many years, I can only join in the chorus of condemnation which his last book provoked. Among the opponents of the Celtic hypothesis one whose influence I consider most harmful was James Douglas Bruce, and yet I must seem ungracious in attacking him since he mentioned favorably my earliest publications. Of living scholars none has been more generous with his help to me than Professor Kenneth Jackson, yet since he took the opportunity at Strasbourg in 1954 to deliver a sharp and unprovoked attack on the upholders of the Celtic hypothesis, I am obliged, however reluctantly, to parry some of his thrusts and to find some chinks in his armor.

Scholarship cannot live without controversy, and personal ties and obligations, even one's own *amour propre*, must be disregarded in the conduct of that needful and not inglorious strife. In a debate as prolonged and complicated as that of the origins of Arthurian romance mistakes have inevitably been made on both sides, and it is only by the frank recognition of such errors that the issues of the conflict can be kept clear and progress can be made toward their settlement.

I cannot claim to be wholly impartial, but I will admit that if the advocates of Celtic origin have met with skepticism in many quarters, they have themselves largely — though by no mean wholly — to blame. From this charge I do not exempt myself. As one of the more pertinacious — and some might say pugnacious — champions of the theory, I confess to having done my share to discredit it. In *Celtic Myth and Arthurian Romance,* published over thirty years ago, I involved myself in a network of speculations and equations which was bound to provoke amazement in those better grounded than myself in Celtic literature. I proposed that the figures Curoi and Cuchulainn, famous in sagas of the Ulster cycle, represented two forms of the same divinity, one huge and old, the other his younger self; that their relationship to each other and the slaying of Curoi by Cuchulainn reflected the same pattern as the Priest of Nemi and his successor, as expounded by Sir James Frazer. I went on to argue that the name Curoi, transmitted to Wales, reappeared as Gwri, the name of the young hero of the *mabinogi* of *Pwyll*, that the names Gwrvan and Gwrnach meant "Little Gwri" and "Big Gwri", and preserved thus the contrast in size between Cuchulainn and Curoi. I have long since realized that not only is there insufficient evidence for these ralationships, but also that Gwrvan and Gwrnach cannot mean what I thought. No wonder that scholars found a book which started out with such propositions difficult to swallow, and I am not suprised that some of the associated ideas which I put forward — the mythical traits attached to Curoi and Cuchulainn, the interpretation of their rivalry over the woman Blathnat, "Little Flower", and the battle between them which lasted from November 1 to the middle of spring as a nature myth — were rejected, though I still consider the evidence to be strong.

Again, in dealing with the Grail problem I lumped together various Celtic vessels of plenty as prototypes of the Grail, and following Brown and Nitze, I included the cauldron of the Dagda, the chief of the Irish gods, from which no one departed unthankful. It was, of course, proper to object that, beyond its food-providing virtue, there was nothing told of the cauldron to suggest a connection with the Grail, and nothing told of the Dagda to remind one of the Fisher King. The result of such a rash coupling of the Dagda's cauldron with a vessel so unlike it in shape was to discredit any claims I made — and have made since — for other vessels which present notable analogies in their narrative setting or their shape to the wide and rather deep dish which Chrétien had in mind when he implied that it could hold a salmon, and which other romancers found suitable for the lamb which Christ ate with his disciples on Sher-Thursday [1].

Thus there were legitimate objections to the Celtic hypothesis as I expounded it over thirty years ago. I was guilty of errors of ignorance, of forcing the story of Curoi and Cuchulainn into the foreign pattern of the Priest of Nemi, of claiming parallelism and a genetic connection when the sole point of resemblance was too common place to prove anything. Needless to say, there were other lapses, and it was natural for Lot and Brugger to dismiss the book altogether [2], and, if there was a baby, to throw it out with the bath.

It may seem presumptuous for me to mention Sir John Rhys with anything but the highest respect, for he possessed a command of Celtic languages, literatures, folklore, and archaeology which far exceeds mine; indeed, in my *Wales and the Arthurian Legend*, I have had occasion to cite him more frequently than any other scholar. But in extenuation of my audacity I may point out that he recognized, himself, the fallibility of some of his major theses. He wrote in the preface

---

1. *PMLA*, LXXI (1956), 845 f. J. Frappier, *Chrétien de Troyes, Perceval ou le Conte du Graal, Cours de Sorbonne* (Paris, 1953), p. 90 : « Il est évident que les vers 6420-21 font allusion aux mets qu'on pourrait normalement s'attendre à voir portés dans un graal. »

2. *Romania*, LIII (1927), 401-06. *ZFSL*, LIV (1930), 81-125. Most of Lot's criticisms, however, I do not consider valid. See *Romania*, LIV (1928), 515-26.

to *Studies in the Arthurian Legend* (1890), excusing his
employment of the terms of the Solar Myth Theory on the
ground of their convenience, forecasting a revolution in respect
of mythological questions, and declaring that "finality is not,
in any case, to be dreamed of in a field where so much remains
to be learned ". Nevertheless, that book, coming from so
erudite a scholar, was naturally taken to represent the strongest
case possible for the Celtic origin of the *Matière de Bretagne*.
Yet few scholars today, even supporters of the same general
position, would accept many of his arguments, and Bruce
went so far as to declare that Rhys's ideas on the Grail legend
struck him as " fantastic to the last degree "[1].

Rhys, though conceding that there might have been a
historic Arthur, with a name derived from the Roman Artorius
(a derivation quite widely accepted today), maintained that this
Arthur had been confused with a culture hero or divinity, corresponding to Irish Airem and the Artaean Mercury of the Gauls,
and that from this mythical personage Arthur inherited certain
elements of his legend[2]. Rhys himself, however, granted that
the comparison between Arthur and Airem might create the
impression that the similarity between them was only to be
seen through the glasses of an etymologist[3]. That impression
seems to me justified, even though Rhys tried to bolster his
hypothesis by the existence in Perthshire and Forfarshire of
stories about Arthur, Modred, and Guenevere which offered a
vague resemblance to the Irish story of Airem, Mider, and
Etain. In fact, not only is the resemblance vague, but the
Scottish stories were not recorded till the eighteenth century
and were inspired by Hector Boece's chronicle, written in the
sixteenth[4].

Without forgetting the beam in my own eye, I cannot but
call attention to the recklessness with which Rhys handled

---

1. J. D. Bruce, *Evolution of Arthurian Romance* (Göttingen, Baltimore,
1923), I, 269, n. 2.

2. J. Rhys, *Studies in the Arthurian Legend* (Oxford, 1891), p. 6-48.

3. *Ibid.*, p. 45.

4. See a paper of mine just published in the Proceedings of the Society
of Antiquaries for Scotland.

proper names. Morgan le Fay, he asserted, was doubtless a Welsh Morgan, meaning "sea-born", and identified in point of etymology with the Irish Muirgen, one of the names of the aquatic lady Liban [1]. Unfortunately for this equation, there is nothing beyond the fact that Morgain la Fée is once referred to as a sea-nymph to connect her with Muirgen. This might suffice, to be sure, if it were not that many more remarkable elements of Morgain's story linked her on the one hand with the Irish Morrigan, as Miss Paton and Zenker showed [2], and on the other with Welsh Modron, who, like Morgain, was the mother of Owein (Yvain) by a mortal father, Urien, king of Reged [3].

Just as Rhys was deceived by the accidental similarity between the names Morgain and Muirgen, he was too easily impressed by the resemblance between the name of Pelles, king of the Grail castle in the Vulgate cycle, and that of Pwyll, prince of Dyved, in the *Four Branches of the Mabinogi* [4]. A fuller and more rigorous examination of the evidence would have shown that the Welsh prototype of Pelles and Pellinor was the Welsh Beli Mawr, apparently a dwarf king of the Other World, euhemerized as king of Britain [5]. Rhys was even more unfortunate in his selection of a prototype for Malory's Balyn [6]. " In Balyn one readily recognizes Geoffrey of Monmouth's

---

1. Rhys, *op. cit.*, p. 22 f., 348 f.

2. L. A. Paton, *Studies in the Fairy Mythology of Arthurian Romance* (Boston, 1903), p. 148-66. *ZFSL*, XLVIII (1926), 82-92.

3. *Speculum*, XX (1945), 190. R. S. Loomis, *Wales and the Arthurian Legend* (Cardiff, 1956), p. 114. J. Loth, *Mabinogion*, 2nd ed. (Paris, 1913), II, 284.

4. Rhys, *op. cit.*, p. 273-96.

5. R. S. Loomis, *Arthurian Tradition and Chrétien de Troyes* (New York, 1949), p. 139-45. On Beli as ancestor god see R. Bromwich in *Studies in Early British History*, ed. N. K. Chadwick (Cambridge, 1954), p. 131 f. On Kair Belli, identified as a " fatale castrum ", a faery castle, and localized at Ashbury Camp in Cornwall see *Revue Celtique*, III, 86 ; J. Loth, *Contributions à l'Étude des Romans de la Table Ronde* (Paris, 1912), p. 64. On Beli as possibly a sea-god see J. Rhys, D. Brynmor-Jones, *Welsh People* (1909), p. 43, n.

6. Rhys, *op. cit.*, p. 119 f.

Belinus, whose name represents the Celtic divinity described
in Latin as Apollo Belenus or Belinus... Belinus or Balyn was,
mythologically speaking, the natural enemy of the dark divinity Bran or Balan. "Though it seems possible, though far
from easy to prove, that Geoffrey's Belinus had some remote
connection with a Gallic Belenus [1], it was certainly a grave
error to derive Balyn from Belinus for no better reason than that
both engaged in battle with their respective brothers, Balan
and Brennius. Combats between brothers are not so uncommon
in legend or story as to serve as proof of identity, and there is
no reason to think that Balyn and Balan existed as characters
before they were created by the author of the *Suite du Merlin*
(*Huth Merlin*) [2].

Accordingly, even those who agree with Rhys as to the derivation of much Arthurian matter from Wales are forced to
admit that the case he presented was weak, too often marred
by rash equations, by ignoring the distinction between early
traditions and demonstrably late traditions, and by mythological
speculations of a very dubious nature.

But if Rhys's book did not inspire confidence, the latest
work of A. C. L. Brown, *The Origin of the Grail Legend*, was,
I regret to say, tantamount to a *reductio ad absurdum*, if not of
the Celtic hypothesis, at least of certain methods when too
carelessly employed by its advocates. I particularly regret this
because a book issued by the Harvard University Press and
written by one who had devoted his life to Arthurian studies
and who read the Irish sagas in the original seemed to offer an
authoritative survey of the evidence by a competent judge. But
one has only to open at random the pages of Brown's book to
come across such passages as these : "It is nowhere said [in
Chrétien's *Lancelot*] that Arthur is prisoner in a Dolorous
Tower; but if we suppose that he is not truly at Camelot but
is lying wounded in an enchanted palace at the outskirts of
the land of the dead and is subject to attacks by giants from a

---

1. Hastings, *Mythology of All Races*, III (1918), 290.

2. E. Vinaver in *Le Roman de Balain*, ed. M. D. Legge (Manchester, 1942),
p. xvii-xxii. There is some evidence, however, to show that Balyn's story
is a deliberate modification of Gauvain's. R. S. Loomis, *Celtic Myth and
Arthurian Romance* (New York, 1927), p. 250-52.

Dolorous Tower, it will explain the puzzles of the romance [1]."
Now all these suppositions are groundless. Again let me quote :
"In *Perceval*, Arthur is not a prisoner, of course, but he is
exposed to raids by giants from a Dolorous Tower. His castle
is not truly at Carduel but in Orcanie, i. e., Orcus or Hades...
The Red Knight is a Fomorian and a king of the dead like
Meleagant. In *Lancelot*, Bademagu's castle, from which he
watches Lancelot cross the sword bridge, is a castle of Maidens [2]."

I doubt whether any scholar of repute has gone farther than
Brown in rejecting what an author has said and making him
say something else in order to build a theory. Such a method
makes it possible to support any hypothesis, however fantastic.
Moreover, Brown endeavored to explain the strange adventures
of Arthur's knights by postulating the existence of an elaborate
narrative which he called a scenario and which "must have
existed somewhere before Chrétien [3]". This scenario Brown
fabricated by putting together motifs from Irish and Welsh
journeys to fairyland and from Aeneas's visit to Hades. It is
from this one arbitrarily devised composite that he would
derive nearly all the material of Chrétien's four traditional
romances. Such a single source is not only imaginary, but,
since the romances are so different, it is most improbable.

As for the Grail, Brown went out of his way to invite incre-
dulity when he took the French word *graal* to be derived
from, or substituted for, the Irish word *criol*, meaning either
a coffer or a basket, which he supposed would become by
mutation in the Welsh stage *griol* [4]. But *criol* is not found in
Welsh, and no such fanciful theory is required to explain the
word *graal*, which is well attested in Old French and meant
a "wide and rather deep dish", a synonym of *platiaus* [5].

---

1. A. C. L. Brown, *The Origin of the Grail Legend* (Cambridge, Mass. 1943),
p. 109.
2. *Ibid.*
3. *Ibid.*, p. 14.
4. *Ibid.*, p. 439-48.
5. *Continuations of the Old French Perceval of Chrétien de Troyes*, ed.
W. Roach, III, part 2, Glossary of First Continuation by L. Foulet (Philadelphia, 1955), p. 139 : « un plat peu profond mais assez large pour contenir

Brown again seemed eager to rouse skepticism when, instead of establishing firmly a connection between the Fisher King Bron and the Welsh Bran [1], he sought to connect the latter with the Irish god Brion, who, indeed, so far as I can discover, bears no significant likeness either to Bran or to the Fisher King [2]. Brown's strange attraction to the most implausible theses forced him to resort to the most desperate methods of establishing them.

It was a misfortune that a man of much learning and great ingenuity devoted his mature years to building an elaborate structure on the sands of guesswork, vague resemblances, and pure imagination. Surely, if this was the best case that could be made out for Celtic origins, the whole position would have to be abandoned. Fortunately Gaston Paris, Kittredge, Cross, and Miss Schoepperle adduced many significant parallels between Celtic literature and the *Matière de Bretagne* [3], and Brugger, though sometimes fantastically wrong [4], was often right in tracing the Welsh and Breton origin of Arthurian names [5]. While it is true that many objections directed against this or that argument in favor of the Celtic hypothesis are fully justified, many others are, in my opinion, fallacious, as misconceived as any of the arguments they are intended to meet. The pro-Celts are not the only culprits, the only fanatics, and it is only fair if I try to expose the methods of certain of their opponents.

Among the opponents of the Celtic hypothesis Bruce was one of the more judicious, the least fanatical. He conceded that a few of the characteristic motifs of Arthurian romance were of Celtic origin [6]; he granted not only that the Tristan

---

une hure de sanglier... M préfère un ' platiaus ' au ' graaus ' de *E*. » *Modern Philology*, XIII (1916), 681. Migne, *Patrologia Latina*, CCXII, col. 814.

1. Loomis, *Arthurian Tradition*, p. 386. Loomis, *Wales*, p. 53-60.

2. Brown, *op. cit.*, p. 240-308. Nothing could be more devious than Brown's methods of connecting Brion with Bran son of Llyr.

3. *Modern Philology*, XXXIII (1936), 226, n. 3.

4. *ZFSL*, XXVII[1] (1904), 69 ff ; XXVIII[1] (1905), 1 ff,

5. " Eigennamen in den Lais der Marie de France ", *ZFSL*, XLIX (1926-7), 201-52, 381-484.

6. Bruce, *op. cit.*, I, 74-91.

legend started in Pictland but also that it underwent a long
process of transmission through Wales, Cornwall, and Brittany [1].
He saw clearly what some anti-Celtists have failed to do, that
Geoffrey of Monmouth and Wace had only a trifling influence
on Chrétien de Troyes and the other early romancers and
cannot therefore be regarded as the begetters of a type of fiction
so different in content and spirit [2]. Nevertheless, in attempting
to discover the sources and the nature of Chretien's material
he made basic errors in judgment and logic.

His first error lay in assuming that all five of the poems
which introduce Arthurian figures and employ an Arthurian
setting are so homogeneous that what can be predicated of one
can be predicated of all. He declared [3] : " It cannot be too strongly
emphasized that the *Cligès* constitutes the proper starting-
point for any study of Chrétien's relation to his sources. We
can analyze with certainty his principles of composition in the
case of this poem, whose sources can be fixed, one may say,
even in the minutest details." Thus, having proved quite correctly that *Cligès*, though showing the literary influence of the
Tristan romance and of Wace, revealed no contact with traditional Celtic material, Bruce argued that the four other
romances were made up in the same way, and that though
incidental features, such as the chase of the white stag and the
Joie de la Cour in *Erec*, were probably derived from Celtic
sources [4], the main plots were of Chrétien's own invention.

Now an argument which starts with the assumption that
Cligès was made up in the same way from the same kinds of
material as *Erec*, *Lancelot*, *Yvain*, and *Perceval* is open to
challenge. In 1898 Kittredge wrote [5] : " The 'Cligés'...
formed no original part of ' the matter of Britain '; its Arthurian
relations are due entirely to Chrétien." In 1903 Gaston Paris
voiced the same opinion : *Cligès* was only superficially connected
with the Arthurian world, and was to be classed rather as a

---

1. Bruce, *op. cit.*, I, 171-91.
2. *Ibid.*, I, 37. G. Paris in *Romania*, X (1881), 488.
3. Bruce, I, 120.
4. *Ibid.*, I, 109 f.
5. *Nation* (New York), LXVI, 150.

roman d'aventure [1]. In 1915 Nitze again made the distinction [2] :
« Le procédé du poète en composant *Cligès* ne nous indique
pas nécessairement ce qu'il fait ailleurs. La combinaison d'un
conte oriental comme *Cligès* avec un thème ' arthurien ' comme
Tristan est évidemment tout autre chose qu'un roman 'arthurien' comme *Erec* ou *Lancelot*, où le thème et les matériaux
ont très certainement une seule et même provenance. »
M. Frappier, last year, formulated the contrast most clearly [3].
In *Cligès* « Chrétien renonce dans une large mesure à la *matière
de Bretagne*... *Cligès* se distingue encore par un air de réalité.
Plus de conte de fée à l'arrière-plan... on constate des correspon-
dances entre la fiction romanesque et nombre d'événements
réels... A la place des 'lieux arthuriens', souvent difficiles à
situer dans le vague et poétique royaume de Logres, nous trou-
vons une Angleterre authentique et des noms de cités bien
connues ». Strange to say, Bruce himself recognized this fundamental difference [4] : " It is generally agreed that no part of
this romance has any genuine connection with the *matière de
Bretagne* and the Arthurian affiliation which Chrétien gives it
is of the most artificial kind. " Yet Bruce based his main argument
for the non-traditional, non-Celtic origin of Chretien's *matière*
on an analogy between *Cligès* and the other romances — an
analogy which by his own admission is, to say the least, very
imperfect.

Bruce supported his thesis by an exposure of the weakness
of A. C. L. Brown's argument for the derivation of Chrétien's
Yvain " from a Celtic Other-World tale of the type represented
by the *Serglige* [the *Sick-bed of Cuchulainn*]" [5]. After sketching the
plot of the French poem and giving a synopsis of the Irish saga,
Bruce remarked [6] : " Most readers, we believe, will agree with
us, that it would be impossible for the French poet to extract

---

1. Paris, *Mediaeval French Literature* (London), p. 64.
2. *Romania*, XLIV, 33.
3. J. Frappier, *Chrétien de Troyes* (Paris, 1957), p. 106 f.
4. Bruce, I, 113.
5. *Studies and Notes in Philology and Literature*, VIII (1903, Boston), 145.
6. Bruce, I, 99.

from such a story the plot of *Yvain*." If we take this to mean
that it is inconceivable that Chrétien had access to a French
redaction of the *Sickbed of Cuchulainn*, remodeled it to give it
an Arthurian setting and a contemporary coloring, and thus
produced the *Chevalier au Lion*, we must agree with Bruce.
Brown was far from clear as to how and in what form the Irish
material reached Chrétien, but in his last book he remedied this
defect by claiming that there were Welsh, Breton, and French
intermediaries [1]. Now since the *Sickbed* goes back to the tenth
century, as linguistic forms show [2], it preceded *Yvain* by some
two hundred years, and there is nothing preposterous in the supposition that the original plot was reduced in transmission to
a mere skeleton, a bare framework, which was filled in with
extraneous matter. To offer detailed proof in support of this
hypothesis is beyond the scope of this article, and I must refer
to pp. 269-308 of my *Arthurian Tradition and Chrétien de Troyes*.
But the Welsh contribution can easily be detected in the
Arthurian setting and the choice of a hero, Owain ap Urien,
while the Bretons added the magic fountain in the forest of
Broceliande. Though Bruce exposed the weakness of Brown's
argument, he did not deal it a death-blow.

As for *Lancelot*, Bruce was obliged to concede that not only
the central theme, the abduction and rescue of Guenièvre, but
also the name of the abductor, Meleagant, and his Otherworld
realm were derived from the Welsh [3]. This, needless to say,
was a major concession. Nevertheless, Bruce denied that the
central figure, Lancelot, was anything but a purely literary
creation, since his name did not appear in Welsh literature, in
Geoffrey of Monmouth and his derivatives, or on the Modena
relief [4]. Now this is plainly the *argumentum ex silentio* — an
argument which in a case like this is valid only when the
records are abundant, and is conclusive only when the records
are complete. But is anyone so daring as to assert that the
records of Arthurian nomenclature for the eleventh and twelfth

---

1. Brown, *Origin of the Grail Legend*, p. 453. See n. 3, p. 54 above.
2. M. Dillon, *Early Irish Literature* (Chicago, 1948), p. 118.
3. Bruce, I, 196-203.
4. *Ibid.*, I, 192.

centuries are complete ? Let us take a figure comparable to
Lancelot, namely Tristan. His name does not appear in extant
Welsh literature till well into the thirteenth century
(*Rhonabwy's Dream*) [1], though he had already been mentioned
as a supreme lover by Bernard de Ventadour about 1154 and
must have been famous in Wales much earlier [2]. To deny the
prominence of Lancelot before Chrétien ranked him in *Erec*
as the third of Arthur's knights is to rely on the notoriously
fallacious *argumentum ex silentio*.

How fallacious it can be is proved by the fact that Bruce
overlooked a figure who appears twice in the *Kulhwch* list of
Arthur's warriors and who distinguished himself on an expedition to Ireland by wielding Caledvwlch (Excalibur) so effi-
caciously that he destroyed Diwrnach the Irishman and all
his host [3]. His trisyllabic name, Llenlleawc, might easily have
become Lancelot under the influence of the name Lancelin,
recorded in Brittany [4]. Now it is a curious fact that this Llenlleawc who slaughtered the Irish host was himself an Irishman,
Gwyddel. It is probably this Hibernian origin which prevented
Bruce from suspecting that this Llenlleawc was Lancelot, yet it
is precisely this Irish descent which makes the identification
probable and in my opinion certain.

According to the *Estoire del Saint Graal*, Lancelot's grand-
father, also named Lancelot, " sen parti de Gaule et ala en la
grant bertaigne et prinst a feme la fille au roy dirlande" [5].
Thus Lancelot du Lac was the great-grandson of the King of
Ireland. In the *Suite de Merlin* [6] we have a knight who, when
Balaain rides away from Arthur's court, pursues him and chal-

---

1. J. Loth, *Mabinogion*, I, 373.

2. *Modern Philology*, XIX (1922), 287. J. Kelemina, *Geschichte der Tristansage* (Wien, 1923), p. 220.

3. Loth, *Mabinogion*, I, 271, 276, 334 f.

4. Bruce, I, 193. G. Paris in *Romania*, X (1881), 492, n. 2 : « Le nom de
Lancelot est peut-être un nom celtique altéré. »

5. H. Sommer, *Vulgate Version of the Arthurian Romances* (Washington),
I, 293.

6. *Roman de Balain*, ed. M. D. Legge, p. 15-24. The inscription on the
tomb is transcribed from the manuscript of the *Suite* in Cambridge Univ.
Lib. Additional 7071, fo. 252.

lenges him to combat. Balaain, with his usual unhappy fortune, kills him, and has inscribed on his tomb : "Ci gist lanceor li fiz au roi dirland." It is a remarkable coincidence linking Lanceor to Lancelot that in the romance which Malory followed in his Book VII Lancelot plays a role similar to Lanceor's [1], though less tragic [2]. When Beaumayns rode away from Arthur's court, he was pursued, for no very good reason, by Lancelot. Beaumayns offered to fight with Lancelot, and handled him so severely that Lancelot cried quits. The differences between the two episodes in which Lanceor and Lancelot figure preclude the possibility that Malory's source borrowed from the *Suite du Merlin*, and the resemblances are such as to warrant the assumption of a common source. In that source Lancelot and Lanceor would have had a common original, and he must have been the King of Ireland's son. Recalling the curious fact that Llenlleawc, besides being an Irishman, accompanied Arthur to Ireland, and destroyed the Irish army, it is a noteworthy fact that Guiraut de Calanson, the troubadour, wrote about 1200 in his instructions to his *joglar* : "Apren, Fadet, De Lansolet, Com saup Islanda conquerir [3]." This has puzzled the commentators [4], since Lancelot, among his many exploits, is never credited with conquering Iceland. But Bruce pointed out in the *Merveilles de Rigomer* an obvious instance where Islande has been mistakenly substituted for Irlande [5], and if we replace the improbable Islanda of Guiraut's poem with Irlanda, Lansolet's achievement matches that of Llenlleawc. In short, the little direct information we have about Llenlleawc corres-

---

1. *Morte d'Arthur*, Bk. VII, chap. iv.

2. The tragic ending of the episode in the Balain is demanded, as Prof. Laura Hibbard (Loomis) pointed out in *Medieval Studies in Memory of G. Schoepperle Loomis* (Paris, New York, 1927), p. 175-86, by the special character of the hero.

3. K. Bartsch, *Denkmäler der provenzalischen Literatur* (Stuttgart, 1850), p. 98.

4. W. Keller, *Das Sirventes « Fadet Joglar » des Guiraut de Calanso* (Erlangen, 1905), p. 104-6. *Romanische Forschungen*, XXII (1906), 200[2].

5. Bruce, II, 252. Ireland was then divided into four provinces, each with its king. According to the poem, four kings in Ireland offer Gauvain the crown.

ponds to what we know about Lancelot, Lanceor, and Lansolet. That this association of Lancelot with Ireland is preserved only in such obscure allusions may be accounted for, at least in part, by the powerful influence of the Vulgate *Lancelot*, which established a new tradition connecting the hero with the kingdom of Benoic in France.

If this explanation seem inadequate, and if the links between Lancelot and Llenlleawc the Irishman seem due to odd coincidences, the answer is provided by ample, though complex evidence, showing that Lancelot goes back through Lllenlleawc to the King of Ireland, Lugh Loinnbheimionach. To go into the intricacies of this connection seems hardly necessary since I have presented them elsewhere [1], and I will content myself with enumerating eight remarkable parallels between the careers of Lancelot and Lugh [2]. 1. Both were reared, not by their mothers, but by queens, until they were fit to bear arms. 2. Both were trained in feats of strength by one or more mermen. 3. Both were nameless in infancy and were not given their names except under special circumstances. 4. Both, on arrival at a royal court, occupied or approached a seat of special honor, and were admired for their bearing and their prowess. 5. Both lifted huge stones and were consequently recognized as heroes who would deliver their peoples from bondage. 6. Both begat in clandestine affairs sons destined to high renown in arms. 7. One had a red color on him from sunset to morning; the other habitually bore red arms. 8. One became king of Ireland; the other was the great-grandson of a king of Ireland. I

---

1. Loomis, *Arthurian Tradition*, p. 187-92.

2. I have already listed the first seven with references in my introduction to Ulrich von Zatzikhoven, *Lanzelet*, trans. K. G. T. Webster (New York, 1951), p. 15-17, and without references in *Bulletin de la Société Internationale Arthurienne*, No. 3 (1951), p. 69-73. For the statement that Lugh became king of Ireland see *Zeits. f. Celt. Phil.*, III, 244. I have omitted in this paper a ninth parallel, which I still consider valid but which rests on the assumption that Lugh's marriage with the kingship, "banais rigi" (*ibid.*), was the equivalent of his marrying the Sovranty of Ireland, who appears together with him in the *Prophetic Ecstasy of the Phantom*. J. Rhys, *Hibbert Lectures* (London, 1892), p. 409-17. On Lugh see J. Loth in *Revue Archéologique*, IVᵉ Série, XXIV (1914), 205 ff.

believe that these eight correspondences between Lancelot and Lugh Loinnbheimionach prove a genetic connection, and it seems clear that the intermediate figure was Llenlleawc the Irishman.

Bruce cannot be blamed, of course, for failing to take cognizance of these resemblances in his chapter on Lancelot, for not even the most ardent champions of the Celtic hypothesis of his day had observed them. But he can be accused of adopting the fallacious principle of *post hoc ergo propter hoc* when in that chapter he concluded that the *Lanzelet* of Ulrich von Zatzikhoven, translated from an Anglo-French poem about 1195, represented merely a pastiche of adventures drawn from Chrétien's poems and arbitrarily attached to Chrétien's Lancelot. Bruce himself was aware that there was at least one strong argument against this view, and admitted that there was one traditional element in Ulrich's poem (the fosterage of the hero by a water-fay) [1]. Nevertheless, he had so convinced himself that Lancelot's story was a literary creation of Chrétien's that he brushed aside all difficulties and proclaimed that the later poem, Ulrich's source, must have been derived from Chrétien's earlier work.

Apart from the evidence of a nexus between *Lanzelet* and the legend of Lugh [2], and apart from the improbability that a poet inspired by Chrétien's *Lancelot* should have so ignored, even contradicted in effect, the central thesis of that work as to provide the hero with a series of four mistresses, Bruce disregarded a conclusive piece of evidence bearing on the independence of *Lanzelet*. Chrétien's account of the abduction of Guenièvre, as Bruce himself recognized [3], was an expansion of the Welsh tradition preserved in cognate form by Caradoc of Lancarvan. Now Ulrich's account of the abduction and rescue of Ginover could hardly be more different from Chrétien's, and as early as 1906 K. G. T. Webster pointed out in *Englische Studien* that it follows a quite different Celtic pattern [4]. In a

---

1. Bruce, I, 213-15.
2. Nos. 1, 2, 3, 4 listed above.
3. Bruce, I, 196-202.
4. *Englische Studien*, XXXVI, 348-50. Webster did not know the Egerton version of the *Wooing*, which presents a clearer parallel than the Book of the Dun Cow version to *Lanzelet*.

twelfth-century version of the *Wooing of Etain* we find anticipated the following features of Ulrich's story [1] : Valerin's
assertion that he had an earlier claim to Ginover than Arthur's;
her rejection of his claim ; his carrying her away forcibly at an
equestrian assemblage ; Arthur's enlisting the aid of a wizard
to recover his queen ; his destruction of Valerin's castle, and
his winning back his wife. Just so, in the Egerton text, Mider
asserted an earlier claim to Etain than that of her husband
Eochaid; Etain rejected his claim ; Mider carried her away
forcibly at an equestrian assemblage ; Eochaid enlisted the aid
of a wizard to recover his queen ; he destroyed Mider's palace,
and took back his wife. By overlooking Webster's discovery or
by failing to realize its significance, Bruce fell into the logical
error of assuming that if there were two versions of the
abduction and rescue of Guenièvre, the earlier must be the
source of the later, no matter how great the differences—an
example of the fallacy of *post hoc ergo propter hoc.*

When Bruce took up the subject of Perceval and the Grail,
he was able, on the whole effectively, to dispose of the pro-
Celtic arguments of Nutt and Brown [2], but his own arguments
follow, as in a groove, the same fallible reasoning as in his
discussion of Lancelot. He cites (p. 247) *Cligès* to show that
Chrétien " always makes up his romances by combining
elements drawn from different sources "— presumably non-
Celtic. He declares (p. 251) : " There is no reason ... to think
that before Chrétien any definite story had ever been attached
to his [Perceval's] name any more than to that of Lancelot. "
Again (p. 275) : " No one has yet brought forward a folk-tale,
Celtic or otherwise, corresponding in incident or setting to
the Grail story. " And, of course, all later versions of the Grail
legend were echoes of Chrétien's poem (p. 294) : " one may

---

1. A. H. Leahy, *Heroic Romances of Ireland* (London, 1905), I, 19-21.
Ulrich von Zatzikhoven, *Lanzelet*, trans. Webster, p. 18 f., 93, 96 f., 117,
120, 125 f., 216. On the composition of the Egerton version see *Zeits. f.
Celt. Philologie*, IX (1913), 356. The story of Etain being carried off by
Midir, in which the parallelism is found, was based on a poem in the Book
of Leinster and therefore earlier than 1150.

2. Bruce, I, 269-76.

safely affirm that Wauchier knew nothing of the Grail, except what he found in Chrétien's fragmentary poem, and Manessier and Gerbert were in the same case—only they had Wauchier's and Pseudo-Wauchier's continuations, besides, to furnish suggestions to their imaginations." Here one recognizes the false analogy between *Cligès* and the other romances; the dubious argument *ex silentio*; the dangerous assumption of *post hoc ergo propter hoc*, in the sense that Chrétien's successors merely added variation upon variation to his *Perceval*.

Bruce was fair-minded enough to mention several facts which conflicted with his thesis : the " folk-lore origin " of the question test (p. 250, n. 33), the Great Fool or *Dümmling* motif, and the Waste Land; the folk-tale spirit of Gauvain's visit to the Grail castle ; Chrétien's statement that he was "putting into verse a prose-romance that the Count gave him "; the heterodoxy of permitting a maiden to administer the Sacrament. He also admitted in a footnote (p. 248) that Zimmer, Nutt, and Pace had adduced parallels between the *enfances* of Perceval and those of Cuchulainn and Finn. But all these suspicious circumstances did not undermine his belief that Chrétien in his last poem produced an entirely original medley of folklore motifs with others of his own invention, and centred them around a mystical version of the Byzantine mass.

Probably those who are convinced by Bruce's arguments will not be led to reconsider by my exposition of their frailty nor by my attempt in *Arthurian Tradition* to show that Perceval, like Lancelot, had a prototype in Welsh literature [1], and that Perceval's story, as told by Chrétien, was a traditional medley of elements from Celtic sagas (not folktales) and, though doubtless improved in the telling, was not the poet's own invention [2]. In any case, I have not room to elaborate the

---

1. *Arthurian Tradition*, p. 341-46.

2. *Ibid.*, p. 355-417, 430-33. A gross misconception, frequently expressed by both pro-Celts and anti-Celts, is to regard the traditional elements in Arthurian romance as derived from folklore, from folktales, and by implication picked up from the lips of swineherds, clodhoppers, fishermen, etc. The Irish sagas, the Welsh *mabinogion*, and the Breton *lais* doubtless contain

matter here. But I should like to ask a question which Bruce
never came near to answering and which casts doubt on Chrétien as the source of all subsequent literature concerning Perceval and the Grail.

How did it happen that the first continuator (formerly known
as Pseudo-Wauchier), following in the Champenois Master's
footsteps, gave an account of Gauvain's visit to the Grail castle
which is nothing less than a complete rejection of every important feature of the Master's own narrative, except the question
test ?

It is an amazing fact, strangely ignored by many recent
commentators on the Grail legend, that this author, who had
of course read Chrétien's unfinished poem, told of a second
visit to the Grail castle which boldly contradicts what Chrétien
had said about the first visit [1]. The castle is situated not in a
valley but at the end of a causeway washed by the sea. The
lord of the castle is not an invalid who cannot walk, but a
stalwart, able-bodied king. There is no Grail bearer, but the
dish itself moves hither and yon without visible agency. It
serves not the host's father in his chamber but the king and his
guest in the hall, and it has no sacramental character. The
lance is not borne in procession but is fixed in a sort of rack.
In the morning Gauvain does not wake to find himself in a
deserted castle, but lying in a field, with no castle in sight.
The consequence of asking the question is different from what
Chrétien had led one to expect ; the land is restored to fertility. As an explanation of these drastic changes Bruce's only

---

many motifs and plot elements which are common in modern folklore and
in primitive beliefs the world over, but the Celtic narratives from which
the Arthurian romances drew much of their material were not the pastime
of peasants but formed the repertoire of professionals. P. Hinneberg, *Kultur
der Gegenwart*, Teil I, Abt. XI, 1 (Berlin, Leipzig, 1909), p. 56-60. H. M.
and N. K. Chadwick, *Growth of Literature*, I (Cambridge, 1932), p. 584-87.

1. *Continuations of the Old French Perceval*, III, Part 1 (1952), p. 458-71,
490-95. This, the short version, is earlier than the long and the mixed
versions. Prof. Roach in *Les Romans du Graal aux XIIe et XIIIe siècles, Colloques Internationaux du Centre National de la Recherche Scientifique* (Paris,
1956), p. 113, wrote : « Dans la version donnée par la Rédaction Courte
rien ne ressemble à la scène racontée par Chrétien. »

comment was [1] : "The poet has undoubtedly caught here the spirit of a folk-tale more distinctively than Chrétien in his corresponding description, only in the legitimate endeavor to gain the effect of mystery he commits some blunders and leaves the narrative in certain particulars unnecessarily obscure."

Now the relation of this Grail visit to Chrétien's earlier account is much the same as the relation of Ulrich's *Lanzelet* to Chrétien's *Lancelot*. In both instances the later poet tells a story in violent conflict with the earlier. I think it will be granted that in both instances Bruce failed to give an adequate explanation of the phenomenon. But an Irish saga, the *Wooing of Etain*, provided, as we have seen, precisely the pattern needed to explain the main features of the abduction and rescue of Ginover in Ulrich's account. The Celtic hypothesis succeeded where its rival failed. Does the same hypothesis explain the astonishing discrepancies between the two versions of the visit to the Grail castle, Chrétien's and his first continuator's ?

Professor Roach has astutely remarked [2] : « Il a dû exister à la fin du XIIᵉ siècle un amas de contes sur Gauvain, ce qui explique l'importance de ce personnage dans l'œuvre de Raoul de Houdenc et dans d'autres romans contemporains. Ce sont ces contes qui auront fourni la matière à la première continuation ». Nitze accepted this view and pointed out that it was also held by Paul Meyer [3]. The question remains : was the *conte* which furnished the *matière* for Gauvain's visit of Celtic origin ?

The *Adventures of Art Son of Conn* survives only in a fifteenth-century manuscript but is mentioned in a list of tales which goes back to the tenth [4]. The version preserved is not to be regarded as the remote source of Gauvain's visit to the Grail

---

1. Bruce, I, 296. On p. 299 Bruce adds : "This conception of the land that becomes a desert under a spell which a certain question will undo is, of course, derived from folklore." For the survival of the question test in Irish folklore (not the derivation of the test from folklore) see my *Arthurian Tradition*, p. 382 f.

2. *Roman du Graal*, p. 117.

3. *Ibid.*, p. 118. M. Marx likewise accepted this view.

4. For text and translation see *Eriu*, III (1907), 149-73; for translation see T. P. Cross, C. H. Slover, *Ancient Irish Tales* (New York, 1936), 491-502. A good summary is in M. Dillon, *Early Irish Literature*, p. 112-16.

castle [1], but it does tell of a quest to an Otherworld palace in order to bring about the fertility of Ireland —a narrative which neatly accounts for certain striking divergences from Chrétien's description. We have the Waste Land motif; Ireland is without grain and milk, and the object of the quest is to bring the blighted earth and withered trees back to fruitfulness. The hero crosses stormy seas to reach the Otherworld palace. His host displays no signs of infirmity. No beautiful woman and no squires serve the meal, but food and drink are provided by invisible agency. It is implied that fertility is restored to Ireland [2]. On all these points the *Adventures of Art* corresponds to those points in the account of Gauvain's visit to the Grail castle which differentiate it from Chrétien's acount of Perceval's visit. Moreover, another feature of Gauvain's visit, his waking to find himself lying in the open, with no castle in sight [3], is matched in three Irish accounts of mortals who were entertained in dwellings of the gods, namely, the *Adventures of Cormac*, the *Fitness of Names*, and *Caoilte's Urn* [4].

---

1. The fifteenth-century text seems to be a composite of the adventures of Conn with those of his son Art, and it is the former which present the similarities to Gauvain's adventures at the Grail castle. The means by which Conn seeks to end the desolation of Ireland, that is, by mixing the blood of the son of a sinless couple with the soil of Tara, is the chief difference between the Irish and the French texts, and it is possible that the motif of child sacrifice was introduced late into the *Adventures of Art* and took the place of the question test. Prof. Fred Robinson discusses this motif in *Anniversary Papers by Colleagues and Pupils of G. L. Kittredge* (Boston, London, 1913), p. 190-92. It represents the survival of a pagan custom, mentioned in the *Metrical Dinnsenchas*, according to which firstlings were sacrificed to obtain grain and milk.

2. Becuma, who was the cause of the sterility, was banished from Ireland.

3. This motif is found also in Potvin, *Perceval le Gallois* (Mons, 1866-71), IV, vss. 26972 ff.; in Heinrich von dem Türlin, *Crône* (Stuttgart, 1852), vss. 14881 ff.; in Gerbert de Montreuil, *Continuation de Perceval*, ed. M. R. Williams, I (Paris, 1922), p. 5; in Renaut de Beaujeu, *Bel Inconnu*, ed. G. P. Williams (Paris, 1929), vss. 5397 ff. See W. H. Schofield, *Studies on the Libeaus Desconus* (Boston, 1895), p. 142 f.

4. *Romanische Forschungen*, XLV (1931), 72, 74, 76. This motif is, of course, common in British and Irish folktales.

In short, if Bruce had taken the Celtic hypothesis more seriously and had carried his researches in that direction, he would have found in these medieval Irish narrative patterns a far more satisfactory explanation of the startling innovations of the First Continuator in relating Gauvain's visit to the Grail castle than in a hypothetical endeavor to catch the spirit of a folk-tale. Perhaps he might have been led to realize the fallibility of the methods by which he had sought to prove Chrétien's independence of early Arthurian traditions and the more or less direct dependence of all later Arthurian romance on Chrétien.

A recent and more extreme critic of the Celtic hypothesis is Professor Hofer. "Die Annahme einer Beeinflussung der Artussage durch irische Sagen kann sich auf keine überzeugenden Beweise stützen [1]." This, of course, is a mere assertion and by no means destroys the detailed parallels which even Bruce recognized in a few cases. Outstanding is the Beheading Test parallel discovered by Gaston Paris and elaborated by Kittredge [2]. As a Romance philologist, Hofer may never have felt any obligation to read the latter's book, but if he had, he would have learned that an episode in the saga of *Bricriu's Feast*, preserved in a manuscript written about 1100, is reproduced in certain specific details in the *Mule sans Frein* and *Hunbaut*, and is easily recognizable in outline in the First Continuation of *Perceval* and in the English romance of *Gawain and the Green Knight*. If anyone, after reading Kittredge's study, denies that there is any convincing evidence that Arthurian romance was influenced by Irish sagas, then it is obvious that literary parallels have no validity for him. But such persons are rarely consistent. Any non-Celtic, and especially any Latin, parallel is readily seized upon as proof of influence. Tatlock even tried to prove the influence of Geoffrey of Monmouth's *Vita Merlini* on *Yvain*, though the only point of resemblance was that both Merlin and Yvain went mad and wandered in the woods [3].

---

1. S. H. Hofer, *Chrétien de Troyes* (Graz, Köln, 1954), p. 34.
2. *Hist. Lit. de la France*, XXX, 71-78. Kittredge, *Study of Gawain and the Green Knight* (Cambridge, Mass., 1916).
3. *Speculum*, XVIII (1943), 284.

If the Irish parallels thus far adduced are not sufficient, there are others. Permit me to quote from *Arthurian Tradition and Chrétien de Troyes* [1] :

The coming of Galaad to Arthur's court was based on the ancient Irish legend of the coming of Lug to the court of King Nuada as related in the *Second Battle of Moytura* [composed before 908]... The relation between the Galaad and Lug episodes is assured by the fact that, though they have followed divergent paths for centuries they retain in common the assembled court, the empty seat awaiting a worthy occupant, the arrival of a youth "with a red color on him", his taking the seat, the demonstration of his superior strength by means of a stone, the recognition by the warriors that this is their destined leader, the king's relinquishing his couch to the stranger, the demand that each warrior should undertake a task, the list of warriors who do so.

What more could one ask as a demonstration that a famous Irish saga influenced a famous scene in an Arthurian romance ? Hofer's sole counter-argument seems to be : "Arthur selbst ist in der irischen Literatur unbekannt." Even if this were true— and it is not [2] — it would only prove that Arthurian literature made no impression on Irish, not *vice versa*.

An unexpected attack on the Celtic hypothesis was delivered in 1954 by Professor Kenneth Jackson of the University of Edinburgh, and, coming from an eminent authority on Celtic matters, it was calculated to give great satisfaction to the anti-Celts. Let me quote his words apropos the Irish contribution to Arthurian romance [3].

L'hypothèse celtique indiquerait l'existence d'un ensemble vaste et dense d'histoires d'origine irlandaise circulant en Grande-Bretagne, et il n'y a pas la moindre preuve qu'il y ait eu quelque chose de ce genre.

He also added [4] : « Les influences de l'Irlande sur le pays de Galles sont difficiles à établir ; elles sont certainement rares ». These two statements taken together would, if true, mean that Irish influence on Welsh literature was very slight, and on

---

1. P. 236.
2. *Lorgaireacht an tSoidhigh Naomhtha*, ed. S. Falconer (Dublin, 1953). Bruce, I, 92, n. 110.
3. *Romans du Graal aux XIIᵉ et XIIIᵉ siècles*, p. 225.
4. *Ibid.*, p. 230.

Arthurian fiction, Welsh or Cornish or Anglo-French, wholly unproved. And if this be so, then Irish influence on French romance would be merely imaginary.

I do not wish to contradict so learned a Celtic scholar as Professor Jackson, but I should like to quote a number of scholars of acknowledged competence on the subject of Irish influence on Welsh literature. L. C. Stern wrote [1] : « Die alten Verbindungen, die die walisische Epik mit der irischen gehabt hat, drängen sich immerfort auf... So mancher Zug in der normannischen und romanischen Sagenüberlieferung trägt noch die Marke des irischen Ursprungs ». Miss Cecile O'Rahilly, who made a special study of the relations between Ireland and Wales, concluded :

To serious students of Welsh the importance of the Irish language and literature can hardly be over-emphasized... To supplement the scanty remains of Old Welsh literature and to appreciate the influence of Irish upon their own most cherished literary possession, the *Mabinogion*, Welshmen must have some acquaintance with the literature of Ireland.

W. J. Gruffydd's brilliant analysis of *Math Vab Mathonwy* has demonstrated its debt to Irish traditions of Lugh and Balor and of Curoi and Blathnat [2] ; in fact, the *mabinogi* is incomprehensible without reference to Irish cognates. Sir Ifor Williams adds his testimony [3] :

Contacts between the two nations in the early centuries of our era, down to the twelfth century, were many and close. Irish tales were borrowed and retold in Welsh, with minor modifications : parts of the Branwen story in the *Mabinogi* are sufficient proof.

According to these experts, then, Irish influence on Welsh literature was extensive and profound. If Professor Jackson, in dissenting, meant that not all the sagas of the Ulster, mythological, and Fenian cycles have left their imprint on the literature of Wales as it has been preserved to us, he is of course right. But he has himself vigorously asserted that among the Celts a vast oral literature once existed which has been lost [4].

1. Hinneberg, *op. cit.*, Teil I, Abt. XI, 1, p. 118.
2. *Math Vab Mathonwy* (Cardiff, 1928).
3. *Lectures on Early Welsh Poetry* (Dublin, 1944), p. 24.
4. *Romans du Graal*, p. 215.

What forbids us to believe that just as the extant tales found in the *Mabinogion* embodied Irish saga material, so did the literature which has perished ? So far as Wales is concerned, there is no good reason to doubt that there was « un ensemble vaste et dense d'histoires d'origine irlandaise » — not, of course, kept separate and retaining their original Goidelic heroes, but rather amalgamated, as in the *Mabinogion*, with native Welsh stories of native heroes.

The proof that such stories must once have existed in great numbers is the fact that there is no other method of accounting for the infiltration of so many Irish plots and motifs into Arthurian romance [1]. Even if we subtract the more preposterous claims of Brown, a very large number of parallels remains, of which I have given only a sampling in this article. Professor Jackson is too wise to challenge the most obvious instances, such as the parallel between the enfances of Cuchulainn and those of Perceval, of which Zimmer once wrote that "es springt in die Augen" [2]. Instead he produced some cases where, in his opinion, the argument from analogy was weak ; and indeed the argument as he presented it *was* weak, but it was not always the argument as originally offered. Let me quote [3] :

> On a expliqué la table ronde par la disposition des sièges dans la grande salle des anciens chefs irlandais. Mais il n'est pas du tout certain que ces salles primitives aient été circulaires ou que la disposition des sièges l'ait été, et les spécialistes du celtique les considèrent en général comme rectangulaires.

I have not maintained that the halls of Celtic chiefs were circular, nor denied that they were rectangular [4]. Jackson has erected a straw man in order to knock him down. He ignores the explicit statement in *Bricriu's Feast* that King Conchobar sat in a hall, and "twelve other couches were set up around him, destined for the twelve chief warriors of Ulster". According to the *Didot Perceval* the knights of the Round Table were twelve, and there is a certain amount of evidence in

---

1. See note 3, p. 54 above.
2. *Göttingische gelehrte Anzeigen*, 1890, p. 520.
3. *Romans du Graal*, p. 222.
4. For my discussion of the Round Table see *Arthurian Tradition*, p. 61-66.

Arthurian romance that this was the traditional number. Even
if this is a mere coincidence, one must consider, what Jackson
also ignores, the fact that a quarrel over precedence arose in
the very hall where Conchobar sat with his twelve warriors
around him, and that Layamon in his account of the Round
Table describes a quarrel over precedence which so closely
resembles that in the Irish saga that even Bruce was convinced.
Is it sound scholarly method to attack an argument from analogy without mentioning the two specific points of the resemblance ?

Another analogy which Jackson criticized concerned the
famous question test in the Grail castle. As everyone knows,
Chrétien represents Perceval as failing to ask the Fisher King,
« Qui sert-on du graal ? ». So far as I am aware, no one has
discovered a parallel to this question in any other literature
except in Irish, where one reads that the beautiful crowned
damsel, the Sovranty of Ireland, asks, " For whom shall this
cup be poured ? ". Jackson admits a certain resemblance between
the two questions, but adds : « Mais les différences n'en sont
pas moins considérables ¹ ». This is, of course, true. There are
marked differences, especially the fact that in the Irish story
the damsel repeatedly addressed the question concerning the
vessel to the host, whereas in the Grail romances it is the hero
who first fails to ask the host concerning the vessel borne by
the damsel, but is expected to do so later. This difference would
be fatal to any theory of connection if the parallel were
confined to the question alone. But the parallel is by no means
limited to the form of the question ; it extends to the whole
narrative setting ². In both the Irish and the French texts the
hero is invited by a royal personage to his dwelling ; in both
the hero, on reaching the palace, finds that his host has
arrived before him ; in both a damsel with a golden vessel
appears and serves food ; in one the host disappears, in the
other he is strangely absent. It is the resemblance between the
narrative settings which makes it reasonable to suppose that

---

1. *Romans du Graal*, p. 224.
2. For the parallel see my *Arthurian Tradition*, p. 374-77, and my *Wales*,
p. 26 f.

the similarity of the questions is not fortuitous. It is hardly fair to remark only on the differences and to ignore the resemblances, especially when the differences can be accounted for by the changes in the Irish story produced by its transmission through Wales.

Professor Jackson dismisses another argument from analogy in the following sentence [1] : « Pwyll est assis sur la colline de Narberth et voit un prodige, et l'on dit que c'est là l'origine du Siège Périlleux ». Here again, it is almost needless to say, the parallelism between the Welsh and French texts has been wonderfully minimized. What are the facts [2] ? In the *mabinogi* Pryderi after a banquet takes his seat on the mound of Narberth. At once there is a roar, and a great mist falls. When this clears, all the land of Dyved, which has been full of well tilled fields and houses, appears desolate and empty. Now in the *Didot Perceval* we read that Perceval, before a banquet, takes his seat at the Round Table. At once the seat breaks with a roar. A great darkness ensues, and a voice declares that the enchantments of Britain have begun. What were those enchantments ? In the First Continuation, as we have already seen, they corresponded to the desolation of Dyved. Once again Jackson has rejected an argument from analogy which I believe far from contemptible.

It is only to be expected that, after such a cavalier treatment of the arguments for the Celtic origin of the Grail legend he should conclude [3] : « L'histoire du Graal est une trame faite de biens des fils, dont certains sont peut-être celtiques, mais dont beaucoup appartiennent à peu près sûrement au fonds commun européen ». But neither Jackson nor anyone else has produced from the general fund of European fiction — from the *chansons de geste*, the *fabliaux,* the saints' lives, the *matière de Rome*, the *Nibelungenlied*, etc. — any parallels to the legend of Perceval, Gauvain, and the Grail comparable to those one finds in Irish sagas and the *Mabinogion*.

Moreover, why should one ignore the fact that the scene of

---

1. *Romans du Graal*, p. 223.
2. Loomis, *Arthurian Tradition*, p. 342.
3. *Romans du Graal*, p. 226 f.

the Grail quest is Britain, that the time is the reign of King Arthur, that the earliest hero of the Grail quest is « Perceval le Gallois », that when Perceval is found at the beginning of Chrétien's poem he is dwelling with his mother not far from the mountain passes of Snowdon, "li destroit desnaudone" [1]. In short, it is not the analogues adduced in favor of Celtic provenance which are defective, but Jackson's account of them.

Not content with these biased and unscientific attacks on the Celtic hypothesis, he challenges the right of anyone to discuss such questions unless he can read the Celtic texts in the original [2]. Let me concede that it is an excellent equipment for the student of comparative literature to be throughly familiar with the languages involved ; and if he is not, he should be careful to have his quotations and translations controlled by an expert. Failure to do so involves grave risks. Nevertheless, Gaston Paris and Bédier had little competence in Celtic languages. Should Paris have been forbidden to write his article on Lancelot in *Romania*, and Bédier to discuss the origins of the Tristan legend ? Since their time, translations of Irish and Welsh texts have been made by such scholars as Thurneysen, Dillon, Gruffydd, and Thomas Jones. Is it necessary to be a better Celtic scholar than these? If not, why is it illegitimate to rely on their work ?

What, apparently, Jackson demands is that all comparative study of the Arthurian legend should be stopped until the non-Celtists become experts in Irish and Welsh, and the Celtists become experts in Old French, Middle English, Middle High German, not to mention medieval Latin. This is an ideal situation but not likely to be realized, though Jackson might set a noble example by reading all the French Grail romances in the original before he again addresses an audience of Arthurians on the subject. Far more important, in my opinion, since authoritative translations are available, are a scrupulous attention to the logical principles involved in the argument from analogy, and some regard to historical probability. After all, who would

---

1. *Mélanges de Philologie romane et de Littérature médiévale offerts à Ernest Hoepffner* (Paris, 1949), p. 230-32.

2. *Romans du Graal*, p. 214 f.

have the strongest motives to create a body of fiction glorifying a British king, Arthur, and a Welsh hero, Perceval? The Champenois and the Picards, or the Welsh and Bretons?

This brings up the question of the transmission of Celtic material to the French. Some contend that the channel of transmission was across England, from the Welsh to the Anglo-Normans, and from the Anglo-Normans across the Channel and the North Sea to the French. This seems a plausible theory—so long as one does not look too closely at the evidence. Jackson himself is content to point out that in South Wales, after the Norman domination of that region, there were friendly contacts between the two races, and seems to think that this establishes a presumption in favor of Anglo-Norman transmission [1]. But, though it is legitimate to speculate about historic possibilities, Jackson fails to take account of the concrete evidence.

It consists of four parts [2]. First, there is the external testimony which consistently refers to the Bretons as the propagators of Arthurian tales. There is the declaration of Wace that Bretons told tales about the Round Table [3]. Giraldus Cambrensis specifies that the "fabulosi Britones et eorum cantores" reported the passage of Arthur to the isle of Avalon [4]. Note that it was Giraldus, a Welshman, who ascribed, not to his countrymen the *Cambrenses* or *Wallenses*, but to the *Britones*, the Armorican Britons, the propagation of the famous legend. A second argument in favor of Breton transmission is the internal evidence of the proper names. As Bédier, Brugger, and others have shown [5], there is a liberal sprinkling of Breton names in the romances of the Round Table; for example, Guingamor, Rivalon, Brian, Guinloie, Rinduran. Only Bretons would have

---

1. *Romans du Graal*, p. 225 f. See Loomis, *Arthurian Tradition*, p. 27-29.

2. On Breton transmission see Bruce, I, 68-70, 78-82; Hinneberg, *op. cit.*, Teil I, Abt. XI, 1, p. 12-14; Loomis, *Wales*, 183-91, 208-13; *ZFSL*, XIII (1891), 86-105; XX (1898), 79 ff.; XLIV (1922), 78. ff.

3. *Moyen âge*, XIX (1916), 234 ff.

4. E. K. Chambers, *Arthur of Britain* (London, 1927), p. 272.

5. Thomas, *Tristan*, ed. Bédier, II, 122 f. See note 5, p. 54 above. *Romania*, XXV (1896), 588. *Modern Philology*, XXII, 405 ff.

introduced these names in such quantity, and it is not to be forgotten that Chrétien's hero, Érec, bears a name strictly Breton. Thirdly, there are affinities between the Breton *lais* and Arthurian romances — such as the similarity between *Desiré* and Chrétien's *Ivain*, between the *Lai du Cor* and the *Livre de Caradoc*, between *Tyolet* and the chase of the White Stag in the Second Continuation of *Perceval* [1]. Fourthly, two compositions written in England in the twelfth century contain proper names which, if they were borrowed directly from Wales, would inevitably approximate closely the forms current in Wales. But if one examines the names in the Anglo-Norman *Lai du Cor*, one finds that they are even further removed from the Welsh than those which occur in French literature [2]; and when one examines the few names which Layamon added to Wace, they are not Welsh at all [3].

All the four kinds of evidence combine to substantiate the hypothesis that, almost without exception, the earliest popularizers of the *Matiére de Bretagne* outside Celtic territory were Bretons. The one clear exception is Bleddri or Breri, but, so far as I am aware, he remains an isolated figure [4]. I have been unable to find, and certainly Jackson has not produced, any other trace of Welshmen who had a share in the dissemination of Arthurian stories outside Wales. Until such evidence is forthcoming, it is safe to conclude that the main channel was through the bilingual Bretons. And Chrétien himself, let us remember, declared [5] :

> Por ce me plest a raconter
> Chose qui face a escouter,

---

1. *Studies and Notes in Philology and Literature*, V (Boston, 1896), 240-43, *Mélanges de Philologie romane dédiés à Carl Wahlund* (Mâcon, 1896), p. 297-99. O. Warnatsch, *Der Mantel* (Breslau, 1883), p. 60-64. J. L. Weston, *Legend of Sir Lancelot du Lac* (London, 1901), p. 30-39.

2. *Modern Philology*, XXXIII (1936), 232.

3. *Ibid.*, p. 233. *Modern Language Notes*, XXVI (1911), 65.

4. On Bleheris see Loomis, *Wales*, p. 193-95 ; J. Van Dam in *Neophilologus*, XV (1929), 30-34. Prof. Kellermann's effort to eliminate Bleheris in *Romans du Graal*, p. 137-45, was by no means conclusive. See on Blaise *Medium Aevum*, XXV (1956), 184-86.

5. *Mélanges Wahlund*, p. 291.

Del roi qui fu de tel tesmoing
Qu'an an parole pres et loing;
Si m'acort de tant as Bretons
Que toz jorz mes durra ses nons.

Yvain, vss. 33-38.

An argument which I have sometimes encountered is the
plea that, if Celtic tradition counts for so much in the Arthurian romances, the French authors of those romances are
stripped of all claim to originality; and thus even Chrétien
de Troyes is reduced to the rank of a mere *remanieur*. In the
first place, it may be said in reply that the advocates of Celtic
origins have by no means excluded contributions of both
matter and manner from other sources. Gertrude Schoepperle
in her study of Tristan has a whole section concerned with
elements derived from popular, non-Celtic tradition, and
includes some features originating in India. Samuel Singer
made the discovery that Tristan's marriage to Isolt of Brittany
and his relations with Kaherdin go back to the Arabic love-
story of Kais and Lobna [1]. In my own book on Chrétien,
which some doubtless consider extreme in its advocacy of the
Celtic position, there are several chapters in which I make no
claim for Irish or Welsh influence. And I would gladly admit
that some of the happiest scenes in Chrétien — Perceval's dialogue with the knights near the passes of Snowdon and
Gauvain's affair with the Maid of the Little Sleeves — have no
analogues in Old Celtic literature. In the second place, even
if Chrétien had as immediate sources Breton *contes* or books
provided by Countess Marie and Count Philippe, and even if
he followed the narrative outline with more or less fidelity,
this concession would not necessarily affect his rank as a poet.
Professor Kellermann well remarked at Strasbourg : « Reconnaître l'importance de cette littérature orale ne signifie nulle-
ment diminuer l'originalité des grands poètes du moyen âge [2] ».
Is Gottfried von Strassburg generally regarded as a mediocre
rhymester because he took over with little change the *matière*

---

1. *Abhandlungen der Preussischen Akad. der Wissenschaften*, phil.-hist.
Kl., 1918, No. 13. *Romania*, LIII (1927), 98 f.
2. *Romans du Graal*, p. 145.

supplied by Thomas ? Is Chaucer rated a slavish redactor because all the *Canterbury Tales* except two adhere fairly closely to antecedent plots, and his *Troilus* is patched together from various versions of the Troy story ? On the contrary, he is still regarded as one of the most individual and versatile geniuses which the Middle Ages produced. If, as I have maintained, Chrétien did not invent the *matière* which he used in *Erec, Lancelot, Yvain* and *Perceval*, his reputation need not suffer, for no one denies that he improved considerably on his sources in style, polish, and charm. And if there are serious flaws in the structure and the concept of *Lancelot* and *Perceval*, the blame does not rest on his shoulders.

I have not tried to rebut all the objections brought against the Celtic hypothesis. I readily grant that many of them directed at this or that particular argument are entirely valid, and among the arguments of demonstrated fragility I would include quite a number in my *Celtic Myth*. But I have tried to point out that some of the criticisms leveled against the hypothesis are by no means logical, and reveal at times an ignorance or a capacity for misrepresentation which is surprising in those who profess an attachment to scrupulous methods. Though one may reject many Celtic parallels adduced by one scholar or another, there remains in my opinion so large a body of striking similarities between the narrative literature of Ireland and Wales on the one hand and the European romances of the Round Table on the other that the position stands secure. And I am convinced that if we possessed Welsh literature of the eleventh century in its entirety, instead of a few scattered fragments, there would be no more doubt about the connection than there is concerning the relation of the *Völsunga Saga* to the *Nibelungenlied* or concerning the relation of the *Odyssey* to Vergil's *Aeneid*. *Nihil ex nihilo* is a sound principle in an age when literature was so largely dominated by the forces of tradition ; and nowhere can one find a more probable source for the tales of Arthur, Gauvain, Yvain, Lancelot, and Perceval than in the literature of Wales.

The Pas Saladin in Art and Heraldry

(Studies in Art and Literature for Belle de Costa Greene pp. 83-91)

The *Pas Saladin* in Art and Heraldry

PAUL GSELL in *Les Matinées de la Villa Saïd, Propos d'Anatole France,* reports a conversation between Edmond Haraucourt, *Conservateur* of the Musée de Cluny, and the celebrated novelist and collector.

Haraucourt.—Vous connaissez bien notre fameux coffre du XIVe siècle si vanté dans tous les manuels d'art?
France.—Assurément!
Haraucourt.—Il est faux!
France.—Allons bon!
Haraucourt.—Voici comment je m'en aperçus. Je voulus célébrer ce coffre dans une pièce de vers, car il m'inspirait. Sur les panneaux de bois, sont sculptés des sujets où je crus reconnaître les *Joyes du Mariage.* Des époux se chamaillent et se pouillent. Des commères coiffent leurs maris de luxuriantes ramures. J'avais accordé mon luth et je préludais, quand je remarquai, sur deux faces, des scènes héroïques qui n'avaient rien de commun avec les autres. C'étaient des chevaliers qui, lance au poing, partaient en guerre. Je sais bien que les militaires peuvent gallament intervenir dans les ménages de pékins. Mais, vraiment, ces paladins étaient trop nombreux. Ils me mirent la puce à l'oreille. Je découvris que mon coffre est un artificieux rafistolage de pièces et de morceaux. Un tiers du couvercle seulement remonte au XIVe siècle. Vous pensez si je déposai mon luth. Mais, pour Dieu, Messieurs, soyez discrets! Car ce coffre, c'est notre gloire. Il est si célèbre que je n'ai pu me résoudre à en frustrer le public.[1]

Doubtless the curator of the Musée de Cluny could detect a forgery or a patchwork, but it was unfortunate that he did not recognize the identity of his paladins and the literary source from which they were derived. For he would have been somewhat reassured. Though the panels on which they appear may have been carved in the nineteenth century, they must be close copies of fourteenth-century originals. Iconographically they are correct and one may still find the chest as a whole one of the finest specimens of the type.

M. Haraucourt can hardly be reproached for not being familiar with the *Publications of the Modern Language Association of America,* but if he had been, he would have found in the volume for 1915, pp. 509-28, an article on "Richard Cœur de Lion in Medieval Art," in which I identified the subject of the two panels containing

[1] References to the chest may be found in Viollet-le-Duc, *Dictionnaire raisonné du mobilier français,* ed. 2, Paris 1868, vol. I, pp. 25-29; E. Du Sommerard, *Musée des Thermes et de l'Hôtel de Cluny,* Paris 1883, p. 105; F. Roe, *Ancient Coffers,* pp. 25-29; E. Haraucourt, F. de Montrémy, E. Maillard, *Musée des Thermes et de l'Hôtel de Cluny, Catalogue des bois sculptés et meuble,* Paris 1925, p. 99. The chest was acquired from A. Gerente in 1869, is of oak, is 66 cm. high, 34 cm. wide, and 1.40 m. long. Du Sommerard described it as "ouvrage lorrain." On Aug. 20, 1923, M. F. de Montrémy wrote me: "Le couvercle seul est du XIVe siècle. Toutes les autres parties du meuble, ainsi que les pentures, sont de la première moitié du XIXe siècle."

knightly figures and noted that it was a familiar one in the art of the thirteenth and fourteenth centuries and was even presented as a spectacle on the entry of Isabel of Bavaria into Paris in 1389. During the thirty-five years that have passed since the publication of the article, I have been able to accumulate more pertinent material and am glad of this opportunity to recall an almost forgotten chapter in the history of medieval secular iconography.

The front panel of the chest (fig. 34) shows a series of twelve knights, who stand in a decorative design obviously inspired by window tracery. There are, as it were, six windows, each containing two lights. In the spandrels are what our ancestors would have called *babuini*—grotesque monsters and masks. The front supports of the chest are carved with wyverns. The right side of the chest (fig. 35) depicts a troop of mounted knights, two bearing odd, heart-shaped shields. The foremost is crowned and his shield bears the charge of a wyvern. He holds out his hand as if in inquiry toward a spearman standing on a height. The latter points, as it were, around the corner to the twelve standing knights, at the same time looking back toward the king.

This scene recalled to me a poem of the early fourteenth century, *Le Pas Saladin*, which Gaston Paris had described and discussed in the *Journal des Savants*,[2] which Lodeman published in *Modern Language Notes*.[3] The subject is the holding of a narrow defile in ·he Holy Land by twelve Christian knights, including Richard Cœur de Lion, against an invading host under Saladin. When the Saracen vanguard is checked and many of the chieftains slain, Saladin despatches a spy, Tornevent, to an eminence overlooking the pass where the fight is raging. Being familiar with the blazonry of the Christian knights, he recognizes each of the twelve shields and reports the names of their bearers back to the sultan. Realizing the sacrifice which further fighting would entail for his forces, Saladin orders a retreat, while the victorious heroes return to their camp and celebrate in feasting their marvelous exploit. It seems obvious that the poem was composed with the object of pleasing the descendants of the celebrated knights, for we read: "Grant honneur firent leur lignage, Tous jours en iert la renommee, On les point en sale pavee." Earlier in the poem there is again the statement: "En mainte sale les point on." There can be no doubt, then, that by 1300 the *Pas Saladin* was a common subject for the decoration of castle halls and that the Christian champions were scrupulously identified by their arms, just as in the later Middle Ages the Nine Worthies were likewise represented in tapestry, murals, and sculpture with equal attention to their heraldry.[4]

Though no painting of the *Pas Saladin* survives today in any medieval hall, yet we have the Cluny chest, an ivory casket in the possession of Lord Gort, and numerous references in literature and in inventories which prove that in the thirteenth and fourteenth centuries it was one of the favorite themes of secular decorative art.

The Cluny chest is remarkable in that it enables us to identify not only Saladin and Tornevent on the side panel, but also eleven of the Christian champions on the

[2] *Journal des savants* (1893), pp. 486-498.

[3] *Modern Language Notes*, xii (1897), cols. 21-34, 84-96. In col. 275 Lodeman described the dialect as that of the Ile de France with Picard and Walloon features.

[4] On Nine Worthies in art cf. R. S. and L. H. Loomis, *Arthurian Legends in Medieval Art*, New York 1938, pp. 37-40, 140, figs. 11-17, 392-394.

front.[5] The first on the left, whose device is a saltire within a border, is also the first to be named in the poem, Hue de Florine, who had estates in the Ardennes and at Florenne in the province of Namur, and whose arms were gold a saltire gules and a tressure vert. The second figure is Jofroi de Lusignan, brother of the King of Jerusalem, Gui de Lusignan, and his arms were barruly argent and azure with a lion gules crowned gold. The third is Thierry de Cleves, count of a territory on the lower Rhine, whose arms were gules a carbuncle *fleurdelisé* gold. The fourth must be Guillaume Longespée, third earl of Salisbury or his son, who bore six lioncels gold on a field azure, though the carver for lack of space has reduced the number to three. The fifth is Simon de Montfort of Montfort l'Amaury near Paris, whose arms were gules a lion rampant argent with a forked tail. The sixth knight bears on both shield and ailette what appears to be a long-necked, long-legged bird, but none of the twelve mentioned in the poem had such a cognizance. By the process of elimination this should be Bernard de Horstemale, a German knight. Since these are not his arms,[6] however, the carver or his model, unfamiliar with German heraldry, seems to have invented a device for him. The seventh figure is Renaud de Boulogne, whose arms were barry argent and azure with a bordure gules. The eighth is Valeran de Lemborc (Limburg), whose shield bore argent a lion gules with his tail in saltire. The ninth is Guillaume de Barre, whose charge was lozengy gold and gules. The tenth is Philippe, Count of Flanders, whose arms were gold a lion rampant sable. The eleventh crowned figure is, of course, Richard, bearing the three leopards of England gold on a field gules. The last is Gautier de Châtillon, whose arms were paly gules and vair with a chief gold.

Needless to say, the fabulous battle in which these warriors wielded their weapons to such good effect was imagined as occurring during the Third Crusade, and at least eight of those mentioned by the poet actually played a part in that heroic but ill-starred venture: Hue de Florine, Jofroi de Lusignan, Thierry de Cleves, Bernard de Horstmale, Guillaume de Barre, Philippe de Flandres, King Richard, and Gautier de Châtillon.[7] Philippe had been a notable fighter in his younger days, but died at Acre in 1191 not long after his arrival. Guillaume de Barre, Bernard de Horstmale, and Jofroi de Lusignan were outstanding for their valor.[8] The latter two, as well as Thierry and Hue, were followers of the most spectacular warrior of them all, Richard Cœur de Lion. Valeran de Lemborc not only took part in this Crusade but also came on a later expedition, reaching Palestine in 1197 and returning home the next

[5] Authority for the coats of arms may be found in *Publications of the Modern Language Association of America*, xxx, pp. 526-528. The first of these, however, is mistaken. The correct arms of Hue are blazoned in Ms. 880 of the Municipal Library at Valenciennes. See below. Cf. also *Romania*, xLVI (1920), pp. 164-178.

[6] The arms of Horstmar were *d'or a vii fasces d'azur au lion de gueules couronné d'or brochant sur le tout*.

[7] See Lodeman in *Modern Language Notes*, xII (1897), cols. 21-34. I do not know on what authority he stated that Guillaume de Barre, Hue de Florine, and the Count of Cleves accompanied Richard to Jaffa.

[8] Ambroise in *Histoire de la Guerre Sainte* mentions Guillaume and Jofroi with high praise. The anonymous author of *De Rebus Gestis Ultramarinis* says of Bernard: "A sua juventute propter plurimas suas virtutes famosissimus . . . cujus militiam et audaciam commendabat Richardus rex Angliae et Philippus rex Francorum et maxime Saraceni et Saladinus ipsorum saldanus."

year. Simon de Montfort is notorious as the leader of the bloody Albigensian Crusade, and it is possible that his name has replaced that of his brother, Gui de Montfort, who fought under Philip of France at Acre and also against the Albigenses.[9] One of the most striking features of the list of twelve champions is that five of them took part in the fateful battle of Bouvines in 1214, and were arrayed on opposite sides. Gautier de Châtillon and Guillaume de Barre fought under Philip Augustus, the latter saving the king's life, while Bernard de Horstmale, the older Guillaume Longespée, and Renaud de Boulogne were on the defeated side and were captured.

The fact that only three of the twelve heroes of the *Pas Saladin* were loyal supporters of the French monarchy and that Richard Cœur de Lion and Guillaume Longespée were treated with such respect shows where the author's sympathies lay. Significant, too, for his origin is the selection of six lords whose territories lay in the region between the Straits of Dover and the lower Rhine. The assignment of so prominent a part to Hue de Florine, who was not an outstanding personage, but who is represented in the poem as choosing five of the knights who were to hold the pass for the Christians, seems to reveal the author's special connection with Florenne or its vicinity.

The heraldry of the side panel is of the fantastic sort usually assigned to Saracens. Saladin's shield and pennon are adorned with a wyvern, which also appears on the shield of a Saracen knight painted on the front of a church chest at Burgate, Suffolk— a knight whom we can reasonably identify as Saladin.[10] The same monster is repeated twice on the housings of a gigantic blackamoor, Isoré, painted about 1270 on the wall of a house at Pernes, Vaucluse.[11] Another Saracen device on the Cluny chest is a frog.

The date of the model copied by the carver of the chest is not easy to determine with precision. The traceried framework may not be an authentic reproduction, and even at best can afford only a general indication. If we fall back on the military costume, we may do a little better, for it can hardly be dissociated from the heraldry, which is certainly authentic. Though ailettes appear as late as about 1340 in the English Lutterell Psalter, and though I have not observed the unusual headpiece worn by Renaud de Boulogne, and known as a kettle-hat, in any earlier illustration than that of Richard Cœur de Lion in the Auchinleck manuscript of about 1335,[12] yet the cyclas, a surcoat cut short in front, which came in about 1340,[13] does not appear on our chest. The costume of the knights is probably that of 1320-1330, and to that period we may assign the original carving.

Another illustration of the *Pas Saladin* occurs on a French ivory casket published for the first time by Dr. David J. A. Ross with a very full description and commentary.[14] He was kind enough to send me an offprint of his article, and the present owner of the casket, Lord Gort, has graciously given permission to reproduce here the back panel which concerns us (fig. 36). Though Dr. Ross was unable to discover

---

[9] De la Chenaye-Desbois et Badier, *Dictionnaire de la noblesse*, vol. XIV, p. 286.
[10] *PMLA*, XXX, pp. 516f.
[11] R. S. Loomis, "La Pourtraicture de Guillaume d'Orange et Ysoré" in *Gazette des beaux-arts*, ser. 6, XXIII (1943), p. 314.

[12] *PMLA*, XXX, fig. 7, opp. p. 521.
[13] R. S. and L. H. Loomis, *Arthurian Legends in Medieval Art*, fig. 267.
[14] *Journal of the Warburg and Courtauld Institutes*, XI (1948), pp. 112-142.

the subject, a comparison with the Cluny chest leaves no doubt. The first compartment on the left shows five bearded, turbaned men, all apparently mounted, two equipped with spears, while at the foot of a tower kneels Tornevent, reporting to his master the names of the redoubtable twelve. These appear in the three succeeding compartments, striding toward the left, headed by the crowned figure of Richard. No ailettes are visible, though they appear elsewhere on the casket. The surcoats are distinctly longer than those shown on the Cluny chest, and six of the knights wear helmets, with open visors, of a type which I do not remember seeing elsewhere. It would seem that the casket was designed before the chest, probably about 1315.

The loss of all other illustrations of the *Pas Saladin* is somewhat compensated for by the existence of several notices from the second half of the century. The first is from a record of payments made in the year 1351: "Pour un jouel d'un pas salladin pesant 22 marcs, 7 onces."[15] Among the pieces of plate listed in the inventory of Louis I, Duke of Anjou, in 1364-1365 our subject is twice mentioned.[16]

Un trés grant pié d'argent doré. . . . Et le hanap siet sur un souage à orbesvoies, et est le dehors d'icellui hanap de viii esmaux azurez, et en chascun esmail a ii chevaliers armez tenant leurs espées et leurs escus de leur armes, et y sont ceulz qui furent au pas salehadin, et quatre autres chevaliers. . . . Et ou fons du dit hanap, par dedens, a un esmail d'azur ouquel est Salhadin à cheval et plusieurs Sarazins derrière lui . . . et dedens le dit couvercle a un grant esmail d'azur, où il a les xii bannières de ceux qui furent au dit pas Salhadin.

Another item in the inventory is a dish for comfits, of which we read:[17] "En l'esmail dudit dragouer a la bataille du roi Salhadin." In 1379-1380 the same Duke had a second inventory drawn up, and in it the two pieces are described in almost the same words.[18] Moranvillé, who edited this inventory, asserted that Louis's magnificent collection of plate was melted up to finance his claim to the throne of Naples; at least, not a single identifiable piece has survived.[19]

We have also a record of payments made in the years 1375 and 1376 for the decoration of the castle of Valenciennes in Hainault, in the centre of those territories held by six of the knights who held the pass.[20]

A Loys, le pointre, pour plusieurs ouvrages de pointure qu'il a fait a le Sale, c'est assavoir le Pas Salehadin, un pan de mur tout armoet des armes Monseigneur et me dame qui est desous le dit pas; item un parkiel dou Geu del eskiek, u li hiermitage est; item le parkiel dou Mierchier as Singes; item le Fontaine de Jouvent. . . .

This is an interesting assortment of secular subjects. In addition to the *Pas Saladin* and the coats of arms, there are the chess game, a common theme for ivories; the Fountain of Youth, represented in ivories, tapestries, a cup belonging to Louis of Anjou, and a mural painting at La Manta;[21] and the sleeping pedlar whose sack is

---

[15] V. Gay, 'Glossaire archéologique, Paris 1928, vol. II, p. 57.

[16] L. E. S. J. Marquis de Laborde, Notices des émaux du Musée du Louvre, Paris 1853, vol. II, pp. 70f.

[17] Op. cit., vol. II, p. 99.

[18] H. Moranvillé, Inventaire de l'orfèvrerie et des joyaux de Louis I Duc d'Anjou, Paris

1906, vol. II, pp. 222, 311, 468.

[19] Op. cit., vol. I, pp. xii-xvi.

[20] C. Dehaisnes, Documents et extraits divers concernant l'histoire de l'art dans la Flandre, l'Artois, et le Hainaut, Lille 1886, vol. II, p. 533.

[21] Journal of the Warburg and Courtauld Institutes, II, pp. 126-128; L'Arte (1905), pp.

being rifled by monkeys—a subject which is found in a miniature on fol. 149v. of the Smithfield Decretals in the British Museum.[22]

The will of the Black Prince, executed in 1376, mentions the bequest of a tapestry to his son, the future Richard II: "Item nous donons et devisons à notre dit filz la Sale d'arras du pas de Saladyn. . . ."[23] The inventory of the possessions of Charles V of France made in 1379 lists a golden seal furnished with a lock. "Item le seel d'or où est le Pas Salladin, fermant à clef."[24]

This ends the list of *objets d'art* illustrating the *Pas Saladin*, but ten years later the famous battle was enacted and witnessed by Froissart on the occasion of the state entry of Queen Ysabeau of Bavaria into Paris.[25]

Après, dessoubz le moustier de la Trinité, sur la rue avoit ung eschafault, et sur l'escha-fault ung chastel, et la au long de l'eschafault estoit ordonné le pas du roy Salehadin, et tous faiz de personnages, les chrestiens d'une part, et les Sarrazins de l'autre, et la estoient par personnages tous les seigneurs de nom qui jadis au pas Salhadin furent, et armoiez de leurs armes ainsi que pour le temps de adonc ilz s'armoient. Et ung petit en sus d'eulx estoit par personnage le roy de France, et entour luy les douze pers de France, et tous armoiez de leurs armes. Et quant la royne de France fut amenee si avant en sa lictiere que devant l'eschafault ou ces ordonnances estoient le roy Richart se departit de ses compaignons et s'en vint au roy de France et demanda congié pour aller assaillir les Sarazins, et le roy lui donna. Ce congié prins, le roy Richart s'en retourna devers ses douze compaignons, et alors se mirent en ordonnances, et allerent incontinent assaillir le roy Salhadin et ses Sar-razins, et la y eut par esbatement grant bataille, et dura une bonne espace. Et tout feu veu moult voulentiers.

It is noteworthy that Richard still retains his position as the commander of the Christian knights, but is obliged in deference to French sensibilities to obtain per-mission from the King of France to engage the enemy. One observes also the insistence in these records on the heraldic tradition.

What may possibly be an extraordinary survival of the *Pas Saladin* as a semi-dramatic entertainment is recorded by the anonymous writer of *The Lives of the Most Eminent Literary and Scientific Men*, who says that he witnessed as late as 1809, "on the borders of Lancashire and Yorkshire, on Good Friday, Saracens and Christians, Saladin, Richard, Edward, and other notable personages, represented by some young men, whose uncouth, fantastic garbs were not the least remarkable feature of the scene. After a long dialogue, in verse, the language of which, though somewhat mod-ernised, was evidently of considerable antiquity, the Soldan and the Lion-heart crossed their tin swords, until the former was sent 'howling to his native hell.' "[26] That the old medieval story should have come down into the nineteenth century in the form of a folk-drama is hardly credible, but stranger things have happened. If only the

183-187; H. Jubinal, *Recherches sur l'usage et les origines des tapisseries*, pp. 25, 35, 42; *Aesculape* (1937), pp. 244-251; (1938), pp. 16-23.

[22] J. J. Jusserand, *English Wayfaring Life in the Middle Ages*, London 1899, p. 234.

[23] A. P. Stanley, *Historical Memorials of Canterbury*, Everyman's Library, New York 1906, p. 170.

[24] J. Labarte, *Inventaire du mobilier de Charles V*, Paris 1879, p. 88.

[25] Froissart, *Chroniques*, Bk. iv, ch. 1.

[26] *Lives of the Most Eminent Literary and Scientific Men, Early Writers*, London 1840, pp. 183f.

observer had recorded the dialogue or the names of the other combatants, we would not be left to mere guesswork.

Before continuing with the later history of the *Pas Saladin* in literature, it is of interest to note that several heroes of the poem were introduced into other romances which had nothing to do with the Crusades. Jean Renart's *Guillaume de Dôle*, written about 1210, describes a tourney held at St. Trond and attended by Gautier de Châtillon, "le Barrois" (Guillaume de Barre), Renaut de Boulogne, and Valeran de Lemborc.[27] In 1285 Jacques Bretel introduced into the *Tournoi de Chauvency* Valeran de Lemborc, Renaud de Boulogne, and Philippe de Flandres.[28] The author of the *Châtelain de Coucy* described a tourney held between La Fère and Vendeuil, supposedly before the Third Crusade, at which Valeran de Lemborc, Jofroi de Lusignan, Guillaume de Barre, Gautier de Châtillon, Hue de Rumegny (and Florenne), and Simon de Montfort displayed their prowess and their coats of arms.[29] The correspondence of these six names with those in the *Pas Saladin* and the blazoning of their shields cannot be due to accident. As M. Prinet suggested, the author of the *Châtelain* must have taken them over from the tradition of the *Pas Saladin*, perhaps as it was painted on some castle wall.

Gaston Paris in his study of the *Pas Saladin*[30] drew attention to a long poem of the fourteenth century, now lost, but preserved in substance in the prose romance of *Jean d'Avesne*.[31] The hero of the poem was probably confused with Jacques d'Avesne, a Flemish knight, whom the chronicler Ambroise likens to Alexander and Hector and who fought with Guillaume de Barre and King Richard against the Turks at Arsuf (1191). In this romance was incorporated the episode of the discomfiture of Saladin by twelve Christian champions, but with some very odd alterations. Saladin was lured into undertaking the conquest of England by two Christians who enjoyed the sultan's confidence and persuaded him that the enterprise would be easy. Richard was warned of the invasion, received as reinforcements eleven knights sent by the King of France, and assembled his host at a mountain pass "between Scotland and Warwick (!)." Saladin on landing found his way blocked by the mountains and first sent a spy, Espiet, to overlook the defile and then made an inspection himself. There he recognized thirteen banners floating over the Christian tents. Nevertheless, he ordered an assault and was twice repulsed. When two of his mightiest warriors were vanquished by Guillaume Longespée and André de Chauvigny, he abandoned the project and reembarked his host.

The names of the twelve defenders of the pass have undergone a few changes. Jofroi de Lusignan, Renaud de Boulogne, and Bernard de Horstemale have been replaced by the Duke of Luxembourg, André de Chauvigny, and the Comte de Joigny.[32] The Duke of Luxembourg was included because Galeran de Lemborc acquired this title by marriage in 1214,[33] and so we have a case of duplication. André

[27] *Roman de la Rose ou Guillaume de Dôle*, ed. G. Servois, Paris, 1893, pp. li, lxv-lxviii.

[28] Jacques Bretex, *Tournoi de Chauvency*, ed. G. Hecq, Mons 1898, vv. 1768, 2685, 2691.

[29] *Romania*, XLVI, pp. 161-176.

[30] *Journal des savants* (1893), pp. 491-495.

[31] Paris, Bibliothèque Nationale, ms. fr.

12572, fols. 227ff.

[32] A Gautier de Joegni appears in *Guillaume de Dôle*. Cf. Servois' edition, pp. liii-lix.

[33] De la Chenaye-Desbois et Badier, *op. cit.*, vol. XII, col. 594.

de Chauvigny was doubtless included on the strength of his feats of prowess as a loyal follower of the Lion Heart on the Third Crusade.[34] He was of a Poitevin family, and Poitevin interest in the *Pas Saladin* is indicated by the fact that at a parliament held at Poitiers in 1425 it was urged on behalf of a certain "le Chabot" that "ses armes sont des premieres au Passeladin et à la Tour de Mauberjon."[35] Antoine Thomas commented: "L'avocat fait manifestement allusion à une représentation figurée du *Pas Saladin* que ses auditeurs devaient connâitre *de visu* et qui était peut-être, comme la célèbre tour de Mauberjon, dans l'enceinte même du palais de Poitiers où siègeait la cour du Parlement."

Paris also noted that both lists of names in the *Pas Saladin* and *Jean d'Avesne* have been laid under contribution by the *Chroniques de Flandre*.[36] All three contain Richard, Guillaume de Barre, Guillaume Longespée, Gautier de Châtillon, and the counts of Limburg, Cleves, and Montfort. The *Chroniques* follows the *Pas Saladin* in naming "le comte d'Oste en Allemaigne," i.e. Bernard de Horstmale, and follows *Jean d'Avesne* in adding Walleran de Luxembourg and André de Chauvigny. It also introduces two newcomers, Droon de Merlo, who was present at the battle of Arsuf, and the baron d'Estanfort (Steenworde in Flanders).

It is a very curious fact, however, that the battle in which the twelve were engaged, according to the *Chroniques*, was not the wholly imaginary defense of a pass, but the historic relief of Jaffa by Richard in 1192.[37] We have a full and reliable account of this event given by Ambroise, who mentions ten knights who fought beside Richard on horseback, but of these only André de Chauvigny reappears in *Jean d'Avesne* and the *Chroniques de Flandre*. Paris argued, nevertheless, that the *Chroniques* preserved an intermediate stage between some authentic narrative of the battle of Jaffa and the *Pas Saladin* tradition, and suggested that it was King Richard himself who ordered the first painting of the historic battle on which the fiction was based.[38] There are several difficulties in this hypothesis; for one thing, the *Chroniques* gives both the count of Limburg and Walleran de Luxembourg, thus duplicating the same person and showing itself to be late; and, for another, the only evidence for Richard's commissioning a mural of the battle of Jaffa is the fact that his nephew, Henry III, ordered the *duellum Regis Ricardi* to be painted at his palace at Clarendon, and the word *duellum* cannot signify a fight in which thousands engaged.[39] It is far more probable, as Leclerc suggested alternatively,[40] that "la chronique de Flandre ait emprunté au trouvère [l'auteur du *Pas Saladin*] ses douze paladins, en changeant quelques noms, lorsqu'à son tour elle a raconté la merveilleuse délivrance de Jaffa par le roi Richard."

A final witness to the fame of the twelve who discomfited the Saracen host and to the interest in their arms is a sixteenth-century manuscript, no. 880, in the Municipal Library of Valenciennes. First, we have on folio 196 an introductory statement:

[34] Ambroise, *Estoire de la Guerre Sainte*, ed. G. Paris, p. 530. See also *Mémoires de la société des antiquaires du Centre*, IX, pp. 96f.

[35] *Journal des savants* (1908), pp. 470f.

[36] *Ibid.* (1893), pp. 492f.

[37] *Le Pas Salhadin*, ed. G.-S. Trébutien, Paris 1836, pp. v-vii.

[38] *Journal des savants* (1893), pp. 491-494.

[39] *PMLA*, XXX, p. 514, note 11; p. 524, note 22.

[40] *Histoire littéraire de France*, vol. XXIII, p. 492.

S'ensuit les armes du Roy Richard dangleterre & de xii nobles prinches et barons qui luy aiderent a garder le pas du pont de norenthon en angleterre contre salhadin soudan de babillonne a compaignie de 4. m. turcs qui volloient descendre audit pais pour destruire le chrestiente. Auquel pas le Sr de chauuigny d[it] le clop fist les plus biaux faitz darmes dont on oit piecha parler.

Then follow in three rows of four columns the names and shields of the twelve (not thirteen) defenders of the pass:

Le Roy Richard dangleterre d[it] coeur de lion. Monseigneur philipes conte de flandres. MonS Waleron duc de lembourg. Monsr conte de cleues. Monsr Regnauld de dommartin conte de boullon de part sa femme. Monsr conte de monffort. Monsr conte de stambourg. Monsr Waleran conte de luxembourg. Monsr andrieu baron de chauuigny d[it] le clop. Monsr gauthier Sr de chastillon. Monsr hue sr de florines. Monsr guillaume longuespee.

Though the reference to the conquest of England seems to reflect the narrative of *Jean d'Avesne*, yet the bridge of Norenthon (Northampton) is a novel element and the list of knights corresponds neither to that in *Jean d'Avesne* nor to any other. The coats of arms and the tinctures of nine knights correspond to those we have assigned to their counterparts on the Cluny chest. Of the others the Count of Stambourg (doubtless identical with the baron d'Estanfort of the *Chronique*) bears a field gules a chief argent; Walleran de Luxembourg bears a field barry argent and azure a lion gules with his tail in saltire and tongue, claws, and crown gold; and André de Chauvigny bears a field argent a fess indented gules a label sable. Even in the seventeenth century some antiquary made a copy of this or some identical manuscript, which is now in the Municipal Library of Lille, Ms. 485 (v. fol. 145).

From all the evidence, it appears that the tradition of the *Pas Saladin* was invented by some romancer who knew something of the Third Crusade, but who had no actual engagement in mind; for, except that the Lion Heart and André de Chauvigny with a comparatively small force defeated the hosts of Saladin, there is no resemblance to the relief of Jaffa. This romancer belonged to the region of Flanders and the adjacent portions of the German empire, as is shown by his choice of the champions of Christendom, his knowledge that most of them took part in the Third Crusade, and his lack of any partisanship between France and England. The emphasis placed from the beginning on the coats of arms suggests that he was a herald; at any rate, heralds must have furnished instructions to the painters who treated the subject in castle halls. As for the date of origin, it is highly unlikely that Guillaume Longespée would have been consistently included among the twelve until after the second of that name, son of the Count of Salisbury captured at Bouvines, had achieved fame as a Crusader and met death in 1250. The tradition remained popular in the same region through the fifteenth century and, as the sham battle of 1389 at Paris and the reference to the Passeladin at Poitiers in 1425 show, it spread to other territories. But new fashions prevailed, the Crusades receded further and further into the past, and so the story was left only to antiquaries. By the nineteenth century even they were completely baffled by the Cluny chest.

Was Chaucer a Laodicean?

(Essays and Studies in Honor of Carelton Brown pp. 129-48)

WAS CHAUCER A LAODICEAN?

IN an essay on Chaucer and Wyclif published in 1916, Professor Tatlock remarks of the poet, 'He was not such stuff as martyrs are made of, but something of a Laodicean.'[1] With this statement and with the substance of Mr. Tatlock's article as a whole I agree; no one nowadays would present the portly poet, pensioner of three orthodox but far from immaculate kings, composer of love allegories and racy fabliaux, as a zealot, a reformer, a devotee of causes. *Something* of the Laodicean there is about him, but was he wholly lukewarm, wholly neutral in the warfare of principles which went on in his day as it does in ours? Can it be said of him, as it was said of the Laodiceans, 'I know thy works that thou art neither cold nor hot'?

The question is a real one since some of the most eminent of Chaucer scholars and literary critics have expressed the conviction that the poet was wholly indifferent or noncommittal as to moral, social, and religious issues. The authority of Lounsbury lies behind the following statements: 'He looks upon all social and political phenomena of his time from the comparatively passionless position of a man of letters who happened to be also a man of genius.'[2] It was not religious sympathy but intellectual clearness 'that led him to draw his famous portrait of the Parson.'[3] 'For his religious rascals he seems, in fact, to have had a sort of liking.'[4] 'Many of the tenets of Wycliffe found favor with the class with which he had become affiliated. . . . It is certainly only in this way that Chaucer can be characterized as a follower of Wyc-

---

[1] *MP*, XIV (1916), 67.

[2] T. R. Lounsbury, *Studies in Chaucer* (New York, 1892), II, 469.

[3] *Ibid.*, 482.

[4] *Ibid.*, 470.—Lounsbury seems to be deaf to the ironic undertones in "a noble ecclesiast," "a gentil harlot and a kynde."

liffe.'⁵ 'He speaks with contempt of the gentility that is based upon position and descent, and not upon character. But his contempt is invariably good-humored and little calculated to provoke resentment.'⁶

Professor Coulton writes in similar vein. 'Where Gower sees an England more hopelessly given over to the Devil than even in Carlyle's most dyspeptic nightmares—where the robuster Langland sees an impending religious Armageddon . . . there Chaucer with incredible optimism sees chiefly a merry England to which the horrors of the Hundred Years' War and the Black Death and Tyler's revolt are but a foil. The man seems to have gone through life in the tranquil conviction that this was a pleasant world, and his own land a particularly privileged spot.'⁷

Professor Root has much the same to say: 'Chaucer is never touched by the spirit of the reformer. . . . He sees the corruption of the Church and clearly recognizes the evil of it; but who is he to set the crooked straight? . . . The good is always admirable; and the evil, though deplorable, is so very amusing. . . . Let us cleave to what is good and laugh goodnaturedly at what is evil.'⁸

Mr. Christopher Dawson observes that Chaucer 'is a courtier and a scholar who looks at the English scene with the humorous detachment of a man of the great world. . . . Chaucer took the world as he found it, and found it good.'⁹ Miss Hadow remarks that Chaucer's 'object is to paint life as he sees it, to hold the mirror up to nature, and as has justly been said, "a mirror has no tendency." '¹⁰ Professor Kuhl asserts: 'Chaucer's rollicking humor and his apparent indifference towards existing conditions give point to his philosophy in *Vache* [*Balade de Bon Conseil*].'¹¹

In that indispensable and judicious guide to Middle English literature, Professor Wells's *Manual*, we find the following pronouncements: 'His [Chaucer's] work is always the product of

---

⁵ *Ibid.*, 479.

⁶ *Ibid.*, 473.

⁷ G. G. Coulton, *Chaucer and His England*, 2d ed. (London, 1909), p. 11.

⁸ R. K. Root, *The Poetry of Chaucer* (Boston, 1906), pp. 28 f.

⁹ C. Dawson, *Mediaeval Religion* (New York, 1934), pp. 160 f.

¹⁰ G. Hadow, *Chaucer and His Times* (New York, 1914), p. 156.

¹¹ *MLN*, XL (1925), 338, n. 90.

poise and control; it is tolerant; it is cool; it is the utterance of an amused spectator, not a participant.'[12] 'Among a nation of writers who had been and were concerned especially for the welfare of their fellows and society, in a period when the literature was responding particularly to the impulse of great political and religious and social needs and movements, Chaucer exhibits scarcely a sign of any reforming spirit, or indeed any direct reflection of those needs and movements.'[13] The dependence of the poet's fortunes on royal and noble patrons may have made wise a diplomatic silence in regard to contemporary conditions; but the silence remains.'[14] 'Slyly he exposed the worldliness and hypocrisy of monk and friar and pardoner and summoner. But it is the individuals that he exposed, not what fostered and lived by such agents. He did not take the matter to heart. . . . He expresses no indignation.'[15] 'As regards religious views Chaucer is as noncommittal as he is regarding most others. . . . Much vain effort was formerly expended in arguing that he was a Lollard, or at least of strong Lollard leanings.'[16]

This conception of Chaucer's bland unconcern with the great issues of his day, thus expressed by eminent scholars, is also to be met with in the work of modern critics who, though making no pretense to specialized knowledge, are deservedly influential. Miss Eleanor Chilton writes: 'There is no conviction in reading him . . . that he was ever more than an amused bystander at the comedy.'[17] Aldous Huxley speaks of Chaucer's 'serenity of detachment, this placid acceptance of things and people as they are.'[18] 'Peasants may revolt, priests break their vows, lawyers lie and cheat, and the world in general indulge its sensual appetites; why try and prevent them, why protest? After all, they are simply being natural, they are all following the law of kind. A rea-

---

[12] J. E. Wells, *Manual of Writings in Middle English* (New Haven, 1916), p. 602.

[13] *Ibid.*

[14] *Ibid.*, p. 603.

[15] *Ibid.*, pp. 603 f.

[16] *Ibid.*, pp. 604 f.

[17] E. Chilton, H. Agar, *The Garment of Praise* (New York, 1929), p. 121.

[18] A. Huxley, *Essays New and Old* (New York, 1927), p. 252.

sonable man, like himself, "flees fro the pres and dwelles with soothfastnesse." '¹⁹

Here, then, is an array of testimony from some of the best critical minds united in the belief that Geoffrey Chaucer looked upon the stormy spectacle of English life with a smiling tolerance, was merely amused by abuses in church and state, was inclined to believe that this was the best of all possible worlds. ·If cross-examined, he would doubtless be, like Calvin Coolidge's minister, against sin; he would also be in favor of virtue; he pitied suffering in remote times and places; he doubtless expressed with sincerity the more sentimental forms of religious emotion. But, according to this view of his nature, he never was moved to indignation by any contemporary evil, never took sides on any issue of moment, never lifted a finger to set the crooked straight. Lounsbury frankly concedes that the influence of environment and an eye to the main chance controlled Chaucer's pen; Coulton lays the major emphasis on his congenital optimism; Root attributes this unruffled surface to his serene Boethian philosophy; while Huxley finds the explanation in an attitude of fatalistic naturalism. But though these critics disagree widely as to why Chaucer remained a neutral observer of the events of his day, they agree that he was neutral, that he must have seemed to those involved in the struggle a sitter on the fence, a Laodicean.

In this paper I am not at all concerned with rendering a moral judgment on a great genius; I am but slightly concerned with probing into the obscure matter of motives; I am mainly concerned with a question of fact. Did Chaucer show an amiable and universal tolerance in dealing with contemporary men and affairs; or did he on more than one occasion make it quite clear on which side he stood?

There would, of course, be no debate if there were not some evidence to support the view that the poet was a neutral by temperament, or by philosophical conviction, or from a discreet regard for his personal fortunes. He was in daily contact with men on opposite sides of the bitter struggle for power between King Richard and his uncles, and yet, as Professor Hulbert has brought out,²⁰

---

¹⁹ *Ibid.*, p. 254.
²⁰ J. R. Hulbert, *Chaucer's Official Life* (Menasha, 1912), pp. 70 f.

he seems to have kept the friendship of both factions. Professor
Kuhl has suggested that Chaucer's selection of the five guildsmen
in the General Prolog was dictated by the consideration that these
guilds were neutral in the conflict between the victualers and the
nonvictualers, and so gave no offense to either party.[21] To retain,
as Chaucer did, his pensions and perquisites during the last years
of Richard's reign and to have them immediately confirmed by
Richard's foe and conqueror implies a prudent neutrality and
superlative tact. But, when all this has been said, does Chaucer's
character suffer? Was there any reason why in any of these quarrels a man was bound to declare himself? In a conflict of interests,
not of principles, a man of sense will try to keep out of trouble and
is not to be censured if he can keep on good terms with both sides.
If Chaucer accepted favors from men as little admirable as King
Richard and John of Gaunt, he might well plead in extenuation
that even a man of stern principle, John Wyclif, owed much of
his early power and influence to these same questionable supporters. We can hardly expect the poet to be squeamish where
the reformer was not. We may be sure that Wyclif's relations to
Richard and his uncle involved no downright betrayal of his
principles, and, if the question be raised as to Chaucer, we may
well give him the benefit of the doubt. There is no evidence that
in his public career or in his relationships with public men he was
guilty of dishonorable conduct. If, in the midst of these factional
struggles and personal rivalries, the diplomat in Chaucer prescribed for him the unheroic role of a friend to both sides, that is
all to his credit as a man of sense.

When we consider his attitude on matters of greater moment,
there is still some confirmation for the view that he avoided controversy and played safe. His references to the Hundred Years'
War and to the Peasants' Revolt are purely casual, and indicate
no attitude whatsoever.[22] Here are two topics on which, we may
be sure, every tongue was loosed. Chaucer twice served as a
soldier in the war, and twice acted as ambassador to bring it to
a termination. During the Peasants' Revolt he must have counted

---

[21] *Transactions of the Wisconsin Academy of Sciences*, XVIII, 652 ff.

[22] Like Professor Tatlock, I cannot detect a slurring allusion to the Peasants' Revolt in
Troilus, IV, vv. 183 f. Cf. *MLN*, L (1935), 277 f.

some of his fellow students at the Inner Temple among the victims, the palace of his friend John of Gaunt was sacked, and the Princess Joan of Kent, who, Miss Galway has given us some reason to believe,[23] was the object of his Platonic devotion, was insulted by the mob. But scholars have repeatedly observed that there is not one serious and specific comment on either the great war or the revolt in all his extant work. Though Minot had written his jingoistic jingles to celebrate the early triumphs of King Edward, and though Gower had loosed his invectives against the insurgent peasantry, Chaucer maintained a neutrality which was certainly not dictated by his personal interests.

In regard to the events of 1381 it is not possible to interpret that silence with certainty. But is it not probable that his failure to match the violent denunciations of his friend Gower is to be explained by the fact that, as a humanitarian and a just man, he knew too well that Jack Straw and his 'meynie' had serious grievances and that the revolt had been crushed only because Richard had broken his solemnly pledged word to the people? On the other hand, the mob had beheaded the innocent archbishop and massacred the harmless Flemings. May not Chaucer have reasoned that, where there was much wrong on both sides, there was no obligation to offer his career as a vain sacrifice to the cause of the oppressed? Once more it is arguable that Chaucer's neutral attitude, even on a great public question, was dictated not by artistic detachment or cowardice, but by a feeling that right and wrong were so mixed that to tell the whole truth would merely bring down on his head the curses of both sides. At any rate, his reticence on the matter proves that he was not one of those gentlemen of property who become more voluble on the sins of the unemployed and the arrogance of labor than on any other subject. And surely it is little short of amazing that, writing the General Prolog within six years of the Peasants' Revolt, this poet of the court should sketch for us a representative peasant, the Plowman, not as a loafer, a scamp, a bolshevik, a sower of class hatred, but as a model of all the social and Christian virtues.

This interpretation of Chaucer's attitude toward the great

---

[23] *MLR*, XXXIII (1938), 145-199.

rising becomes the more plausible when one realizes that one of his favorite topics is the responsibility of the gentleman to behave like one. As Chesterton has acutely remarked, 'Though Chaucer is called a courtier, it is Chaucer, much more than Langland, who is always saying that true nobility is not in noble birth but in noble behaviour; that men are to be judged by worth rather than rank; and generally that all men are equal in the sight of God. And similarly, though Langland is treated as a revolutionary, it is Langland much more than Chaucer who is always saying that up-starts have seized power to which their birth does not entitle them; that the claims of family have been disregarded through the insolence of novelty, and that men are bragging and boasting above their station.'[24] Not to mention the passage which Chaucer translated from Boethius and the evidence that he had also care-fully noted what Dante and Jean de Meun had to say on the subject,[25] he inserted in his Parson's Tale, as Professor Patch has observed in his discerning article on 'Chaucer and the Com-mon People,'[26] remarks not found in Peraldus to the effect that 'of swich seed as cherles spryngen, of swich seed spryngen lordes.'[27] He dragged into the Wife of Bath's Tale a long and vigorous discourse on the text that he is 'gentil that dooth gentil dedis.' He wrote one of his best balades on the same theme. It is, of course, true, as Professor Robinson asserts,[28] that these ideas were official doctrines of the Church. But surely the poet did not reiterate them and go out of his way to introduce them because they were harmless platitudes, but rather because he thought that, if repeated often enough, they might make some impression on the snobs and titled cads whom he counted among his readers. After all, the sentiment is precisely that of Burns's *A Man's a Man for A' That*, which critics have not been wont to treat as a rhetorical commonplace. Was Chaucer less revolutionary than Burns because he harped on the same theme in the fourteenth instead of the eighteenth century?

---

[24] G. K. Chesterton, *Chaucer* (London, 1932), p. 247.

[25] J. L. Lowes, "Chaucer and Dante's Convivio," *MP*, XIII (1915), 19–27.

[26] *JEGP*, XXIX (1930), 379.

[27] *The Complete Works of Geoffrey Chaucer*, ed. F. N. Robinson (Boston, 1933), p. 300.

[28] *Ibid.*, p. 808.

As for the Great War, though he voiced no judgment on it specifically, he does have a good deal to say about war in general. We must discount the lines in *The Former Age* which proclaim among the blessings of an ideal society that 'No flesh ne wiste offence of egge or spere,' 'No trompes for the werres folk ne knewe.' For other blessings of the Golden Age enumerated in the same poem are a diet of mast, haws, and water of the cold well, and the enthusiasm of the vintner's paunchy son for a vegetable and teetotal diet is open to grave suspicion. But we may take far more seriously the Melibeus. True, Chaucer introduces it jestingly as a little thing in prose. But it is incredible that he should have deliberately set himself at his desk and spent good days and weeks translating a work of edification only in order that he might bore himself and his readers. He did not translate the *Rose* or the *Boethius* or the *Astrolabe* or the Parson's Tale with any such ponderously subtle effort at humor. Chaucer, the humorist, like Mark Twain, Dickens, Thackeray, and many another master jester, had his grave aspect, and was capable of translating a work of instruction for no more recondite a purpose than instruction. Professor Robinson rightly avers[29] that for the poet and his age the Melibeus was an interesting treatment of a very live topic—the practical futility of force, the wickedness of revenge, the beatitude of the peacemaker. We may agree with Professor Cowling that 'its appearance amongst the *Canterbury Tales* seems to indicate that the strain and loss in blood and treasure due to the Hundred Years' War with France had caused the prudence and pacifism of this allegory to appeal to others besides Chaucer.'[30]

The portrait of the Knight in the General Prolog also carries its meaning. As the late M. Legouis has remarked, 'The virtues of his [Chaucer's] Knight, of his Clerk, of his Parson are in fact so many hidden sermons.'[31] In all these we have obviously ideal portraits, and it is noteworthy that the ideal knight as depicted by Chaucer had devoted his military career, incidentally perhaps to

---

[29] *Ibid.*, p. 13.

[30] G. H. Cowling, *Chaucer* (London, 1927), p. 162.

[31] E. Legouis, *Geoffrey Chaucer*, trans. L. Lailavoix (London, 1913), p. 155.

'his lordes werre,' wherever that may have been, but mainly and specifically to fighting for our faith against the heathen on all fronts. This emphasis was probably deliberate. In the single volume of Wyclifite writings collected by Matthew there are seven direct attacks on war waged by Christians on Christians.[32] Of Wyclif himself, Workman writes that he maintained that wars waged for 'God's justice,' 'in the cause of the Church or for the honour of Christ,' are right, and no other.[33] If Chaucer's listing of the campaigns of the Knight, if the phrases 'foughten for oure feith' and 'again another hethen' are a part of the doctrine implied in the description of the Knight, that doctrine coincides with the doctrine of Wyclif on the subject of war.

Chaucer's attitude toward the Hundred Years' War may also be inferred from his silences. M. Legouis makes the statement, startling but true: 'There is not a single patriotic line in his work.'[34] There is no disparaging reference to Frenchman or Italian or German as such. He was a better Wyclifite, a better Catholic, a better internationalist than the great majority in his day. He believed that Christendom must at least defend itself by the sword against Islam—and what agnostic of today would deplore the victory of Charles Martel at Tours?—but within the bounds of Christendom Chaucer believed profoundly in peace. The mature Chaucer of 1387 must have been convinced of the futility of war, except for some high cause far transcending the territorial pretensions of monarchs, and must have deplored the waste and destruction and barbarity that characterized the conflict between his own people and a people whom he had all the reasons of a poet to admire. His protest he put into the Melibeus and the portrait of the Knight, where his contemporaries, I feel sure, caught his drift more easily than do most of his interpreters today.

Readers or hearers of the General Prolog in the year 1387 would also have felt that on another vital controversy of the time Chau-

[32] *English Works of Wyclif*, ed. F. D. Matthew, *EETS* (London, 1890), pp. 73, 91, 99, 100, 132, 152, 176.—The view is not, of course, exclusively Wyclifite. Cf. Gower, *Vox Clamantis*, Bk. III, vv. 663–666, 945–947; Bk. VII, vv. 491 f.

[33] H. B. Workman, *John Wyclif* (Oxford, 1926), II, 28.

[34] Legouis, *op. cit.*, p. 31.

cer was deliberately taking sides and shaping the evidence. Three years after Wyclif's death Lollardy was still powerful and popular in London; though partially suppressed at Oxford, it was still alive there; it found favor with a party of the lesser nobility and knights, including Sir Lewis Clifford, Sir Richard Stury, and other friends of Chaucer's. Now if Chaucer displays any bias in his selection of characters for idealization or satiric treatment, it is in this very matter. I am not going to revive the legend that Chaucer was an avowed Wyclifite and propagandist,[35] nor am I proposing that his attacks on the vices of the clergy proclaim him unorthodox. It has not been brought out, however, so far as I am aware, how heavily the scales are weighted in the General Prolog in favor of the supporters of Wyclif and against the classes who opposed him. Who are the ideal types depicted?

There is the Knight, who has already stood for Chaucer's protest against warfare between Christians. But he was also a member of a class notorious at this time for their support of Lollard preachers and anticlerical doctrines. Under date of 1382 we read that Sir Thomas Latimer, Sir Lewis Clifford, and Sir Richard Stury forced their tenantry to attend Lollard sermons and stood by armed to see that the evangelists were unmolested.[36] In the very year of the General Prolog, 1387, the attack of Pateshull on the morals of the friars pleased, we are told, these same knights, as well as Sir John Clanvowe, Sir William Neville, and Sir John Montague.[37] This group was called the *milites capuciati,* or

---

[35] H. Simon, *Chaucer a Wycliffite, Essays on Chaucer,* Ser. 2, Chaucer Society (1876).

[36] Henry Knighton, *Chronicle* (Rolls Series), II, 181. On the Lollard Knights, cf. Workman, *op. cit.,* II, 380–404, and W. T. Waugh, "The Lollard Knights," *Scottish Historical Review,* XI, 55 ff. Mr. Waugh seems unduly skeptical of the genuine Lollard feeling among these knights. Yet the testimony of contemporary chroniclers, the fact that four of them risked the anger of the king by their support of the radical *XII Conclusions,* the self-accusation in the wills of Clifford and Latimer supply a firm foundation for belief in their sincerity. Montague sheltered Lollards at Shenley, including probably Nicholas Hereford, and removed images from the chapel. Latimer's manor of Braybrook seems to have been a center for the copying of Lollard literature. Such an accumulation of evidence is not to be offset by the fact that some of these men went on crusade or were executors of the wills of the orthodox.

[37] *Chronicon Angliae, 1328–88,* ed. E. M. Thompson (London, 1874), II, 377. Cf. G. M. Trevelyan, *England in the Age of Wycliffe* (London, 1925), p. 327.

'hooded knights,' because they did not doff their hoods at the sacrament of the altar. 'Fuerunt et alii multi milites male scientes de fide catholica.'[38] The Lollard document of 1388 known as the *XXV Points* concludes with the prayer that God will light the hearts of lords to know and destroy the heresies of the official church.[39] The protest to the pope in 1390 against the corruption of the clergy and the usurpations of the papacy might be construed as an answer to this prayer, since it was signed by John of Gaunt, the Earl of Salisbury, and the knights, Clifford and Stury.[40] Clifford, Stury, Latimer, and Montague formed a group of knights who in 1395 attempted to bring the whole issue before open parliament.[41] As late as 1399 Archbishop Arundel warned convocation against certain knights in parliament[42] whose identity is obscured since all the knights formerly prominent had been by this time reduced to silence by royal and ecclesiastical pressure.

There is a special significance in these facts, for five of these most conspicuous Lollard knights were at one time or another members of Richard's privy council: Clifford, Stury, Neville, Clanvowe, and Montague. They were not humble country gentlemen or mere soldiers; they were powers in the land. Moreover, of these five knights all but Montague were Chaucer's close friends.[43] The witness of their contemporaries makes it abundantly clear that knights as a class were suspected of anticlericalism and some were regarded as outstanding supporters of Lollardy during the decade after Wyclif's death. We know that the poet was linked by ties of friendship to leaders of this group. In idealizing the Knight he was not only flattering a class with which he had close associations, but he may have deliberately held up to admiration a class which because of certain prominent members was popularly identified with the cause of Lollardy.

It is, of course, fair to object that Chaucer's Knight had been on a crusade and was going on a pilgrimage—both practices of

---

[38] *Ibid.*

[39] Workman, *op. cit.*, II, 390.

[40] *MLN*, XL (1925), 322 f.

[41] *Annales Ricardi II* (Rolls Series), 173 ff. Workman, *op. cit.*, II, 390 f.

[42] *Annales Henrici IV* (Rolls Series), 290.

[43] Chaucer, *Canterbury Tales*, ed. J. M. Manly (New York, 1928), pp. 40 f.

which Lollards disapproved, and that therefore his author could not have conceived him as in any sense a representative of the cause. It is true, nevertheless, that four conspicuous Lollard knights fought for the faith against the infidel in Tunis in 1390: Clifford, Montague, Neville, and Clanvowe.[44] Montague, it would seem, continued his crusading career in 1391 by service in 'Lettow' and in 'Pruce.'[45] In 1394 or 1395 Clifford joined the Order of the Passion founded for the recovery of the holy places.[46] All these crusading activities, it is important to note, took place while Clifford and Montague were still prominently identified with the Lollard cause and before there were any signs of defection among the other knights. Wyclif himself, we remember, had declared that wars waged in the cause of the Church and for the honor of Christ were right. The crusading career of Chaucer's Knight, though it might have been denounced by Lollard extremists,[47] does not remove from him the associations with Lollardy that attached to his class. On the other hand, that he should promptly on his return from his 'viage' seek the shrine of 'the hooly blisful martir' does disqualify him as a good Wyclifite. For the Reformer and his disciples were consistently opposed to pilgrimages.[48] It cannot be maintained—and I do not maintain—that the Knight was a Lollard. Nevertheless, no matter how orthodox the individual, knights as a class were in the public mind of 1387 tinctured with Wyclifite sympathies; just as in the public mind of today professors as a class are regarded as reds, no matter how large a percentage votes the straight Republican ticket. Chaucer's unrestrained laudation of the Knight might be taken as an expression of sympathy with a suspect class.

This supposition is reinforced by the fact that Chaucer next chooses for serious and unqualified laudation a secular clerk of Oxford. Though nothing identifies him individually as a disciple

---

[44] Workman, *op. cit.*, II, 382, 385. *Scottish Historical Review*, XI, 77.

[45] *Scottish Historical Review*, XI, 73. *DNB* (1921–22), XIII, 652. A. S. Cook in *Transactions of the Connecticut Academy*, XX (1916), 207.

[46] Workman, *op. cit.*, II, 382. *MP*, I (1903), 12. N. Jorga, "Philippe de Mézières," *Bibl. de l'Ecole des Hautes Etudes* (1896), 491.

[47] Wyclif, *Select English Works*, ed. T. Arnold, III (1871), 140 f.

[48] Workman, *op. cit.*, II, 18.

of Wyclif, yet it was the secular clerks of Oxford who till 1382 had been open supporters of his teachings.[49] Though the University in that year condemned the heretical doctrines, and they were studied henceforth surreptitiously, in the western counties in the year 1387 three of Wyclif's foremost disciples, all secular clerks who had been associated with the master at Oxford, Purvey, Hereford, and Aston, were active in propaganda.[50] It is reasonable to suppose that in 1387 a secular clerk of Oxford would still, in spite of all appearance to the contrary, belong to a highly suspect group. And Chaucer portrays for us such a man as a wholly admirable type.

The third idealized figure is the Parson. He is not labeled a Wyclifite; he is not one of the itinerant poor priests; but not only his fellow pilgrims, the Host and the Shipman, smell a 'loller' in the wind, but many a modern scholar as well. Moreover, he never denies the accusation. If there was one fundamental thought characteristic of Wyclif, it was the authority of the Bible and especially the gospels as opposed to the Fathers, philosophers, councils, and all commentators and canonists whatsoever. Dr. Workman writes: 'Wyclif's insistence on the supreme authority of Scripture was not less than that of Luther and won for him at an early date the proud title of 'doctor evangelicus,' while he desired that the title of 'viri evangelici,' 'men of the Gospel,' should be given to his adherents.'[51] How close was the association in orthodox circles between reference to the gospel's authority and heresy, we know from the witness of Margery Kempe, who, when she pleaded before the Archbishop of York that 'the Gospel giveth me leave to speak of God,' was promptly answered by one of the Archbishop's clerks, 'Here wot we well that she hath a devil within her, for she speaketh of the Gospel.'[52] Now three times Chaucer hammers home the point that the Parson took his doctrine from the gospel. He 'Cristes gospel trewely wolde preche.'

---

[49] *Ibid.*, 141 ff.

[50] *Ibid.*, 136, 162, 336.

[51] *Ibid.*, 149 f.

[52] *The Book of Margery Kempe*, ed. W. Butler-Bowdon (London, 1936), p. 189. Cf. Workman, *op. cit.*, II, 150, n. 2, 198.

'Out of the gospel he tho wordes caughte.' 'Cristes loore and his apostles twelve/He taughte, but first he folwed it hymselve.'

In this final couplet there is a further hint that Chaucer intended his ideal priest to be recognized as a Lollard—a hint which no one seems to have publicly exposed though doubtless some scholars have realized its significance. If there is one phrase which occurs inevitably and often monotonously in the English writings of Wyclif and his followers, it is the phrase 'Crist and his apostles.' It is a phrase notably absent from the contemporary writings of the orthodox, though a diligent search would presumably turn up a few examples. But in the literature of Lollardy it is to be found, with variations, as a familiar leitmotif. In the *De Papa* of 1380 Wyclif wrote, for example, in the space of two paragraphs: 'Thes prelatis blasfemen in Crist and in His hooly apostlis'; 'Crist forsok it in word and dede, and bi His lore His apostlis'; 'Crist ordeynede that His apostlis . . . shulden be scaterid'; 'thus may Cristen men lerne bothe of Crist and His apostles.'[53] The so-called *Complaint* of 1382 is full of references to Christ and the apostles.[54] In *The Church and Her Members*, written by Wyclif in the last year of his life, we find: 'Crist . . . movede apostlis to do his dedes'; 'apostlis of Crist'; 'Crist or his apostlis'; 'thus lyvede Crist with his apostlis'; 'so diden Cristis apostlis.'[55] In the anonymous English *De Officio Pastorali* we read: 'Crist and his apostlis never cursiden ne pletiden for ther dette'; 'Crist and his apostlis weren not gredy of worldly godis.'[56] In the anonymous declaration of 1388 the same motif recurs: 'Anticrist, adversary of Jesus Crist and of his apostlis'; 'That Crist and his apostlis durste never do'; 'contrarie ageyne Crist and his apostlis';[57] and so forth and so forth. The same document contains passages describing the perfect priest not unlike Chaucer's: 'Hit is not leefful to a preste for to sette to hire his bysynes of werkis. . . . Lete prestis lif wele that thai be ly3t of worldly men by holy ensaumple, . . . techynge tho gospel, . . . as Seint Jon Crisostome

---

[53] Wyclif, *Select English Writings*, ed. Winn, pp. 72 f.

[54] Wyclif, ed. Arnold, III, 509–522.

[55] Wyclif, *Select English Writings*, ed. Winn, pp. 121 f., 130, 133, 138.

[56] Wyclif, ed. Matthew, pp. 415, 423.

[57] Wyclif, ed. Arnold, III, 457–459.

wittenessys by techynge taken of Cristis apostilis.'[58] The phrase reëchoes through the Lollard tract *Of Clerks Possessioners*.[59] The text of the *XII Conclusions* put forth by the Poor Priests in 1395 begins thus: 'We, poor men, tresoreris of Christ and his apostles.'[60] In the Lollard tract of 1402, *Jack Upland*, the author sharply demands of the friars, 'Why make ye you so many maisters among you; sith it is agaynst the techinge of Christ and his apostels?'[61] In 1407 Sir William Thorpe, when examined for heresy, declared: 'This foresaid learning of Master John Wycliffe is yet holden of full many men and women the most agreeable learning unto the living and teaching of Christ and his Apostles.'[62] The quotations from this and other documents could be extended to many pages. It is safe to say that when Chaucer spoke of the Parson as teaching Christ's lore and that of his apostles, he left no doubt in the minds of contemporary readers that here was the ideal parish priest conceived according to the Lollard view.

The Parson's later reproof to the Host in the matter of swearing confirms this interpretation.[63] Wyclifite opposition to this practice was notorious.[64] It was, for instance, one of the accusations of heresy against Margaret Backster in 1428 that she warned her neighbor to abstain from all swearing, either by God or by any saint.[65] The Parson's Prolog, probably composed after the

[58] *Ibid.*, 492.

[59] Wyclif, ed. Matthew, pp. 121–139.

[60] Workman, *op. cit.*, II, 391.

[61] Chaucer, *Complete Works*, ed. W. W. Skeat, supplementary vol., *Chaucerian and Other Pieces* (Oxford, 1897), p. 196.

[62] A. W. Pollard, *Fifteenth Century Prose and Verse* (Westminster, 1903), p. 119.

[63] Chaucer, ed. F. N. Robinson, p. 90. Cf. Workman, *op. cit.*, II, 28; G. G. Coulton, *Medieval Panorama* (Cambridge, New York, 1938), p. 466. Tatlock seems to be doubly mistaken when he asserts that the Shipman's calling the Parson a "loller" because of this reproof has no significance, for it is not the Shipman but the Host who uses the word, and the Lollard objection to swearing, as the following notes indicate, was notorious. (*MP*, XIV, 259, n. 2.)

[64] Workman, *op. cit.*, II, 27 f. Pollard, *op. cit.*, pp. 149–153. Wyclif, ed. Arnold, III, 332, 483. The objection to swearing was, of course, not confined to Lollards. Cf. Chaucer, ed. Robinson, p. 183; Coulton, *Medieval Panorama*, pp. 465 f.; *The Book of Margery Kempe*, ed. W. Butler-Bowdon, pp. 64, 150, 186, 189; G. R. Owst, *Literature and Pulpit in Medieval England* (Cambridge, 1933), pp. 414–425.

[65] Coulton, *Medieval Panorama*, p. 707.

disintegration of the Lollard party in 1395, still contains two suggestions of Lollard puritanism. Bluntly, the priest declares in response to the Host's invitation, 'Thou getest fable noon ytoold for me'; and later, 'I kan not geeste "rum, ram, ruf," by lettre, / Ne, God woot, rym holde I but litel bettre.'[66] Both these views regarding the use of 'fables' and of rime in sermons can be matched in the Lollard *De Officio Pastorali*, in which we read: 'Certis that prest is to blame that shulde so frely haue the gospel, and leeueth the preching therof and turnyth hym to mannus fablis. . . God axith not dyuysiouns ne rymes of hym that shulde preche.'[67] But though Chaucer consistently maintains the definitely evangelical coloring of his Parson through the Parson's Prolog, the Tale one must acknowledge is wholly conventional and orthodox. Here is no talk of 'Cristes lore and his apostles twelve,' but much concerning the seven deadly sins and the formalities of confession— topics sanctioned, even specifically prescribed, by the hierarchy.[68] Unfortunately, there is no clue to the date of the Parson's Tale, and we are left to conjecture for an explanation of the incongruity between all Chaucer had led us to expect of the man and all that finds expression in the sermon. One conjecture which may be as good as any other is that the sermon belongs to the last years of the century, when Lollardy was patently a lost cause. Chaucer was approaching the mood in which he arranged for his interment in Westminster Abbey and wrote his *Retractions*.[69] This was no time for him to round off his *magnum opus* with a heretical sermon, which would, even if he felt inclined, get him into trouble and might rouse an indignant hierarchy to burn every copy of the *Canterbury Tales*.

If Chaucer's relation to Lollardy followed the evolution thus outlined, it would parallel that of two of his oldest friends, Sir Richard Stury and Sir Lewis Clifford. As has been noted above, under the date of 1382 they are named as active supporters of the

---

[66] Chaucer, ed. Robinson, p. 272.

[67] Wyclif, ed. Matthew, pp. 438, 532. Cf. Wyclif, ed. Arnold, III, 147.

[68] D. Wilkins, *Concilia Magnae Britanniae et Hiberniae*, III (London, 1737), 59.

[69] G. G. Coulton, *Chaucer and His England*, 2d ed. (London, 1909), pp. 71–73. Tatlock in *PMLA*, XXVIII (1913), 521 ff.

poor priests; and thirteen years later, in 1395, they are still listed as advocates of the extremist *XII Conclusions*. But Stury was promptly forced to recant under royal pressure, and soon after died.[70] Clifford in 1402 not only recanted but also informed on his associates in the movement; and in his will, two years later, spoke of himself as a false traitor to God, unworthy to be called a Christian man, and directed that his body be buried in the furthest corner of the churchyard, unmarked by any stone whereby one might know where his stinking carrion lay.[71] These two intimates of the poet fell away after 1395 from a movement that had become dangerous. Their motives we do not know and cannot judge. The difference between the decidedly free-spoken Chaucer of the General Prolog and the entirely correct Chaucer of the Parson's Tale and the *Retractions* may be attributable likewise to the ebb of the Wyclifite tide. But he who would apportion the degree of policy and the degree of sincere contrition which motivated Chaucer's change of front would be a bold man.

The General Prolog of the *Canterbury Tales*, then, furnishes three wholly ideal portraits; of these one is plainly sketched in accordance with Wyclif's ideas, and the other two represent members of classes known to be sympathetic to his program. On the other hand, the Prolog furnishes portraits of several rascals. The rascality of the Miller and the Merchant is briefly and lightly touched upon; that of the Shipman is offset by admiration for his hardihood and seamanship; and that of the Reeve and the Manciple is offset by admiration for the cleverness with which they cheated their wealthy masters. But there are three rascals whom Chaucer seems to have labored to make morally repulsive— the Friar, the Summoner, and the Pardoner—and the two latter he made physically loathsome as well. The Friar would cajole a farthing out of a widow in barefoot penury. The Summoner's face was covered with white-headed pustules, and he was so generous that he would let a man keep his doxie for a whole year in return for a quart of wine. The Pardoner sold sham relics of Our Lady and St. Peter, was a pompous hypocrite, had glaring eyes,

---

[70] Workman, *op. cit.*, II, 400.

[71] *Ibid.*, 402 f. Chaucer, *Canterbury Tales*, ed. Manly, p. 657.

and a goatlike voice; 'I trowe he were a geldyng or a mare.' If contempt and loathing can be expressed in words, they are found in these three portraits. Now, of course, satire on clerical scoundrels was no monopoly of the Lollards; Catholics in good standing were loud in their denunciation of these same traitors to the faith.[72] But the fact remains that Wyclifite literature is full of attacks on the mendicant orders, ecclesiastical courts, and the veneration of relics. As Professor Tatlock puts it: 'Everybody assailed the clergy, but the reformer's club and the poet's rapier made for the same points; there is a striking resemblance in what they say, and they clearly thought much the same.'[73]

The impression made by the General Prolog on the public of Chaucer's day may perhaps be appreciated if we imagine a novel published in 1936, say, in which three characters were idealized— a Middle Western farmer, a college professor, a Democratic politician of liberal views—and three characters were pilloried—a journalist in the employ of Hearst, a syphilitic banker, a homosexual stockbroker. Though the novel contained no downright New Deal propaganda, would a modern reader have any doubt as to where the author's sympathies lay? Neither can there be much doubt as to where Chaucer's sympathies lay when he wrote the Prolog of the *Canterbury Tales*.

Finally, there is a subject which Chaucer thrice treats in passages for which he has no source and in which he seems to be expressing his own mind. That subject is the use and the abuse of the royal power. The balade, *Lack of Steadfastness*, which is undeniably a humble remonstrance on the part of the poet to his sovereign, Richard II, depicts in general terms the lawlessness and confusion of the times, and calls on the king to show forth his sword of castigation, dread God, do law, and wed his folk again to steadfastness. Again, since in the Prolog to the *Legend of Good Women* we find Alceste urging a course of mercy and

---

[72] G. R. Owst, *Literature and Pulpit in Medieval England* (Cambridge, 1933), pp. 216–286. G. G. Coulton, *Five Centuries of Religion* (Cambridge, 1927), II, 504–660. D. Chadwick, *Social Life in the Days of Piers Plowman* (Cambridge, 1922), pp. 7–37. J. Gower, *Confessio Amantis*, Prolog. C. Dawson, *Mediaeval Religion* (New York, 1934), pp. 185–189. J. B. Fletcher in *PMLA*, LIII (1938), 971–988.

[73] *MP*, XIV, 264.

justice on the God of Love, who is also a king, many scholars have
been inclined to see here another tactful reminder to Richard.
Such an interpretation does not necessarily involve any complete
identification of the God of Love with Richard or of Alceste with
any queen or princess. When we note that Alceste recommends to
the god-king some courses of action which seem to have little to
do with the immediate situation—for example, to keep his lords
in their rank, to do right to both poor and rich, not to listen to
envious tattlers[74]—then we may reasonably surmise that the poet
had in mind not only the fantastic and half-humorous situation of
his dream, but also the real situation of the realm. The poem was
to be sent to Queen Anne; doubtless her husband would see it
too, and it is quite like Chaucer to offer a little advice to his king
in a form which might prove palatable and which could surely
not give offence.

A few years before, in what was to be the Knight's Tale, Chaucer had created a situation which had marked analogies with the
scene of Alceste's intercession for the poet.[75] Theseus, it will be
remembered, discovers Palamon and Arcite in mortal combat, is
resolved to execute them, is swayed to clemency by the entreaties
of his queen and Emelye, and then reflects, 'Fy / Upon a lord
that wol have no mercy. . . . That lord hath litel of discrecioun /
That in swich cas kan no divisioun, / But weyeth pride and
humblesse after oon.'[76] Here it is possible that Chaucer is gently
hinting that Richard is doing well to heed the pleas of Queen
Anne for a policy of magnanimity and mercy. We know, then,
that Chaucer undertook to advise his sovereign openly once; and
it is more than likely that in these two other passages he sought
in more indirect ways to guide the royal will into the right
channels.

The facts and the inferences I have adduced in this paper
justify our rejecting any notion of Chaucer as either a sycophantic
timeserver, who merely echoed the sentiments of his patrons and
associates, or of a cheerful philosopher who looked upon the follies

---

[74] Chaucer, ed. Robinson, pp. 578 f. Cf. H. R. Patch in *JEGP*, XXIX (1930), 380 f.

[75] Tatlock in *Studies in Philology*, XVIII (1921), 419 f.

[76] Chaucer, ed. Robinson, p. 40.

and struggles of mankind with an amused detachment. Needless to say, he was no martyr for any cause; he never, in modern parlance, 'stuck his neck out' too far or kept it out after it became dangerous. Perhaps it was his modesty which led him to feel that nobody would be much concerned or much the better if he sacrificed his pensions or his person for a principle. In the *Balade de Bon Conseil*, addressed to the son-in-law of his Lollard friend, Clifford, a poem in which he seems to have distilled the essence of his practical philosophy, he frankly advises Vache not to meddle in situations where he can only harm himself and achieve nothing. 'Stryve not as doth the crokke with the wal. . . . Be war also to sporne ayeyns an al.' But Chaucer does not counsel his younger friend to remain a detached spectator of life if we are to judge by his own practice. He did speak out, we have seen, on various controversial subjects more than once, presumably when he thought his efforts would not prove vain. The line in the same balade, 'Tempest thee noght al croked to redresse,' should therefore be read with some stress on the 'al.' For certainly on some occasions Chaucer did exert himself to set the crooked straight.

If in the light of the foregoing facts any one chooses to point the finger of scorn at Chaucer as something of a Laodicean and a trimmer, if any one living in a country where speech on political and religious questions is still free chooses to adopt an attitude of moral superiority to a poet of the Middle Ages who observed for the most part a politic discretion in his utterances, 'lordynges, by your leve, that am not I.'

Edward I, Arthurian Enthusiast

(Speculum Vol. XXVIII, No. 1, pp. 114-27)

EDWARD I, ARTHURIAN ENTHUSIAST

SIR MAURICE POWICKE in his fine study, *King Henry III and the Lord Edward*, has this to say on the relation of Edward I to the Arthurian tradition.[1]

He knew . . . how to appeal to history. He tried to comprehend in his own rule the traditions of his land. He would not allow Llywelyn and the Welsh to rely upon the memories of King Arthur and the belief in his return to save them. When he and Queen Eleanor were at Glastonbury at Easter in 1278, he had the tomb of Arthur and Guenevere open and the remains placed elsewhere. Few people know why, adds the annalist of Worcester; but the reason was doubtless to link the English royal house with the great patron of Glastonbury and to confirm the truth of his burial. After the defeat of the Welsh Edward is said to have possessed himself of the traditional crown of Arthur, a Welsh treasure, just as later he removed the stone of Scone to Westminster. The conquest of North Wales appealed to contemporaries as an Arthurian adventure, and the feast and 'round table' which he celebrated at midsummer at Nefyn, 'in the farthest limits of Snowdonia by the sea,' suggest that he himself was not averse to this association of ideas. At least one foreign chronicler [Lodewijk van Velthem] gave a highly romantic Arthurian rendering of the campaign.

In these brief remarks Sir Maurice implies that Edward's interest in the legendary king of Britain was dictated by expediency, by political considerations; and one must grant that this was in large part true. But a more complete survey of the subject will show, I believe, that sentiment too was involved, and that in his cult of Arthur Edward was influenced by a vogue not exclusively English but shared by most of the aristocracies of Christendom in his day.[2] The earliest Table Round, imitative of the festivities and tourneys described in the romances, was held in Cyprus in 1223. The quixotic Austrian knight, Ulrich von Lichtenstein, in 1240 made a tour of Styria and Austria in the rôle of 'Künic Artus,' jousting with all comers. In 1278, according to the *Roman de Ham*, Robert II, Count of Artois, played the part of the 'Chevalier au Lyon' in elaborate semi-dramatic festivities and tourneys. Some of the handsomest illuminated copies of the Vulgate Arthurian romances were produced in Picardy at this time,[3] and we read of 'taules redones' held in Spain in 1269, 1286, and 1290. Surely political calculations had little if anything to do with this extraordinary addiction to matters Arthurian in lands remote from Britain, and part of Edward's interest in these same matters cannot be connected with his Welsh wars, but may be attributed simply to the fact that he was a man of his time.

The association of the kings of England with the legends of Arthur may be

---

[1] F. M. Powicke, *King Henry III and the Lord Edward* (Oxford, 1947), II, 724.

[2] On the Round Tables and other imitations of Arthurian fiction cf. R. S. Loomis, 'Chivalric and Dramatic Imitations of Arthurian Romance,' *Mediaeval Studies in Memory of A. K. Porter* (Cambridge, Mass., 1939), I, 79–97; E. Sandoz, 'Tourneys in the Arthurian Tradition,' SPECULUM, XIX (1944), 389–420; R. H. Cline, 'The Influence of the Romances on Tournaments of the Middle Ages,' SPECULUM, XX (1945), 204–211; L. Keeler, *Geoffrey of Monmouth and the Late Latin Chroniclers, University of California Publications in English*, XVII, No. 1 (Berkeley and Los Angeles, 1946), pp. 131–137; N. Denholm-Young, 'The Tournament in the Thirteenth Century,' *Studies in Mediaeval History Presented to F. M. Powicke* (Oxford, 1948), pp. 240–268.

[3] R. S. and L. H. Loomis, *Arthurian Legends in Medieval Art* (New York, 1938), pp. 89–97.

assumed to start with the dedication of one of the manuscripts of Geoffrey of Monmouth's *Historia Regum Britanniae* to King Stephen about 1136,[4] and it can be followed through the reigns of Henry II, Richard, John, and Henry III.[5] Not one of them, however, can be proved to have had more than a passing interest; not one of them is recorded as owning an Arthurian romance in the technical sense, though, of course, Henry II must have owned a copy of Wace's *Brut*.[6] It is only with Edward that we possess a series of indications, from his thirty-second to his sixty-sixth year, of a strong concern with both the historic and the romantic traditions of Arthur.

The first of these comes from the Italian romancer Rusticiano da Pisa, the same who took down from Marco Polo's lips the remarkably veracious account of his travels. Rusticiano states in his French romance, *Meliadus*, that it was compiled from the 'livre monseigneur Edouart, le roi d'Engleterre, en cellui temps que il passa oultre la mer ou service nostre seigneur Dame Dieu pour conquester le saint sepulcre.'[7] Now Edward spent the winter of 1270–71 in Sicily and returned to it in 1272, but it was probably not until the spring of 1273 that there was likely to be any contact between Edward, now king on the death of his father, and Rusticiano. The book which Edward brought with him and which he left behind in Italy was either a *Prose Tristan* or a *Palamède* or a combination of both.[8] At any rate, Tristan and his father Meliadus were prominent, but also others whom the world has chosen rightly to forget. The prolixity and the banality of the narrative forecast the romances of the Renaissance, burlesqued in *Don Quixote*.

Tournaments were recorded in complete detail, and though for us these narratives are more dead than the personal combats in the *Iliad*, yet for Edward these passages of arms were something between a hobby and a professional duty. The conduct of war was part of a king's business, and tournaments furnished practice in warfare. Besides they were a form of sport — a sport to which Edward had already proved his devotion.[9] There can be little doubt that Edward's love of tourneys was one reason for his interest in the romances of the Round Table.

Already the hero of the baronial war and of a crusade, Edward in 1277 had made his first victorious expedition into North Wales and on 11 November had forced Llywelyn to do homage. The following Easter he and his wife visited Glastonbury, and on 19 April he ordered the opening of Arthur's tomb. To quote Adam of Domerham:[10]

---

[4] J. S. P. Tatlock, *Legendary History of Britain* (Berkeley and Los Angeles, 1950), p. 436.

[5] R. S. Loomis, 'Tristram and the House of Anjou,' *Modern Language Review*, XVII (1922), 24–30. E. K. Chambers, *Arthur of Britain* (London, 1927), pp. 110–115, 124, 270–274.

[6] Tatlock, *op. cit.*, pp. 503, 530. The copy of the *Brut* presented to Queen Eleanor would surely have been seen by her husband.

[7] E. Löseth, *Roman en Prose de Tristan* (Paris, 1890), pp. 423 f.

[8] E. G. Gardner, *Arthurian Legend in Italian Literature* (London and New York, 1930), pp. 46 f.

[9] Matthew Paris, *Chronica Majora*, ed. Luard, V (London, 1880), 557.

[10] Adam of Domerham, *Historia de Rebus Gestis Glastoniensibus*, ed. T. Hearne (1727), p. 587. Chambers, *op. cit.*, pp. 125, 280 f.

Die vero Martis proxima sequente . . . in crepusculo fecit Dominus Rex aperiri sepulchrum incliti Regis Arturi. Ubi in duabus cistis, imaginibus et armis eorum depictis, ossa dicti regis mirae grossitudinis, et Gwunnarae reginae mirae pulchritudinis, separatim invenit. Ymago quidem reginae plene coronata; ymaginis regis corona fuit prostrata, cum abscicione sinistrae auriculae, et vestigiis plagae unde moriebatur. Inventa eciam fuit scriptura super hiis singulis manifesta. In crastino vero, videlicet die Mercurii, Dominus Rex ossa Regis, Regina ossa Reginae, in singulis paliis preciosis involuta, in suis cistis recludentes, et sigilla sua opponentes, praeceperunt idem sepulchrum ante maius altare celeriter collocari, retentis exterius capitibus et genis utriusque propter populi devotionem.

When Leland visited the abbey in 1534 and 1539 he saw the tomb, and described it as of black marble, with two lions at each end and an effigy of the king at the foot.[11] No trace of what must have been an impressive monument of the best period of English mediaeval art survived the dissolution and destruction of the monasteries.

Edward's main motive in causing the opening of the twelfth-century tomb and the transfer of the bones of Arthur and Guenevere was doubtless that attributed to him by Sir Maurice, but one may also allow some weight to mere disinterested curiosity. Edward would have been less than human had he felt no desire to look upon the remains of the supreme glory of British monarchy and of his beautiful if erring wife. For a reader of romances what glamorous associations hovered about those white bones!

Whitsuntide of the following year, 1279, saw Edward and his queen at Amiens,[12] and it may well have been on this occasion that Girard d'Amiens presented to her his *Escanor*, one of the latest French romances of the Arthurian cycle.[13] It is very prolix, running originally to more than 27,000 lines, and contains an unusual number of principal characters, making the plot very complicated. It is a sign of the times that Dinadan is allowed to remark in strong terms on the futility of random fighting, but how such unknightly sentiments went down with Edward we shall never know, but can only guess.

In Michaelmas of the same year, when Edward was past his fortieth birthday, he was the guest of his close friend and supporter, Roger Mortimer, at Kenilworth castle. It must have been a magnificent occasion, for it is mentioned by many chroniclers.[14] From these we gather that Mortimer invited a hundred knights and a hundred ladies, and held on Thursday a 'Round Table,' at which he won a prize of a golden lion and also celebrated his farewell to arms. Edward knighted Mortimer's three sons. Mortimer received as a present from Edward's sister-in-law, the Queen of Navarre, some barrels which appeared to contain wine, but

---

[11] Chambers, *op. cit.*, p. 125.

[12] *Annales Monastici*, ed. Luard, IV (London, 1869), 477.

[13] J. D. Bruce, *Evolution of Arthurian Romance* (Baltimore and Göttingen, 1928), II, 283 f.

[14] Dugdale, *Monasticon* (London, 1830), VI¹, 350. Thomas of Walsingham, *Historia Anglicana*, ed. H. T. Riley (London, 1863), I, 19. Walsingham, *Ypodigma Neustriae*, ed. Riley (London, 1876), p. 173. W. Rishanger, *Chronica*, ed. Riley (London, 1865), p. 94. *Annales Monastici*, IV, 281 f., 477. *Chronicles of Mayors and Sheriffs, and French Chronicle of London*, ed. Riley (London, 1863), p. 239. Nicholas Trivet, *Annales*, ed. T. Hog (London, 1845), p. 300.

when opened were found to be full of gold. One is not astonished, therefore, to learn that he had all the guests transported at his own expense to Warwick on the fourth day.

In her interesting article on the Wigmore manuscript in SPECULUM, XVI (1941), 109–120, Professor Giffin is inclined to explain Mortimer's lavish display and the celebration of a Round Table as a calculated effort to associate his family with Arthur, from whom he claimed descent through his Welsh mother. But Dr Ruth Cline has weakened the force of this argument, in SPECULUM, XX (1945), 294, n. 5, by showing how often before and after 1279 Round Tables were held without any possible use of Arthur's prestige for political or dynastic ends.

From 1283, however, we have a record which was of undoubted political significance. In the preceding year Llywelyn, the last native prince of Wales, had rebelled and been slain; whereupon Edward proceeded to attach the principality to the English throne. He received as tokens of submission certain relics treasured by the Welsh, among them the crown of Arthur. The Waverley annalist adds: 'et sic Wallensium gloria ad Anglicos, licet invite, est translata.'[15] When Edward returned to London in the summer of 1285 after an absence of three years, he brought this alleged crown of Arthur along with other trophies, proceeded in solemn procession to Westminster Abbey, and presented them at the high altar.[16] What subsequently became of this precious diadem is a mystery, for there is no further record of it. But it is obvious that Edward regarded the possession of Arthur's crown as symbolizing his sovereignty over Wales, just as in 1296 he removed the coronation stone of Scone to Westminster and in 1299 seized the crown of John Balliol to signify his overlordship of Scotland.

Edward also celebrated the conquest of Wales by holding a Round Table at Nevyn, Carnarvonshire, 27–29 July 1284.[17] It was attended by many English and foreign knights, who engaged both in 'choreis et hastiludiis.'

The next records involve the close relations which Edward established with Brabant. In 1290 he gave his daughter Margaret in marriage to John, son of the Duke of Brabant, at Westminster,[18] and in the following years he became, according to Huet,[19] 'une sorte de héros national' for the Brabançons. Two English chroniclers assert that in 1294 the duke himself held a Table Round at Bar-sur-Aube,[20] and though the Continental writers say nothing of the

---

[15] *Annales Monastici*, ed. Luard, II (1865), 401; IV (1869), 489. *Chronicles of the Reigns of Edward I and Edward II*, ed. Stubbs (London, 1882), I, 91. H. Knighton, *Chronicon*, ed. J. R. Lumby (London, 1889), I, 277. Rishanger, *Chronica*, p. 107.

[16] *Chronicles of the Reigns of Edward I and Edward II*, I, 92. L. Keeler, *op. cit.* (note 2 above), p. 102. On Arthur's crown cf. *Revue celtique*, XII (1891), 281.

[17] Rishanger, *Chronica*, p. 110. *Annales Monastici*, II, 402; III, 313; IV, 491. *Flores Historiarum*, ed. Luard (London, 1890), III, 62. Fordun, *Chronica*, ed. Skene (Edinburgh, 1871), I, 308. For date cf. H. Gough, *Itinerary of Edward I* (London, 1900), p. 157.

[18] *Chronicles of the Reigns of Edward I and Edward II*, I, 98. For Edward's relations with Brabant cf. J. de Sturler, *Les Relations politiques et les échanges commerciaux entre le duché de Brabant et l'Angleterre au moyen âge* (Paris, 1936), pp. 141–163.

[19] *Moyen Age*, XXVI (1913), 175, n. 1.

[20] *Annales Monastici*, III, 388 f. *Flores Historiarum*, III, 88.

Table Round they mention a great tournament, and Lodewijk van Velthem, a Brabançon priest, recounts with some elaboration how the duke arranged this assemblage to celebrate the return of the Count of Bar from England with his new bride, Edward's other daughter, Eleanor.[21] The tragic outcome of the jousting, in which the duke was fatally wounded in the arm, created quite a sensation in the Low Countries. If this was a Round Table, one should not overlook the fact that both the unfortunate duke and the Count of Bar were allied by marriage with King Edward.

It is this intimate connection between England and Brabant which explains the extraordinary space allotted to Edwardian affairs in the chronicle which Lodewijk completed in 1316 and the fact that here we find a most elaborate account of a Round Table held by Edward himself. Though at least three scholars, Hoogenhout, Huet, and Chotzen,[22] have discussed this account and have concluded that it bore some remote relation to the actual festivities of the period, they were so impressed by its manifest historical blunders that they failed to take it as seriously as it deserved. Huet stated flatly:[23] 'Nous devons admettre que le narrateur avait quelque connaissance de la Table Ronde de 1284, mais qu'il inventa librement les circonstances et tous les détails de son récit.' Such a reaction was natural, as one may see from the following summary of Lodewijk's narrative.[24]

After Edward had captured the town of Cornuaelge, he sent to Spain for the daughter of the Spanish king, and on her arrival in London held a great feast to celebrate the wedding. 'In the course of the feast there was prepared a Round Table of knights and squires.' 'According to custom a play (*spel*) of King Arthur was enacted. . . . The best were chosen and named after the knights of old who were called those of the Table Round.' The king instructed his squires to introduce into the play the wrongs that he had suffered from certain towns so that the chosen knights might be pledged to avenge them. The parts of Lanceloet, Walewein, Perchevael, Eggrawein, Bohort, Gariet, Lyoneel, Mordret, and Keye were taken. The tournament had been proclaimed all over England and a great assembly including many ladies had gathered. At sunrise the Round Table began, and the knights aforementioned had the better of their opponents, except 'Keye,' who was set upon by twenty young men; his saddle-girths were cut, all in fun, of course, and he himself was hurled to the ground. He was not seriously hurt, and the spectators laughed lustily to see him filling his traditional rôle.

The king, declaring that everything had taken place as in Arthur's time,

---

[21] *Monumenta Germaniae Historica, Script.*, x, 406; xvii, 79. *Chroniques des Ducs de Brabant*, ed. P. F. X. de Ram (Brussels, 1854), ii, 465, 734 f. Lodewijk van Velthem, *Continuation* of *Spiegel Historiael*, ed. Van der Linden, De Vreese, and De Keyser (Brussels, 1931), ii, 187–191 (Bk. III, ch. 40 f.)

[22] N. M. Hoogenhout, *Untersuchungen zu Lodewijk van Velthem's Spiegel Historiael* (Leiden, 1902). *Moyen Age*, xxvi, 173–197. *Bulletin of the Board of Celtic Studies*, vii (1935), 42–54.

[23] *Moyen Age*, xxvi, 176.

[24] Lodewijk van Velthem, *op. cit.*, i (1906), 295–321 (Bk. ii, ch. 15–20). The summary is based on a translation kindly made for me by Professor Adriaan Barnouw.

turned from the field to the banquet hall and caused the knights who had assumed Arthurian names to sit at the table with him. After the first course, a page rapped on a window for silence, and the king announced that he must hear tidings before the next course. Presently a squire rode in, spattered with blood, called the king and his courtiers cravens, and prayed God to destroy them unless they took vengeance on the Welsh for what he had endured. The king and those of the Round Table promised to do so. After the second course, there was the same suspense till a squire rode in on a sumpter, his hands and feet tied, and, after taunting the circle of knights, begged 'Lanceloet' to release him. When his hands were freed, he gave 'Lanceloet' a letter from the king of Irlant, denouncing him as a traitor and daring him to meet him on the coast of Wales. The hero was somewhat overwhelmed by this challenge till 'Walewein' and the king promised their support. After the third course and the customary pause the Loathly Damsel entered, her nose a foot long and a palm in width, her ears like those of an ass, coarse braids hanging down to her girdle, a goitre on her long red neck, two teeth projecting a finger's length from her wry mouth. She rode on a thin limping horse, and of course she addressed her first remarks to 'Perchevael' and told him to ride to Licester and win the castle from its lord, who was assailing his neighbors. She bade 'Walewein' ride to Cornuaelge and put an end to the strife between commons and lords. The two knights undertook these adventures, and the Loathly Damsel, who, we are informed, was a squire thus disguised at the king's command, slipped away and removed his make-up. The king then proclaimed what his knights had not suspected, that the messengers had been part of the festival, but he held them sternly to their pledges; and so a date was set for starting on the campaign against Cornuaelge, Wales, and Irlant.

In this narrative, as throughout the rest of Van Velthem's treatment of English affairs, the chronological and geographical confusion is shocking to the sober historian but amusing for the mere *littérateur* to contemplate. The marriage between Edward and Eleanor of Castile took place in Spain, not in London, and in the year 1254, eighteen years before he succeeded to the throne. The capture of the town of Cornuaelge shows a confusion between the county of Cornwall and the castle of Kenilworth,[25] a stronghold of the rebel barons, which surrendered to Edward and his father in 1266, twelve years after the prince's wedding, not before. There was no attack on the town of Leicester during the baronial wars, but the Earl of Leicester, Simon de Montfort, was of course the leader of the baronial party. There was no expedition against Ireland in Edward's time; but there is a satisfactory explanation of the error in the hypothesis that Lodewijk identified Scotia with Ireland,[26] carrying over into the thirteenth century a bit of knowledge which was true for the Dark Ages. Everyone knows that Edward's last years were devoted to the subjection of Scotland. Such a mass of anachronisms and blunders and the obviously fictitious account of Edward's

[25] *Bulletin of the Board of Celtic Studies*, vii, 43.
[26] *Ibid.*, vii, 49, n. 4. *Moyen Age*, xxvi, 179, n. 1.

Welsh campaigns, abounding in adventures as fantastic as any encountered in the romances of the Round Table or of Alexander the Great, are enough to put the reader on his guard against accepting the story of Edward's Round Table as strictly veracious.

Nevertheless, the evidence is not altogether unfavorable. Chotzen has demonstrated that behind the confusion and the romancing lay a real acquaintance with the outstanding events of Edward's reign — the marriage with a Spanish princess, the barons' wars, and the many campaigns against the Welsh and the Scots. However unreliable, Lodewijk cannot be dismissed altogether, and when we reconsider his narrative of the Round Table which accompanied Edward's marriage, we discover several reasons for taking it seriously.

First of all, for this account he expressly invokes a Latin authority: 'Die gene diet dlatijn bescreef, Seide so vele van der saken.' Secondly, we know that Edward was present at Mortimer's Round Table of 1279 and that he himself sponsored another in 1284, and we shall see that he held still a third in 1302. Thirdly, if we make allowances for Lodewijk's confusion of Kenilworth with Cornuaelge and of Scotland with Irlant, the three messengers calling for expeditions against the Welsh, Irlant, and Cornuaelge would correspond to the three outstanding wars of Edward's time, against the Welsh, the Scots, and the barons. Fourthly, if we realize that such a rehearsal of his military triumphs in the form of Arthurian interludes, though utterly anachronistic on the occasion of Edward's first marriage in 1254, would have been quite possible and appropriate on the occasion of his second marriage in 1299 to Margaret, sister of Philip IV of France, we get rid of at least two objections to the credibility of the narrative. For Lodewijk was more likely to have read an account or heard a report of an event of 1299 than of an event which took place forty-five years earlier, and he would be correct in placing that event in England. Finally, a remarkable confirmation comes in an unexpected form and from an unexpected quarter. A monk of St Albans, composing his *Annales Angliae et Scotiae* about 1312, after describing the magnificent ceremonies which accompanied the wedding of Edward and Margaret of France on 10 September 1299,[27] followed it immediately, as Professor Laura Keeler detected,[28] by an account of the festivities which he lifted from Geoffrey of Monmouth's description of Arthur's coronation banquet and the ensuing knightly sports.

Professor Keeler naturally inquired: 'What was the chronicler's motive for transcribing virtually verbatim from the *Historia*?' She made three suggestions, and the first probably comes close to the truth. 'Perhaps being a monk, unfamiliar with wedding festivities at court, yet desiring to do justice to the magnificence of his sovereign's nuptials, he turned to what he did know — a description in the *Historia* which could, he thought, be adapted by omitting what seemed antiquated.' The two accounts of Edward's nuptials become understandable if

---

[27] Rishanger, *Chronica*, pp. 394–397.
[28] Keeler, *op. cit.* (note 2 above), pp. 55–58. SPECULUM, XXI (1946), 28–31.

we put them together. The Brabançon priest had heard or read a detailed account of the elaborate interludes[29] which glorified the victories of Edward
under the guise of an Arthurian masquerade, but he completely discredited his
version of the proceedings by assigning them to the first marriage which took
place in Spain in 1254. On the other hand, the monk of St Albans got the date
and place of the second marriage correctly but knew only that there had been
some effort to reproduce the festivities of King Arthur's time. Rather than admit
his ignorance of so notable an occasion, he went to what purported to be a
trustworthy account of Arthur's coronation ceremonies and followed that. Thus,
though neither chronicler gives us an accurate description, between the two of
them we get a pretty good notion of the feast at which Edward presided in his
sixtieth year, assuming the rôle of King Arthur.

If there is still any doubt as to the plausibility of Lodewijk's report, let us
consult the *Roman de Ham*, already mentioned, which describes in full detail
an Arthurian assemblage and tournament which took place at Hem-Monacu
between Péronne and Bray in 1278.[30] We know that historic figures imperson-
ated those of Arthur's time, Count Robert II of Artois taking the part of the
Chevalier au Lyon and being actually accompanied by a lion or some Snug the
Joiner in a lion's skin. The presiding genius was Queen Genievre, who may be
identified with great probability with the Queen of France herself, to whose
coterie the Count of Artois belonged.[31] Now this queen was Marie de Brabant,
mentioned incidentally by Dante, the sister of that Duke of Brabant who
lost his life at the Round Table of Bar in 1294 and mother of the young Margaret
whom Edward married in 1299 and for whom he put on his Round Table masquerade. The dramatic features of the tournament of 1278, over which presumably Marie de Brabant presided, were much more elaborate than those which
attended the Round Table of 1299, which presumably celebrated the marriage
of her daughter. But on both occasions Sir Kay furnished comic relief, and we
have on the former occasion the entrance of a distressed damsel corresponding
to the entrance of the maltreated messengers on the latter. There is abundant
reason, therefore, to take Lodewijk's story of Edward's Round Table as a fairly
trustworthy report of what actually took place at Canterbury in September
1299.

The next demonstration of Edward's interest in Arthurian precedents took
quite a different form. The Scots had appealed to the Court of Rome against
the injuries inflicted on them by the English, and Edward commanded his
secretaries to collect materials to substantiate the rights of the English crown
over Scotland. A letter, addressed to Boniface VIII, was drawn up and to it on
7 May 1301 a hundred English barons affixed their seals. Most of the claims were

---

[29] On 'interlude' as meaning a play given between the courses of a banquet cf. L. B. Wright in
Modern Language Notes, XLI (1926), 98–100.

[30] *Histoire des Ducs de Normandie*, ed. F. Michel (Paris, 1840), pp. 222–283. Sarrasin, *Roman du
Hem*, ed. A. Henry (Paris, 1939). On location of tournament cf. *Romania*, LXII (1936), 386 ff.

[31] *Mediaeval Studies in Memory of A. K. Porter*, I, 95. *Histoire littéraire de la France*, XXIII, 473.

based on Geoffrey of Monmouth's *Historia*, and among them occurs the following:[32]

Item, Arturus, Rex Britonum, princeps famosissimus, Scotiam sibi rebellem subjecit, & pene totam gentem delevit: & postea quemdam, nomine Anguselum, in Regem Scotiae praefecit. Et cum postea idem Rex Arturus apud civitatem Legionum festum faceret celeberimum, interfuerunt ibidem omnes Reges sibi subjecti; inter quos Anguselus, Rex Scotiae, servitium pro regno Scotiae exhibens debitum, gladium Regis Arturi detulit ante ipsum; & successive omnes Reges Scotiae omnibus Regibus Britonum fuere subjecti.

As Professor Keeler pointed out,[33] the secretaries who composed this letter were not too scrupulous in their citations from the *Historia*, and added and omitted to suit their purpose. It is true that Geoffrey represents Arthur as handing over the kingdom of the Scots to Anguselus, but the chronicle makes it clear that in so doing he was merely restoring the land to its rightful sovereign.

We have a brief record that Edward in the course of a somewhat futile incursion into Scotland in 1302 ordained 'la table rounde' at Falkirk.[34] This was probably in commemoration of the great victory he had obtained over William Wallace at this same place four years before.

The last event of the reign which had an Arthurian coloring occurred on Whitsunday, 1306, when the king was almost sixty-seven years old.[35] News had come of a new uprising of the Scots. A great assemblage of nobles and their sons gathered at Westminster. The venerable king knighted his son, Edward of Caernarvon, and invested him with the duchy of Aquitaine; the prince then knighted three hundred of his companions in the abbey. Afterwards when the company had adjourned to the banquet hall, two servitors bore in on a large tray two swans covered with a network of gold. First of all, the King vowed before God and the swans that he would avenge on Robert Bruce the wrong which he had done to God and the church, but after that would bear arms no more against Christian men, but would go to the Holy Land, never to return. Thereafter, Prince Edward vowed that he would not sleep two nights in the same place but would help in the fulfilment of his father's undertaking against the Scots. The other knights followed suit, but what the precise nature of their vows was is not revealed to us.

The king's vow combines the obligations of chivalry and piety. To dedicate oneself to the service of God against the Turks was doubtless the highest ideal; but scarcely lower and even more pressing were the obligations of honor and of feudal right. The vows of Edward and his son were surely taken in the full consciousness that thus, according to the romancers, Arthur and his knights

---

[32] Thomas Rymer, *Foedera*, ed. A. Clarke, F. Holbrooke (London, 1816), I, 932. Keeler, *op. cit.* (note 2 above), pp. 52, 103, 130.

[33] Keeler, *op. cit.*, pp. 53 f.

[34] *Chronicles of the Reigns of Edward I and Edward II*, I, 104.

[35] Nicholas Trivet, *Annales*, pp. 408 f. *Flores Historiarum*, III, 131 f. E. K. Chambers gives in *Mediaeval Stage* (Oxford, 1903), II, 234–238, a list of minstrels who performed on this occasion. We also learn from the Wardrobe Accounts, 34 Edw. I, that 80s. 6d. were paid for the swans. C. P. Cooper, *Proceedings of His Majesty's Commissioners* (London, 1833).

had been wont to pledge themselves to high and perilous emprises. The earliest example of these vowings in the Matter of Britain is furnished by Chrétien de Troyes in his *Conte del Graal* about 1180. This is the fine scene laid at Arthur's court at Caerleon when the Loathly Damsel rebuked Perceval for his silence at the castle of the Fisher King, and announced the adventures of Chastel Orguelleus and Montesclaire.[36]

> Et mes sire Gauvains saut sus,
> Si dit que son pooir fera
> De li rescorre et s'i ira.
> Et Girflez li filz Do redit
> Qu'il ira si Deus li aït,
> Devant le Chastel Orguelleus.
> 'Et je sor le Mont Dolereus,'
> Fet Kahedins, 'monter irai
> Ne jusque la ne finerai.'
> Et Percevaus redit tot el:
> Qu'il ne girra an un ostel
> Deus nuiz an trestot son aage . . .
> Tant que il del graal savra
> Cui l'an an sert. . .
> Et bien einsi jusqu'a cinquante
> An sont levé, et si creante
> Li uns a l'autre et dit et jure
> Que mervoille ne avanture
> Ne savront qu'il ne l'aillent querre,
> Tant soit an felenesse terre.

Though Chrétien makes no mention of a banquet, the hour is noon and the court is assembled in the hall. Here, then, we have a scene which may have suggested the vowing at Westminster in 1306, particularly Perceval's swearing that he would not sleep two nights in the same place till he had achieved the object of his quest, as the same scene had suggested the entrance of the Loathly Damsel and her challenge to 'Perchevael' seven years before at Edward's wedding feast.

While Chrétien's *Conte del Graal* was one of the favorite romances of the late thirteenth and early fourteenth centuries, as indicated by the extant manuscripts, the *Prose Lancelot* enjoyed an even greater vogue. And this, too, contained a vowing scene.[37] Bohort distinguished himself above a thousand other knights at a tourney organized by King Brangoire, and was afterwards seated with twelve companions in a tent, when the king's daughter called on each of the thirteen to promise her some reward for her service. The knights then vied with each other in making the most preposterous vows. A much finer use of the same motif is found in the *Queste del Saint Graal*, where we read that after the Grail, covered with white samite, had floated into the hall at Camelot and ministered to all the company, Gauvain first and then the other knights vowed to seek for a year

---

[36] Chrétien de Troyes, *Percevalroman*, ed. A. Hilka (Halle, 1932), vss. 4718–46. For these and other vows cf. J. H. Reinhard in *University of Michigan Publications, Language and Literature*, VIII (1932), 25–57.

[37] *Vulgate Version of the Arthurian Romances*, ed. H. O. Sommer (Washington, 1909–13), IV, 266 f.

and a day till they saw the vessel openly; and the next morning the vows were repeated on holy relics.[38] As I have shown in SPECULUM, VIII (1933), 419 f., this scene is ultimately derived from the Irish saga, *The Second Battle of Moytura*, which goes back to the tenth century at latest.

We have illustrations of the practice in English literature also. Malory adapted the scenes from the *Queste* in his thirteenth Book. The fourteenth-century poem, *The Avowing of Arthur*, tells how the king, Gawain, Kay, and Baldwin undertook certain hard tasks,[39] and the ballad of *King Arthur and King Cornwall* quotes Arthur as saying:[40]

> 'Ile make mine avow to God
> And alsoe to the Trinity
> Ile never sleepe one night there as I do another
> Till that round table [King Cornwall's] I see.'

Arthur set out with four of his knights, and on their arrival at Cornwall's castle all made extravagant boasts and succeeded in accomplishing them. Professor Reinhard in *The Survival of Geis in Arthurian Romance* (Halle, 1933), pp. 316–324, has cited other examples from the Matter of Britain and from Irish sources. Though the taking of vows, needless to say, was practically a universal custom, there can be little doubt that the Arthurian examples bear an intimate relation to their Celtic analogues.

Evidently, then, the ceremonies of 1306 had an Arthurian background, but in none of the Arthurian texts is there anything resembling the oath by a brace of swans. So far as one can tell today, this was an innovation. Of course, the presence of the fowl on the high table was nothing new, for game of all kinds furnished a considerable, if not the major, part of a great banquet. Four hundred swans constituted only a small fraction of the provender for the installation of Archbishop Neville at York in 1467.[41] But I have found no precedent for Edward's taking a solemn oath on these decorative birds. Whether he was the first to do so or not, he certainly, in the modern colloquialism, 'started something.' For it seems pretty clear that all subsequent observances of this kind, as described in literature or recorded in history, were inspired directly or indirectly by the ceremonies of 1306.

Professor Ritchie has pointed out[42] the probable connection between this spectacular occasion and the famous poem, the *Voeux du Paon*, composed before 1313, by Jacques de Longuyon at the instance of Thiébaut de Bar, bishop of Liège.[43] Thiébaut had intimate connections with England, being presented by

[38] *Vulgate Version*, VI, 13 f., 18.

[39] W. H. French, C. B. Hale, *Middle English Metrical Romances* (New York, 1930), pp. 611 f.

[40] *English and Scottish Popular Ballads*, ed. H. C. Sargent, G. L. Kittredge (Boston, 1904), p. 50. On this ballad cf. K. G. T. Webster in *Englische Studien*, XXXVI (1906), 351 f., and R. S. Loomis, *Arthurian Tradition*, pp. 133–138.

[41] W. E. Mead, *English Medieval Feast* (London, 1931), p. 33.

[42] *Buik of Alexander*, ed. R. L. Graeme Ritchie (Edinburgh, 1925), I, xxxix f. I see no good reason to conclude that Edward's vow on the swans was based on a local custom of Bar, as Ritchie suggests. Cf. SPECULUM, XX (1945), 266, n. 3.

[43] Professor Peckham of Columbia is engaged in preparing a new edition.

Edward to the rectory of Pagham, Sussex, and most important, was the brother of Edward's son-in-law, the Count of Bar, in honor of whom the the Duke of Brabant held the Round Table of 1290.[44] Thiébaut's niece and Edward's granddaughter, Joan of Bar, was married in London to John de Warenne, Earl of Surrey, 20 May 1306, and two days later the young bridegroom was among those who were knighted and who followed King Edward and his son in making their vows.[44] Thiébaut must have listened to accounts of this impressive affair. One can hardly be wrong in assuming that when a few years later he prompted the composition of the *Voeux du Paon*, in which the knights of Alexander the Great take vows on a roasted peacock, he recalled the presence of his niece and her husband at Edward's historic Pentecostal feast. Thiébaut seems to have had so strong a fixation on this theme that he also commissioned a poem, the *Voeux de l'Epervier*, in which he himself and Emperor Henry VII are represented as making vows on a sparrow-hawk during a banquet at Milan.[45]

The *Voeux du Paon*, we know, was widely read, was translated into many languages, and inspired at least three other literary treatments of the theme of vowing on a bird. The *Voeux du Héron*, so cogently and learnedly discussed by Professor Whiting in Speculum, xx (1945), 261–278, was an anti-English burlesque, which ascribes the origin of the Hundred Years War to a series of grotesque oaths sworn on a heron by Edward III and members of his court in 1338. In 1463 David Aubert transcribed for Philip the Good, Duke of Burgundy, a pseudo-historic romance called *L'Histoire des Trois Nobles Fils du Roi*, containing a scene in which the King of Sicily holds a banquet at Naples and all present, including three kings' sons, make vows to a peacock.[46] The motif also occurs in the late romance of *Cleriadus et Méliadice*.[47]

The spectacular ceremonies which in the reign of Edward I were taken with utmost seriousness had become more and more of a hollow mockery. When in 1453 the fall of Constantinople had revived the idea of a crusade, Philip the Good arranged in the following year a 'Banquet du Phaisan,' the *ne plus ultra* of wasteful extravagance, at which he personally swore to lead an expedition against the Turks and to challenge the sultan to a duel — a vow which he conspicuously failed to accomplish.[48]

Edward I has been recognized by historians as one of the most successful of English kings in shaping the destinies of Britain. He subjugated Wales and laid the groundwork for the ultimate conquest of Scotland; he has been called the English Justinian. Yet it seems clear from the facts I have presented that he was strongly influenced by literary tradition, not so much in regard to his practical policies, but in regard to the romantic atmosphere, the Arthurian pageantry,

[44] *Buik of Alexander*, i, xxxix f.

[45] *Ibid.*, i, xxxviii, n. 2.

[46] *Ibid.*, i, xliii.

[47] *Ibid.*, i, xlii, n. 6. H. L. D. Ward, *Catalogue of the Romances in the British Museum*, i (1883), 383 f.

[48] G. Doutrepont, *La Littérature française à la cour des ducs de Bourgogne* (Paris, 1909), pp. 106–117. R. L. Kilgour, *Decline of Chivalry* (Cambridge, Mass., 1937), pp. 253–257.

with which he enveloped them. He evidently liked to think of himself in the rôle of *Arthurus redivivus*.

Contemporary writers and those of the next generation also made the association between Edward and his British predecessor. In an Anglo-French poem, *Le Rossignol*, composed by a certain John, prebendary of Howden in Yorkshire and clerk of the household to Edward's mother, John asserts that the heart which is armed with the love of God is worthier than any hero — Gawain, Lancelot, Iwain, or Arthur, worthier even than Edward, 'qui a beau viaire,' and who has performed such exploits against the Saracens and at the tourney of Chalons (1273).[49] In the first years of his reign, then, Edward was ranked with the knights of the Round Table. After his death one John of London wrote in 1307 a Latin elegy, addressed to his widow, comparing him to his advantage with great warriors of the past.[50] Though Arthur had laid under tribute all the western lands from Aquitaine to the Orkney Isles, he failed to destroy the Saxons, was finally wounded and disappeared. 'Non sic succubuit Edwardus rex noster.'

Not long after, the Yorkshire chronicler, Peter de Langtoft, included in his account of Edward's reign no less than seven references to Arthur, which I cite briefly.[51] Arthur never held his fiefs as securely as Edward. Philip of France tried to rob Edward of his lands in Aquitaine, which Arthur had given to Beduer. In a list of the falls of princes Lucius the emperor and Arthur appear. Edward in his campaign against France failed to win the support of his barons because he had not followed the example of Arthur in distributing gifts. Arthur had been a model of justice tempered with mercy. Edward's great Pentecostal feast of 1306 was the most splendid ever celebrated in Britain, except Arthur's coronation at Caerleon. Peter concludes his poem by twice asserting that Edward was the most glorious king since Arthur's day.[52]

> De chevalerye, après ly reis Arthure,
> Estait ly reis Edward des Cristiens la flure;
> Tant fu beals e grantz, tant pussant en armoure,
> De ly poet homme parler tant cum le secle dure.

Moreover, several manuscripts of the chronicle add a French translation of Edward's claim to sovereignty over Scotland, including the precedent established by Arthur.[53] And the conception of Edward as a hero of adventures as fantastic

---

[49] *Romania*, LXIX (1946-7), 496-519, especially pp. 508-511.

[50] *Chronicles of the Reigns of Edward I and Edward II*, II, 15. Keeler, *op. cit.* (note 2 above), pp. 59 f.

[51] Pierre de Langtoft, *Chronicle*, ed. T. Wright (London, 1868), II, 266, 278, 284, 296, 326, 368.

[52] *Ibid.*, II, 378, 380. Van Veltem also, when speaking of the death of Edward (*op. cit.*, III, 64; Bk. v, ch. 26), says that there had never been a king so mighty in war since Arthur's time.

[53] Langtoft, *Chronicle*, II, 404, 406. On p. 266 Langtoft quotes a poem about Edward which asserts that 'Merlyn de ly ad prophetez,' and certain manuscripts of his chronicle (Cambridge University Library, G.I.i, and Sidney Sussex College 43) contain Anglo-French prophecies assigned to Merlin concerning the six kings who followed John, in which Edward appears as 'une dragoun de mercy.' Versions of these prophecies exist also in Latin and English. Cf. Rupert Taylor, *Political Prophecy in England* (New York, 1911), pp. 48-51, 157-164; H. L. D. Ward, *Catalogue of Romances . . . in the British Museum*, I (London, 1883), 299 f., 308-310, 312, 322.

as any recounted in the Matter of Britain is found, as Powicke observed, in Lodewijk van Velthem's narrative of the Welsh campaign of 1282–83.[54] We have a guiding stag and a guiding bird, a storm-making spring and a ferocious bear, ancient weapons and a cave where lay huge bones; perhaps, Lodewijk suggests, the weapons and the bones were those of Arthur himself. We see once more, then, how persistently the career of Edward Plantagenet reminded men of his own and the next generation of the fabulous deeds of the British king and of his Round Table knights.

Seldom, I think, has the impress of literature on events and of events upon literature been more curiously illustrated than in the preceding pages. To borrow a phrase from my friend and colleague, Professor Emery Neff, 'the poetry of history' and the history of poetry are inextricably intertwined.

[54] Lodewijk van Velthem, *op. cit.* (note 21 above), II, 132–170 (Bk. III, ch. 22–34). Huet has a summary and an excellent comment in *Moyen Age*, XXVI, 179–197, in which he points out parallels in romance.

Was Chaucer a Free Thinker?

(Studies in Medieval Literature in Honor of A.C.Baugh pp. 21-44)

Was Chaucer a Free Thinker? [1]

Many critics have refused to accept Geoffrey Chaucer as a thinker at all. Matthew Arnold denied him the quality of high seriousness. Many readers, I feel sure, even though they admit that Chaucer had ideas about such topics as true gentility and Christian piety, take him as a representative of the Middle Ages, of the Age of Faith, and assume that he never came up against the problems which have haunted the eighteenth century, the so-called age of reason, and the nineteenth century, the age of science, and our own age, in which it seems possible that mankind together with its problems may cease to exist. For such readers, Chaucer speaks only through the Prioress and the Second Nun, as an unquestioning devotee of the Trinity and the Blessed Virgin. They fail to take into account, or dismiss as rhetorical flourishes, the heterodox ideas which he sometimes expressed.

When I say that Chaucer *expressed* these heterodox opinions, I do not mean that he actually held them as firm convictions; I do not mean that they formed articles in his creed. What I do mean to say is that these skeptical ideas crop up again and again in his poems when there was no particular occasion for them and when there was nothing in his sources to suggest them. What I do mean is that certain basic doubts, which went beyond Wyclif's questioning of the authority of the papacy and denunciation of the mendicant orders—doubts of God's justice and wisdom in dealing with mankind, doubts as to the freedom of the will, doubts as to immortality of the soul—were sufficiently familiar to Chaucer as to obtrude themselves into the *Troilus*, the Knight's Tale, the *Legend of Good Women*, the Franklin's Tale, and even so pious a legend

289

as the Man of Law's Tale of Custance. It is noteworthy that these questionings crop up in writings of the period when Chaucer was making his translation of Boethius, in which these very problems were raised.

Of course, there is plenty of evidence that the poet was no confirmed skeptic but a devout and orthodox Christian. The *ABC* may be discounted as evidence of Chaucer's personal devotion to the Virgin, since it is essentially a translation from Deguileville and was, according to Speght, made at the request of Blanche the Duchess for her private use. The pious tales related by the two nuns may also be discounted as required by the profession of the narrators. But no such objection can be raised against the epilogue to *Troilus*, against the *Balade of Good Counsel*, or against the *Retractions*. Even the portrait of the Parson, though it displays from a Catholic point of view a heretical taint, from the Protestant point of view is orthodoxy itself.[2]

In the *Retractions*, though the poet frankly confesses to inditing worldly vanities, tales that "sounen unto sin," and many a lecherous lay, he apparently feels himself innocent of any provocation to skepticism. If more proof were needed, there are the references to Chaucer by such impeccably orthodox writers as Hoccleve and Lydgate, who probably would have heard if their master had been *at any period* notorious as an agnostic. I am quite ready, therefore, to agree with those who maintain that Chaucer was, in spite of a temporary sympathy with the heresiarch Wyclif and in spite of temporary lapses into ribaldry, a professing Christian and, *in certain moods* at least, a devout one.

I have used two expressions which show perhaps how I would reconcile my belief in Chaucer's religious orthodoxy with my belief in the skeptical tendency of certain passages in his writings: those expressions are "at any period," and

"in certain moods." For it is characteristic of most human be-
ings to change with the passing of time and to respond to
different moods. Professor George Stewart in a penetrating
essay on "The Moral Chaucer," in the *University of California Publications in English,* remarked thirty-two years
ago:[3] "Even the simplest of us play in our lives, often in the
same day, many and sometimes incongruous parts: a keen-
eyed friend may see in *us*

> Buffoon and poet, lover and sensualist,
> A deal of Ariel, just a streak of Puck,
> Much Antony, of Hamlet most of all,
> And something of the shorter Catechist.

So with Chaucer—a little of the Miller, more of the Squire,
a bit of the Wife, a touch of the Manciple, something (not
very much I feel) of that strange elvish creature with down-
cast eyes, most of all probably of the Clerk, and finally no
inconsiderable portion of the Parson." To Professor Stewart's
analysis of the many-sided Chaucer I would add that there
was in him something of the rationalist, something of the
skeptic. Can we not all agree that the greatness of Chaucer,
as of Shakespeare, lies in his universality, his ability to enter
sympathetically into the thoughts and feelings of the most
diverse characters? Can we not agree that a poet who expressed with such poignancy and naturalness the contrary
views on marriage of the Wife of Bath and of the Clerk of
Oxenford was able to feel and to express very diverse attitudes toward the ultimate problems of man's destiny? Permit
me to quote a passage from an essay on Bernard Shaw written
by one of the best of American critics, Edmund Wilson. Wilson wrote:[4]

One of the prime errors of recent radical criticism has been the
assumption that great novels and plays must necessarily be written

by people who have everything clear in their minds. People who have everything clear in their minds, who are not capable of identifying themselves imaginatively with, who do not actually embody in themselves, contrary emotions and points of view, do not write novels and plays at all—do not at any rate write good ones. And—given genius—the more violent the contraries, the greater the works of art.

If Edmund Wilson was right in enunciating this by no means novel idea, and if it applies to Shakespeare, it surely applies to the author of the *Canterbury Tales* and *Troilus*. If it applies to the creator of Hamlet and Falstaff, it applies to the begetter of Troilus the romanticist and of Pandarus the ironist, to the begetter of the Parson, who caught his words out of the Gospel, and also of the Doctor, whose study was but little on the Bible. So, granting that Chaucer regarded himself and was regarded by others as essentially a conformist to the religion of his day, let me ask you to consider a number of passages which show a questioning spirit.

But before reviewing these passages, may I remind you that this also was in conformity with the spirit of his day. It was a period of doubt and challenge. Kittredge in his excellent book, *Chaucer and His Poetry*, declared:[5]

We hear . . . that our times are blessed with a critical or questioning spirit, whereas our medieval ancestors believed what they were told, with blind faith. This, however, is at best a very crude antithesis, and it has no merit whatsoever when applied to Chaucer's lifetime. Then, if ever, the spirit of radicalism was abroad in the land. To describe as an era of dumb submissiveness the age of Wyclif, and John Huss, and the Great Schism, of the Jacquerie in France and Tyler and Ball in England, is to read both literature and history with one's eyes shut.

Anyone who surveys the literature of the fourteenth century for evidence of this questioning spirit will quickly discover that it not only challenged, as the Protestants did later, the validity of excommunication, the spiritual value of pilgrimages, the miracle of transubstantiation, and the authority of the Pope, but also went far beyond, to question the justice of God, the freedom of the will, the doctrine of the fall of man and his redemption, and the immortality of the soul.

One of the most representative and popular homiletic works of the later Middle Ages was the *Gesta Romanorum,* written probably in England about 1330. It contains two exempla, or parables, particularly designed to answer doubts as to the justice of the divine dispensation. One is the famous, perhaps notorious, parable of the Angel and the Hermit.[6] A hermit, who lived in a remote cave, one day saw a shepherd tending his flocks. The shepherd fell asleep and a sheep was stolen, whereupon his master had him put to death. Appalled at this injustice, the hermit cried out: "O Lord, see how this man placed blame on an innocent person and killed him. Why do you permit such things to happen? I will go out into the world and live as other men do." Leaving his cave, the hermit set out into the world. An angel appeared to him in human form and became his travelling companion. In the course of the next few days the angel killed the child of a knight who had given them shelter, stole a gold cup from a burgess who had entertained them, threw into a river a pilgrim, and presented the stolen cup to a man who had refused them the shelter of his home. Thus the hermit was even more deeply convinced that injustice prevailed in the world. But the angel revealed his celestial mission, explained the divine plan to prevent sin and reform character by means of his acts, and concluded saying: "Know that nothing on earth is done without reason." The second exemplum tells how a knight accused an innocent servant of theft, cut off his foot, and left him to die.[7] A hermit went to the servant's aid and was moved by his story to reproach God for permitting such wrongs to exist. Once more an angel was sent to justify the Deity. "All His ways are truth and His judgments equity. Do not say: Why did He make me and then let me fall?"

The presence of these two exempla in a manual for preachers is evidence that the problem of the theodicy was one with which preachers of the fourteenth century found it necessary to deal. Among their parishioners doubtless there were those who asked, "Why did God make me and then let me fall?"

In Chaucer's own time the monk and chronicler Thomas of Walsingham wrote that the Londoners were of nearly all peoples the most arrogant, and had no faith in God.[8] Walsingham also referred to the lords who believed that there was no God, no sacrament of the altar, no resurrection after death, but that as an animal dies, so also ends man. Chaucer's friend Gower in the *Mirour de l'Homme* confirms this accusation as regards the merchant class.[9] "One of them," he writes, "said to me the other day that he who can have the sweetness of this life and rejects it, would in his opinion act like a fool, for after this life no one knows the truth, whither to go or by what way." Langland asserts that men of high degree were accustomed to mock at the most sacred doctrines.[10] "I have heard high men, eating at table, talk as if they were clerics, of Christ and his power. They found fault with the Father who formed us all. . . . Why would our Savior allow such a serpent into His garden of bliss, who beguiled first the woman and the man after, and through whose wily words they went to hell, and all their seed for their sin suffered the same death? Why should we who now live rot and be rent for the sins of Adam? Reason would never have it." Here in Christian England of Chaucer's day men were anticipating the charge which Fitzgerald made in the nineteenth century in his *Rubaiyat:*

> O Thou, who didst with pitfall and with gin
> Beset the road I was to wander in,
> Thou wilt not with predestined evil round
> Enmesh and then impute the fall to Sin.

Again Langland speaks of the blasphemous talk of the rich.[11] "Now it is the mode at meat when minstrels are silent for laymen to dispute about holy lore with the learned, and talk of the Trinity, how two slew the third. . . . Thus they drivel on the dais to explain the Deity, and gnaw God with the gorge when their guts are full." It will be remembered that Dante assigned a whole circle in hell to the Epicureans, "those who with the body make the spirit die." And among those who denied the after-life were Farinata degli Uberti, Cavalcante Cavalcanti, Cardinal Ubaldini, and the Emperor Frederick II. Dante speaks of more than a thousand of these unbelievers, and his commentator Benvenuto da Imola remarks that it would take too long to enumerate the eminent men of the Epicurean sect.[12] "Ah, how many heretics there are who hypocritically pretend to be Catholics for fear of punishment or infamy!" It would seem that these men, and other skeptics, such as those mentioned by Langland and Gower, conformed outwardly to all the teachings of the Church, heard mass, went to confession, took the sacraments, and except for the Emperor Frederick were not excommunicated. But among their intimates they made no secret of their sadduceeism.

It is to be noted that Dante classed even the Cardinal Ubaldini among the Epicureans, and Ubaldini seems not to have been unique among the clergy in his materialistic philosophy. Froissart, the chronicler, was in orders and became a canon of Chimay. For eight years he moved in the same court circles as Chaucer. When he returned to England in 1395, he made inquiries of a certain squire as to how Richard II's campaign against the Irish had gone. The squire explained that four Irish kings had submitted to the King of England "by the grace of God." Froissart, churchman though he was, could hardly believe that this was sufficient cause, and, as he tells us himself, he remarked: "La grâce de Dieu est moult bonne, qui la puet avoir, et puet grandement valloir, mais on voit petit de seigneurs terriens présentement augmenter leurs seigneuries, se ce n'est par puissance." [13] Here is a sentiment exactly analogous to the cynical dictum often, though mistakenly, attributed to Napoleon, that God is always on the side of the big battalions. Froissart was essentially a worldling, and his worldliness extended itself beyond a fondness for the fleshpots and for the pageantry of life to something very close to a materialistic interpretation of history.

It may perhaps be thought that I have overdrawn the picture. Of course, I have said nothing about the millions who never wrestled with doubt, and the other millions who after wrestling with doubt came for one reason or another to the conclusion that the clergy were wiser than they. And when it comes to estimating the exact proportion of believers, secret doubters, and downright skeptics, it would be impossible even for a contemporary, even for Chaucer himself, to make more than a rough guess. All that one can say is that there was a considerable minority who though conforming to the demands of the Church sufficiently to escape excommunication and burning, actually were agnostics, Sadducees, or even atheists. Some of the more powerful and wealthy even indulged in open mockery at the most sacred doctrines. It is necessary to remember the existence of these scoffers when the Middle Ages are pictured as an Age of Faith, exempt from any taint of materialism, fatalism, or rationalism.

Now Chaucer lived in the same world with Thomas of Walsingham, Gower, Langland, and Froissart, and he, if anyone, knew what was going on in the minds of his contemporaries, not to mention the ideas they discussed openly. It is well to remember that though he was a bookworm and though much of his poetry consists of translation and quotation, he was also very much a man of affairs. John Livingston Lowes, one of the greatest interpreters of the poet, declared in an article over fifty years ago that [14] "Sources other than the books Chaucer read—sources that lie in his intercourse with men and in his reaction upon the interests, the happenings, the familiar matter of his day—entered likewise into 'that large compasse' of his, and must be taken into account in estimating his work."

Now, given Chaucer's contact with men and women who were covertly or openly skeptical of the most sacred dogmas of Christianity, it would be strange if he did not in some measure feel the impact of their skepticism. His was a mind which combined a strong element of docility and imitativeness with an equally strong element of originality and inventiveness. His was a spirit given to inquiry and exploration. And when he was presented with some of the perennial questions which men have asked about the universe and man's place in it, about undeserved suffering and the immortality of the soul, about fate and free will, he more than most men was likely to examine with tolerance and understanding the various answers. The poet who could so sympathetically present the erotic feminism of the Wife of Bath and portray so admiringly the Wyclifite Parson, was not one who saw life entirely from a conventional angle. So it is only natural that in reading Chaucer we should find him repeatedly expressing in his own person or through the mouths of his characters certain heterodox opinions. Let me repeat that I do not believe that he was an agnostic, a materialist, a rebel by conviction, but simply that such speculations were familiar to him, that they were much on his mind, and that they crop up in his work with significant frequency even when nothing in his sources called for them.

Thus Chaucer seems to have passed through a period of disillusionment and dark musings, a period when the sense of assurance and hope was weakened by doubts. Between 1379 and 1385 he was probably writing the *House of Fame*, which, with all its fun, manifests a completely ironic, disillusioned view of the inequities of fame and reputation; the Knight's Tale, with Palamon's violent outburst against the inequities of man's lot and Arcite's despairing "What is this world? What asketh men to have? Now with his love, now in the colde grave, alone withouten any companye." Certainly in this period he wrote the *tragedye* of Troilus, told of his "double sorwe," and concluded with this comment:

> Swych fyn hath al his grete worthynesse,
> Swich fyn hath his estat real above,
> Swich fyn his lust, swich fyn hath his noblesse.

And it was in this period that Chaucer took the time to translate into English the *De Consolatione Philosophiae* of Boethius, which offered a reasoned antidote to all these doctrines of doubt and despair.

Let me quote again from Professor Stewart's article on "The Moral Chaucer." [15] "Like Hardy's *Dynasts*, although not quite so schematically, the *Troilus* attempts to probe the motivation of human existence, and again like the *Dynasts* its conclusion is strikingly black." Stewart goes on to make the following personal comment: "The Knight's Tale, the Boethius, and *Troilus and Criseyde,* make me believe that in this middle period Chaucer became greatly interested in the deeper problems of life, to which he was able to see no solution except through religion." Indeed the *Troilus* may be regarded as an exemplum as much as the story in the *Gesta Romanorum* of the Angel and the Hermit—an exemplum in which the fickleness of Fortune, the undeserved torment of a noble soul, are in the end reconciled with a belief in Him who died upon a cross our souls to redeem, and who will betray the trust of no man, I dare say, who will lay his heart wholly on Him.

But Chaucer reaches this solution not by logic but by faith. He puts into the mouth of Troilus the long discussion of fate and foreknowledge, taken over from Boethius, but he does not add the defense of human freedom which Boethius supplied. He allows Troilus to stop with a fatalistic conclusion.[16] Now it is highly significant that Chaucer's principal source, Boccaccio's *Filostrato,* has not the barest suggestion of this debate on God's foreknowledge and man's free will. It is Geoffrey Chaucer who has introduced it, rather inappropriately, since it is odd to find the Trojan prince an adept in metaphysics and pondering this complex problem with all the subtlety of those great clerics "who have their tops full high and smoothly shorn." There can be no doubt that it is the poet's own interest in the problem which has foisted it, somewhat artificially, upon the Trojan prince as a soliloquy.

Much the same problem is introduced by Chaucer into the Knight's Tale, this time, I believe, much more naturally. Again there was little to correspond in the Italian source, the pseudo-classical epic, Boccaccio's *Teseida.* In fact, the Knight's Tale reveals a preoccupation with the idea of destinal forces moulding men's lives. The planets Mars, Venus, Diana, and Saturn

exercise their conflicting influences and determine the outcome of the lovers' rivalry. The notion of chance and its
ironies is a sort of *leitmotif*. The Theban queen who greets
Theseus on his return to Athens addresses him as "Lord, to
whom Fortune hath given victory," and ascribes her wretched-
ness to Fortune and her false wheel. Arcite ascribes his im-
prisonment to Fortune or to some disposition of the stars.
"So stood the heaven when that we were born." Palamon likewise refers to his destiny shaped by the eternal word. Arcite
indulges in a longish soliloquy on the ironies of life. There is
mention of Fortune's dice and Fortune's mutability. Straight
from Boethius comes a passage on man's ignorance of where
his true happiness lies. We are like a drunk man who knows
he has a house, but does not know the way thither. Later in
the poem Chaucer repeats from Boccaccio the comment on
the role of chance: "Sometyme it shal fallen on a day that
falleth not eft within a thousand yeer."

The chief expression, however, of protest against the divine
order is put into the mouth of imprisoned Palamon. Shut off
from his Emelye, he inveighs against the gods.

> "O crueel goddes that governe
> This world with byndyng of youre word eterne,
> And writen in the table of atthamaunt
> Your parlement and youre eterne graunt,
> What is mankinde more unto you holde
> Than is the sheep that rouketh in the folde?
> For slayn is man right as another beest,
> And dwelleth eek in prisoun and arreest,
> And hath siknesse and greet adversitee
> And ofte times gilteless, pardee.
> What governance is in this prescience
> That giltelees tormenteth innocence?
> And yet encresseth this al my penaunce

That man is bounden to his observaunce,
For Goddes sake, to letten of his wille,
Ther as a beest may al his lust fulfille.
And whan a beest is deed he hath no peyne;
But man after his deeth moot wepe and pleyne,
Though in this world he have care and wo.
Withouten doute it may stonden so.
The answere of this lete I to dyvynys,
But wel I wot that in this world greet pyne ys."

Palamon's protest begins with paraphrasing a metrical pass-age in Boethius, but the words are more audacious, the passion more violent. And Chaucer added the complaint that man-kind is bound by God's law to curb his desires, whereas noth-ing hinders an animal from indulging its appetites. Man alone is doomed to suffer after death, but when a beast is dead, he has no pain. Is there in English literature, except in James Thomson's *City of Dreadful Night,* a stronger appeal against "the governaunce which gilteless tormenteth innocence"?

And it is to be remarked that this charge of Palamon's against the cruel gods receives no direct refutation such as Boethius attempted. Later the old Egeus, who knew this world's transmutation, gives the cold comfort that the world is but a thoroughfare full of woe, and death is the end of every worldly sore. Theseus himself, after a discourse on the inevitability of change and death, declares:

"Then is it wisdom, as it thinketh me,
To maken vertu of necessitee,
And take it weel that we may not eschue. . . .
And whoso gruccheth ought, he dooth folye,
And rebel is to him that al may gye."

This is, of course, no real answer to Palamon's complaint. In fact, there is, according to the Knight's Tale, no rational justification of the universe. It is folly to rebel. Submit to what cannot be helped. That is the moral. I think we may safely conclude that the poet had found no satisfactory *rational* answer to the problem; otherwise he would have given it to us. His failure to answer is practically a confession of agnosticism—at least of incompetence so far as this particular difficulty is concerned.

Two generations ago, in 1892, Professor Lounsbury of Yale University published his erudite *Studies in Chaucer,* in which he adduced another passage in the Knight's Tale which seemed to strengthen the case for Chaucer's agnosticism.[17] He quoted the lines about the fate of Arcite's soul after death.

> His spirit chaunged hous and wente ther,
> As I cam never, I can not tellen wher.
> Therefore I stinte, I nam no divinistre.
> Of soules finde I noght in this registre,
> Ne me ne list thilke opinions to telle
> Of hem, though that they writen wher they dwelle.

Lounsbury commented: "Can modern agnosticism point to a denial more emphatic . . . of the belief that there exists for us any assurance of the life that is lived beyond the grave?" Lounsbury had a point; the lines are capable of such a construction; but they are also open to another interpretation which relieves them of any unorthodox tendency. One of the issues on which there was debate among the orthodox was the fate of the righteous heathen—men who never had heard of the Christian's God or of His plan of salvation, who by no possibility could have received God's grace through baptism and the sacraments.[18] Dante, you will remember, brought up the problem in the *Paradiso.*[19] "A man is born upon the bank of Indus, and there is none to tell of Christ, nor none to read, nor none to write; and all his volitions and his deeds are good so far as human reason seeth, sinless in life or in discourse. He dieth unbaptized and without faith; where is that justice which condemneth him? Where is his fault in that he not believes?" [20] In England and in Chaucer's own day the question of the salvation of righteous heathen was argued pro and con. The problem weighed heavily on the mind of Langland.[21] The author of the Middle English *Saint Erkenwald* makes it possible through a miracle for a pagan judge of King Belinus's time to escape from limbo and join the celestial cenacle.[22] Dame Juliana of Norwich, on the one hand, accepts as an article of faith the damnation of those who die out of the faith of Holy Church, that is, the heathen;[23] but on the other hand approaches the doctrine of universal salvation.[24] "In mankind that shall be saved is comprehended all; that is to say, all that is made and the Maker of all; for in man is God, and God is in all." It seems pretty clear that Chaucer preferred not to impale himself on the horns of that dilemma. In confessing his ignorance as to the house where Arcite's spirit dwelt, Chaucer was merely refusing to commit himself as to the fate of so noble a pagan as Arcite. That is all that we can infer from the passage.

Not long after the completion of the *Troilus,* Chaucer began the *Legend of Good Women,* and it opens with some lines which show that the question of the after-life was still much on his mind. The passage is written in imitation of Froissart's agnostic lines about the Fountain of Youth. Froissart wrote:[25] "I have heard talk of the Fountain of Youth and of invisible stones. But these are impossibilities, for never, by the faith I owe to Saint Marcelli, have I seen anyone who has said: 'I have actually been there.'" Now Chaucer deliberately rejected the Fountain of Youth as a place about which there was no valid testimony and substituted heaven and hell. "A thousand times have I heard men tell that there is joy in heaven and pain in hell, and I accord well that it is so. Nevertheless I wot well also that there is no one dwelling in this country who has ever been in heaven or hell or who knows of it in any other way but as he hath heard said or found it written. For by experience no man may prove it." After making the point that the existence of heaven and hell has never been verified by anyone living in England in his day, Chaucer goes on to assure us that this is no reason for disbelieving. "But God forbid that one should believe only what one sees with the eye. One should not consider everything a lie unless he has seen or done it himself. Then may we give full credence to books through which old things are kept in mind, and to the doctrine of wise men of old. . . . Well ought we then to honour and believe these books, when we have no other proof." Chaucer when he revised the Prologue of the *Legend of Good Women* some nine years later retained these lines intact. Obviously they do not mean that the poet rejected the belief in heaven and hell, as Lounsbury maintained; in fact, they state emphatically that we ought to accept many things of which we have no ocular demonstration. Nevertheless, they furnish another instance in which Chaucer departed from his source in order to bring up and to state clearly a case for unbelief. Even though he rejects it, he had at least entertained it, and if we may take the witness of his contemporaries, Gower and Thomas of Walsingham, there were men in business and among the aristocracy who were known to deny the immortality of the soul. It was a live issue, not a dead one.

If we hark back to the problem of God's tolerance of evil and unmerited suffering, it is noteworthy that it crops up again and again as a *leitmotif* in several other poems where the source had no corresponding note. Even in that most pious legend of Custance, the Man of Law's Tale, the tendency of which is to counsel patience under misfortune, to see a beneficent Providence operating through calamity and wrong, and to bring about a happy ending, this cry is heard, though uttered in all meekness. The Constable, having received the Uriah letter about the innocent Custance, exclaims:

> "O mighty God, if that it be thy wille,
> Sith thou art rightful juge, how may it be
> That thou wolt suffren innocents to spille,
> And wikked folk regne in prosperitee?"

Custance herself, about to be set adrift on the sea, though welcoming God's dispensation, cannot resist turning to the babe in her arms, and asking "O litel child, allas! What is thy gilt, That never wroghtest synne as yet pardee?" The opening lines of "Filomena" in the *Legend of Good Women* raise the question why the Creator created so black-hearted a villain as Tereus. "Thou giver of the forms, who hast wrought this fair world and borne it in thy thought eternally before thou didst begin thy work, . . . why dost thou suffer Tereus to be born, who is so false in love and so forsworn, that when folk name his name he corrupteth all, from this earth to the first heaven!" Here Chaucer in his own person expresses the same bewilderment that Dame Juliana of Norwich, his contemporary, felt and recorded:[26] "I wondered why, by the great foreseeing wisdom of God, the beginning of sin was not letted, for then, methought, all should have been well."

Dorigen in the Franklin's Tale finds unaccountable the existence of the black rocks off the Breton coast, rocks which serve only to destroy God's own creatures.

> "Eterne God, that thurgh they purveiaunce
> Ledest the world by certein governaunce,
> In ydel, as men seyn, ye no thing make.

But, Lord, thise grisly feendly rokkes blake,
That semen rather a foul confusioun
Of werk than any fair creacioun
Of swich a parfit wys God and a stable,
Why han ye wroght this werk unresonable? . . .
See ye nat, Lord, how mankynde it destroyeth?
An hundred thousand bodyes of mankynde
Gan rokkes slayn, al be they nat in mynde,
Which mankynde is so fair part of thy werk
That thou it madest lyk to thyn owene merk. . . .
I wot wel clerkes wol seyn as hem leste,
By argumentz, that al is for the beste,
Though I ne kan the causes nat yknowe.
But thilke God that made the wynd to blowe
As kepe my lord! this my conclusioun.
To clerkes lete I al disputisoun."

Here once more is poignantly expressed the agonized perplexity of a soul faced with the problem of reconciling the
benevolence and wisdom of the Creator with the hostility and
confusion of the world He created.

It is possible to argue that these complaints, addressed to
the Deity and questioning His ordinances, which we find in
the tales of Custance, and Filomena, and Dorigen, were mere
literary commonplaces, samples of the rhetorical question and
the apostrophe. It is also possible to argue that in two out
of the three cases the sentiments are not those of Chaucer
himself but those of his characters; and he canont fairly be
held responsible for every emotional outburst to which they
give vent.

But neither of these arguments seems to stand up against
the force of certain facts. One of these protests, in the "Filomena," is that of Chaucer speaking in his own person. Moreover, in no case is the protest to be found in the source whence
Chaucer derived the narrative setting. This is also true of the

passage on heaven and hell which opens the *Legend of Good Women*, and of Palamon's passionate protest to the cruel gods in the Knight's Tale, and of Troilus's dissection of the problem of free will versus foreknowledge. According to the testimony of Chaucer's contemporaries, these were live issues. Least of all can the notion that these passages are hackneyed commonplaces or mere "colours of rethorike" stand up against the fact that Chaucer went to the trouble of making a careful translation of Boethius's work, which raised precisely these problems and offered ingenious and plausible solutions. In the face of these facts I see no other conclusion possible than that in his later thirties the poet went through a period of *Sturm und Drang* and was almost obsessed with these disturbing theological and metaphysical issues. Though he pretended to no special competence as a philosopher and more than once transferred to the "grete clerkes" the task of solving the riddles, he could not dismiss them from his mind. He may be placed, then, in the line of those men of letters who have taken seriously the problems of undeserved suffering and of evil in our world, a line which includes the author of the Book of Job, Plato, Boethius, Voltaire in *Zadig* and *Candide*, Matthew Arnold in *Mycerinus*, Fitzgerald in the *Rubaiyat*, and Thomas Hardy in *Tess of the D'Urbervilles* and *The Dynasts*. Some of these authors, needless to say, answered the problem with mockery or a sad irony. They found no reasonable creed which would justify the ways of God to man, and declared the heavens empty.

But Chaucer came to no such conclusion. Though he may *in a sense* be considered an agnostic since he repeatedly leaves the doubt he has raised without any answer, and repeatedly disclaims his ability to find an answer in logic, he seems to have found, like multitudes of others, an answer in faith. I believe that he was essentially a modest man, ready to kiss the steps where he saw pass Virgil, Ovid, Homer, Lucan, and Stace; ready also to put his trust in the "olde bookes," particularly Boethius's golden book. And for the benefit of his compatriots he rendered it into English, for here if anywhere there was a reasoned theodicy, a Christian apologetic (at least it was accepted as such) to counter the infidelity of his day, an apologetic which could be read by the layman—though, strange to say, the style must have discouraged most laymen from reading it.

But what is remarkable and highly significant is the fact that though Chaucer chose the way of faith and supported it with his translation of the *Consolation of Philosophy*, he does not, so far as I can remember, attack those who were lost in perplexity or who were vocal in their complaints against an omnipotent Deity. Indeed his doubters and complainants— Palamon, Troilus, Dorigen—are sympathetic, noble figures. They come in for no such castigation, in spite of their wild and whirling words, as do the hypocrites, not even for such gentle ridicule as the Prioress. Why such tolerance for persons who dared to question the decrees of Heaven and the teachings of the Church? The only explanation I can offer is that Chaucer himself had felt too keenly the force of their questionings and complaints, and though he could not go along with them and in fact opposed them, he could not blame them very much for following their reason to its logical conclusion. After all, unless the authority of reason is to be rejected, they could not honestly do otherwise.

It is pertinent to note that four of Chaucer's literary contemporaries, all four of English birth, displayed a similar tolerance, even a sympathy, for those who did not hold the Christian faith. Three of the four were unquestionably devout believers. The author of *Piers Plowman* was much exercised over the problem of whether Saracens, that is the heathen, could be saved, and in four passages he asserts the possibility of their salvation. At the end of the *A* text Scripture declares: "It is our belief that an unchristian, because of his just belief may have heritage in heaven, as truly as a high Christian." In the *B* text, Passus XI, Trajan, the Roman Emperor noted for his justice, interrupts the argument to cite his own case to prove that without singing of masses he could be saved. The poet continued: "Thus loyal love and living in justice pulled out of torment a pagan of Rome." Later in the twelfth Passus the case of Trajan is cited, and the principle is laid down that for him who lives as his religion teaches, and believes there is no better, a just God would never permit but that such a true man were approved. And finally, in Passus XV of the *B* text, in accordance with the same principle, Langland declared: "So may Saracens be saved and Scribes and Jews." The author of that contemporary masterpiece *Saint Erkenwald,* as I have already remarked, tells a story much like that of Trajan and of how a heathen judge of Belinus's time had executed justice with such flawless impartiality that not only was his corpse preserved uncorrupted for centuries in the tomb, but also his spirit was released from purgatory and joined the cenacle above because of a single tear shed by the Saxon saint.

The author of Mandeville's *Travels,* who now, thanks to Professor Josephine Bennett,[27] may be regarded as an Englishman, wrote of the Brahmins of India.[28] "Albeit that these folk have not the articles of our faith as we have, nevertheless, for their natural good faith and their good intent, I trow fully that God accepts their service, right as he did of Job, who was a paynim, and held him for his true servant. And therefore, albeit there be many diverse religions in the world, yet I trow that God loveth always them that love him meekly in truth. . . . No man should have in despite none earthly man for their diverse religions, for we know not whom God loveth, nor whom God hateth." As I have already noted, the devout visionary Dame Julian of Norwich wrote in her *Revelations of Divine Love:*[29] "In mankind that shall be saved is comprehended all; that is to say, all that is made and the Maker of all; for in man is God, and God is in all."

To such a doctrine of universal salvation Chaucer never approaches. But I think it is safe to say that, though he was not in our modern sense a free thinker, an agnostic, he displays in his poetry a broad tolerance and even a sympathy with honest doubt. He might have been willing to accept Tennyson's dictum:

> There lives more faith in honest doubt,
> Believe me, than in half the creeds.

¹ In 1950 Miss Mary Edith Thomas published a doctoral dissertation under the title *Medieval Skepticism and Chaucer* (William–Frederick Press, 391 East 149th St., New York). It was met with skepticism by several reviewers. Since it was prepared chiefly under my direction, I consider myself responsible for the material and the conclusions; and I am by no means ready to concede that the testimony of Dante, Benvenuto da Imola, the author of *Piers Plowman*, John Gower and many others, cited by Miss Thomas, is negligible or mendacious, as her critics imply. Accordingly, with acknowledgments to Miss Thomas, I propose to present the case briefly again, since I regard it as essential to the estimate of the poet as a serious thinker.

² R. S. Loomis, "Was Chaucer a Laodicean?", *Essays and Studies in Honor of Carleton Brown* (New York, 1940), pp. 141-46. Reprinted in *Chaucer Criticism*, ed. Richard J. Schoeck and Jerome Taylor (Notre Dame, 1960), pp. 302-4.

³ P. 109.

⁴ *The Triple Thinkers* (New York, 1948), p. 180.

⁵ G. L. Kittredge, *Chaucer and His Poetry* (Cambridge, Mass., 1915), pp. 7 ff.

⁶ *Gesta Romanorum*, ed. H. Oesterley (Berlin, 1872), pp. 397 ff.

⁷ *Ibid.*, pp. 478 ff.

⁸ Thomas Walsingham, *Historia Anglicana*, ed. T. H. Riley (Rolls Series, London, 1863-64), II:208.

⁹ Gower, *Complete Works*, ed. G. C. Macaulay (Oxford, 1899-1902), I:287.

¹⁰ *Piers Plowman*, B text, X:101-3, 105-12.

¹¹ *Ibid.*, C text, XII:35-7, 40 ff.

¹² *Comentum super Dantis Aldigherij Comoediam*, ed. J. P. Lacaita (Florence, 1887), I:357.

¹³ *Oeuvres de Froissart*, ed. Kervyn de Lettenhove; *Chroniques*, XV (Brussels, 1871):179.

¹⁴ *MP*, III (1905): 45 ff.

¹⁵ *University of California Publications in English*, I (1929), p. 000.

¹⁶ In *Speculum*, VI (1931):234, Prof. Howard Patch writes: "In the famous soliloquy of Troilus in Book IV, the hero gives, it is true, considerable expression to what, for the sake of argument, we may call determinism—although I think he is rather complaining against predestination and trying to exonerate himself without impiety. In any case, there is no reason to suppose that this monologue is spoken for other than dramatic effect."

¹⁷ T. R. Lounsbury, *Studies in Chaucer* (New York, 1892), II:514 ff.

¹⁸ R. W. Chambers, "Long Will, Dante, and the Righteous Heathen," *Essays and Studies by Members of the English Association*, IX (Oxford, 1924):50-69.

¹⁹ *Paradiso*, Canto xix.

²⁰ *The Divine Comedy*, Carlyle–Wicksteed translation, Modern Library (New York, 1932).

[21] Chambers, *loc. cit.*, p. 54.

[22] *Saint Erkenwald,* ed. H. L. Savage (New Haven, 1926).

[23] Juliana of Norwich, *Revelations of Divine Love,* ed. Roger Hudleston (London, 1927), p. 57.

[24] *Ibid.,* p. 17

[25] *Oeuvres,* ed. A. Scheler (Brussels, 1870-72), II:24.

[26] Juliana of Norwich, *op. cit.,* p. 48.

[27] Josephine W. Bennett, *Rediscovery of Sir John Mandeville* (New York, 1954), pp. 176-80.

[28] *Ibid.,* p. 73.

[29] See note 24.

Pioneers in Arthurian Scholarship

(Bulletin Bibliographique de la Societe International Arthurienne No. 16, pp. 95-106)

PIONEERS IN ARTHURIAN SCHOLARSHIP

Many of you will have read of a Connecticut Yankee who distinguished himself at Arthur's court as a mechanic, advertising expert, social reformer, forecaster of eclipses, and humorist. Though now a resident of Connecticut and though descended on both sides from Connecticut Yankees, I cannot lay claim to any of the varied talents of Mark Twain's hero, but I should like to resemble him in one respect, his sense of justice and fair play. I should like in this paper to correct an injustice in Arthurian scholarship and give a " square deal " to three British scholars whose pioneering work on the Matter of Britain is seldom recognized by scholars today.

The names of the three are : Sharon Turner, Joseph Ritson, and Lady Charlotte Guest. These scholars not only did much of the spade-work in Arthurian studies, but they planted and watered a healthy garden. None of them held an academic post, but between them they published nearly all the significant material concerned with the origins and early stages of Arthurian literature, or at least called attention to the most significant passages. They went to the manuscripts ; they made translations ; they surmounted difficulties. Of course, there have been better translations ; more evidence has been gathered for the solution of the problems ; mistakes have been corrected. But, in the large, it may be said that these three amateurs anticipated over a hundred years ago many of the solutions of fundamental problems 'which are at last being accepted today by professional scholars.

Yet these pioneers have been curiously neglected by their successors. A glance at the bibliography in Bruce's standard work on the *Evolution of Arthurian Romance* will suffice to reveal this neglect. Turner and Ritson are completely ignored, and there are only the briefest references to Lady Guest. Another instance of this undeserved neglect is to be found in Lucy Paton's *Fairy Mythology of Arthurian*

Romance, first published in 1903 (republished with supplement in 1960). This was an admirable work, still enormously useful, but though a large part of it was devoted to Morgan le Fay and her origins, Miss Paton overlooked the equation pointed out by both Ritson and Lady Guest, the equation of Morgan le Fay with Modron, which is fraught with supreme significance. For this equation demonstrates the descent of Morgan le Fay from one of the great Celtic goddesses, Matrona, worshipped from Cisalpine Gaul to the lower Rhine, and apparently also in Britain. And this descent is confirmed by the many characteristics of Morgan which are paralleled by one or another of the Celtic deities.

To be sure, Professor Annette Hopkins in an article in *PMLA,* 1928, did justice to Ritson's energy and acumen, and Lady Guest's name is familiar to every Arthurian today, but we tend to think of her condescendingly as an adapter of the Welsh romances to children. Unless I have overlooked other tributes by modern scholars to their forerunners of the late eighteenth and early nineteenth century, the pioneers of Arthurian study are today largely forgotten.

The first of them was Sharon Turner, a London solicitor and a selfmade scholar, whose interest in Northern antiquities led him to spend his leisure hours poring over the Anglo-Saxon manuscripts and documents in that hospitable home of scholars, the British Museum. After sixteen years of study he produced in 1799 the first installment of a *History of England from the Earliest Period to the Norman Conquest.* This work, completed in 1805, uncovered a literature which had lain buried under the dust of libraries, the literature of Wales, and startled the world almost as much as the excavations of Layard at Nineveh and Babylon. The chapter wich Turner devoted to Arthur's life and campaigns displayed the zeal of a collector but no great critical judgment : in fact Turner pronounced the discovery of Arthur's bones at Glastonbury Abbey in 1189 (or rather 1191) as the first clear and historical certainty about this celebrated man. Nevertheless the chapter was notable for the citation of many Welsh texts, the triads, the Welsh *Brut,* and poems attributed to Llywarch Hen. The use of the *cynfeirdd* as valid evidence bearing on the activities of the historic Arthur was challenged by certain critics who knew nothing of the matter. Turner picked up the gauntlet and defended himself in a work which seems to me of great significance, *A Vindication of the Genuineness of the Ancient British Poems of Aneurin, Taliesin, Llywarch Hen, and Merdhin,* published in 1803.

Considering that date, the book is remarkable for the familiarity it displays with all the Welsh material available at the time and for the sobriety of the reasoning. Turner proved that the poems were no modern forgeries, like Macpherson's *Ossian.* He described and dated the Four Ancient Books of Wales. It was no ordinary solicitor riding a hobby who took the trouble to learn Welsh when, as he· expressed it, the English were as ignorant of that language and its early monuments as they were of the language and monuments of Great Tartary. He printed numerous passages side by side with their translations : in spite of the admitted obscurity of the language, he rendered Taliesin's poem on the Battle of Argoed Llwyfain accurately enough, so that it coincides in sense for the most part with the rendering of the same poem by Sir Ifor Williams, the eminent modern interpreter of the *cynfeirdd.* Perhaps the most daring feat which Turner essayed was the translation and publication of the poem entitled *Preiddeu Annwn,* or the *Spoils of Fairyland,* even though he admitted that all connection of thought seems to have been studiously avoided, and asked : " Could Lycophron or the Sybils or any ancient oracle be more elaborately incomprehensible ? " Much of its meaning is still matter for guesswork, but it remains a tribute to Turner's ardor and discernment that it compares quite favorably with the one which Sir John Rhys published ninety years later. In a footnote Turner remarked that if the *Mabinogion* and all Welsh remains were to be accurately studied, enough might be gathered to elucidate some of the allusions of Taliesin to the opinions, tales, and traditions of his day. His prophecy has been slowly realized, and perhaps when Sir Ifor Williams has edited *Preiddeu Annwn,* as I hope he soon will, the mysteries of this most mysterious text about Arthur will be clarifed. Turner pioneered in the Arthurian field where the territory was most rugged and the obstacles most formidable, and won the approbation of the omniscient Southey and the interest of Sir Walter Scott and Tennyson ; even Matthew Arnold, though pointing out weaknesses in the *Vindication,* conceded that Turner's critical sense was at bottom sound.

In the same year, 1803, which saw the publication of Turner's *Vindication,* another book was completed, though not published then, a book which was even more important, more perspicacious, and more solid. This was *The Life of King Arthur* by Joseph Ritson. Strange to say the author of this, the most lucid and judicious work yet to appear on the subject, died a few months later a mental wreck. The last we hear of him, he was gathering books and loose papers, setting them ablaze in a grate, throwing his furniture about, breaking windows and threatening callers with a dagger. A melancholy end to the most eccentric, but also the most scientific of Arthurian pioneers.

Ritson had come to London from Stockton-on-Tees in 1775 and established himself as a conveyancer. But he already had literary and antiquarian tastes and knew some of Bishop Percy's ballads by heart. Like Turner he devoted his spare time to reading and notetaking in the British Museum. In later years he visited the Bodleian Library and Cambridge. He used his knowledge to comment on Warton's *History of English Poetry,* Percy's *Reliques,* and Johnson's Shakespeare, and to edit several anthologies of Middle English poetry.

Ritson, as an author, was a paradox incarnate. On certain subjects, he was a faddist and a fanatic ; on others, he was the essence of accuracy and logic. He was in politics at first a Jacobite, later a Jacobin ; he was a spelling reformer, and an erratic one ; a propagandist for vegetarianism so rabid that on this subject all his common sense deserted him. At the same time he was far more learned, more scrupulous, more perceptive than any of his contemporaries in the field of medieval English literature. Unfortunately to his intellectual eccentricities he added a pugnacious temper, and insisted not only on saying what was true of the scholarship of Thomas Warton and Bishop Percy, but he ascribed base motives to the Professor of Poetry at Oxford and to the Bishop of Dromore. These were unforgivable sins, particularly since Ritson had a talent for insult. To Bishop Warburton, he referred as that " confident and mendacious prelate ". To Pinkerton, the author of *Hardyknute,* he wrote : " Your success has doubtless fully gratified your expectations : and the dexterity of a pickpocket may vie with the impudence of a highwayman. " To Thomas Warton,

author of the *History of English Poetry* he wrote apropos
of a third volume : " I love to speak out, Mr. Warton. I
really believe you will not willingly close the work so long
as you can make a single guinea by it ", and concluded by
charging him with being " guilty of such low, paltry and
dishonorable and even dishonest artifices as almost to deserve
the name and punishment of a *Swindler* ".

Of the famous and powerful Thomas Percy, author of the
Reliques of Ancient English Poetry, Ritson wrote : " Forgery
and imposition of every kind ought to be universally
execrated, and never more than when they are employed by
persons high in rank and character... A man who will forge
a poem, a line, or even a word will not hesitate when the
temptation is greater and the opportunity equal to forge a
note or steal a guinea ".

Such language was, of course, undiplomatic, to say the
least. It is not the language of scholarly controversy. But
evidently Bishop Percy was *touché*. He *had* tampered with
the text of his ballads, sometimes drastically, as Ritson
suspected and later was able to prove. Percy had published
them without notifying his readers of his extensive alterations. This magnanimous pontiff went so far in his hatred
of Ritson as to use all his influence with reviewers to see
that the little atheist was damned on earth. And when he
heard the news of Ritson's death, he gloated over the pro-
spect of his damnation in another world.

The fact is that as an accurate recorder and as a literary
detective Ritson was greatly the superior of Warton and
Percy. Let me offer some examples of his acumen. When
the Shakespearean forgeries of William Henry Ireland were
exhibited to the public as genuine, Ritson was one of the
first to examine them, and Ireland later testified that " The
sharp and piercing eye and the silent scrutiny of Mr. Ritson
filled me with a dread I had never before experienced ". The
brain behind Ritson's eye was equally acute : it detected the
amusing fact that St. Amphibalus, introduced by Geoffrey
of Monmouth as the companion of St. Alban, was a nonentity, being only the name given by Gildas to St. Alban's
cloak. Ritson was properly scornful of the statement in one
of the Welsh *Bruts :* " I Walter, archdeacon of Oxford,
translated this book out of British into Latin, and afterwards,
in my graver years, have again done it into British. "

Ritson in 1803 perceived what many amateurs and some scholars have not yet learned in 1964, that the *De Antiquitate Glastoniensis Ecclesiae* of William of Malmesbury, as it has come down to us in a unique manuscript, is full of interpolations. The nature of these interpolations was characterized by Ritson as follows : " These worthless monks [of Glastonbury] filled their monastery with forgery and falsehood. The *charta sancti Patricii* seems to have been one of their first attempts : this they forged in the person of St. Patrick and made him tell a parcel of fables about their pretended antiquities and supposititious saints. " The rightness of this judgment on the *De Antiquitate* has been fully demonstrated by the late Dean of Wells and Fellow of the British Academy, Joseph Armitage Robinson.

Of course, Ritson, the relentless bishop baiter, did not overlook " that right reverend father in god, Geoffrey, lord bishop of St. Asaph, " and though he was uttering no *new* heresy when he rejected the *Historia Regum Britanniae* as unworthy of trust, seldom has a more sober critique been pronounced on that book than his. " The fact is glaring and notorious that with the exception of the extracts here and there interspersed in Geoffrey's book from Caesar's *Commentaries,* Bede's *Ecclesiastical History,* Gildas's querulous epistle on the destruction of Britain, and Nennius's *Eulogium Britanniae,* the legends of St. Alban, St. Dubricius, St. Ursula and others, not a single name or incident, which occurs in that work is to be found mentioned or alluded to by any writer or in any book before his own era. That the Britons had popular stories concerning Arthur, previous to the publication of Geoffrey's history, is not to be denied : since, beside the evidence of William of Malmesbury and what Geoffrey himself says, Master Wace observes : ' Fist Arthur la ronde table, Dunt Breton disent meint fable. ' " Ritson went on to say : " It may be possible that Walter the archdeacon had actually brought some book upon the subject of the British kings out of Britanny, a book which Geoffrey made use of, perhaps translated, interpolated and enlarged, and in his conceit amended, improved, and rendered more palatable to men of learning or to the taste of his times, but that his own work, as we now have it, existed in whatever shape or language before his own time or that the modern Welsh can produce his indubitable original in the British tongue is utterly incredible ". In the main this 150 year old pronouncement agrees with the conclusions of the latest scholar to discuss the subject, the late Professor John Tatlock in his monumental *Legendary History of Britain*. Where the two differ, as to the existence of stories about Arthur before Geoffrey, it is Ritson who has the evidence on his side, not Tatlock.

Enough has been said about Ritson's surprising acumen : and perhaps a word should be added about his surprising range and his knowledge of obscure details. He was evidently familiar with all the materials about Arthur which Sharon Turner had used. He complimented Turner, in fact, as the only Englishman who had ever been known to acquire or even to cultivate the British language, and it is probable that Ritson acquired some familiarity with it himself. At any rate, he knew the dialogue between Arthur and the gate-warden in the Black Book of Carmarthen, the poetic dialogues between Trystan and Gwalchmai, and between Arthur and the Eagle. He knew the title *Mabinogi Jesu Crist* as applied to a story of the childhood of Christ, though he, like some later experts, wrongly concluded that *mabinogi* meant a " childish book, a book for children ", instead of the meaning now accepted — a story of a hero's birth and youthful exploits. He was properly sceptical of the historic value of the Welsh triads. He not only knew Nennius but he even recorded the manuscript variants of the place names assigned to Arthur's battles. He quoted from many Latin documents the legend of Arthur's survival, and even included Cervantes' reference to the British hero's adopting the form of a crow. He cited passages from Marie de France and from the Franklin's Tale to show that the Bretons cultivated a form of narrative known as the lay. In this instance, however, his sceptical tendency, elsewhere so valuable, led him to conclude that the Bretons had little to do with the transmission or dissemination of the Matter of Britain. He refers to them as " this pitiful nation ", and denies that as emigrants from Great Britain they had any other fictions than such as they had carried over with them. It is true that no vernacular literature from the early Middle Ages has survived in Brittany, but to call the Bretons a pitiful nation and to ignore the striking fact that two of the greatest geniuses of the twelfth century, Peter Abelard and Adam of St. Victor were Bretons is a curious lapse of judgment on Ritson's part. Broadly speaking, however, Ritson made use of nearly all the texts and the critical literature about them which were available to him : he examined them in minute detail, was able to collate Malory's statement that Urien's wife and Owain's mother was Morgan le Fay with the Welsh triad which makes her Modron. A few serious blunders there were in his book such as the reiterated statement that Giraldus Cambrensis was bishop of St. David's when actually Giraldus's failure to obtain the election was the great disappointment of his life. Nine times out of ten his opinions have been borne out by more recent scholarship as Professor Annette Hopkins showed in her article mentioned above. By and large, Ritson's *Arthur* was in truth a pioneering work ; and its author, as Miss Hopkins wrote, deserves the title of the first modern Arthurian scholar.

It is pleasant to record that despite the attacks upon his character and the cold reception of his work by the envious or the biased, Ritson was not unappreciated in his own day. Southey wrote to Coleridge : " Ritson is the oddest but the most honest of all our antiquaries, and he abuses Percy and Pinkerton with less mercy than justice. " Scott, after Ritson's death paid him handsome tribute. In a letter to Surtees, Sir Walter wrote : " I loved poor Ritson with all his singularities... I do not believe the world could have made him say a word he did not think. I wish we had his like at present. " Again in Edinburgh Scott publicly declared : " Let it be remembered to his honour, that, without the encouragement of private patronage or of public applause, without hopes of gain and under certainty of severe critical censure, he has brought forward such a work on national antiquities, as in other countries has been thought worthy of the labour of universities and the countenance of princes. "

It will be noticed that one great source of Arthurian tradition was not used by Turner and Ritson — the collection of Welsh prose tales known to us as the *Mabinogion*. Though Turner knew of its existence, it was another amateur, Lady Charlotte Guest, who unlocked this rich treasure-house of story not only to antiquaries but also to the wider public of cultivated readers.

Her father was ninth Earl of Lindsey, and she as a

wealthy heiress was naturally destined to marry a peer and live a life of gay frivolities. But instead at the age of 21 she married John Guest, one of the most successful steel manufacturers in Britain and in the world, twenty-eight years her senior. The discrepancy in age and in social position might have foreshadowed disaster, but it was a love match. Lady Charlotte bore the ironmaster ten children, took the keenest interest in the business and actually kept the accounts. Though ostracized at first by society, she was able within a few years to regain her place in the fashionable world of London. And this busy life was occasionally interrupted by tours of the Continent.

But these were not the whole of her activities. As a girl she had been an ardent reader, and Chaucer was her favorite poet : already she was not to be daunted by a strange language. When, as a result of her marriage in 1833, she settled in South Wales where the steel plant lay, she interested herself in the people and almost at once started taking lessons in Welsh — as well as in Persian ! She wrote of Arthur as her countryman, and when a translation of *Culhwch ac Olwen* by Justice Bosanquet fell into her hands in 1837, she seems at once to have conceived the idea of translating all the tales in the Red Book into English. Her diary records : " I returned at dusk and read part of the tale of *Kilhwch and Olwen* from the *Mabinogion*. It pleases me much. There is a great field for annotation." There emerges the spirit, not of a dilettante but of a genuine scholar. On New Year's day 1838 she began her task, making her own translation with the aid of dictionaries. By July she recorded that, though she had forgotten to take her dictionary to Newbridge, she was surprised to find that she could understand the old Welsh words without one. She had the good sense to consult with the best Welsh scholars of her own day about difficult or doubtful passages. For example, we learn from her diary that in December she read over her translation of *Geraint* with the Rev. Thomas Price, and they corrected it together.

We find her working in the British Museum, for, not content with the task of translation, she investigated the analogues of the Welsh romances, took notes on the *Chevalier au Lion,* and compared Hartmann's *Iwain* with the *Iarlles y Fynnawn,* and a few days later doing the same for the Icelandic *Sir Gawain* — the *Valversthatr*. The same month her diary proudly notes the birth of her fifth child and third boy with less suffering than she had believed possible ; two days afterwards she was correcting proof with the assistance of her husband. It is a strangely happy picture which recurs throughout the diary — Plugson of Undershot taking time out from manufacturing steel rails to read his wife's proofs, thus contributing to a work which was destined to inspire the *Idylls of the King.*

Early in March, 1839, Lady Guest faced with characteristic boldness a typical scholar's peril, the danger of being forestalled. She learned that the Breton *littérateur* (one cannot call him a scholar), La Villemarqué, who owed his acquaintance with the *Mabinogion* to her, had obtained a transcript of *Peredur* and was intending to publish it. Alarmed, she changed her own plans and, at the end of seven weeks, was able to write triumphantly that she had transcribed the text of *Peredur,* translated it, written the notes, provided the decorations and brought it almost out of the printer's hands. La Villemarqué was beaten in the race.

In 1840 we find her transcribing with her own hand the 2288 lines of the Middle English text of *Sir Perceval* from the manuscript. Having performed this same task myself in the summer of 1911, I must pay her the tribute of acknowledging that she must have worked more assiduously than I, for she began it on a Monday morning and seems to have finished it on Saturday — six days. It took me almost a month.

An entry a year later runs as follows : " I sat up late this evening and had the pleasure of finishing my *Kilhwch* notes before going to bed. Hardly any portion of my life has passed more agreeably than the days which I have spent working hard with them. " This testimony, coming from a lady of fashion, who moved among peers and statesmen and enjoyed the luxuries of foreign travel, that writing notes to *Kilhwch* was almost the greatest pleasure of her life, is the final proof that at heart she was a born scholar.

By 1843 she saw the end of her labors approaching. She wrote : " Now that my seven babies are growing up and require so much attention, it is quite right that I should have done with authorship. I am quite content with what will have been done when the present work is concluded, and I am sure if a woman is to do her duty as a wife and a mother, the less she meddles with pen and ink the better. " In 1845 the work was done. It was with well warranted pride that she wrote as the work progressed : " Whatever I undertake I must reach an eminence in. I cannot endure anything at a second grade... I am happy to see we are at the head of the iron trade. "

She could also claim that she had accomplished a supreme service for the literature of the Celts. M. Joseph Loth once denied her the credit due her, saying that Lady Charlotte Guest « ne savait guère le gallois : elle a travaillé sur une version littérale d'un savant gallois ». This was almost a complete misconception. We know that before she attempted the task she knew modern Welsh, and the evidence of the diary shows that she plowed through the text with a dictionary before she submitted her translation to the Welsh scholars she consulted. She had the good sense and modesty to take advantage of the superior knowledge of such men as the Rev. John Jones and the Rev. Thomas Price, but she made the translation herself, and her name rightly appears on the title page. Of course, the work has some curious flaws. Victorian ideals of propriety led her to omit the account of Pwyll's model behavior in the bed of Arawn's wife, and to introduce a note deprecating the medieval practice of women riding astride and pointing to the mention of a woman's saddle in *Geraint* as rescuing the ladies of the tale from the imputation of so unbecoming a practice. Her introduction does not display the perspicacity of Ritson, and, unless I am mistaken, she neglected his work because his controversial manners were not genteel. But she recognized two strata in her tales, correctly perceived that one stratum had been contaminated by the culture of the French and Normans, and correctly proclaimed the other to be a purely Cymric tradition, the cradle of Arthurian romance.

Her notes which bear testimony to her wide ranging curiosity are still useful. They must, however, be carefully sifted, many of the worthless inventions of Iolo Morganwg and of earlier fabricators being mixed in with the genuine traditions derived from medieval manuscripts. Iolo was the La Villemarqué of Welsh scholarship and his dubious practices were not fully exposed till much later than those of his Breton counterpart. It is no discredit to Lady Guest, therefore, that she included in her notes much that the best scholars of her day accepted but which are rejected today. She brought together an amazing amount of relevant matter from sources not only Welsh and English, but also Latin, French, German and Icelandic. She quoted from Chaucer and the Middle English romances, from the *Gododdin* of the seventh century and from David Thomas of the 18th century, from the *Tournoiement Antechrist* of Huon de Méry, from Froissart, from the sermons of John Herolt and *Piers Plowman's Creed*. Though much of this accumulation is now absorbed into the common heritage of Arthurian scholarship, there are references and remarks which are still useful today. If I may be personal, I should like to record my own obligation to her notes for calling attention to the Thirteen Treasures of the Isle of Britain which contained the Horn of Bran and the Dish of Rhydderch, which, unless I am much mistaken, provide essential clues to the unravelling of the Grail problem. It was among these notes also that I came across the legend of St. Collen which provided an illuminating description of Annwn, originally a Celtic elysium, but transformed into the Christian hell.

I cannot put it more strongly than this. It is my belief that if Arthurian scholars had meditated more deeply on Lady Guest's translation, whatever its faults, and on her notes, there would be far less confusion and agnosticism about the question of Arthurian origins. The Welsh materials (excepting the poetry) are there. But the students of French romances have rarely been Celtic scholars. They have read rapidly through the book, seen little resemblance between *Kilhwch and Olwen* on the one hand and the *Conte del Graal* or the *Queste del Saint Graal* on the other, and sometimes in disappointment, sometimes in triumph, have intoned the obsequies of the Celtic hypothesis. But Lady Guest's *Mabinogion* lives on, not wholly superseded by later editions and translations.

ROGER SHERMAN LOOMIS

Bibliography

compiled by
Ruth Roberts

BIBLIOGRAPHY

Books:

The Romance of Tristram and Ysolt by Thomas of Britain. Translated by Roger Sherman Loomis. New York: E. P. Dutton, 1923; revised edition, Columbia University Press, 1932; new revised edition, 1951. Dutton Paperback, 1967.

Celtic Myth and Arthurian Romance. New York: Columbia University Press, 1927; revised edition, 1935. Reprinted, New York: Haskell House, 1967.

The Play of St. George. Based on the version in the *Return of the Native* and completed from other versions and local tradition by Thomas Hardy. Together with a modernized version by Roger S. Loomis. New York: Samuel French, 1928.

Arthurian Legends in Medieval Art (Part II in collaboration with Laura Hibbard Loomis). London: Oxford University Press; New York: Modern Language Association of America, 1938.

Representative Medieval and Tudor Plays (in collaboration with Henry W. Wells). New York: Sheed and Ward, 1942.

Medieval English Verse and Prose in Modernized Versions (in collaboration with Rudolph Willard). New York: Appleton-Century-Crofts, 1948.

Arthurian Tradition and Chretien de Troyes. New York: Columbia University Press, 1949.

Wales and the Arthurian Legend. Cardiff: University of Wales Press, 1956

Medieval Romances (in collaboration with Laura Hibbard Loomis). Modern Library Edition. New York: Random House, 1957, 1965 (Paperback).

The Development of Arthurian Romance. London: Hutchinson University Library, 1963; Harper Torchbook, New York: Harper and Row, 1964.

The Grail: From Celtic Myth to Christian Symbol. Cardiff: University of Wales Press; New York: Columbia University Press, 1963.

A Mirror of Chaucer's World. Princeton: Princeton University Press, 1965.

327

Editorial Works; Bibliographies; Supplemental Critical Essays and Notes:

Lot-Borodine, Myrrha and Gertrude Schoepperle. *Lancelot et Galahad Mis en Nouveau Langage.* Introduction by Roger S. Loomis. New York: Oxford University Press, 1926.

Introduction to Medieval Literature, Chiefly in England: Reading List and Bibliography. New York: Columbia University Press, 1939; second edition, 1948.

Ulrich von Zatzikhoven. *Lanzelet.* A Romance of Lancelot translated from the Middle High German by Kenneth G. T. Webster. Revised and Provided with Additional Notes and an Introduction by Roger Sherman Loomis. New York: Columbia University Press, 1951.

Arthurian Literature in the Middle Ages. A Collaborative History. Edited by Roger Sherman Loomis. Oxford: Clarendon Press, 1959.

Paton, Lucy Allen. *Studies in the Fairy Mythology of Arthurian Romance.* Second edition, enlarged by a Survey of Scholarship on the Fairy Mythology since 1903 and a Bibliography by Roger Sherman Loomis. New York: Burt Franklin, 1959.

Loomis, Gertrude Schoepperle. *Tristan and Isolt: A Study of the Sources of the Romance.* 2 vols. Second edition, expanded by a Bibliography and Critical Essay on Tristan Scholarship since 1912 by Roger Sherman Loomis. New York: Burt Franklin, 1960.

Van Duzee, Mabel. *A Medieval Romance of Friendship: Eger and Grime.* Preface by Roger Sherman Loomis. New York: Burt Franklin, 1963.

Fletcher, Robert H. *The Arthurian Material in the Chronicles, Especially Those of Great Britain and France.* Second edition, expanded by a Bibliography and Critical Essay for the Period 1905-1965 by Roger Sherman Loomis. New York: Burt Franklin, 1966.

Textbooks: Readings and Rhetorics:

Freshman Readings. Boston Houghton Mifflin Co., 1925; revised edition, 1927.

Art of Writing Prose (in collaboration with Mabel Robinson, Helen Hull, and Paul Cavanough). West Rindge, New Hampshire: R. R. Smith, 1930; revised edition, 1936 (New York: Farrar).

Models for Writing Prose. West Rindge, New Hampshire: R. R. Smith, 1931; revised edition (in collaboration with T. H. V. Motter), 1937 (New York: Farrar).

Modern English Readings (in collaboration with Donald L. Clark). New York: Farrar, 1934; revised editions, 1936, 1939, 1942; Rinehart, 1946, 1950, 1956 (in collaboration with John H. Middendorf); Holt, 1963.

Fight for Freedom: College Readings in Wartime (in collaboration with G. M. Liegey). New York: Farrar, 1943.

Articles:

"A Sidelight on the *Tristan* of Thomas." *Modern Language Review*, X (1915), 304-9.

"*Richard Coeur de Lion* and the *Pas Saladin* in Medieval Art." PMLA, XXX (1915), 509-28.

"In Praise of Spoon River." *Dial*, LX (1916), 415-6.

"Spoon River Once More." *Dial*, LXI (1916), 14-5.

"Illustrations of Medieval Romance on Tiles from Chertsey Abbey." University of Illinois Studies in Language and Literature, II, no. 2. Urbana: University of Illinois Press, 1916.

"A Medieval Ivory Casket." *Art in America*, V (1917), 19-27.

"Note on the *Areopagitica.*" *Modern Language Notes*, XXXII (1917), 437-8.

"A Phantom Tale of Female Ingratitude." *Modern Philology*, XIV (1917), 751-5.

"Verses on the Nine Worthies." *Modern Philology*, XV (1917), 211-9.

"The Tristran and Perceval Caskets." *Romanic Review*, VIII (1917), 196-209.

"The Allegorical Siege in the Art of the Middle Ages." *American Journal of Archaeology*, XXIII (1919), 255-69.

"Defense of Naturalism." *International Journal of Ethics*, XXIX (1919), 188-201.

"Notes on the *Tristan* of Thomas." *Modern Language Review*, XIV (1919), 38-43.

"Tom Jones and Tom-mania." *Sewanee Review*, XXVII (1919), 478-95.

"How They Captured Castles with Roses." *International Studio*, LXXI (1920), 67-70.

"Vestiges of Tristram in London." *Burlington Magazine*, XLI (1922), 54-64.

"Tristram and the House of Anjou." *Modern Language Review*, XVII (1922), 24-30.

"On the Slopes of Etna." *Outlook*, CXXXIV (1923), 593-4.

"Modena, Bari, and Hades." *Art Bulletin*, VI (1924), 71-4.

"Bleheris and the Tristram Story." *Modern Language Notes*, XXXIX (1924), 319-29.

"The Story of the Modena Archivolt and Its Mythological Roots." *Romanic Review*, XV (1924), 266-84.

"Medieval Iconography and the Question of Arthurian Origins." *Modern Language Notes*, XL (1925), 65-70.

"Romance and Epic in the Romanesque Art of Italy." *Nuovi Studi Medievali*, II (1925-6), 105-11.

"The Date of the Arthurian Sculpture at Modena." *Medieval Studies in Memory of Gertrude Schoepperle Loomis*. Paris: Champion; New York: Columbia University Press, 1927, pp. 209-29.

"Problems of the Tristan Legend: Bleheris; the Diarmaid Parallel; Thomas's Date." *Romania*, LIII (1927), 82-102.

"La Legende Archeologique a la Cathedrale de Modene" (in collaboration with A. Kingsley Porter). *Gazette des Beaux Arts*, XVIII (1928), 109-22.

"Calogrenanz and Crestien's Originality." *Modern Language Notes*, XLIII (1928), 215-22.

"Gawain, Gwri, and Cuchulin." PMLA, XLIII (1928), 384-96.

"Cause or Coincidence? A Reply to Monsieur Ferdinand Lot." *Romania*, LIV (1928), 515-26.

"Geoffrey of Monmouth and Arthurian Origins." *Speculum*, III (1928), 16-33.

"The Legends of Arthur and the Round Table"; "Welsh Literature." *Columbia University Course in Literature*. New York: Columbia University Press, 1929, Vol. IV, pp. 65-73; 243-52.

"Bron and Other Figures in the *Estoire del Saint Graal.*" *Modern Language Review*, XXIV (1929), 416-36.

"Reproductions of Medieval Art Furnished by the Metropolitan Museum" (in collaboration with Margaret Scherer). *Parnassus*, I (1929), 41-2.

"Some Names in Arthurian Romance." PMLA, XLV (1930), 416-43.

"The Head in the Grail." *Revue Celtique*, XLVII (1930), 39-62.

"The Scientific Method in Arthurian Studies." *Studi Medievali*, III (1930), 288-300.

"The Magic Horn and Cup in Celtic and Grail Tradition" (in collaboration with Jean Stirling Lindsay). *Romanische Forschungen*, XLV (1931), 66-94.

" 'Chastiel Bran,' 'Dinas Bran,' and the Grail Castle." *Miscellany of Studies in Romance Languages and Literatures in Honour of L. E. Kastner*. Cambridge: Heffer and Sons, 1932, pp. 342-50. Reprinted with revisions in *Wales and the Arthurian Legend*, pp. 42-52.

"Isdernus Again." *Medium Aevum*, II (1933), 160-3.

"The Visit to the Perilous Castle: a Study of the Arthurian Modifications of an Irish Theme." PMLA, XLVIII (1933), 1000-35.

"Irish *Imrama* in the *Conte del Graal.*" *Romania*, LIX (1933), 557-64.

"The Irish Origin of the Grail legend." *Speculum*, VIII (1933), 415-31. Reprinted as "The Irish Origin and the Welsh Development of the Grail Legend" in *Wales and the Arthurian Legend*, pp. 19-41.

"Notes on Layamon." *Review of English Studies*, X (1934), 78-84.

"*Sir Orfeo* and Walter Map's *De Nugis.*" *Modern Language Notes*, LI (1936), 28-30.

"By What Route Did the Romantic Tradition of Arthur Reach the French? " *Modern Philology*, XXXIII (1936), 225-238.

"The Modena Sculpture and Arthurian Romance." *Studi Medievali*, IX (1936), 1-17.

"Gawain in the *Squire's Tale.*" *Modern Language Notes*, LII (1937), 413-6.

"Baudemaguz." *Romania*, LXIII (1937), 383-93.

"Geoffrey of Monmouth and the Modena Archivolt: A Question of Precedence." *Speculum*, XIII (1938), 221-31.

"Chivalric and Dramatic Imitations of Arthurian Romance." *Mediaeval Studies in Memory of A. Kingsley Porter*. Cambridge, Massachusetts: Harvard University Press, 1939, pp. 79-97.

"Malory's Beaumains." PMLA, LIV (1939), 656-68.

"Was Chaucer a Laodicean? " *Essays and Studies in Honor of Carleton Brown*. New York: New York University Press, 1940, pp. 129-48. Reprinted in

Chaucer Criticism, Vol. I. Edited by Richard J. Schoeck and Jerome Taylor. Notre Dame, Indiana: University of Notre Dame Press, 1960, pp. 291-310.

"King Arthur and the Antipodes." *Modern Philology*, XXXVIII (1941), 289-304. Reprinted in *Wales and the Arthurian Legend*, pp. 61-76.

"The Spoils of Annwn." PMLA, LVI (1941), 887-936. Reprinted with revisions as "The *Spoils of Annwn:* an Early Welsh Poem" in *Wales and the Arthurian Legend*, pp. 131-178. Nominated the most significant article published in the Arthurian field in PMLA (1883-1958). PMLA, LXIII, no. 5, Part 2 (Dec., 1958), 47, 52-3.

"The Arthurian Legend before 1139." *Romanic Review*, XXXII (1941), 3-38. Reprinted in *Wales and the Arthurian Legend*, pp. 179-220.

"Arthurian Legend." *Dictionary of World Literature.* New York: Philosophical Library, 1943, pp. 52-4.

"More Celtic Elements in *Gawain and the Green Knight.*" *Journal of English and Germanic Philology*, XLII (1943), 149-84. Reprinted with revisions as "Welsh Elements in *Gawain and the Green Knight*" in *Wales and the Arthurian Legend*, pp. 77-90.

"Chaucer's Eight Years' Sickness." *Modern Language Notes*, LIX (1944), 178-80.

"Evidence for the Existence of the Secular Theatres in the 12th Century." PMLA, LIX (1944), 1339.

"The Combat at the Ford in the *Didot Perceval.*" *Modern Philology*, XLIII (1945), 63-71. Reprinted in *Wales and the Arthurian Legend*, pp. 91-104.

"Were There Theatres in the Twelfth and Thirteenth Centuries? " *Speculum*, XX (1945), 92-5.

"Morgain La Fee and the Celtic Goddesses." *Speculum*, XX (1945), 183-203. Reprinted in *Wales and the Arthurian Legend*, pp. 105-30.

"Some Evidence for Secular Theatres in the 12th and 13th Centuries." *Theatre Annual*, III (1945), 33.

"From Segontium to Sinadon---the Legends of a *Cite Gaste.*" *Speculum*, XXII (1947), 520-33. Reprinted as "Segontium, Caer Seint, and Sinadon" in *Wales and the Arthurian Legend*, pp. 1-18.

"Two Cruces in the Text of Chretien de Troyes." *Melanges de Philologie Romane et de Litterature Medievale Offerts a Ernest Hoepffner.* Paris: Les Belles Lettres, 1949, pp. 227-35.

"A Parallel to the Franklin's Discussion of Marriage." *Philologica: The Malone*

Anniversary Studies. Baltimore: The Johns Hopkins Press, 1949, pp.191-4.

"Le Folklore Breton et les Romans Arthuriens." *Annales de Bretagne,* LVI (1949), 203-27. English version: "Breton Folklore and Arthurian Romance." *Comparative Literature,* II (1950), 289-306.

"Arthur"; "Grail"; "Lancelot"; "Mabinogion"; "Merlin"; "Mordred or Modred"; "Morgan le Fay"; "Percival or Perceval"; "Tristan, Tristram, or Tristrem" (in collaboration with MacEdward Leach); "Vivien or Vivian". *Standard Dictionary of Folklore, Mythology, and Legend.* 2 vols. New York: Funk and Wagnalls Co., 1949-50, pp. 76-8; 461-2; 602; 658-9; 708-9; 746-7; 856; 1125-6; 1161.

"Lincoln as a Dramatic Centre." *Melanges d'Histoire du Theatre du Moyen-Age et de la Renaissance Offerts a Gustave Cohen.* Paris: Librire Nizet, 1950, pp. 241-7.

"The Descent of Lancelot from Lug." *Bulletin Bibliographique de la Societe Internationale Arthurienne,* III (1951), 69-73.

" 'Ci falt la Geste que Turoldus declinet.' " *Romania,* LXXII (1951), 371-3.

"The *Fier Baiser* in Mandeville's Travels, Arthurian Romance, and Irish Saga." *Studi Medievali,* XVII (1951), 104-13.

"Arthur's Round Table and Bran the Blessed." *Modern Language Quarterly,* XIV (1953), 131-2.

"Edward I, Arthurian Enthusiast." *Speculum,* XXVIII (1953), 114-27. Abstract in *Bulletin Bibliographique de la Societe Internationale Arthurienne,* III (1951), 105-6.

"Bruce's Conception of the History of Lancelot." Abstract in *Bulletin Bibliographique de la Societe Internationale Arthurienne,* VI (1954), 101-2.

"Was There a Play on the Martyrdom of Hugh of Lincoln? " *Modern Language Notes,* LXIX (1954), 31-4.

"Grail Problems." *Romanic Review,* XLV (1954), 12-7.

"The *Pas Saladin* in Art and Heraldry." *Studies in Art and Literature for Belle da Costa Greene.* Princeton: Princeton University Press, 1954, pp. 83-91.

"How Did the Grail Legend Arise? " *History of Ideas News Letter,* I, iii (June, 1955), 2-3.

"Vandeberes, Wandlebury, and the *Lai de l'Espine.* " *Romance Philology,* IX

(1955), 162-7.

"Scotland and the Arthurian Legend." *Proceedings of the Society of Antiquaries of Scotland*, LXXXIX (Session 1955-56), 1-21.

"Les Legendes Hagiographiques et la Legende du Graal." *Les Romans du Graal dans la Litterature des XIIe et XIIIe Siecles.* Paris: Editions du Centre Nationale de la Recherche Scientifique, 1956, pp. 233-45.

"Bran the Blessed and *Sone de Nausay.*" *Wales and the Arthurian Legend*, pp. 53-60.

"Onomastic Riddles in Malory's *Book of Arthur and His Knights.*" *Medium Aevum*, XXV (1956), 181-90.

"The Grail Story of Chretien de Troyes as Ritual and Symbolism." PMLA, LXXI (1956), 840-52.

"The *Esplumeor Merlin* Again." *Bulletin Bibliographique de la Societe Internationale Arthurienne*, IX (1957), 79-83.

"Arthurian Tradition and Folklore." *Folklore*, LXIX (1958), 1-25.

"A Common Source for *Erec* and *Gereint.*" *Medium Aevum*, XXVII (1958), 175-8.

"Objections to the Celtic Origin of the 'Matiere de Bretagne.'" *Romania*, LXXIX (1958), 47-77. Abstract in *Bulletin Bibliographique de la Societe Internationale Arthurienne*, IX (1957), 131-2.

"The Oral Diffusion of the Arthurian Legend"; "The Legend of Arthur's Survival"; "Layamon's *Brut*"; "The Origin of the Grail Legends"; "The *Livre d'Artus*" (in collaboration with Frederick Whitehead); "The Latin Romances"; "Arthurian Influence on Sport and Spectacle." *Arthurian Literature in the Middle Ages*, pp. 52-63; 64-71; 104-11; 274-94; 336-8; 472-9; 553-60.

"Morgain la Fee in Oral Tradition." *Romania*, LXXX (1959), 337-67.

"Some Additional Sources of *Perlesvaus.*" *Romania*, LXXXI (1960), 492-9.

"Was Chaucer a Free Thinker?" *Studies in Medieval Literature in Honor of Professor Albert Croll Baugh.* Philadelphia: University of Pennsylvania Press, 1961, pp. 21-44.

"Pioneers in Arthurian Scholarship." *Bulletin Bibliographique de la Societe Internationale Arthurienne*, XVI (1964), 95-106.

"Did Gawain, Perceval, and Arthur Hail from Scotland?" *Etudes Celtiques*, XI (1964-65), 70-82.

"The Grail in the *Parcevals Saga.*" *Germanic Review*, XXXIX (1964), 97-100.

"Discussion: the Development of Arthurian Romance" (with D. D. R. Owen). *Forum for Modern Language Studies*, I, 1 (1965), 64-77.

"The Strange History of Caradoc of Vannes." *Franciplegius: Medieval and Linguistic Studies in Honor of Francis Peabody Magoun, Jr.* New York: New York University Press, 1965, pp. 232-9. French version: "L'etrange Histoire de Caradoc de Vannes." *Annales de Bretagne*, LXX (1963), 165-76. Abstract in *Bulletin Bibliographique de la Societe Internationale Arthurienne*, XII (1960), 133-4.

"Literary History and Literary Criticism: a Critique of C.S. Lewis." *Modern Language Review*, LX (1965), 508-11.

"Fundamental Facts about Arthurian Origins." *Studi in Onore di Italo Siciliano.* Firenze: Olschki, 1966, pp. 677-83.

"The Structure of Malory's 'Gareth.' " *Studies in Language and Literature in Honour of Margaret Schlauch.* Warsaw: Panstwowe Wydawnictwo Naukowe, 1966, pp. 219-25.

"The Heraldry of Hector or Confusion Worse Confounded." *Speculum*, XLII (1967), 32-5.

"Romance, Medieval," *The New Catholic Encyclopedia*, New York, 1967, XII, 613-21.

"The Library of Richard II", *Studies in Language, Literature, and Culture of the Middle Ages and Later.* University of Texas Press, 1969, 173-8.

Reviews:

Koechlin, R. *Les Ivoires Gothiques Francaises.* 3 vols. Paris, 1924 (*Art Bulletin*, VI (1924), 109-12).

Bruce, James D. *The Evolution of Arthurian Romance.* Gottingen: Vandenhoeck & Ruprecht, 1923 (*Journal of English and Germanic Philology*, XXIII (1924), 582-91).

Griscom, Acton. "The *Book of Basingwerk* and MS. Cotton Cleopatra B. V." *Y Cymmrodor*, XXXV (1925), 49-116; XXXVI (1926), 1-33. Parry, John J., ed. *The Vita Merlini.* University of Illinois Studies in Language and Literature, X, no. 3. Urbana: University of Illinois Press, 1925 *(Journal of English and Germanic Philology*, XXVI (1927), 423-7).

Gruffydd, William J. *Math vab Mathonwy.* Cardiff: University of Wales Press,

1928 (*Modern Language Notes*, XLIII (1928), 558-9; *Speculum*, IV (1929), 139-44).

Krappe, A. H. *Balor with the Evil Eye*. New York: Institute of French Studies, 1927 (*Modern Language Notes*, XLIII (1928), 559-60).

Paton, Lucy A. *Sir Lancelot of the Lake*. London, 1929 (New York Herald Tribune *Books*, January 26, 1930, p. 21; *Modern Language Notes*, XLV (1930), 274-6).

Vinaver, Eugene. *Malory*. Oxford: Clarendon Press, 1929 (New York Herald Tribune *Books*, September 14, 1930, p. 10).

App, August J. *Lancelot in English Literature, his Role and Character*. Washington: Catholic University of America Press, 1929 (*Speculum*, V (1930), 104-5).

Faral, Edmond. *La Legende Arthurienne. Premiere Partie: Les Plus Anciens Textes*. Paris, 1929 (*Modern Language Notes*, XLVI (1931), 175-9, 181-2).

Nitze, William A. and T. A. Jenkins, eds. *Perlesvaus, The High History of the Holy Grail*. Vol. I, Text. Chicago: University of Chicago Press, 1932 (*Romanic Review*, XXIII (1932), 265-6).

Gabrici, Ettore and Ezio Levi. *Lo Steri di Palermo e le Sue Pitture*. Regia Accademia di Scienze, Lettere ed Arti di Palermo, Supplemento agli Atti, N. 1. Milan, 1932 (*Speculum*, IX (1934), 105-6).

Carman, J. Neale. *The Relationship of the "Perlesvaus" and the "Queste del Saint Graal."* University of Kansas Humanistic Studies, V, no. 4. Lawrence: University of Kansas Department of Journalism Press, 1936 (*Romanic Review*, XXVIII (1937), 351-5).

Nitze, William A. and others. *Le Haut Livre du Graal: Perlesvaus*. Vol. II, Commentary and Notes. Chicago: University of Chicago Press, 1937 (*Romanic Review*, XXIX (1938), 175-80).

Burdach, Konrad. *Der Gral: Forschungen uber seinen Ursprung und seinen Zusammenhang mit der Longinuslegende*. Stuttgart: Kohlhammer, 1938 (*Germanic Review*, XIV (1939), 221-2).

Weekley, Ernest. *Jack and Jill, a Study in our Christian Names*. New York: Dutton, 1940 (*American Speech*, XV (1940), 423-5).

Roach, William, ed. *The Didot Perceval according to the Manuscripts of Modena and Paris*. Philadelphia, 1941 (*Romanic Review*, XXXIII (1942), 168-74).

Brown, Arthur C. L. *The Origin of the Grail Legend*. Cambridge, Massachusetts: Harvard University Press, 1943 (*Romanic Review*, XXXV (1944), 82-4;

Review of Religion, VIII (1944), 294-7).

Closs, August, ed. *Tristan und Isolt: a Poem by Gottfried von Strassburg.* Oxford: Blackwell, 1944 (*Speculum,* XX (1945), 111-3).

Tatlock, John S. P. *The Legendary History of Britain.* Berkeley: University of California Press, 1950 (*Romanic Review,* XLII (1951), 150-3).

Jones, Thomas. *Gerald the Welshman's "Itinerary Through Wales" and "Description of Wales."* National Library of Wales Journal, VI, nos. 2,3. Aberystwyth: National Library of Wales, 1950 (*Speculum,* XXVI (1951), 393-4).

Nelli, Rene, ed. *Lumiere du Graal: Etudes et Textes.* Paris: Cahiers du Sud, 1951 (*Romance Philology,* V (1952), 322-5).

Marx, Jean. *La Legende Arthurienne et le Graal.* Paris: Presses Universitaires de France, 1952 (*Speculum,* XXVII (1952), 407-11).

Kurvinen, Auvo, ed. *Sir Gawain and the Carle of Carlisle in Two Versions.* Helsinki: Finnish Academy of Sciences, 1951 (*Erasmus,* VI (1953), 591-2).

Cross, Tom Peete. *Motif-Index of Early Irish Literature.* Indiana University Publications: Folklore Series. Bloomington: Indiana University Press, 1952 (*Midwest Folklore,* III (1953), 250-1).

Emmel, Hildegard. *Formprobleme des Artusromans und der Graldichtung.* Bern, 1951 (*Speculum,* XXVIII (1953), 158-9).

Gruffydd, William J. *Rhiannon: An Inquiry into the Origins of the First and Third Branches of the Mabinogi.* Cardiff: University of Wales Press, 1953 (*Speculum,* XXVIII (1953), 882-3).

Ackerman, Robert W. *An Index of the Arthurian Names in Middle English.* Stanford University Publications, University Series, Language and Literature, X. Stanford, California: Stanford University Press, 1952 (*Speculum,* XXIX (1954), 244-6).

Jones, Francis. *The Holy Wells of Wales.* Cardiff: University of Wales Press, 1954 (*Midwest Folklore,* VI (1956), 171-3).

Carney, James. *Studies in Irish Literature and History.* Dublin: Dublin Institute for Advanced Studies, 1955 (*Medium Aevum,* XXVI (1957), 197-9).

Rickard, Peter. *Britain in Medieval French Literature, 1100-1500.* Cambridge: Cambridge University Press, 1956 (*Speculum,* XXXIII (1958), 316-9).

Ashe, Geoffrey. *King Arthur's Avalon: the Story of Glastonbury.* New York: Dutton, 1958 (*Speculum,* XXXIV (1959), 90-5).

Schirmer, Walter Franz. *Die fruhen Darstellungen des Arthurstoffes.* Cologne:

Wesdeutscher Verlag, 1958 (*Speculum*, XXXIV (1959), 677-82).

Adolph, Helen. *Visio Pacis, Holy City and Grail.* University Park: Pennsylvania State University Press, 1960 (*Speculum*, XXXVI (1961), 439-41).

Pickford, Cedric E. *L'Evolution du Roman Arthurien en Prose vers la Fin du Moyen Age.* Paris: A. G. Nizet, 1960 (*Speculum*, XXXVI (1961), 483-4).

Legge, M. Dominica. *Anglo-Norman Literature and its Background.* Oxford: Clarendon Press, 1963 (*Studia Neophilologica* (Uppsala), XXXVI (1964), 346-9).

Rumble, Thomas C., ed. *The Breton Lays in MiddleEnglish.* Detroit, Michigan: Wayne State University Press, 1965 (*Speculum*, XLI (1966), 366-8).

Olschki, Leonardo. *The Grail Castle and its Mysteries.* Trans. J. A. Scott. Manchester: Manchester University Press, 1966 (*Medium Aevum*, XXXVI (1967), 83-5).